Reading from Left to Right

In memory of

LEONARD W. BROCKINGTON, Q.C., LL.D.
1888-1966

First Chairman of the Canadian Broadcasting Corporation and
sometime Rector of Queen's University

H.S. FERNS

Reading
from Left to Right:
One Man's
Political History

Foreword by Malcolm Muggeridge

UNIVERSITY OF TORONTO PRESS

Toronto Buffalo London

© 1983 University of Toronto Press
Toronto Buffalo London
Printed in Canada

ISBN 0-8020-2518-8

Canadian Cataloguing in Publication Data

Ferns, H.S. (Henry Stanley), 1913-
Reading from left to right

ISBN 0-8020-2518-8

1. Ferns, H.S. (Henry Stanley), 1913-   2. College
teachers – Canada – Biography.   I. Title.

LA2325.F47A3   378'.12'0924   C83-098608-1

This book has been published with
the assistance of the Canada Council
and Ontario Arts Council
under their block grant programs.

Foreword

There are many varieties of autobiography since we all live several lives. Thus, St. Augustine of Hippo called his autobiography – the first ever, in our sense of the word – *Confessions,* and based it on his conversion; Casanova based his on his seductions, Doughty his on his travels in Arabia, Jean-Jacques Rousseau his on his lies, and so on. Professor Harry Ferns gives away the theme of his autobiography in its title, *Reading from Left to Right: One Man's Political History*. What could this possibly be but an account of his political adventures and misadventures? Such a theme, as any experienced reviewer knows, can be excruciatingly boring – like the party political broadcasts from which all but the most politically obsessed recoil. Actually, Ferns' *apologia pro vita politica sua* (dog Latin, if that!) is, at once, eminently readable and a shrewd contribution to the everlasting conundrum as to why the most favoured children of capitalism and bourgeois-style living tend to enlist with their avowed enemies and destroyers; why no Marxist turn-out is complete without a few tame millionaires and ecclesiastical dignitaries, and why it is in the lush groves of academe rather than in the slums and shanty towns of the poor that the Red Flag most proudly flies.

A pleasing feature of Harry Ferns' treatment of this inexhaustible subject is the absence of dramatization, even in his account of his own journey from Left to Right. As a student, he became a Marxist and card-carrying communist, dazzled by Marx's elephantine assumptions and conclusions, and prepared to justify, or at any rate tolerate, the murderous goings on in the Kremlin and in the countryside, especially in the Ukraine, under Stalin. He was at Cambridge in the heyday of leftist enthusiasm, when the élitist and quasi-secret Apostles Club included members like Guy Burgess and Anthony Blunt, whose championship of the toiling masses did not preclude or restrict their proneness to snobbishness and sodomy. Ferns' duties as a party member were confined to ideologically respectable activities like anti-imperialism, without any taint of espionage.

Thus, in his journey from Left to Right, there is no sudden enlightenment, no Damascus Road experience. Nor does he feel constrained to expose or denounce fellow-communists as he moves away from communism, which he increasingly sees, in party political terms, as merely an instrument for promoting a Sovietized version of traditional Russian imperialism under the Tsars. Indeed, he defends at some length and much earnestness friends who, like Herbert Norman, have been plausibly charged with acting as Soviet agents. I have felt the same myself in certain cases – for instance, Philby, until he was finally exposed. Likewise, no doubt, there were those who sympathized with the Jesuits who came to England clandestinely in the reign of Queen Elizabeth I at the peril of their lives, even though the sympathizers were by no means sharers of their faith.

It was the late Arthur Koestler, another traveller on the Left to Right road, who said that the last battle would be between the communists and the ex-communists. Nor would it be fanciful to suppose that the melancholy which overtook Koestler as he grew old and led to his suicide was fostered in some degree by a growing conviction that the ex-communists would be the losing side. There are many varied wayfarers along Professor Ferns' journey – indeed, I count myself one – and whatever brave words they may utter, they are liable to be afflicted by the sense of being on the losing side that so distressed Koestler. The only ultimate antidote is to withdraw from the power struggle that governs history in favour of another sense altogether of what is our true destiny here on earth – a destiny whereby the quest is for love, not power, for faith, not knowledge, whose inspirer was nailed to a cross and died in ignominy two thousand years ago. I detect in this *apologia* intimations of this other destiny.

MALCOLM MUGGERIDGE

Contents

Acknowledgements

The autobiographer is ill advised who relies entirely on his own memory and his own records. In telling my story, I have not done so. I have been greatly helped by others, both in establishing the substance of what I have written and in bringing my work to the point of publication.

My wife, Maureen, has not been much mentioned in this book. To do justice to Maureen and to express what I owe to her, I would have to write a quite different book from this one. But even in writing this I have been enormously helped by her memory and her assistance in making some sense of what we singly and jointly remember about the last half century. Our children have helped me, too, each in his or her own way, and I am grateful to them.

I am indebted to old friends from Cambridge and particularly to Professor Victor Kiernan for permission to quote from his private diary and to Dr Hugh Gordon for his comments and criticisms.

I am grateful to Professor A.R.M. Lower and Professor A.M. Schlesinger Jr. for permission to quote from their correspondence with me.

The list of those in both Britain and Canada who have helped me with facts, the analysis of facts, and comments on the sense or otherwise of what I have written is a long one; the late Professor Harry Crowe, Mrs. Jean Crowe, my father Mr S.J. Ferns, Mr Douglas Fisher, Professor Jack Granatstein, Lord Harris of High Cross, Mrs Margaret Hilton, Ms Christine McCall, Mr Malcolm Muggeridge, Mrs Irene Norman, Mr Richard Nielsen, the late Mr Friedl Simkin, Dr Bessie Touzel, Professor Albert Tucker, and Dr K.W. Watkins.

But what I have written is my responsibility alone. Finally I am grateful to Miss Marjorie Davies and Miss Gillian Briggs for typing a difficult manuscript. This book has been published with the help of a grant from the Social Science Federation of Canada, using funds provided by the Social Sciences and Humanities Research Council of Canada.

Birmingham 1983   H.S.F.

Reading from Left to Right

CHAPTER ONE

Plato on the Prairies:
the aspiration to think

Lately some political scientists have turned their attention to what they call 'the politicization of children.' How do children become conscious of politics and how do they develop political attitudes and values? The child is father of the man. Maybe, but not necessarily so.

My earliest memory of a political question goes back to the autumn of 1920, when I was six going on seven years old. It was put to me by 'an American kid' in the schoolyard in Strathmore, Alberta, Canada, in the shape of a dogmatic assertion: 'It is better to have a president than a king.' I asked the American kid why, and he replied: 'anybody can be president, but anybody can't be a king.' At that time I could only answer my challenger in terms of asserting that we people in the British Empire had a king and that was better than having a president. But the question implied in the argument of the American kid was a beginning.

Unless one is acquainted with the circumstances of time and place, it may seem odd that children of six or seven should engage in political discussion of a rather fundamental kind. It must be borne in mind that the town in which I lived had only been in existence for twenty years; the province of Canada where I was born was only fifteen years old in 1920, and Canada, which was my home and native land, had only been a political community for fifty-three years. The British Empire to which my country belonged was, of course, much older and even at the age of six this was a considerable satisfaction to me. Why?

In my part of Alberta thirty or so miles east of Calgary, where I was born, there were many Americans, mostly farmers, who had come there in search of land either freely given under the homestead acts of the Canadian Parliament or purchasable from landholders of which the Canadian Pacific Railway and the Hudson's Bay Company were the largest. Naturally there were many American children in the public school in Strathmore just as there were many Canadians whose parents, like my own, had come from eastern Canada before the First World War. There were very few 'foreigners' in Strathmore or in any part of Alberta. Most

3

people had Anglo-Saxon or Irish names, but there were a few Dutch, Germans, and Scandinavians. Eastern Europeans – Poles, Ukrainians, Russians, Galicians – were hardly known in Alberta at that time, and we tended to think of people who were not English-speaking in origin as foreigners. On the whole foreigners were not people we naturally liked, and I can remember very well the indignation I felt when, in an American adventure story, the hero, Tom Swift, referred to an Englishman as 'a foreigner.'

But being English-speaking had its political problems. Here was an American kid challenging the political order of which I was a part, and I did not like it one little bit.

This question of the king cropped up again. My father was a poultry farmer. One day I was watching him replacing panes of glass in a poultry house which had been broken by some sheep. I was fascinated by glass-cutting and the puttying of the window frames, but not entirely so. I asked my father: 'What is the difference between the king and Mackenzie King?' Mackenzie King had lately become the prime minister of Canada and he was a subject of conversation among the farmers from whom my father used to buy eggs on behalf of the Dining Car and Hotel service of the Canadian Pacific Railway.

My father explained to me that there was King George V in London, who was king of the British Empire, but that we Canadians had a leader whom we elected and that this leader, called a prime minister, had a name, Mackenzie King, in the same way that my name was Harry Ferns. Mackenzie King was not a king, but George V was. I accepted what my father told me, and so far as I can remember I never thought about the matter again until we began to learn about responsible government in grade VII in the public school in Calgary, where we went to live in 1923. It seemed to me that the Americans were not any better than we were because we elected our leader just as they elected a president.

The Americans and their children had another important effect on my political understanding in childhood. They used to assert, not once but very often, that 'the Americans won the war,' that the British and the French could not beat the Germans in the war just over, but that the Americans did. None of the Canadian children liked this bragging and boasting. I know that in my case I got a great deal of satisfaction and comfort out of looking at the map of the world on the wall at school and seeing how much of it was in red, indicating the British Empire. The British Empire was everywhere on all the continents, and the United

4

States was only in North America. It may have turned out that the most constant of my political beliefs centres on anti-imperialism, but there can be no doubt that as a child the existence of the British Empire, its growth and its glory, exercised my mind and imagination more than anything else. Part of the largest and greatest empire in history! That was something to be proud of. That was the answer to loud-mouthed American braggarts.

Part of political consciousness involves an awareness of laws and their importance. Such awareness of rules of conduct as I had as a child was unconnected with people like the king and Mackenzie King. Long before I went to school my mother taught me to say my prayers before I went to bed at night. These prayers were short and followed a rigid pattern starting with an invocation 'Gentle Jesus, meek and mild, look upon this little child' and ended with a petition that 'God bless Mummy and Daddy and make Harry a good boy for Jesus Christ's sake, Amen.' Although I have no recollection of the instruction, I had obviously been made aware that there is good conduct and bad behaviour, and that I needed help in embracing the first and avoiding the second. There was, likewise, a hymn for children which was sung in church, lines of which stuck in my mind: 'Yield not to temptation, For yielding is sin.'

When I went to school I encountered temptation. A little girl who sat across the aisle from me in grade I possessed a splendid, long, lead pencil with gold lettering on the side and a white rubber at one end fixed to the pencil by a glowing brass band. It was a finer pencil than anyone else possessed. I coveted it and I stole it. The girl complained to the teacher. We were obliged to turn out our desks, and my theft was discovered. The teacher ordered me to stay behind after the class was dismissed for lunch.

In that age of innocence all teachers in the schools of Alberta were issued with straps, a strip of gutta percha belting about $2^{1}/_{2}$ inches wide and 12 inches long. Miss Fairley called me to her, took the strap from a drawer in her desk, and ordered me to hold out first one hand and then the other. The pain was very considerable, but I felt I ought not to cry. Much to my surprise I felt better after this punishment. I was deeply ashamed of having yielded to temptation. I was sure I deserved punishment, and I rejoiced after it was over. I did not tell my parents what had happened, because I knew two things: that they would be even more ashamed of me than I was myself, and that my parents and the teacher were on the same side as far as my behaviour was concerned. And so was God.

5

My first encounter with the laws of the state was a rather different experience. This occurred when I was fourteen years old, and it happened in this way.

My father possessed a 22-calibre revolver which was kept in a trunk in a closet in one of the bedrooms in our house in Calgary. I discovered this one day when curiosity prompted me to investigate what I supposed were some of my parents' secrets. Naturally I did not ask about the gun, but I was fascinated by it. The revolver had a long shiny nickel-plated barrel and a handle of hard black rubber. It was in fact not much more than a toy, which my father subsequently told me he had obtained many years previously as security for a loan of five dollars which had never been redeemed. But to me it was an impressive object. From time to time when no one was at home I used to get the gun out of the tortoise-shell box where it reposed in the trunk, and I used to practise in front of a mirror at becoming a fast gun like one of the heroes in the novels of Zane Gray.

I had a friend named Fred Seymour. I told him about the gun. He made me a proposition: if I would get the gun out of the house, he would buy a box of cartridges. He delivered newspapers and had money to spend, which I did not.

I agreed. I hid the gun in my room until the day came when Fred had procured a box of 22 'shorts,' to use the terminology of the trade. We both lived on the North Hill on the edge of the city, and a walk of a mile or two beyond the Regal golf course brought us to the valley of a little river called Nose Creek, which in those days was more or less part of the prairie wilderness. After firing a dozen or so experimental shots, which was a wonderfully exhilarating experience, I proposed that we see how good we were at hitting a target. To this end I spread out a muslin handkerchief with a faded fawn and yellow pattern on a bank of the creek, and we took turns firing. We were anything but accurate, but finally I put a bullet through one corner of the handkerchief and Fred followed with an even better shot quite near the centre. Unfortunately, that was our last bullet.

This evidence of our growing skill as gunmen made us decide to buy some more ammunition. Fred threw caution to the winds, and declared that another 35 cents on cartridges would be nothing. And so we set out to civilization – to the hardware store on 16th Avenue North East where ammunition was sold.

In those days not many of the streets were paved and there were many vacant lots and open spaces. One did not have a sense of being confined in a city with people and passers-by everywhere. We walked along examining our revolver and noting the powder marks on the magazine. We passed by a parked motor car in which a man was sitting. Suddenly he called out sharply. 'What have you kids got there?'

We stopped. 'Come here,' the man said. 'Let me see that.'

We were too startled to do aught but obey.

'Where did you get this?' he asked, examining the gun.

I told him it was my father's gun. He wanted to know whether I had my father's permission to have it. I told him the truth.

'I'm keeping this, and your father's going to hear more of this.'

I considered myself a rather shy boy, but for some reason I became indignant, and demanded that he give me back my gun and I asked him who he was.

The man shouted to someone, and a policeman in uniform but without his helmet came out of the house in front of which the car was parked.

'Tell these kids who I am,' the man said.

The policeman came over to the car, and told us that the man in the car was a detective inspector of the Calgary City Police. This frightened Fred and me, and we fell silent. We were told to get along home, and we would hear more in due course.

I was afraid to tell my mother about what had happened, and my father was away on business. I could not sleep that night, nor the next. My mother asked what was the matter, but I could not tell her. Some days passed, and I began to relax in the hope that the matter would blow over and the gun would never be missed. After all, I reasoned, my father never uses the gun and perhaps he has forgotten its existence.

Then one day almost a week after our shooting expedition, I was in the garden helping my mother dig potatoes. The phone rang in the distance and my mother went to answer it. After a short interval my mother came out on the porch and shouted angrily.

'Harry, you come here at once.'

She was extremely angry, but also crying. What had I done? She could see at once a criminal career ahead of me. I had to be taken to the police station tomorrow, and she would not go near a police station. 'Your father's going to have to attend to this.'

Making a long distance call on a telephone was something of an event in those days, and this crisis seemed to my mother to warrant one. She called my father at his hotel in Ponoka, Alberta, and demanded that he return home at once.

This he did by the afternoon train from Edmonton. I dreaded his coming. To my great surprise, he was not nearly so angry as my mother. I suspect that he regarded me as having a too bookish and sissified character, no good at games and not much good at anything, and that this pistol shooting and an encounter with the police was welcome evidence of manliness and enterprise in his elder son.

There was a consultation between Fred Seymour's father and mine. Fred and I were ordered to dress in our Sunday clothes, and the next morning we set out for the Central Police Station in downtown Calgary. The station sergeant bade us to wait on a bench, and soon my father and Fred's were summoned to go upstairs. After perhaps fifteen minutes of great trepidation Fred and I were summoned upstairs. We did not know what was going to happen. Maybe we would be locked up; maybe we would be given a beating.

Nothing like this happened. We were shown into an office. There was the detective inspector. The gun was on his desk. Our fathers were seated opposite the inspector. Fred and I stood there pale and anxious.

The inspector demanded that we tell him what exactly we had been doing on the day he found us with the pistol, where we got the money for the ammunition, and where we had been shooting.

When this interrogation was over, the inspector said sternly, 'I want you two to listen to this.'

He turned to a shelf and reached down a heavy black volume.

'Do you know what this is?' he inquired. Of course, we did not know. 'It is the Criminal Code of Canada.'

He leafed through the volume, and when he had found what he wanted, he said,

'I want you to listen carefully.'

Then he proceeded to read the section of the Criminal Code relating to concealed weapons. By the time he came to the end there was no doubt in anyone's mind, and certainly not in my own, that persistence in the carrying of concealed weapons could earn us, on conviction, five years of hard labour in a federal penitentiary.

When the inspector had finished reading he said, 'Do you understand what I have read to you.'

We agreed that we understood. Then he said,

8

'I don't want to see either of you again, but if you are ever brought here I can tell you you will be in serious trouble.'

He then turned to our parents and said,

'Here is your gun, Mr Ferns. Both of you keep an eye on these kids. We don't want to see them back here.'

So ended my first encounter with the laws of the state. When I reflect on this experience and analyse it I am impressed by the simple common sense and humanity of the entire proceeding. This policeman assumed that Fred Seymour and I were rational beings, and that we ought to know and understand the choices before us. He left it up to us to determine our conduct in the light of the law. We were only fourteen years old, but he treated us as men and as citizens and not as cases to be investigated and personalities to be manipulated by people who presumed to know why we had gone shooting. He made no allegations about our relations with our fathers and mothers or our motives. The inspector had not flattered us by telling us he knew we were good boys. He did not know, and he did not care. He told us the facts about the law and what could happen if we broke it again. That was enough.

It is reported of Maurice Duplessis, the famous (or infamous as some might say) Quebec politician, that even as a child he was absorbed by politics, and that he used to memorize the electoral returns over many years in the provincial and federal constituencies of his native province much as some children fill their minds with the statistics of games and sports. In another quite different way fascination with politics shaped my childish imagination and determined the context of the only activity I really liked – reading books. Mine was not an interest in parliaments or oratory or political principles, but in fighting, violence, patriotic heroism, and the victories and defeats of great commanders and individual soldiers, or the struggle of the 'good guys versus the bad guys' to create peace and civilization on the American frontier.

What I read was determined by circumstances. My parents were not much acquainted with 'book learning.' My mother had left school in London, Ontario, after one year of secretarial education following the completion of eight years in the public school. My father had left school before he was thirteen years old. What they had of education was good by any standard inasmuch as they both wrote 'a good hand,' spelled correctly, wrote grammatical sentences, and conveyed written information more clearly and accurately than many students admitted to universities in Canada and Britain nowadays. Their arithmetic was always accurate and quick. In his ninety-first year my father accompanied me to a supermarket where he wished to return sixteen bottles on which there was a refund of eight cents a bottle. The cashier, who earned $6.00 an hour operating a computerized register, was non-plussed by a situation in which she had herself to make a calculation, and she began to count on her fingers. Impatiently my father said, 'Sixteen times eight is $1.28.' But, of course, he had had an accurate, if limited, computer built into his head in a school in London, Ontario, in the 1890s.

My parents' education enabled them to work. It did not prompt them to speculate, and they never had any leisure to read very much or acquaint themselves with literature. My father educated himself but only for the purposes of his work. When he was competing by examination for a post in the Department of Agriculture, in the federal civil service he excelled several college graduates, but none the less what he possessed in the way of knowledge and understanding had only to do with his work, and it was not possible for him or for my mother to guide me in reading. They did, however, forbid the reading of 'penny dreadfuls' partly on account of their presumed content and partly because the small print was 'bad for your eyes.' They frowned on pulp magazines like *Western Story*, *Aces*, and *War Stories*, but they did not actually forbid me to read them. Occasionally my mother used to advise me to 'read some good books' and she directed my attention to *David Copperfield* which was among her possessions. Unfortunately I could never get beyond page 40 on account of crying abundantly about the behaviour of Mr Murdstone to poor little David.

A sympathetic heart moved by the sufferings of David Copperfield was no obstacle to omniverous reading about the heroic death of Nelson on HMS *Victory* or the carnage at Borodino. I once came upon a volume of Fortescue's *History of the British Army*. Fortescue's account of the desolation after the battle of Laswaree in the Punjab moved me greatly, but not with revulsion or horror. How noble! How sad! How wonderful!

My particular enthusiasm was for the great aviators of the First World War, and especially the Canadian aviators. They were the very best. Billy Bishop VC, had brought down, so I liked to believe, more planes than any airman Allied or German, and he was a Canadian. A Canadian had shot down the Red Baron Richtofen. No American came anywhere near the Canadians in the Royal Flying Corps. Years later when I had been through Norman Angell, Bertrand Russell, Tolstoy, and Henri Barbusse, I was introduced to Billy Bishop in Ottawa. I could not resist the feeling of awed admiration of my childhood. Here I was clasping the hand of the Marshal of the Royal Canadian Air Force W.A. Bishop, and there he stood a trim, plumpish man with greying hair in a uniform, the breast of which bore the sacred signs of heroism: the ribbons of the Victoria Cross, the Distinguished Service Order with bar, the Croix de Guerre with palms, etc., in two lines of glowing silk. He was a quiet modest man with sharp, piercing blue eyes. I told him he was the hero of my young days and he said, 'Yes, there used to be a lot of kids like that.'

Calgary was, of course, better stocked with books than Strathmore. There I had had to rely on reading matter supplied by my parents and grandparents, aunts and uncles in London, Ontario, in the shape of the *Chatterbox* and the *Boys Own Annual*. In Calgary there was a handsome public library, and there I used to spend hours. I borrowed stacks of books and renewed them as often as three times a week during the long summer vacations from school. One gripped my imagination more than any other – *Deeds That Won the Empire*, an extensive survey of military operations and individual acts of heroism in Europe, India, China, North America, the East Indies, West Indies, the Mediterranean, and Africa where British armies had triumphed and civilization been protected and extended.

Not long after I read this, the father of a school friend took his son and me for a walk along a prairie trail across the farther part of the North Hill. I started enthusiastically describing the casual calm with which the Duke of Wellington and the Marquis of Anglesey had regarded the shattering of the latter's leg by a cannon ball during the last stages of the Battle of Waterloo. My friend's father was an electrician by trade and a socialist by conviction who later became the mayor of Calgary. Although he used to beat his son quite frequently in order to improve his attitude towards life and authority, he was a pacifist, and on this occasion my youthful enthusiasm for war provoked him. He told me gravely and firmly that I was much mistaken in supposing war to be glorious and wonderful. It was in fact the most odious, destructive, and stupid of all human activities and was caused by the greed, ignorance, and foolish arrogance of the upper classes, and he said he could not understand why my parents allowed me to read the trash I did.

I was very startled by this view. Up to this moment I had regarded war as not only part of the natural order like education or farming, but much more exciting and ennobling than working or learning. It was a far, far better thing than anything I ever did or my parents and their friends ever did. I rather regretted that my father and my uncles had never 'gone to the war,' and I counted it a redeeming fact of the family history that my father's cousin, Charlie Dickens, had been killed by shell shock while in an advanced observation post in France, and that his father, Joe Dickens, had been in the army at the time of the Second Riel Rebellion and had fought in France in the Canadian army.

James Watson's assertion that war was immoral and bestial shook me, but I am afraid that it did not change my reading preferences. These only altered as I grew up and my circumstances changed.

In 1929 my parents moved to Winnipeg. I found myself among quite different people from those I had known in Alberta. Much to the chagrin of my mother who always aspired to live in 'a nice house in a nice part of the city' my father had bought a house in the North End of Winnipeg. At the turn of the century the North End had been a 'nice part of Winnipeg' where St John's Cathedral and St John's College School were located. Not so any longer. The cathedral was still there, and so was the school, but the eminent citizens living in 'nice' homes had nearly all departed. The archbishop of Rupertsland still dwelt in Bishop's Croft on Scotia Street on the banks of the Red River. Not far from our new house on Inkster Boulevard, across the city boundary in West Kildonan, was the home of the Hon. Colin Inkster, High Sheriff of Manitoba, who had been born a British subject in the territory of the Hudson's Bay Company and whose forbears had been servants of the company and Indians. He was a tall dignified gentleman who always wore morning dress when he attended church, and, although he had a white moustache, his face had the strong, composed features one sees in surviving photos of chiefs like Poundmaker and Big Bear.

But Anglo-Saxons of Canadian and American origins were now a small minority in the North End of Winnipeg. The majority were Jews, Ukrainians, Poles, and Russians who had come to Canada before and after the World War seeking opportunities and escape from pogroms and revolution. I entered St John's Technical High School in September 1929, and when Yom Kippur rolled around a few weeks after the beginning of the autumn term, the school was more than half empty.

My school fellows may not have come from 'nice' homes, but they were energetic and competitive at school and many were highly intelligent and talented. In the first class in English I attended, taught by a man we called 'Babyface,' a stoop-shouldered boy with heavy, straight hair, dressed in a dark double-breasted suit was asked to read a passage from *Hamlet*. He did this in a histrionic manner pausing over the phrases and savouring the words as if they were hard candies. Some of the boys guffawed, and were told by 'Babyface' to be silent. The boy reading Shakespeare was Max Freedman who became the *Manchester Guardian*'s correspondent in Washington for many years. He had a voracious appetite for books, a flowing English style, and an extraordinary talent for flattery. He once publicly declared that he passionately loved President Lyndon Johnson.

There was a high order of musical talent in the school. Bohdan Hubicki, whom we called Bohdan da Fiddler, was a member of the London Symphony Orchestra when he was killed in a German bomb attack. Eugene Nemish became an internationally known concert artist, and so did Zara Nelsova.

The brother of a boy who sat opposite me in 11A became a physicist at Los Alamos and the first man to die in a radiation accident. The list is long of those who became physicians, surgeons, lawyers, research scientists, and literary men and women. Another boy whose desk was near mine in 11A was Morris 'Tubber' Kobrinsky who became a celebrated football player and a physician with a considerable reputation.

I had never been a star student. In a school like St John's Tech. I was nobody, always down near the bottom of the class. Too lazy, too lacking in self-discipline, too imprisoned in my imaginative world of heroes, and too uncompetitive, I managed only to survive in this atmosphere of habitual and energetic striving. Some of my teachers thought there was something in me, but none of them succeeded in bringing out whatever it was and converting it into academic success. Once I failed an examination in French grammar and the mother of a friend, whose parents were French from France where both had been teachers, undertook to tutor me for a 'supplement' examination. She asked me first to write a short essay in French. She read it through, and then said, 'Harry, you have a good French style, but oh dear, you cannot make the adjectives agree with the nouns and your knowledge of verb endings is dreadful.' This about summed me up. I had not done the hard work, and what was true of my French was true of everything I did at school. The only crumbs of comfort for my self-esteem given to me by a teacher was the remark in a school report to my parents made by a bosomy lady with disordered hair and a pince-nez: 'In history, Harry should go far.' In St John's Tech. I did not seem to be going anywhere and it took a sharp shock in the real world of work to awaken me from the dream world in which I lived.

13

School from first to last was a neutral experience of which I have very little detailed recollection. No teacher ever terrified me, and no boys ever bullied me. Once a class teacher entered me in a competition for a prize in Canadian history, but I did not win. For some reason I never understood I had been appointed a platoon commander in the Stanley Jones School Cadet Corps in Calgary and in my final year in the school there the commander of the corps. I was the Duke of Wellington, but I lost my Waterloo on the inspection day, when a colonel of the Canadian militia came to look at the corps' performance. He ordered me to form the platoons into columns of four, march them past the saluting point, and then reform the platoons into lines of two. In the concluding part of the operation I gave the wrong order with the result that the lines of two looked like the teeth of a saw instead of a smooth ranking with the small boys in the centre of the lines and the tall boys at each of the ends.

And yet I learned some important lessons at school, and particularly from the subjects which excited me least. In those days the educational authorities prescribed a balanced curriculum. Those who aspired to professional education were required to pass the matriculation examinations held by the provincial department of education at the end of one's career in high school, and these examinations obliged all students to reach an acceptable standard in English, history, mathematics, one or more sciences, and one or more modern foreign language and Latin. Boys and girls could choose more science and less language study or *vice versa*, but all were obliged to study some science and some language. There was no nonsense about boys and girls from 14 to 18 following their own inclinations and doing what they liked best to the exclusion of what was conceived as a necessary foundation for further education.

I had no natural inclination to study chemistry, physics, and biology, and I had no talent for the performance of experiments and the preparation and study of slides. None the less I was deeply and permanently impressed by the way the teachers of chemistry and physics set about proving propositions about energy and chemical elements which were not at once evidently true by their mere statements. I could not see atoms or molecules, but I was compelled to believe in the truth of what was said about them by the visible and measurable evidence which flowed from the simple experiments we were obliged to witness or perform ourselves.

Mathematical reasoning may have bored me, and I may have had no talent for the activity, but I was deeply respectful of those who could, by following the rules of reasoning about quantities and forces, lay out on paper what it is necessary to do in order to build a bridge capable of bearing the weight of great express trains crossing hundreds of feet above a wide river. By the time I was fifteen or sixteen I was strongly aware that there is a truth about the physical world which does not flow from feeling or wishing or imagining but requires for its apprehension the use of reason and procedures of observation, which men and women can learn, can develop, but which they cannot arbitrarily manipulate. Thus it was from study of subjects which attracted me least that I learned the most.

Physics, chemistry, biology, and geography as they were taught to us in St John's Technical High School did not, of course, constitute a cosmology or provoke in me speculation about the creation of the universe or the origin of life. In so far as I thought at all about these larger questions I accepted the account of the creation as presented in the Bible. My family were conventional Christians and members of the Church of England. They were not very active church-goers, but on the other hand they respected their religion and they saw to it that their children always regularly attended Sunday School. Religion itself was not taught in the schools of Alberta and Manitoba which I attended, and the nearest we came to religion in school was the recitation on some occasions of the Lord's Prayer. Sunday school was an obligation, but not one which ever influenced me; at least not very consciously. As far as I was concerned and as far as my parents were concerned, Christianity was a matter of morals. The Bible taught one how to behave, and the object of going to church was to learn how to behave. Going to church was itself a kind of improving discipline. In church one acknowledged in a general way that one had either done wrong or was capable of wrong-doing, and one asked God both to forgive us for our sins and to help us to do better. The notion that going to church or praying or taking the holy communion had any magical power in itself was absolutely repudiated, not in so many words but in the felt belief that to so regard the ceremonies of the church was hocus-pocus and a form of superstition characteristic of Roman Catholics, pagans, and savages.

In so far as I thought about the matter at all, I believed the Bible was true. Much of it was boring and incomprehensible, and the miraculous elements were regarded as being possible in the time and places where they had happened but not likely of repetition in Canada in the twentieth century. The central miracle of Christ's crucifixion and resurrection was something I accepted as fact, and when Jewish school fellows sometimes

15

asked me how I could believe such garbage I answered in two ways: firstly, I said that the crucifixion and resurrection was no more impossible than the parting of the waters of the Red Sea when the Lord brought the Israelites out of Egypt and, secondly, inasmuch as the Jews had instigated the crucifixion of Christ it was not surprising that they refused to accept the consequences. But even in this controversy the moral element was uppermost, for I believed, as I think my fellow Christians believed, that the main thing about Christ was not his death or resurrection but His teaching about loving one another, turning the other cheek and regarding all men as brothers. Religion had to do with behaviour. Christ was an example much more than a redeemer.

Religion taught us the difference between right and wrong, between good behaviour and bad behaviour. What was good and right and what was bad and wrong were so because God said they were. He had said it to Moses, and His Son had repeated this when He was on earth. And furthermore God punished the wrong doers and He rewarded those who were good and did right.

In his *Autobiography* R.G. Collingwood tells us how at the age of eight he came upon *Kant's Theory of Ethics*, and that reading this provoked in him an intense excitement so that he 'felt things of the highest importance were being said about matters of the utmost urgency.' I was more than twice Collingwood's age when I had a similar experience. The book was not by Kant but by Plato.

For a reason which I shall endeavour to explain, I had come to the conclusion in my eighteenth year that I did not know how to think. I confessed this to a bookseller in Winnipeg named Bruno Lasker. He searched about on his shelves and produced a small, brown, leather-covered volume, which he said he would sell me for ninety-five cents.

'This should help you to think,' he said, as he presented it to me. The book was *The Republic of Plato* translated by Davies and Vaughan, described on the title page as late fellows of Trinity College, Cambridge. Here I was with a book of which I had never heard before. It had been written by a man who had been born 430 years before Christ; who knew nothing of Moses or of God; and who in his discourse referred to gods in a casual way as we might refer in Canada to hockey players or other objects of popular worship. And yet this man had a conception of the good, of right and wrong which he was himself endeavouring to explain and justify without reliance on the authority and authorship of God.

I do not wish to leave the impression that I understood all or even very much of the *Republic*. What electrified me was the way Plato argued. A conception of good and bad, right and wrong, could exist independently of God, or so it seemed to me – certainly independently of the God of Moses about whom Plato obviously knew nothing.

When the magnitude of my discovery dawned upon me I rushed down to the basement of my home where my mother was washing clothes. I explained excitedly what I had read.

'You shouldn't believe everything you read in books,' she said.

'But what about the Bible?' I replied.

'That's different,' she said and went on with her washing.

The dawning or the enlightenment had, however, happened, and I was never the same again.

How was it that I had come to the conclusion that I did not know how to think? The answer to this question is to be found in the first friendship I ever had of an intellectual character. Until I met Lea Lardner some time early in 1930 I had never encountered anyone nearly my own age who was capable of exciting my mind and of challenging me with unfamiliar ideas.

I was still a schoolboy, and Lea was not. He was three or four years older and even older in experience of life. Having early exhibited a talent for drawing, he had left school at the age of 14 or 15, taken employment with a firm of printers and lithographers, and had learned there and at night classes the trade of commercial artist and engraver. He had simultaneously developed an interest in mathematics, astronomy, and philosophy. His aspirations to become learned had prompted him to buy books, mostly in English but some in French and German, which he was able to do because he earned rather more money than young men of eighteen or nineteen years of age. He did not read them all, but they were an expression of intellectual ambition and love of learning – particularly of mathematics and science.

When I first met Lea he had just left the employment of the printing firm and had become an elevator boy (or lift attendant) in order that he would have the time and energy to study those subjects necessary to pass the matriculation examinations for entry into the University of Manitoba. His father had very reluctantly agreed to this course of action, but he had promised to back him in his educational ambition to the extent of providing him with board and lodging. The fees at the university were low in those days and Lea expected to be able to pay them out of his savings.

Apart from his intellectual interests the real tension in Lea's life was

17

the problem of his father. George Lardner was a widower who with his son shared a family home with a Mr and Mrs Smith and their son Harold. Mr Lardner was an Englishman of the kind who prompted the Canadian saying 'You can always tell an Englishman but you can't tell him much.' He had once been a stoker petty officer in the Royal Navy. In Canada he had qualified as a steam heating engineer and had become the building superintendent of the Winnipeg Electric Company, which owned two large office buildings in the city. He was a clean, carefully dressed man, very efficient at his business, and a firm disciplinarian in his dealings with his employees and his son and indeed with anyone in any way dependent upon him. He was always in command. I once went with Lea and his father on a camping holiday near Fort Frances in the far northwest of Ontario near the US border and I shared with Mr Lardner the driving of his heavy splendid Studebaker car. I must have driven this a few hundred miles with Mr Lardner beside me. Never for a minute did he takes his eyes off what I was doing and hardly a minute passed without him issuing an order about what to do.

This authoritarian disposition was complicated by religious fanaticism. He belonged to a pentecostal group which held meetings on Wednesdays and Sundays and on other occasions when the spirit moved the brethren. Given his religious views it was surprising that he even agreed to his son's proposals to attend the university, for he was deeply suspicious of godless learning. Lea was of the opinion that the critical event in the decision to approve of his son's plan was a terrible row which had developed when his father discovered some drawings of a naked woman which Lea had been obliged to make at one of the life classes he had attended at the art school. Mr Lardner appears then to have decided that university was the lesser of two evils. Mathematics and astronomy were not so tinged with evil as art appeared to be. As it was he snooped among Lea's books, but nothing profane could be found on shelves which held a book on quaterions by Sir William Rowan Hamilton and another on quantum theory by Max Planck. Books by Anatole France were fortunately in French, and Lea kept well out of sight works by Bertrand Russell.

Lea was a thin young man with a heavy head of brilliant red hair. His skin seemed almost transparent and he had a pinkish tinge about him. Perhaps he even then in 1930 harboured in his body the tuberculosis bacilli which killed him early in 1936.

But when I knew him best and saw him almost daily during part of

1930 and 1931 and 1932 Lea was very much alive and full of energy. For me he opened a window on a world of which I knew nothing or next to nothing. Lea introduced me to books and ideas which challenged the mind; his mind more than mine. Although I had no interest in or talent for mathematics, physics, and astronomy, his interest and enthusiasm none the less excited me and prompted me to listen and even argue about the implications of what he was seeking to do. In some respects he was as ignorant as I was, and in his own way he was struggling out of the darkness towards a light which he could see in the distance. For him that light was science. What constituted light was for me less certain. But we shared the same sense of searching: I with no maps at all and he with ones he could as yet imperfectly read.

This can be illustrated best by analysing what was the closest we ever came to quarrelling. Lea, of course, had never gone very far in high school and had never been long exposed to academic teaching. I on the other hand had, little though I had profited from the experience. The activity which first turned him towards an interest in mathematics and astronomy was the study of astrology when he was fifteen or sixteen years old.

He was initiated into this study by the man at his place of work who was teaching him engraving. This man was a fanatic on the subject. Lea was fascinated by astrological calculations and by the signs of the zodiac. When I knew him he still used absent-mindedly to draw in his neat, methodical way the sign for Pisces or Taurus or Sagittarius while engaged in a discussion. He still had sheets of neatly arranged astrological calculations which he had made a few years before I met him, all carefully set out with an eye to appearance as well as information.

By 1930 Lea was finished with astrology. One day I told him a joke which turned upon the superstition of pilgrims to the shrine at Notre Dame de Lourdes and we went on to talk about superstitions in general. Without thinking I condemned astrology as total nonsense. Lea flared up in indignation and embarked upon a defence of the subject. I stuck to my view. My only information about the subject consisted in knowing that astrologers were supposed to be able to foretell events because events involving human beings were controlled by conjunctions of heavenly bodies. This seemed to me most improbable, and the whole notion in any case contradicted what seemed to me to be the self-evident truth that men and women make their own decisions, and that the events in which they are involved are the consequences of what they decide to do. This may have been a very simple-minded view, but it was one which I then thought was true and incontrovertible.

Lea, however, was determined to sustain his view of the matter, and because his view was grounded on what seemed to me a physical absurdity I would not yield. It looked as if we were going to quarrel, when I said something like this: 'Look, Lea, why don't you test these theories of yours in a simply way. Why could you not build a greenhouse which could be kept at a constant temperature and then plant beans selected for their uniformity? Then calculate the conjunctions or influences under which they were planted and compare the life histories of beans planted under one conjunction compared with those planted under a different conjunction. If you then found significant differences in the life histories of the beans which could not be explained as pure chance then you might make me begin to believe in astrology.'

Lea thought this over, and he never mentioned astrology again. Some weeks later I remember him endeavouring to explain to me how certain astronomical observations could best be explained by Einstein's theory of relativity. I am not sure that Lea fully understood Einstein's theory, and I certainly did not, but I was gratified to know that in this matter Lea accepted that a theory was said to be true because it explained an observation.

Had Lea and I focussed our attention simply on mathematics, astronomy, and physics I am sure that our friendship would not have flourished as it did. Fortunately, Lea was interested in the implications of his mathematical and scientific interests for human life and the activities of human beings which could not be described as scientific. I shared this interest. Lea bought a book *Aspects of Science* by J.W.N. Sullivan, and I found that I could read, even if I could not understand, this book. Lea could understand the book better than I could, but he couldn't make it intelligible to me. Re-reading the book much later in life I came to see why I could not understand it, and Lea could not explain it. Both of us were too ignorant really to read it, even though it was written in clear and simple English.

Our joint endeavour to understand Sullivan's book produced a kind of despair: quite marked in my case, less so in Lea's. This is what prompted my confession that I did not know how to think which in turn caused Bruno Lasker to recommend Plato's *Republic*.

When I was so electrified by the *Republic* I, of course, knew nothing about the history of philosophy or religion. Reading the *Republic* had the effect of awakening me and causing me to think in a new way because it offered man-made arguments about good and evil, right and wrong, which carried conviction and yet did not require for that conviction a belief in the direct instruction of mankind by God either in the form of depositing tablets of stone for Moses to discover or by sending into the world His Son to tell us what to do. The arguments of Plato seemed to me an extraordinary revelation, even though they did not appear, in so far as I could understand the book, to require patterns of behaviour essentially different from those prescribed in the Holy Scriptures by God the Father and God the Son.

Bearing in mind the authoritarian temper and the religious fanaticism of Lea's father and the regime of 'meeting-going' which was a condition imposed on Lea in order to retain parental support for his educational ambitions, I am still surprised how little attention either of us paid to the truth or otherwise of the Bible or the Christian religion. At the time of our friendship the Rationalist Press Association was sponsoring the publication of the Thinkers' Library, which featured cheap reprints of works by Ernst Haeckel, Charles Bradlaugh, Charles Darwin, and so on. Lea bought several of these little volumes, but they never seemed to make any impact. Lea had read *Gibbon on Christianity* which was a reprint of the 15th and 16th chapters of *The Decline and Fall of the Roman Empire*, but he regarded this as too dangerous a book to have in his room, and he recommended that I read these chapters in the public library. We were both of us enormously amused and impressed by Gibbon's wit. Gibbon, of course, satirized just the sort of mindless enthusiasm and absurdity which Lea almost daily experienced. 'Too bad the brethren could not imitate Origen,'' Lea said more than once. 'Disarm the tempter is what they ought to do and at least the next generation might be rid of them. No balls, no breeding; that's the policy for them.'

But Lea was not concerned to argue about the Christian religion. He regarded those believers whom he immediately knew as beneath contempt and simply morons and hypocrites. Their dogmas were unworthy of any kind of answer, and in any event his mind was occupied with mathematics and science.

For my part I too laughed at Gibbon and admired his way of writing and the breadth of his knowledge, but I had experience only of the mild regime of the Anglican Church. What I knew of religion was acquired almost unconsciously through going to church which at first I did with my parents but later on my own for no better reason than that I liked to go to St John's Cathedral in Winnipeg. The Rt. Rev. S.P. Matheson, the Archbishop of Rupertsland who presided over the church, was known to have said in respect of sermons: 'If a man cannot say what needs to be said in ten minutes he should say nothing.' There was, therefore, no reason to be oppressed by or bored by tedious sermons. The prayers and the litany were there in the Prayer Book as they had been for centuries, and they were written in language which was moving to hear. I used to like to attend the evening service just to hear the 'Nunc dimittis.' Between 1936 and 1949 I was scarcely ever in church and I had utterly repudiated religion, but when with my family I went to the village church in Bottisham in Cambridgeshire in October 1949 for no reason but to meet some of the village people, I found myself weeping when I heard again the sacred service I had known in my boyhood. 'Blessed be the Lord God of Israel: for he hath visited and redeemed his people.'

Thus for quite different reasons than Lea there was not cause for me to seek an intellectual confrontation with Christianity. The *Republic* of Plato opened my eyes, but, as later I was able to see, it did not for all its pagan origins constitute a critical attack on religion as such.

It seems to me now very fortunate for our intellectual development that neither Lea nor I ever became entangled in attempts to challenge the Christian religion or the authenticity of the Bible. Our endeavours were positive: a lively concern with knowledge and methods of analysis of the physical and social world, which we both believed could be perfected by attending a university.

In the autumn of 1931 I entered the University of Manitoba, and Lea gained admission to St John's Technical High School in order to qualify for entry into the university. This was the beginning of a separation between us, at first a separation imposed upon us because we became very busy in separate institutions and then a separation brought about by Lea falling in love with a girl he met in the high school.

Lea's story can be quickly told. His year in St John's Technical High was an academic and social triumph. He passed all the examinations in exemplary fashion. He edited the school year book. He organized school entertainments and he taught some of the teachers things they never knew. At the University of Manitoba, I did not see much of him because he was in the Junior Division which functioned on the campus in downtown Winnipeg, and I was obliged to work in the new buildings on the

Fort Garry campus erected as a 'cure' for unemployment by the federal government and opened in the autumn of 1932. Again Lea's academic life was a triumph, and already he was planning a career as an astronomer. Then he was visited by a double disaster.

A few days before he was about to enter the Senior Division of the university to study physics and mathematics, his father took him aside and announced that he was no longer willing to support him in his studies. The reasons were clearly stated. Lea was not growing in grace. He was in fact treading a path to damnation: girls, frivolity, godless arrogance, and pride in learning. George Lardner was adamant.

In the autumn of 1933 Canada was at the very bottom of the most terrible depression in its history. There were no jobs in Winnipeg. This did not deter Lea. He told his father that he could support himself, and that he wanted no more of his assistance. He would go to Montreal, where he had an uncle, and would make his way as a free-lance commercial artist. There were no tears. It is a moving memory to recall how he got out his drawing board, his paints, and his pencils and produced some samples of his work while he waited for his uncle to reply to his appeal for accommodation. One sample in particular still fascinates me: an advertisement for a cigarette in the form of a microscope drawn with great precision and attention to technical detail in which, in place of the magnifying column there was a cigarette. Underneath was the legend in bold distinctive lettering, 'As pure as science can make it.'

The other disaster was Winnie. She said she did not intend to marry him. Winnie was a very ordinary girl, but Lea had invested her with intellectual, moral, and aesthetic qualities to be found in comparatively few women in Winnipeg or anywhere else. She had neither the inclination or the means to go to the university, and she had no intention of waiting to marry an astronomer. Indeed she did not like Lea very much judging by the way she treated him, and I suspect she was very uncomfortable on the pedestal on which he had located her.

It was in these circumstances that Lea departed from Winnipeg. When I saw him off on the platform of the Union Station, he pressed both my hands with his frail and delicate ones, but he shed no tears. 'To hell with them. To hell with them all,' he said and climbed aboard the pullman car.

But in early spring he was back in Winnipeg too sick even to walk to his father's car. He was taken directly to the hospital stricken with tuberculosis. His father was upset but triumphant. Lea had been judged, and now he would be brought back to health. Winnie returned to his bedside.

For some months he was in the hospital in Winnipeg. He seemed to show some signs of recovery, and he was always optimistic when I visited him. His books and notes were stacked beside his bed. Then he was transferred to the sanitorium at Ninette. He was still there when I was preparing to depart to Queen's University in the autumn of 1935. I drove to see him late in August. He talked about how he was going to marry Winnie when he 'got out of here.' But he was now very frail and tired. I wrote to him from Kingston, but there were no replies. In the winter, shortly after the death of King George v, I learned that Lea had died. Before Christmas Winnie had thrown him over once again. My father was a pall bearer at his funeral. With characteristic realism my father wrote: 'That coffin was so light you'd think there was nothing in it. But old Lardner looked O.K.'

CHAPTER TWO

Graduating in the Great Depression; a university in western Canada fifty years ago

I entered the University of Manitoba in the autumn of 1931 and graduated in the spring of 1935. These were years of acute depression everywhere in the world and in few places was the depression worse than in the prairie provinces of Canada. When I hear Englishmen raking over memories of the 1930s and luxuriating in grief at the unemployment and the road to Wigan Pier, I call to mind the shock I had when I first came to England in 1936 and encountered the prosperity of Britain – not just in London and Cambridge but in Lancashire and Yorkshire – a state of affairs so different from that which prevailed in Manitoba.

In the Trinity College (Cambridge) magazine in 1939 someone endeavoured to epitomize members of the college in brief rhymes, and it was written of me 'Henry Ferns Marx and learns.' This fairly described me. By the standards then prevailing I was quite a learned Marxist to whom someone like Maurice Dobb would listen with attention. It would be tempting to explain my Marxism in terms of a response to the depression. But this would be wrong. I was anything but a Marxist when I left Manitoba in 1935, and if there is any connection between my experience of depression in Manitoba and my Marxism at Cambridge it is not direct and obvious. I most certainly did not interpret my experience of depression in terms of 'the failure of capitalism.' This came later.

And yet the depression most surely did shape my thoughts, beliefs, and emotions, but not in the way one might expect. Looking back and sorting out my reactions to the social, economic, and political circumstances in which I found myself in the 1930s, I can, I think, discern a pattern.

There were some emotional reactions which were very compelling, but these had no immediate intellectual consequences. I can remember very vividly as if it were yesterday the beginning of the depression – not the beginning as an economic historian might record it, but its emergence as a public event. On a cold, windy autumn night in October 1929, I was waiting for a tram near the corner of Portage and Main in Winnipeg. Nearby a man was selling newspapers. He was crying the headlines, and this night there was only one: 'Wall Street Crash! Read all about it! Wall Street Crash!' I had only a vague idea of what went on in Wall Street; my only firm knowledge was that it was a street of bankers and financiers in New York. But there was something so urgent and so apprehensive in the man's cry that suddenly I felt a sense of doom and foreboding. When I boarded the tram I could still hear that cry and it echoed in my head as the tram rattled along Main Street towards the North End.

This feeling of apprehension passed. The price of wheat fell catastrophically. Businesses began to go bankrupt. More and more men were being 'laid off,' but these events did not affect me. I still lived in my private world, day-dreaming or arguing with or listening to my friend Lea. My father was a federal civil servant. He did not earn much money – less than $2000 a year – but he was supposed to be immune from the troubles everywhere. I could, however, see the connection between his income and my aspirations, and when in 1932 there began to be talk about 'cuts' in the civil service, I began to worry not about society but about myself and my family. I used to scan the reports from Ottawa and especially the federal estimates to see whether my father's department was the object of economy, and I do not readily forget the day when my father reported that a colleague in another branch of the federal Department of Agriculture had been fired. Would he be next?

For a substantial proportion of the people of Winnipeg – and particularly the young people – the experience of not working was their most compelling memory of the depression. For me it was the experience of working. I was lucky. I actually worked for eight weeks between 1931 and 1935 and I earned eighty dollars. It was not the fact of working for four weeks during two vacations from the university which deeply affected me, but what I had to do. This was the shock which awakened me to the world outside my head.

My father knew a number of men in the poultry trade in Winnipeg, and he asked around about the possibility of a summer job 'for his boy.' One man, Roy Calof, who owned and ran the Dominion Poultry Sales Ltd., said he might have a job for a few weeks when things were busy. Could I come to see him?

Roy Calof looked me over. 'Your dad says you're going to college. Well, the job I've got is not for a college boy, but it's all there is. How about it? I can pay you $10.00 a week.'

Thus I was appointed a chamber maid for the chickens brought from farmers for killing in the plant of the Dominion Poultry Sales, an old leather warehouse taken over by Roy Calof and converted into a slaughterhouse. My job was filthy and boring, and it started at eight o'clock in the morning and went on until five o'clock in the evening or longer if circumstances required.

Farmers brought crates full of chickens to the slaughterhouse. When Roy Calof or his assistants had struck a bargain with the farmer, the chickens were transferred to large four-storied cages on wheels called batteries. There they were given water and left overnight for slaughter the next day. My job was to water the chickens and keep the batteries clean. This was effected by removing a steel tray covered with chicken dung, scraping the dung into a barrel, whitewashing the tray, and returning it to the battery. My additional duty was to help clean up the slaughter room after the killing session was over by hosing the floor and removing the barrels of feathers to a platform where they were collected by a contractor who disposed of them. Sometimes when there was an urgent need to 'get off a shipment,' I was taken with others to the Manitoba Cold Storage where the dressed chickens were graded and packed for despatch by rail to other parts of Canada or to the United Kingdom. The cool clean rooms of the Manitoba Cold Storage seemed like paradise.

What made my work in the Dominion Poultry Sales a formative experience was not its filthy, boring nature, which I was quite willing to endure, but the knowledge that this work or something like it was what I might conceivably have to do for a very long time unless I had some qualification beyond possessing a pair of hands and a few muscles. My day-dreaming was at an end. I realized that I had been a very lazy boy and I might become a man worth only $10 a week.

There was nothing in the activity of the Dominion Poultry Sales which I could find attractive, even though I appreciated that Roy Calof and his organization were doing a necessary and useful job. Even if I could be like Roy Calof, and I knew I could not, this kind of life was not for me. And yet the men and women who worked for and with Roy Calof seemed content and even happy. One boy, a powerfully built German about my own age, became a kind of friend, and I used to talk to him about alternatives to what we were doing, assuming naturally that he would wish to escape from the fate which I feared. But he wanted nothing but what he had. 'This is a good job. I like it here. Roy buys us beer all around Saturday nights. When things get better maybe I'll go to the coast. There's big money in the lumber camps.'

Roy Calof left some kind of mark on me. No matter what kind of ideas I formed subsequently or what conclusion I came to on economic and social questions my close daily observations of an independent business man in action produced in me a positive respect and caused me to value him as a type more than the others in the enterprise which he ran. No amount of contact with gentlemen, scholars, aristocrats, revolutionary intellectuals, acute critics and satirists, trade union leaders, and politicians ever extinguished in my mind the feeling of admiration I developed for Roy Calof in the short time I worked for him – only for two spells of four weeks in 1931 and 1932.

My father who was a government inspector used to say, 'You've got to watch Roy like a hawk. He'll cut corners if you give him half a chance. But he's a good scout. He's made something out of nothing. I'll say that for him.'

Roy Calof was physically a big man: tall, sallow-faced with a shock of coarse straight hair pushed back from his forehead. There was no fat on him. A public face and figure which calls him to mind is that of the film actor George C. Scott. Just as he stood out from his employees he stood out from his family: his old father and mother who sometimes appeared on the scene and were spoken of with respect when absent but were usually the centre of rough argument when present in the flesh. There were sisters whom I never saw, and two brothers: Sammy and Maxie. Sammy worked in the Dominion Poultry Sales in an indefinite role as a conveyor of orders to others. He was a muscular, dull man. More than once I heard Roy roar at him: 'Sammy, how can you be so goddamned stupid? I told you ...' but Sammy used only to reply, 'O.K., O.K.'

Maxie was a fat, dandified type, probably as stupid as Sammy was reputed to be, but vain. He was not content to work for Roy: he wanted to be like Roy. He ran his own business and had failed in doing so more than once. Inexplicably Roy bailed him out and set him up again at least twice. I came into the office once when a loud row between Roy and Maxie was in progress. The occasion which was something I had observed – the attention Maxie was paying to a handsome young Ukrainian girl who plucked chickens.

Roy never beat about the bush in an argument. The row was not many minutes old. I had entered the office only a minute or two before Roy, but I heard him shouting at his brother.

'So you've got a big deal on, eh? So why the hell are you hanging around here, eh? Running your hands over the ass of some girl, eh? I'm not having you interfering with my people, see. They got their work to do. How would you like I should call up Rose and tell her what goes on, eh? Now get the hell outa here.'

I was embarrassed to have intruded on this family scene and I hastily withdrew. A few minutes later Maxie got into his car and drove off with an angry clashing of gears.

Usually the buying of chickens was a routine matter handled by an underling like the accountant or Roy's brother Sammy. Sometimes, however, a farmer would challenge the price or the grading of his birds. Then Roy would be summoned if the farmer could not be persuaded. 'You'll have to talk to Roy,' was the final answer to a challenge. Most mornings Roy was about, and he would come out to the buying platform.

He always started politely.

'They tell me you gotta problem, Mike,' he would say. 'What's the trouble?'

The farmer would protest the price or the grade or both.

Roy would look at some of the chickens.

'Whatta you think they're worth?'

The farmer would name his price.

Roy would say 'Ya must be kidding, Mike. I'll tell ya what to do. You take your birds to Joe Kerschott, or Canada Packers. You just see what they offer. This is a free country. You get the best prices you can. I'm telling you *my* price. If you can do better, then do it. That's how it is, Mike, and I don't want you holding things up any longer.' He would then go back to his office. Sometimes the farmer would go away with his chickens, but more often than not he indicated that he would sell to Dominion Poultry Sales.

The other man in the Dominion Poultry Sales I learned to like and respect – the man whom I regard as one of the most admirable men I have ever encountered – was Hymie Lepkin, the truck driver. Hymie was a short, round, muscular man with a fat, round, red face. He never shaved oftener than twice a week with the result that his fat red cheeks were usually covered with short, coarse bristles. I rode with him in the cab of his truck when I was taken to work in the Manitoba Cold Storage and sometimes he gave me a lift home in the evening. Sometimes, too, we sat in the shade in the loading platform and ate our lunch together. He had a mildly protective attitude towards me, and sometimes when there was still work to do at 5 o'clock he would say, 'Ah, knock off. The work'll get done. You do as much as you're paid for.'

Like the other employees of Dominion Poultry Sales, Hymie seemed content with his lot, but it was not so much contentment as a rational acceptance of his life in the light of alternatives. Hymie did not want to succeed. I naturally assumed that everyone wanted 'to get somewhere' and that if one failed to do so this must be due to stupidity or laziness or some moral failing; indeed to those faults which I was beginning to see in myself. Hymie, however, was not stupid; he most certainly was not lazy, and I could detect in him no obvious moral faults. He seemed to me to know as much about the packing business as Roy Calof.

Once I asked him why he did not set up in business for himself; why he seemed content to be a truck driver.

'I'll tell you why not,' he said. 'It isn't worth it.' This I could not understand. Hymie lived in a poor part of town. He shared a house with another family. His wife, a jolly, fat coarse girl, worked in a garment factory. His idea of amusement was to go on a Sunday to Winnipeg Beach for a swim.

Why was it not 'worth it'?

'You can't judge business just by looking at Roy. In the first place he is comparatively honest, and he makes out O.K. You have to look at all the schmuks in business. Most of them will steal ya blind; their employees, their customers, one another. And what does it get them? Nothing but a lot of ulcers. I don't want any part of it. And I'm not talking about just the Jews in business. The Goys are worse in my experience. They just don't look so crude. I tell you, Harry, it just isn't worth it. I'd rather let Roy do the worrying.'

Hymie said he envied me. 'You're a college boy. You stick at your books. Maybe some day you'll know something. Maybe you'll be a professor.'

For Hymie this seemed to be the best a man could aspire to. In this he shared Roy's opinion. On my last day with Dominion Poultry Sales, Roy gave me my cheque for $10 dollars, and we stood on the loading platform to say good-bye. He put his arm around my shoulder.

'Harry,'' he said, 'You stick at your books. I wish I could have gone to college. Maybe when the season's over my wife and I'll go to New York. See a few shows. And go to the Met. You ever heard any good opera? There's nothing like it, boy!'

My weeks in Dominion Poultry Sales were a good preparation for entry into the University of Manitoba. At least for me.

It is worth remembering that the University of Manitoba founded in 1877 is nearly as old as the province from which it takes its name, and it speaks well for the men and women who established the province as the means of governing an isolated community of a few thousand people that they considered the creation of an institution of higher learning as an essential part of their political economy. In a small community, however, faced with formidable problems of building their connections with the larger society of North America and the world beyond the oceans, the pursuit of learning could not be given more than an ideal priority. By 1931 when I entered the university it was still far from being an institution comparable in quality with any of the great universities of the English-speaking world. But it served its purpose well enough and the young people it trained were well able to hold their own in the professions and in practical scientific and technological activities in Canada. Even in the more rarified intellectual activities of scholarship and research graduates of the University of Manitoba were able to contribute respectably to the international world of learning and discovery in the great seats of learning mainly in the United States and Britain.

Compared with anything I have experienced in universities in the United Kingdom, where I have spent most of my life as a teacher, the University of Manitoba was an informal do-it-yourself institution of higher education. A student was admitted to the university without question provided he or she could show evidence of having passed the required examinations in high school subjects set by the provincial educational authorities and paid the required fees. These fees were modest: in 1931 they were $65.00 for two terms to which was added $5.00 for membership in the student union. In 1932 the fees were more than doubled for two reasons: the straitened financial circumstances of the provincial government and the looting of the university's endowment fund by the honorary treasurer of the university.

There were some scholarships originally sufficient to pay a student's fees. These were few in number and were awarded each year to the ten or so students in each faculty who stood highest in the examinations. Thus, less than half of one per cent of students had any assistance in so far as fees were concerned, and there were no maintenance grants of any description. The assumption and the practical fact was that the students provided for themselves; either their families did so, or they supported themselves.

The organization of the courses made self-support as easy as the state of the economy would allow. One graduated when one had acquired so many units; i.e., had passed examinations in courses, which were arranged in sequence and combinations but which could be taken at any time, either in the normal university terms or at the university summer school. Provided one registered for a course and wrote the examination one could theoretically graduate without ever attending a lecture or coming near the university. Of course, in science, engineering, medicine, agriculture, and home economics there was laboratory and practical work which made it impossible totally to absent oneself and in these subjects opportunities for study at a summer school were restricted or non-existent. None the less the system was very flexible and students could study in the university for a year, and work for a year or so to accumulate the means of paying their way and then return to the university and so on. During the prosperous 1920s students could often earn enough in vacations to finance themselves. In the 1930s this was not easy to do, but on

31

the other hand, the great fall in prices made it possible for parents, like my own, who remained in employment, to help their children in a way which they could not have done so easily when the cost of living was higher in relation to their incomes.

The flexibility of the system worked also to the intellectual advantage of students. They could change courses in response to changing interest. Not many did so, but it was possible without argument or loss of time. After two years in the university I, for example, decided that an understanding of economics was more important to me than the study of literature and languages. I did not have the knowledge or the course requirements to study the economics offered to students in their senior years. All I had to do in this circumstance was pay a small fee to write the examinations in the required courses, get some books, and do some work. For eight or ten weeks I read Adam Smith, John Stuart Mill, Ricardo, and the prescribed text books. Then I sat the examination in September intended for failures and odd people like myself. I never attended a lecture or talked to anyone about economics. I did it myself, and although I never became a professional economist I think I understand how an economy works better than many PhDs in the subject. Many years later I was both flattered and amused, and grateful for what it had been possible to do in the University of Manitoba, when a world-famous economist, brought to Birmingham to participate in an intellectual war among the professionals on the merits of 'quantitative methods,' sought me out, and said, 'I have so wanted to meet the author of that splendid book on Argentina.' But I am not an economist. I just know something about economics because of what I was able to do in the University of Manitoba in response to a felt, personal intellectual need.

Flexibility worked to advantage in another way. No one was obliged to do more than their capacities or career required. Most students, except in subjects like medicine, engineering, or agriculture, aimed at a 'general degree' which involved a scatter of subjects in a variety of combinations: some mathematics, some history, some French, etc.; better than a smattering but nothing studied very deeply. Any student, however, who wanted more and could do more had only to score better than 67 per cent of the marks in an examination and he or she was qualified to drop those subjects they cared least about and double the amount of study in subjects of their own choice. This was possible in their final year, and they could then go on to earn an honours degree by a further year of study. An honours degree was a necessary qualification for postgraduate study in Manitoba and in other Canadian universities.

Going to the university was an enterprise about the merits of which there were no doubts on the part either of my parents or myself. The only question was whether they could afford to send me there. We had very small means, and there were five children in the family of which I was the eldest. As far as my parents were concerned they – and particularly my mother – conceived of a university education as a 'good thing' in a very generalized way but mainly as a means of 'getting on in the world,' of getting a better job than either of them had ever had. They had no specific ideas on this subject, and they never thought of me as becoming a lawyer or a doctor or an engineer or an agricultural scientist or an accountant. What I studied was left entirely to me.

In some respects I shared this goal of 'getting on in the world' but my principal motives were intellectual. As Hymie Lepkin suggested I should, I wanted to know something, to understand something about the life of the world. The study of history and literature and perhaps philosophy seemed to me the keys to the knowledge I wanted. But I also believed that I could not accomplish anything unless I knew languages. I believed that I could not become learned unless I mastered Latin and Greek and at least French and German. Although I had taken Latin and French at school, I did not in any practical sense know these languages. None the less I enrolled to study Latin and French at the level the university required and to start on German. Because there was no room in my program for Greek, I undertook to start this on my own and to pass a university examination. And I enrolled too to study history and English literature.

For two years I laboured away at university courses, three-quarters of the content of which were concerned with language and literature. I am sure that the work itself had some beneficial effect, but the rewards from the effort were disappointing. I was not naturally a good linguist, and I had no sense of satisfaction which comes from the easy exercise of an acquired skill, and the amount of information and understanding I gained from reading in Latin and Greek was very small in proportion to the effort expended. What was the use of being able to read a few pages of Xenophon in as many hours? One Christmas vacation I borrowed from the university Library a fat volume of Sallust, determined to enjoy the experience of reading a Roman historian who I was informed from an encyclopaedia was 'good stuff.' I read a few pages in the time in which

I could read the whole of the Everyman's Library edition of Thucydides in translation. I was not, however, reconciled to this easy road to a knowledge of the classical authors, but instead felt much depressed by my incapacity to travel along the original highroad to learning. I read Sir George Otto Trevelyan's life of Lord Macaulay, and the account therein of Macaulay's feats as a reader of the classical texts made me feel I belonged to another species.

Because I borrowed books like the volume of Sallust, I attracted the attention of an old and eccentric assistant librarian named Wallace. On several occasions he invited me to drink tea with him and his wife in their cramped and cluttered cottage on the outskirts of Winnipeg. There he would recite long passages of Homer in Greek. From time to time he would pause and exclaim: 'Isn't that wonderful!' and repeat the passage. I did not understand a word, of course, but I was impressed by the sonorous flow of sound and I was willing to believe that the images and meaning matched the music. He liked me because I would listen, and it did not matter to him that I had no understanding. I think he was satisfied because it was evident that I respected and admired him in a way that probably no one else in Manitoba did.

Even French and English literature in the end seemed unrewarding. Here there was no great barrier of language which painfully had to be surmounted. But given the content of the courses French and English were more foreign languages than I perhaps fully appreciated. It was, of course, no bad thing to explore and learn to understand something of the literature of other communities and other ages than one's own. Indeed I do not see how anyone can claim to understand anything without such an experience. Far from having regrets I count as very much worthwhile the time I spent reading Corneille, Racine, Montesquieu, Hugo, and Balzac, Chaucer, Shakespeare, Jonson, and so on. None the less there developed in me a feeling of boredom associated with these studies. Some years later I had as a colleague in the wartime civil service in Ottawa, E.K. Brown, a distinguished professor of English and the author of several perceptive and rewarding books on literary topics. I discussed with him the impressions I had about the study of literature as I had experienced it in Manitoba, where he had himself been a professor of English after my time there.

The source of my dissatisfaction, I argued, was the fact that literature – English literature in particular – seemed to be about something I had never experienced. It was interesting and entertaining, of course, but literature had happened somewhere else – not in Canada and not in North America. I used a phrase that became very popular in the days of student revolt twenty-four years on. I said English literature is not relevant, and explained myself in terms of my own experience by fastening on nature in English poetry and particularly the conception of spring.

'I could never understand the enthusiasm for spring. What is spring like in Manitoba? It happens in a few days, and it means cold winds, mud and misery lightened only by the knowledge that in a few days it will be hot as hell. I never appreciated spring in poetry until I did experience spring in Cambridge, England, in 1937. It is no use talking about beauty if there is no truth in it for the reader.'

I then went on to generalize wildly about the impossibility of making North American experience into literature. Brown then made a suggestion. 'I think you ought to read Thomas Wolfe.'

A few years ago I tried to re-read Thomas Wolfe and I could not. He had all the worst vices of American literature: prolixity, self-absorption, false sentimentality, and yet when I read him at Brown's suggestion in 1943 I was electrified. For all his badness there was something real about him in terms of my own experience.

God alone knows what would have happened to me had I responded to the suggestion old Professor Perry made in 1933 that I showed some talent as a Chaucerian scholar. As it was, I had already found a real guiding stimulus from the teachers of history. There were two who had great significance for me: H.N. Fieldhouse and R.O. Macfarlane.

Professor Fieldhouse gave the first lecture I ever attended in a university. I was immediately fascinated by the man and what he had to say. In a few minutes he made me feel that the university was worthwhile, a place to which I wanted to return. There is a mystery about a great teacher which cannot always be explained. This was certainly so in Fieldhouse's case. He was not a great scholar. He was not a clear thinker. He had no political or religious message which could arouse enthusiasm. Later when I came in close contact with him briefly as a colleague I found he had very little sense of conscientious duty. He despised students, most of his colleagues, and the Manitoba community. Those more his own age who knew him as well as I suppose anyone ever knew him thought him an unhappy man. But for me, naive, ignorant, knowing nothing but the conventional liberalism of western Canada, Fieldhouse was a great teacher.

Noel Fieldhouse was younger than most of the heads of departments in the University of Manitoba. He was English and he spoke with what

I took to be a cultivated English accent. Mostly he wore a well-cut tweed sports jacket and a club tie of a sort not seen around the necks of Canadian males. He wore good shoes and he smoked a pipe. Although not a handsome man, he was large, well proportioned, and had something of a military bearing.

When eventually I began to see through him I realized he was a great actor. He was able from the very moment he opened his mouth to convey an impression of authority based upon an acquaintance with a great world away from Manitoba where people were more interesting, more intelligent, engaged in greater intellectual and political enterprises than anything we knew or could know in Manitoba. He projected an image of an English gentleman. In fact he was of modest social origin: the son of a non-commissioned officer of the British army born in Gibraltar. Nevertheless he had something of the character of an English gentleman: self-confident, uninhibited in what he said, and a great contrast to the cautious, secretive, dull men and women of Canada who taught, preached, and lectured the public.

Fieldhouse's lectures to students in the Junior Division of the university were devoted to the French Revolution. I cannot recall that he had any well-developed theory or doctrine which he wished to establish. He made it plain that he regarded everything which had happened in human history since the Protestant Reformation as a disaster for mankind. But he was not a Roman Catholic. Indeed he implied, if he did not state outright, that he held all religion in contempt, a source of hysteria and enthusiasm the consequences of which were brutality and degradation. He was an English Tory with the religion left out. Bolingbrooke and Halifax were the only English men of politics he esteemed, and we were all led to believe that he was labouring on a great work about the first of these. The French Revolution he depicted as a disaster of a kind which human beings were only too prone to bring upon themselves. Two men of the Revolution for whom he had considerable regard were Danton and Talleyrand: Danton because he seemed to understand what he was doing and Talleyrand because he survived and prospered while others perished, victims of their illusions. He advised us to read *Les Dieux ont soif* by Anatole France.

Subsequently I 'took' Fieldhouse's course on English history. He never treated any theme systematically and he skipped about mainly in the late seventeenth and early eighteenth centuries talking about people and events which had attracted his attention. We were led to believe that there was only one contemporary academic historian of any merit – Keith Feiling – and he also praised extravagantly *The Endless Adventure* by F.S. Oliver. It was difficult for a student to know how to prepare for an examination set by Fieldhouse, but he seems to have given credit to anyone who followed his own inclination to display knowledge of and interest in odd characters whom it was possible to invest with importance. I did well in the examination in English history, but I could not imagine why, and some time later I asked one of the examiners why this had happened. 'You wrote an essay on Bishop Jewel,' he said. 'Nobody else did, and this intrigued Noel. I don't think he read anything else in your paper. He just said, 'Ferns must have a good mark' and I agreed because I liked what you wrote and what's more I read the whole paper.'

It was in the lectures on English history that there occurred what seemed to me the best example of Fieldhouse's style. There were twenty or thirty students in the class, and he was discussing the activities and views of some English aristocratic politician whose name I cannot now recall. 'And he admired and appreciated equally,' Fieldhouse said, 'the beautiful limbs of horses and women.' In Manitoba in 1934 this was a bold, risqué remark to make in the presence of a mixed audience. Fieldhouse paused momentarily and without the suggestion of a leer or of any feeling at all he allowed his eyes to scan the form of the most beautiful girl in the class sitting with her wonderfully attractive legs crossed in the front row. She blushed, and Fieldhouse went on as coolly as ever.

In my final year I enrolled in Fieldhouse's seminar course entitled 'The Origin of the World War,' i.e., the war of 1914-18. Inasmuch as I was the only student who did so I used to meet him alone in his office once a week in the depressing 'temporary' Broadway buildings in the centre of Winnipeg. The course consisted in reading extensively British papers on the origin of the war published by H.M. Government in London, a variety of memoirs of statesmen and diplomats, and books like the Erich Brandenburg's history of German foreign policy, *From Bismarck to the World War*. I read and then discussed with the professor what I had read. If there was any objective to the course apart from discovering who said what and who agreed with whom about something, it was in attempting to assess where mistakes were made, much as one might do in studying a chess game. There was no theory introduced into the study; no talk about imperialism, no conception of an international political system. The catastrophe which followed the outbreak of war was never considered. Fieldhouse himself was, I think, rather bored by the whole enterprise. For my part I benefited from the work, if only because I read an enormous number of official despatches, and was obliged to discover, if I could, their meaning. In close contact Fieldhouse had no opportunity to display his talents as an actor, and he was to that extent diminished. But I remember well, and perhaps I could have profited by taking to heart one of his observations, which on the surface seemed only witty, but revealed a thoughtful man with an acute critical faculty which it has taken me many years fully to appreciate.

I had been reading the memoirs of the British Foreign Secretary, Lord Grey of Falloden, and I had a few things to say about Grey. 'You have to remember that Grey was a Liberal,' Fieldhouse said, 'And you have to look carefully at what he says. Liberals, like Russians, *prefer* lying. Most people lie if they are obliged by circumstance to do so, but Liberals and Russians *prefer* to lie.' So far this was only an expression of Fieldhouse's hatred of British Liberals, whom he regarded as confidence tricksters and of whom Lloyd George was the most conspicuous and accomplished example.

Then he added something which upon reflection I now regard as profound. 'It is not just that they regard truth as rustic and uncouth and lying as a superior form of art. Lying gives them control of situations and arguments. When truth is assumed to reside in theories, it is possible and advantageous to lie about everything else.'

It was said of Fieldhouse that he never produced any evidence of scholarship. This is true, but how many were there in the Canadian academy of the 1930s who, though they published and prospered, could have made a remark like this? And the irony of it is that it was made to one who only understood it after thirty-odd years of experience.

The other historian from whom I learned much was R.O. Macfarlane. He was a Canadian of much the same age as Fieldhouse. He had attended Queen's University in Kingston and he had earned a Ph.D. at Harvard. Many academics also had traversed his path, and ended up pedantic bores. Not so Macfarlane. He was probably not very satisfied with academic life as such. He never published much, and when war came he joined the army. Thereafter he was deputy minister of education in the province of Manitoba and after a quarrel with the politicians he organized a school of administrative studies in Ottawa.

Macfarlane was none the less a first-rate teacher, but not in the way Fieldhouse was. His experience in the Harvard Graduate School – the hard work, the insistence on much prescribed reading and study, the requirement to research and write up to publishable standards – was evident in his teaching. He gave courses on English Constitutional history before 1485 and on Canadian history and on the history of the United States. One sweated away on Stubbs' *Constitutional History of England* and the more recent writings of men like McIlwain. Stubbs' *Select Charters* was indispensable reading for anyone who aspired to do well for Macfarlane. There was no impressionism in his courses. Dates, institutions, and laws mattered, and people, the social structure, economic forces were nowhere.

It was otherwise in his course on Canadian history. At this time the writing of Canadian history was undergoing a great revolution. Although Macfarlane himself was not an intellectual leader in this revolution he was well equipped to understand what was being done and he made sure that students in Manitoba learned something about the new insights into Canadian development which were being brought about by the work of Harold Innis and the iconoclastic discourses of Frank Underhill. The old staples of Canadian historical study – the evolution of constitutional arrangements and political tensions – were not neglected, but the new understanding of the historical evolution of the Canadian economy was emphasized. Innis' great and difficult book *The Fur Trade in Canada*, first published in 1930, became an indispensable work for anyone wishing to understand what Macfarlane had to say. He was, too, a bit of a Canadian nationalist and a Canadian liberal, who fully appreciated that the conservatism of the age of Macdonald was over and the Conservative party as it existed in the 1930s was becoming increasingly bankrupt politically and intellectually. Macfarlane never directly attacked the concept of empire or the British Empire in particular, but he did plant in my mind a critical understanding of empire which made it very easy for me to sympathize with Indian nationalism when I went to Cambridge. Listening to Macfarlane and thinking about what he had to say my assumptions about politics began to change more than I at that time fully realized. Instead of assuming that political institutions could be understood in terms of ideas about the working of government which find their expression in constitutional arrangements and positive laws, I began dimly to see that, if not entirely the result of economic activities, these were powerfully influenced by the efforts of interests to accomplish economic objectives. The idea of an economic interpretation of history was beginning to germinate in my mind, and equally the notion that political entities like empires could be dissolved by economic forces. It was the analysis of

Innis presented by Macfarlane which moved my thinking in the direction of Marxism and not any acquaintance with the writings of Marx. Indeed, I hardly knew who Marx was and nothing at all about his arguments.

This experience of an economic interpretation of history was the effective factor in causing me to abandon the study of literature and languages. I cannot recall that the fact of acute depression in the economy of western Canada and the catastrophic economic collapse in the United States were compulsive factors in my change of interest. I did not say to myself that wheat at 35 cents a bushel, the army of unemployed, and riots in the soup kitchen in Market Square, Winnipeg, made Chaucer irrelevant. I listened to and was as confused as anyone else by the paradoxical economic panaceas of the time. I had welcomed the election of R.B. Bennett and the Conservatives in 1930 because of Bennett's promises to blast Canada's way into the markets of the world. Doing more business with Britain and less with the United States sounded good and made me feel good, but I did not understand what Bennett's policies meant. Nor was I moved by the plight of the unemployed, even though I feared for my father's job and the dire implication for me should he be fired. I remember watching one cold spring day a demonstration of unemployed men outside the Legislative Buildings in Winnipeg. I felt neither sympathy nor fear. In fact I shared with the demonstrators, who were quiet and orderly, a sense of bewilderment. And I can remember just as vividly an impression I had one day when working in the library in the Legislative Building. I was there reading some of the *Jesuit Relations* of which the library had a complete set, but I began to leaf over some of the learned journals only to discover that more than one series ceased in 1931. I looked about the handsome room, and then a thought came to me. Was this the way the Roman Empire began to come to an end? There must have been a day when new books ceased to be added to the libraries founded by Augustus and Trajan. Was this now happening in Manitoba?

No. These were not the factors which turned me to economics. Particularly I was excited by the economic interpretation of history and negatively I was repelled by what seemed to me the aridity, pedantry, and arbitrary and artificial nature of literary studies. I simply wanted to know more about economics, and I set about this in the way that I have described.

The Professor of Economics in the University of Manitoba at that time was Archibald Brown Clark. He was a Scotsman, a thin, wiry example of the breed. For him Adam Smith was the Great Discoverer, and the whole duty of economists consisted in explicating the sacred texts. He himself had edited the works of the Scottish economist, John Shield Nicolson, and John Shield Nicolson had been a true disciple. One day a student challenged Professor Clark on a point. 'But, sir,' he shouted, for Clark was very deaf, 'Smith says ...' He was interrupted. 'Not Smith! *Adam* Smith!' Clark declared indignantly.

Clark's method of teaching was a logical consequence of his dogmatic belief in the truths of *laissez-faire*. The way to know the truth was to memorize it as one memorized the catechism. He dictated notes, which the class copied down. Those students with parents who had studied under Clark were spared much labour, because they had the notes of their fathers or mothers. Those of us not so fortunate copied what was dictated to us. Success in the examinations depended upon exact reproduction of the lectures. My future brother-in-law and I took one of Clark's courses at the same time. I came out with a mark of something like 85 and Colin had 87. We tried to figure out his better mark and we discovered that he had put down two sentences which I had missed out.

In spite of his dogmatism, Clark provided his students with a good education in economics. Courses in money and banking and the organization and functioning of markets were available. He himself was an expert on taxation. His course on the shifting and incidence of taxation was the centre piece of the academic program in economics. It was presented as a logical deduction from *laissez-faire* principles. If men and women were perfect beings living by the light revealed to them by Adam Smith, government would not be required, and hence taxes would be unnecessary. But men and women were less than perfect, and so government and taxes, the means of sustaining government, were necessary. He did not say necessary evils. Taxes are the cost of sinful and inadequate human nature. The business of the economist is to discover what taxes can be levied which interfere least with the functioning of the economy. Indirect taxes like sales taxes on commodities or on services interfered with pricing and were therefore undesirable. Direct taxes were the best set of taxes because people then knew what the cost of government is. But Clark showed that direct taxes such as poll taxes levied equally on all citizens are undesirable, partly because incomes are unequal and therefore the weight of taxes on individuals is unequal; but more importantly because poll taxes take most money from the productive factors in the economy, i.e., from wage workers and from investors of capital. The proper tax is the graduated income tax. Then by a series of ingenious arguments Clark showed that graduated income taxes are in the long run paid principally be rentiers, i.e., by those whose incomes are derived not from working with hand and brain, nor from investment in enterprise, but from the ownership of resources such as land, mines, etc., and from capital assets the costs of which had been recovered from profits or by capital appreciation due to changes in demand. The whole had a compelling logic about it.

There was, however, another teacher of economics, a young man named W.J. Waines. I attended his course on economic theory given to students in their final honours year. Waines had a great gift for clear exposition, and what he explained was the doctrines and analysis contained in Marshall's *Principles of Economics*. In this course there were opportunities for argument and the consideration of alternatives to authoritative pronouncements. Mastering Marshall's *Principles* was a great labour. By doing so I learned really to think. One day after puzzling over one of Marshall's arguments until I was nearly exhausted I felt something happen in my head, and suddenly I found I could understand.

Argument about Marshall's doctrines generated some new thinking in the students. Marshall's analysis led to the conclusion that all the factors in an economy – labour, capital, and resources – are 'naturally' fully employed and that, if they are not, an explanation can be discovered in non-economic or quasi-economic factors interfering with the natural propensity of an economy to achieve an equilibrium in which the demand for factors of production evokes the necessary supply of factors and *vice versa*. Vested interests, for example, can induce governments to levy tariffs which interfere with trade. Another vested interest can force up or keep wages higher than they might otherwise be if a free market operated and so on. The first published thoughts of my own were contained in a letter of the *Winnipeg Free Press* signed with the pseudonym, 1846 (the year of the repeal of the Corn Laws in Britain), in which I denounced the Canadian tariff system.

But some of us in the class began to question whether the 'natural' factors operated as Marshall suggested. The conventional wisdom of the time held that much economic trouble was caused by insufficient saving. F.D. Roosevelt had during the election campaign of 1932 attacked the Hoover administration for imprudent public expenditure and for setting a bad example in the matter of saving. It was widely believed that miseries of individuals suffering unemployment or long lay-offs could be attributed to their failure to save for a rainy day. These bits of folk wisdom were not, of course, the same as Marshall's analysis of savings and investment, but there was nothing in his argument which contradicted the folk wisdom or asserted that there could be saving without investment. It was on this front that some of us began to raise questions. We had never heard of Keynes, and *A Treatise on Money* had not yet reached Manitoba. By our own unaided reasoning we asked the questions: was saving necessarily a 'good thing?' Was there too much saving? Did saving lead to investment? Did savers just leave their money in the banks and do nothing at all with it and maybe the banks did nothing with it either? Suppose, I put it to myself, Roy Calof had plenty of money. Would he want to slug his guts out running Dominion Poultry Sales? He might prefer to see some shows in New York and go to the Met. This would, of course, give employment to people in New York, but what would be the effect in Winnipeg? And maybe he would not create any employment anywhere, if he just left his money in the bank, and there was no one willing to borrow it for financing production.

In 1936 after I had left Manitoba, I heard that J.M. Keynes had published *The General Theory of Employment, Interest and Money*. I rushed to get a copy. Here was a well-developed argument which confirmed the doubts we had expressed in Waines' class about the behaviour of savers. Another milestone on the road to Marxism without knowing anything about Marx! The classical economists whom we had studied, and particularly Ricardo and J.S. Mill, had identified rentiers, and Archibald Brown Clark had indicated that they were the legitimate subjects of taxation because rentiers are unproductive, being neither wage workers nor investors. Now it was becoming evident that capitalists as distinct from rentiers were ceasing to fulfil their function of investing, organizing production, and buying labour. A paradox was beginning to present itself to my mind. As savings accumulate the stock of capital grows and the price of capital must therefore fall, i.e., profits must diminish. The inducement to invest declines, and the very abundance of capital could itself be a deterrent to investment. Possessors of money do not *need* to invest, at least in the short run. And I responded with enthusiasm to Keynes' quip; 'in the long run we are all dead.'

A university is not just teachers and books and laboratories. It is also a community of students. One has to ask what can be attributed in one's education to one's fellow students. In my case I do not think I was very much influenced, if at all, by my fellow students, and owed very little to the challenge and response which comes from mental discourse with them. In this respect my experience in the University of Manitoba differed greatly from my experience in the University of Cambridge.

This cannot be attributed solely to the superior calibre of the Cambridge students. There were young people in the University of Manitoba with lively and enquiring minds who would have flourished and left their mark in Cambridge University or in any institution where they studied. But I encountered few of them. In *The Making of a Secret Agent*, which is a 'life and letters' book about Frank Pickersgill, who perished at the hands of the Nazis, there is, for example, a gallery of Manitoba students, all contemporaries of mine. Save for one man, I knew none of these young people personally.

Why did I not associate with these able, lively, young men and women who figure in the Pickersgill book? I think the explanation has to do with the nature of the University of Manitoba as a social organization. In the 1930s it drew its students very largely from the city of Winnipeg and its suburbs, and a high proportion of the students lived at home. The circle of one's friends tended to be drawn from one's neighbourhood. I lived in the North End which was socially 'the wrong side of the tracks.' Although I had many Jewish, Ukrainian, and Polish friends and ac- quaintances and we all mixed together easily at school, there was little socializing out of school. I belonged to the Anglo-Saxon minority as- sociated with one of the Protestant churches. I was a member of the St John's Cathedral Anglican Young Mens' Bible Class in much the same way as Jewish school friends were associated with their synagogue or the Young Men's Hebrew Association, or Ukrainians with an Orthodox church or the Ukrainian Labour Temple.

Once the transition was made to the university I was almost alone. The only 'English' school companion who went to the university aspired to be a dentist, and as time passed our paths diverged physically as well as intellectually. Many of the Jewish boys and girls went to university, but mainly to the faculties of medicine, law, engineering, and science. Thus I was rather alone in the university, and furthermore I felt I had much work to do in order to make good to some extent the years I had allowed myself to waste at school. I might have made a greater effort than I did to form friendships in the university, but instead I stuck to my own ethnic-religious minority in the North End.

The St John's Cathedral Anglican Young Men's Bible Class was my club, society, and means of enjoying myself when I wanted to turn from books and university work. As I recall it, I was the only university student among three dozen or so young men varying in age from eighteen to thirty: bank clerks, clerks in the Grain Exchange and insurance offices, a young medical doctor, a telephone linesman, and several who had never had more than casual jobs in shops and offices and could be properly described as unemployed. Some of them were very average citizens. Others were out of the ordinary or were related to people who rose in society. The brother of the telephone linesman became an Anglican bishop. One of the unemployed I last saw in Canada in the summer of 1938; I next met him in a blacked-out court of St John's College, Cambridge, in October 1939, where he had just been rejected by the RAF. I next saw him in a picture on the cover of Life magazine dangling his feet in the sea while waiting to be taken off at Dunkirk. I next heard of him as a brigadier and the military adviser of the Emperor Haile Selassie; then as the proprietor of a doughnut-baking enterprise in Florida, and finally as a victim of heart failure.

The leader of the bible class was G.J. Reeve, the principal of St John's Technical High School. George Reeve was an Englishman who had become a teacher through Ruskin College, Oxford. He was not in any way a typical Canadian high school teacher inasmuch as he seemed outside society while being very active in it. He had an easy-going self-confidence based on tolerance and freedom from social prejudice, which in the 1930s were still very present in Winnipeg. He was, for example, a summer resident at Victoria Beach, a resort organized as a joint stock company, whose directors ensured that none but approved people had cottages there. In practice this meant no Jews or 'foreigners.' Every few years Reeve used to challenge this policy and kept on chipping away at the prejudices of his fellow vacationers. More than once he invited the rabbi of one of the principal synagogues to speak to the bible class. One autumn we worked our way through George Bernard Shaw's *Intelligent Woman's Guide to Socialism*. When the legislation to establish the Bank of Canada was before Parliament he invited me to give a lecture on central banking and the significance of the legislation, having heard that I knew something about the subject on account of my study of banking at the university. On another occasion he induced Professor Fieldhouse to talk to us about events in Spain. Added to all this we had an annual dinner in the parish hall and parties at times like Hallowe'en. Years later when I was organizing a co-operatively owned daily newspaper in Winnipeg, I asked George Reeve to become a director. He readily agreed and succeeded me as president of the company when I was forced out of office.

As far as I was concerned the bible class resembled the university in being an institution in which I learned more from the leader, or the opportunities created by the leader, than I did from the members.

There was one individual in Winnipeg, associated with no institution, to whom I owe an intellectual debt. He was an unemployed stock-brokers' clerk named James H. Gray. I met Jimmy by chance in a lecture in the Playhouse Theatre by Luigi Villari on Mussolini's Italy. I used to visit him in a little cottage he and his wife had across the Red River in Elmwood. At that time he was launching himself on a successful career in journalism and he was living the life he has described so well in *The Winter Years*. In that book he told about the important part H.L. Mencken and the *American Mercury* played in his self-education. He introduced me to Mencken, George Jean Nathan, and the essayists and critics in the *Mercury*. At the university R.O. Macfarlane used to urge upon us that there was another side to American life than that depicted in the *Saturday Evening Post* and the *Literary Digest*, and he recommended *The Education of Henry Adams* as an antidote for the boosterism and the flatulent American dogmas about progress and democracy. Mencken was stronger stuff and funny into the bargain. Reading him led on to Veblen, Lincoln Steffens, and the muckrakers. By 1935 I lost interest in the *American Mercury* because the depression was a more telling indictment of the American 'booboisie' than anything Mencken could say, and this had turned him sour and into a sympathizer with German fascism. But I have often much regretted the loss of the scepticism about politicians and ideologists which Mencken stimulated and I was soon to abandon. It is a useful assumption in contemplating politics and one not much inculcated in the Canadian universities of my day, that political leaders are as often as not the 'con' men Mencken described them as being.

CHAPTER THREE

Book Learning about Art and Love

The young man who wrote letters to the *Winnipeg Free Press* denouncing obstacles to international trade and lectured to a bible class on the saving merits of a central bank modelled on the Bank of England can properly be described as a classical and, indeed, old-fashioned liberal. He believed in the virtue of the free market economy. He, of course, recognized the shortcomings of the market economy as it existed in Canada in the 1930s, but he attributed these to imperfections of the market system which could be remedied by reform and institutional innovation. There were some niggling little doubts generated by the study of history and theoretical economics, but he was *in esse* a liberal individualist whose aim was to become a rational man and to assist in making society equally so.

There were to be many ironies in the life of this young man. One of them relates to his practice of planning. While he held to the faith in free enterprise, he was a very careful planner of his life. Once he became a Marxist and a partisan of plans for everything, he ceased to plan for himself and lived by impulse.

During my last year in the University of Manitoba I was obliged to take stock of my circumstances and to consider what I was to do next; how I was going to find an income to support life and how I was going to realize my not very well defined ambitions. I was at the university and I was happy there. And so naturally I thought in terms of more university. But how? My parents had five children and small means. It never for a moment entered my head that I could do anything else but 'stand on my own feet.' I had to find the means of life in the world at large and no longer in my family. As it was I had lived in and off my family for a much longer time than most Canadians were accustomed to do.

To continue in a university one could not in those days expect any assistance except that which universities were themselves able to give or which the charitable endeavours of private citizens created. Two major possibilities presented themselves: to get a scholarship, studentship, or assistantship in one of the graduate schools in the United States or to get a scholarship which would enable me to study in Britain. There existed, of course, a small number of opportunities for graduate study in Canada assisted by scholarships, but in the 1930s such opportunities were regarded, not entirely with justice, as second best. Whatever may be said of them they were very few.

In calculating my own prospects, I came to the conclusion that I could not expect to move directly from Manitoba to one of the prestigious American graduate schools like Harvard or Chicago, nor could I at once expect to get a scholarship which would enable me to study in Britain. I believed that I was insufficiently prepared and that the University of Manitoba was not itself a sufficiently prestigious institution to command entry for its students into the more exalted institutions of learning. I decided to concentrate on getting something in an eastern Canadian university as a step in the direction of what I considered 'better things.'

I did not put my thoughts so frankly to R.O. Macfarlane, but he agreed with me about the desirability of a modest objective. He undertook to explore the possibility of getting something in his old university, Queen's. And so it turned out. Queen's was willing to consider me for a teaching fellowship worth $700 dollars a year and the opportunity to work for a Master of Arts in history. In order to build up this sum sufficiently to cover the cost of travel to Kingston I asked H.N. Fieldhouse's advice. He was planning to go to England and France during the vacation, and recommended that I be appointed to teach his course in the Summer School. Another $220. Altogether I had enough money for the first step up.

Then I had a piece of luck which came disguised as injustice. It is worth explaining my good fortune as an example of informal politics.

First, the setting. In 1935 the University of Manitoba was beginning to recover from what was known as the Machray scandal. John A. Machray, KC, was what today would be called an 'establishment figure': nephew of the first archbishop of Rupertsland, born in Scotland but educated in the University of Manitoba and at Cambridge, chancellor of the archdiocese of Rupertsland, and honorary bursar of the University of Manitoba. In his career as a respectable, model citizen of high social standing, he looted the treasuries of both the university and the Anglican Church. Altogether he got away with $1,700,000 from the endowment funds of the institutions with whose financial affairs he had been entrusted. He was such a shameless villain that before he went to jail he endeavoured by legal chicanery to keep possession of the large paid-up insurance policies he possessed.

In addition to the Machray defalcations others of a lesser kind were discovered, the independent work of minor administrative officials in the university. An eastern lawyer, Sidney Smith, was appointed president to restore the University and make it cleaner than a hound's tooth, free of any suggestion of lax administration and nepotism.

Second, a little episode of a gold medal in which I figured. Gold medals were awarded each year to the graduating students who stood highest in the examinations in the several faculties of the university. Because the marks awarded in the several subjects of study differed considerably, and students of mathematics, for example, tended to earn numerically high marks compared with, say, students of English, there had been devised a system of 'raised averages' designed to make comparisons of achievement possible, i.e., the student scoring highest in a particular subject was assigned a mark of 100 and other students proportionate percentages of marks according to their rank order. Thus the student having the highest marks in mathematics was accorded a score of 100%; in English 100%, and so on. The system of raised averages was published in the university calendar as a publicly acknowledged rule of administration.

When the names of the graduating class were published, a student of classics in the Faculty of Arts was declared the winner of the University Gold Medal in Arts with the name of H.S. Ferns added followed by the words *proxime accessit*. I knew I had done well in the examinations, but at first I thought that, perhaps, some account had been taken of the fact that I was the only student writing one examination and had thus scored 100 in an easy way and without competition. I was, however, rather puzzled, and I mentioned my puzzlement to W.J. Waines. He said that the matter seemed strange to him inasmuch as I had the highest marks in all the courses. He declared that he intended to look into the matter.

He did, and he was indignant to learn that the registrar's office had decided in this case simply to use the numerical marks and not use the system of raised averages. Because the winner of the gold medal was the son of a professor in the university, this arbitrary proceeding contrary to the publicly declared rules of the university left an unpleasant impression. Waines declared that henceforward he would always give the highest students in his courses 100 in order to prevent injustice to them, and in my case he recommended that I complain to the president of the university.

This I did in a letter setting forth the reasons why I was puzzled by the *proxime accessit*. I very soon received a phone call from the secretary of the president asking me to see him.

President Smith received me in his office. He was a large, plump man, well barbered and carefully dressed in a manner just a little less sombre than the average business executive. He exuded charm and bonhomie.

'Now,' he said, 'Tell me about your problem.'

I replied that I had no problem, but maybe the university had one. My information suggested that the people who made decisions about the award of medals did not observe the regulations of the university.

The president continued to smile, and then said, 'I believe you are being considered for a teaching post in the Summer School.'

I said nothing. This statement just hung in the air. Then he said: 'What do you want me to do?'

I told him that what had been done could not be undone. I did not care about the gold medal, but what did concern me was the fact that in seeking for scholarships I was competing with other students, and whether I was first or second could be a matter of some importance in this connection. The president said I should not let this worry me. References written on my behalf would do full justice to me. 'You can take my word for it,' he said. I told him that this suited me fine, and I had nothing more to say. We shook hands.

A few days later there was a letter in the post for me from the university. It informed me that I had been awarded a travelling scholarship worth $425.00. This was my luck: something I never expected and something I did not really need. I had *in toto* $1320 to finance my first year away from home – a sum only $530 less than my father had to maintain a family of six.

While I was engaged in planning the immediate future in the way I have described, I was simultaneously planning further ahead: what to do after Queen's University and how to do it?

There were two alternatives: to find the means of graduate study in Britain or the United States, or to try for the federal civil service. This alternative had been created by a new, experimental endeavour of the Civil Service Commission to recruit university graduates by selective examination for undefined administrative posts following the pattern of the British civil service. I applied for an opportunity to write the necessary examinations and I did so before leaving Winnipeg.

As to further university work I established in my mind what needed to be done. About opportunities in the United States I decided to wait until I was settled in Queen's University and able to command their assistance in getting into Harvard or Chicago. Going to Britain required immediate attention because the means of doing so was under the control of people in Manitoba. The means were two in number: a Rhodes scholarship or a scholarship provided annually by the Imperial Order of the Daughters of the Empire.

Both of these opportunities owed their existence to an enthusiasm for and a belief in the beneficient civilizing influence of British imperial power around the world. The first, of course, owed its existence to Cecil Rhodes, the immensely rich mining entrepreneur and land speculator whose scene of operations was half of Africa south of the Sahara. The second was the work of thousands of Canadian women, mostly mothers and/or wives of Canadians who had served overseas in the First World War. They believed equally in the virtues of education and being British. None of the Daughters whom I ever met were rich or high-born. Mrs MacQuillan, the secretary of the IODE in Manitoba, was a matriarch who lived in a very modest house off Portage Avenue in Winnipeg. She had no social or intellectual pretensions, but she obviously believed firmly in the value of what she was doing and she had a talent for raising money in small sums from a lot of people and for its administration. She and Cecil Rhodes were at one in so far as their ideals were concerned, and behind her were thousands of a like mind.

I decided against attempting for a Rhodes scholarship. I was a good student, but I had never displayed any of the capacities for leadership and physical prowess on the playing fields which Rhodes considered necessary. An IODE scholarship, on the other hand, seemed a possibility, and it had the additional merit of allowing a holder, who might be either male or female, to study at any university institution in the United Kingdom. It was not nearly so rich a scholarship as a Rhodes scholarship, but it was generous and adequate so far as I could see.

I calculated, I think rightly, that I needed some sponsorship additional to what I could expect from my teachers in the university: the recommendation of someone in the upper reaches of Winnipeg society. But where to find such support? I had no friends nor did my family have friends in the Winnipeg establishment. One day a solution of this problem occurred to me. My father had met in the course of his work, Major H.G.L. Strange, a man who had won the 'World Wheat Championship,' and who was married to Kathleen Redman Strange, a writer of some repute. Major Strange at this time had ceased farming in Alberta, and had established himself as a public relations man with the grain trade. Would my father go to see Major Strange? He did, and Major Strange asked me to come for a talk. I visited him in his office in the Winnipeg

Grain Exchange. He was a raffish, uninhibited Englishman who was rather intrigued by what I wanted, and he agreed to support me.

Once I had formally applied for the scholarship I was sent to see the assessor and academic adviser of the IODE, Professor Watson Kirkconnell. He taught in a church college, United College, then an affiliated institution of the University of Manitoba. Kirkconnell was a shy, thin man who peered at people through round horn-rimmed spectacles. He had a great gift for languages, and he had translated much poetry from Polish, Czech, and Ukrainian. Publicly he was known as a bitter and outspoken critic of Bolshevism and Communist Russia, and he was a member of one of the Polish orders of chivalry. Because he was a vague and taciturn man in private conversation, I could not guess what impression I had made upon him. So having carefully tied up the ends of all my plans and with a purse full of money I set out for Queen's University in Kingston, Ontario.

Queen's was on the whole a disappointing experience for me. The professor under whose direction I was to work was R.G. Trotter. He was a distinguished scholar well known in the 1930s for his book *Canadian Federation*, which in its day helped to advance the understanding of nation-building in Canada by getting away from the concern with personalities and parties and by giving 'due weight to non-political factors.' He was a kind, modest, methodical man, but he was very boring. He had been trained as a scholar in the United States where at that time the supreme goal was to achieve an unimpassioned objectivity and to concern oneself strictly with well-documented facts. This by itself was a worthy way, but in Trotter's case it seems to have reinforced a natural suspicion of all feeling, so that by comparison with R.O. Macfarlane, whose scholarly achievements in no way matched Trotter's, he seemed to have little to say and little capacity to create excitement about the history of Canada. It used to be said at this time that Canadian history was as dull as ditchwater and full of it. Trotter's studies suggested that the ditchwater was in fact clear and drinkable, but not very refreshing none the less. In talking with him I was sometimes baffled by the cautious way he avoided questions about the meaning of nationhood in Canada's case, and finally I formed the impression that, perhaps, Trotter really was more aware of the ambiguities of Canadian political life than he would ever openly admit and that his caution was a way of putting out of his mind conflicts of values too hard and too disturbing to contemplate. In this respect Trotter was a very common Canadian type, believing, as it were, that if one doesn't think about difficulties and dilemmas they will go away. And they often do.

As a challenging intellectual experience my year at Queens amounted to nothing. It did, however, contribute two opportunities which added to the felicity of life.

The first had to do with visual art. In order to understand my experience in this regard one has to appreciate what it was like to grow up in the Canadian west in the 1920s and 1930s. There was very little there that was more than fifty years old and very, very little that had not been built for immediate use in commerce, agriculture, and industry or for domestic comfort. There were some examples of an effort to create the magnificent in the way of architecture and decoration. The Legislative Building in Winnipeg is an instance of this. By and large, however, there was little in western Canada which one can describe as high art. This was something one learned about at second hand in books and from illustrations, but one had neither direct knowledge of nor a firsthand acquaintance with the works of man which one was led to suppose are supreme achievements of skill, understanding, and feeling.

One's ignorance was reinforced in my case by attending to the throw-away opinions of Professor Fieldhouse. The views he expressed were very likely different from what he might have been willing to stand by under challenge by knowledgeable people, but the impression he did create in my mind was that Anglo-Saxons everywhere were philistine brutes incapable of appreciating anything which could not be translated into money and that the higher sensibility was the prerogative of the French, the Italians, and the people of Mediterranean Europe and the Near East. I felt that not only was I ignorant of high culture but probably suffered from a racial handicap in this regard. Reading *The Education of Henry Adams* did not help either.

When I arrived at Queen's I found there was a course which I could take concerned with the Renaissance and the Reformation and which included a study of the art of the Renaissance. I inscribed myself for this course which was taught by a bald-headed little Englishman named Professor A.E. Prince. There were no examples of the art about which Prince lectured and his only visual aids were a large collection of small rotogravure reproductions in brown and white of the work of Giotto, Bellini, Raphael, *et al*. In spite of these handicaps Prince had the capacity to generate feeling and understanding, and to establish in the minds of his auditors that there is good and bad art and that one can develop one's taste. He did not lay down any rules concerning what is good or bad. Rather he inculcated the view that beauty was in the eye of the beholder, but also that the beholder ought to cultivate a sensibility which historical knowledge and technical understanding could articulate and enhance. In short, one could learn to see and to feel.

Prince further told us that, if the opportunity ever presented itself, we ought to visit the National Gallery in Ottawa, where it was possible to see a few examples of the work about which he talked. Nowadays Canada has a number of splendid art galleries, but in those days the national gallery was a series of rooms at the top of a museum largely given over to the display of dinosaur bones, Indian pipes, tomahawks, canoes, and feather work. None the less, there one could see some examples of European art. And what a revelation this was! Following Prince's precepts I just looked and then decided for myself what was the best to me. Then I looked at the catalogue. The result: El Greco top of the list!

Whenever I feel sour and disillusioned about faculties of arts and of the social sciences, and this has been a not infrequent experience during the past fifteen years, I remember A.E. Prince and the course he gave in Queen's. Then confidence returns that, amid the cacophony of cant, young people can still discover and hear the voice of cultivated feeling and disinterested reason, if they will but search.

The second of the beneficial effects of Queen's University upon me had to do with sex. Anyone acquainted with this university in the 1930s will probably think this a most surprising statement. And it is. Some explanation is required.

The part played by the university was this. The Douglas Library kept under lock and key a copy of Van de Velde's book *Ideal Marriage*. At this time the discussion of sex was just beginning to emerge from the shadows as far as the general public was concerned, and in this matter I was very much part of the general public: ignorant, bewildered, and full of fears. I learned in one of the popular journals – probably in the pages of *Time*, which I always used to read – that there was this book by a Dutch medical man and that it was both sensible and explicit. I looked it up in the catalogue of the Douglas Library and discovered the library had a copy marked for restricted circulation. I asked to borrow the book and I was told I would have to see the university librarian. It required a considerable degree of boldness actually to admit to a university official that one was interested in such a taboo subject. However, curiosity prevailed over shame and I went to see the university librarian. He demanded to know why I wanted to borrow a book 'like that.' I said I was engaged to be married, as I was, and I wanted to discover the way to ideal marriage, an answer which seemed to me to have some sort of logic. And it did so far as the librarian was concerned for he consented to my request.

For me Van de Velde's *Ideal Marriage* was like Plato's *Republic* – a great means of liberation; an *aufklärung* or enlightenment, a book the understanding of which changed my view of myself and my life. Why this should be so requires some explanation and the principal explanation lies in a description of the circumstances of the time forty years or more ago in Canada.

For me, and I suspect for a very great many people of all ages and descriptions, sex was an agonizing mystery. It was not that the crude facts were not known. These were only too well known. What produced the agony and the mystery were the moral miasma and the 'official' silence and shame which enveloped the subject. My parents, for example, never discussed the subject with me, and it was unthinkable that they should do so. My father was past eighty before we ever exchanged any views on the subject, and with my mother I never discussed the subject at all. But it was equally the case that no one whom I recognized as an authority ever discussed sex: no teacher, no priest, and certainly no political leader. The nearest I ever came to hearing a view on the subject occurred during a confirmation class in St John's Cathedral held by an old and amiable Anglo-Irish canon. Referring to the 'lusts of the flesh,' which we were instructed to conquer, he stated that at certain times young men had certain impulses and when they did they ought to go for a long walk – a local version of the cold baths strategy.

This absence of guidance, this almost total silence on the part of those who in other matters were a constant source of advice and guidance about behaviour was matched by a great flow of 'information' among one's equals and all of it expressed in a language which one dared not use in the presence of one's superiors: parents, teachers, and so forth. Furthermore the language employed to describe the genitalia, copulation, and perversions of sexual activity were used either to make jokes or to express derision, contempt, and hatred.

While sexual intercourse was conceived of being at least a necessary evil – and this is how the Articles of Religion of the Church of England described it – the activity itself was beset with ill-defined but real physical and social terrors: the fear of venereal disease and the fear of social ostracism occasioned by pregnancy outside of wedlock. The only way to sexual gratification approved by society and pleasing to God was marriage.

This seemed reasonable enough. The marriage service of the Church of England was to me, as it still is, a sane and sensible document which defined the purposes of the institution and clearly established the terms on which a man and a woman were able freely to commit themselves to live together. But it did not answer all questions, and particularly not those generated by the presumption that sexual intercourse was anything but a positively good activity, or by the prevailing and powerful impression gained from the way it was discussed by boys and men as a secret, crude, and filthy proceeding. My parents, a great many of my teachers, and the clergymen as well as leaders in public life had all obviously engaged in sexual intercourse, but to a youngster their silence suggested they were ashamed of what they did and popular discussion only proved that they were right in this.

To a young man then there was the further complication that he knew nothing about women except what he learned in coarse and prurient conversation. This was knowledge of a kind, but it was contradicted by the fact, reinforced by the romantic impressions created by the popular literature and by the movies, that women were objects of great respect – like one's mother – who were purer, better, and more untroubled by sex than men. One might suppose that the co-educational schools which I always attended would have prevented this notion establishing itself in my mind. But no. From the age of six onward I was always in love with some girl or other who was 'in my room' at school. They were always pretty, nice girls but they never excited in me sexual fantasies. The girls who figured in my fantasies were the ones with swelling bosoms or 'nice legs' or saucy manners. There was no relationship between adoration and love on the one hand, and sexual desire on the other. The girls one loved were pure, sweet, and far removed from those who figured in the world of lust and desire. In spite of this it was not supposed that these girls were any different to the stereotype of virgin purity which described all women.

Given this kind of bewilderment, it is easy to see why Van de Velde's *Ideal Marriage* was the book for the times and the book for me. It was not a book about sex in general. It was about sex in marriage, and therefore it did not challenge a known and respected institution. Nor did it challenge the position of men (except in love-making) and it depicted them as the

56

initiators and active agents. Thus it did not demand too much of the male reader as he existed in 1935.

That said, Van de Velde's book was a revolutionary book inasmuch as its author dogmatically asserted that sexual activity is good in itself and that sexual pleasure is not only what people seek but should seek in order to have a full and even bearable life. Van de Velde depended in his arguments upon analogies. A recurrent analogy was violin-playing – a worthy art about which there can be little dispute. Making love was like playing the violin, a skill from which pleasure and more could come if one studied and practised enough. More than this, the violin on which one played was another human being capable, perhaps, more capable than the violinist himself of experiencing delight. Indeed, the man had a great moral responsibility to the woman, not just to keep her in sickness and in health, but to give her the most complete pleasure of which she was capable. Only by doing this could a man satisfy himself.

This blessed Dutchman rescued me from the morass of ignorance in which I was wallowing. His book had the added advantage that it saved me from another morass; the one created by Freud. When I went to Cambridge Freud was being much studied and discussed there. I bought his *Selected Writings*, and I studied them and other books on themes Freud and his followers dealt with, but I came to the conclusion that Freud was no scientist, as it was argued by many, and that his hypotheses were not susceptible to convincing proofs. Without these proofs his theories were arbitrary statements, and his work was little more than an intellectualized and higher form of dirty talk with no more or no less value than confessional conversation ever has. By no means a fashionable judgement, but one I have never had cause or reason to change.

Graduate work at Queen's involved 'original' research and the production of a thesis. I decided on a quite simple exercise: to ascertain what the Canadian political leader and father of Confederation, George Brown, had thought about the American Civil War and to do so by reading the *Globe* newspaper which he owned and the opinions of which he determined. I cannot say whether this piece of work was good or bad. The examiners approved of it, but I have never been able to bring myself to re-read it. A copy has reposed on my bookshelves for more than forty years, but it has never been opened. I cannot burn it, and I cannot read it. Curious.

In the week in January 1936 when King George V died all my plans made

57

six or eight months previously began to work out favourably. One day I received a letter from the Civil Service Commission in Ottawa informing me that I had passed the administrative entry examination in third place. I was invited to come to Ottawa as soon as possible. A few days later I was told that I had been awarded an IODE scholarship. What I later came to think of as 'the Canadian way' seemed to be working for me, or, to use the popular and morally accurate phrase, 'paying off.' Hard work was producing what I supposed was intellectual enlightenment, and this I valued for its own sake, and at the same time and by the same means, hard work plus planning was carrying me forward and upward.

I went at once to Ottawa by bus and put up at the YMCA. My appointment was to meet the chairman of the Civil Service Commission, Charles Bland. He was a polite, kind, and considerate man, and this was no facade for he treated me in the same polite, kind, and considerate manner when I met him thirteen and a half years later in very adverse circumstances. I told Mr Bland about my scholarship and how much I was attracted by the prospect of going to England. I enquired about the possibility of sitting for examinations for entry into the Department of External Affairs as a third secretary. This was the best known and most highly regarded opportunity then open to public competition and a third secretaryship was regarded as the best post a young man could get in the non-technical part of the civil service: better paid and more prestigious certainly than the new experimental entry as an administrative clerk, grade III. Mr Bland told me that examinations for third secretaryships would likely be held within a year or eighteen months and he suggested that I see Dr O.D. Skelton, the under secretary of the department. He reached for the telephone and arranged a meeting at once. He said that he would like me to meet a man in the Civil Service Commission who could tell me about an opening in the Civil Service Commission itself, and that he hoped I would give this opportunity some consideration. I was very much impressed by Mr Bland, and I decided then that the civil service had more attractions than the security which my parents had always declared was the only feature worth considering of 'working for the government.'

I saw Dr Skelton, visited the National Gallery as Professor Prince had recommended, and made a brief reconnaissance of the Public Archives, then back to Kingston. I had already decided to go to Britain. But where?

The impression existed in Canada that Oxford was *the* university in Britain. There were other places, of course, but none matched Oxford. This impression was reinforced by the effect of twenty-five years or so of appointments to Rhodes scholarships tenable only at Oxford. Ex-Rhodes scholars occupied positions of influence and authority in the professions, in journalism, universities, and in politics and the civil service. I decided against Oxford mainly for the negative reason that I was more likely at Oxford than elsewhere to be drawn into a Canadian community overseas. If I was going overseas, I wanted to be overseas and to be sure of meeting English people and whomsoever else fate might put in my way. The only other place I seriously considered was 'the other place,' Cambridge. The current holder of an IODE scholarship from Manitoba, Marshall McLuhan, was at Cambridge. This had no influence on me, but it did indicate that people like myself did go to Cambridge. And there was in St John's Cathedral in Winnipeg a young professor of theology, Canon H.G.G. Herklots, whom I liked and respected and who had been the president of the Cambridge Union. The great economist Marshall and J.M. Keynes were Cambridge men, and more remotely there were Bacon and Newton, Milton and Cromwell, Macaulay and Darwin, Wordsworth and Byron. I wrote to Canon Herklots for advice about Cambridge.

He was delighted at my choice of university. Although he had been at Trinity Hall, he advised me to seek entry into Trinity College on two grounds: it was a rich college with more scholarships than the other colleges and it was the institution which had produced 80 per cent of all the British winners of Nobel prizes. This was surprising advice from so other-worldly a Christian as Canon Herklots, but it was good advice and very much in line with my own prudential and intellectual inclinations.

As a precaution in case of disappointment I applied also for Emmanuel and Peterhouse, mainly because I was intrigued by the names. Like Trinity, Emmanuel accepted me, but Peterhouse turned me down, largely, I think, on account of the solecism I committed in addressing the admissions tutor there.

My university career in Canada was finished by July 1936. Where did I then stand intellectually and politically?

I had had no vote in the Canadian general election of 1935. Had I had the residential qualification to vote then I would have cast my vote for the Liberal candidate, not because this was the least worst choice, but because I genuinely thought the party led by Mackenzie King was the right party to govern Canada at that time. When I returned to Manitoba I was entitled to vote in the provincial election, and this I did. Winnipeg in those days was a ten-member constituency designed to hive off the urban vote and to ensure the political predominance in the province of the farmers and rural interests. A system of proportional representation determined the outcome of the election in Winnipeg. I did not share the popular belief propagated by the newspapers and the farmers themselves that farmers are somehow purer and more deserving citizens than anyone else in the community. When I went to the polling booth I cast my vote for the candidates sponsored by the Co-operative Commonwealth Federation first and then for the 'Bracken' candidates, i.e., the supporters of the existing provincial government. I did not vote for the Communist candidates or for the extreme radical ex-judge, Louis St George Stubbs.

On my way home to Winnipeg there occurred a conversation which enabled me exactly to fix my views of Marx and Marxism as they existed in July 1936. I was travelling in a tourist sleeping car. In one of the sections there was a young couple – I presumed they were man and wife – whom I judged on account of their dress and general bearing to be atypical Canadians: neither business people nor conventional members of the minor professions nor wage workers. During the journey I spent a good deal of my time reading in the smoking compartment where there were no children and for most of the time only the sleeping car porter. And I was reading C.E.M. Joad's *Guide to Philosophy*.

While I was so engaged the young man came into the smoking compartment and, after he came out of the lavatory, he sat down. From the bright yellow dust jacket of the book he could see what I was reading, and, after a pause, he started to talk to me about Joad and what did I think of this and that. Then he said to me, 'What do you think of Marx?'

I have a very precise recollection of my answer. I said that I did not know very much about Marx, but as I understood it he was concerned to state certain laws of history. Maybe it was possible to do this, but in my view we did not know enough about history to generalize about the past. Maybe some day we might be able to do so, but not now in our state of comparative ignorance.

The young man then began to argue, but I never yielded, and he gave up and returned to his wife.

Underlying my view were some assumptions about the nature of knowledge and the laws of nature. Knowledge is an acquaintance with facts. I asked no questions about facts. I simply assumed we can know a fact. From facts we can draw conclusions about relationships. If we want to call these conclusions laws, so be it, but conclusions derive from facts, and have no other source. That is where I stood in July 1936.

A Revelation on the Road to Cambridge: the encounter with Marxism

In mid-September 1936 I set out from Winnipeg for Cambridge. Still the prudent planner but also moved by family affection, I stopped my journey to visit my grandmother in London, Ontario, in order to get her agreement to lend money, should I need it, to finance my second year in Cambridge. This she willingly did and even offered to forgo interest on any money lent to me until I should be in paid employment. I stopped off, too, at Kingston for an examination connected with my Master's thesis, and at Montreal I embarked on a vessel of the Cunard line, the *Ausonia*.

The Cunard vessels which sailed regularly from late March to early December between Montreal and London had been built for the transport of immigrants to Canada as well as for general passenger and cargo purposes. But in the 1930s there were no immigrants. In fact the flow was west to east, for when I made the passage some 20 per cent of the two hundred or so passengers in the third class were people going to seek work in Britain. A few were being deported because they were both troublesome and unemployed. The fares were absurdly cheap – $108.00 return, as I remember it, and the ticket was good for three years. Inasmuch as one was boarded and fed abundantly for eleven days there and eleven days back, travelling third class on a Cunard liner was cheaper than boarding in hotels ashore. At least this was how one of my fellow passengers explained it to me; 'And the booze is cheaper and better than it is ashore,' he added.

The object of my voyage was to discover England and Europe. This happened, of course, but I discovered something else which I did not at all expect: Marxism. The 'road to Damascus' syndrome operated in me during this voyage, and I experienced enlightenment – sudden, comprehensive, compelling. It came about in this way.

At dinner while we were making our slow progress between Montreal and Quebec I fell into conversation with a man who I supposed was fifty or so years old. He introduced himself as Major Hooper, Indian Army retired. He was a little on the small side physically and obviously fit, neat, and dressed in clothes which were of good quality, well worn but also well cared for. After dinner he invited me to play chess. I hesitated to do this because, although I liked the game, I had only played with three friends, two of whom always beat me. I agreed, however, and to my surprise I won two matches the first evening. Chess led on to conversation and the discussion of political questions of one sort or another, and particularly events in Spain where civil war had broken out in the previous July. I had no views on the war for I knew nothing about Spain and I had paid little attention to events there. Major Hooper on the other hand had very well defined views and he talked forcefully about the issues of fascism, the dangers that he saw for the balance of power in Europe, and about the military aspects of what was happening. All very interesting, but nothing calculated to cause a mental earthquake in me.

After we passed the Straits of Belle Isle and the ship entered the open ocean I was knocked out by sea-sickness for twenty-four hours. When I had recovered my equilibrium we returned to playing chess and discussing politics. Major Hooper continued without much success to galvanize me about the Spanish Civil War. I supposed I sympathized with the Republic but nothing more. Then Major Hooper put to me the same question that I had encountered in the sleeping car of the train to Winnipeg. 'What do you think about Marxism?'

I gave the same answer as I had done in July, but this time I had encountered an interlocutor who had no wife to claim his attention and eight days more at sea to press his views. Major Hooper was not an acute or consistent reasoner, but he was armed with *The Handbook of Marxism*, edited with an introduction by Emile Burns, which had been published in 1935 by Gollancz. He urged me to read this volume and particularly the 'Communist Manifesto' first and then Lenin's pamphlet 'The State and Revolution.'

It speaks well for Major Hooper's judgment of my state of mind that he should have especially recommended these short and succinct bits of Marxist argument as teething dummies. He seems to have detected two elements in my thinking which might make me susceptible to the arguments in the manifesto and in 'The State and Revolution': firstly my evident interest in an explanatory concept useful for analysing the three revolutions to which I had alluded in my arguments about political evolution; and secondly, my scepticism about the value and role of the state as a social institution.

I followed the Major's advice with consequences more profound than,

I think, he had anticipated. I experienced this sudden surge of enlightenment. My mind seemed to work at this moment like one of the old-fashioned electric calculating machines. Punch in the data, then punch the key for multiplication or division or addition or subtraction, and almost instantaneously an answer appeared. Eureka!

Why should this have happened? What were the answers to what questions?

In the course of my studies at the University of Manitoba I had been obliged to consider the English Civil War, the American Revolution, and the French Revolution. Of the Russian Revolution I knew absolutely nothing and of the Revolution of 1848 very little. I had studied the French Revolution, and I had lectured on this subject in the University of Manitoba Summer School in 1935. Of course, I had no knowledge of the French Revolution which was my own. I had followed books like *The French Revolution* by Louis Madelin and my lectures were simply an endeavour to explain to students more ignorant than myself the meaning of what I invited them to read.

None the less in my studies of this revolution, the English Civil War, and the American Revolution, I had always done more than establish in my mind the simple chronology of events. I had tried to find some meaning in the events, and the reasoning that emerged in my mind was not unexpectedly the conventional notion that these revolutions were steps in the direction of democracy and evidence that man, or at least European man and his brothers overseas in the Americas and Oceania, was making progress.

These conclusions of mine, taken by themselves, were not startingly unlike what I discovered in the 'Communist Manifesto.' But there was this very important difference. I conceived of this progress towards democracy as being the product of moral development and the work of men and women, not necessarily heroic in character, who by the exercise of their mental and spiritual powers, had first imagined and then brought into being the laws and the institution which expressed and protected the equal rights of individuals. As I saw it moral energy had produced, and was continuing to produce, a democratic order which was an advance on less morally evolved political communities. Marx and Engels, on the other hand, seemed to attach no importance to moral understanding. Society evolved without dependence upon moral insight or moral leadership. Society is a form of material matter like water or a biological species. These change and evolve without the intrusion of moral forces.

What Marx and Engels had to say seemed to me more consistent with the facts than my own conceptions at this time.

After all, I thought, the researches of Harold Innis on the development of Canada showed pretty clearly that society in Canada had been created by economic activity, not by politicians and soldiers. Fur trading, cod fishing, and lumbering were not moral activities, but they were the activities which had created Canada. Indeed those who engaged in these activities were often not over-scrupulous in their morality. Greedy and violent men were often successful men, not just in the sense that they became wealthy, but in the sense that they created great enterprises beneficial to large numbers of people. They conquered the wilderness and made it flourish. What was wrong with that?

Without any promptings from Marx, I already was more than halfway to an economic interpretation of history. Marx and Engels did add a new dimension to thinking along these lines. They opened my eyes to the political aspects of economic relations among producers. *Laissez-faire* economics was based on the assumption that in markets of all kinds there is an opposition of interest among the participants which the mechanism of the market resolves by establishing prices. But participants in markets rig markets. Had not Adam Smith asserted that the natural propensity of traders is to engage in conspiracies to control prices in their own interest, in other words to co-operate as groups to secure their collective interest? Marx's conception of class interest seemed a natural and more all-embracing conception than any I at that time entertained.

What finally clinched the Marxist argument for me was Lenin's promise that the triumph of the working class would cause the state to wither away. I had no clear doctrine about the state, but my predisposition to doubt the value of the state as an institution was quite strong. Adam Smith had employed his talents to demonstrate the idiocies of the mercantilist system of state control of trading. Canadian governments had repeatedly interfered with the economy by levying tariffs beneficial to some interests and detrimental to others. The history of the United States was one of constant intrusions of political power into the economy on behalf of vested interests. As recently as 1922 the Fordney-McCumber Act had made it almost impossible for Canadian producers to compete fairly in American markets, and the Hawley-Smoot tariff of 1929 piled up more and more obstacles to trade. And then there were the constant interferences in the labour market by the state. I had no particular affection for trade unions, but I did think that in both Canada and the United States the power of the state was used more often than not to the disadvantage of wage workers. But, of course, my view of the state was a liberal one, and it was making a vast jump to move from doctrinaire liberalism to an acceptance of Lenin's promise that the state would disappear. But I made that jump none the less. Major Hooper was very well satisfied with his work.

Why a few answers to questions concerning revolution and a promise about the disappearance of the state should have had the quality of a revelation puzzled me once I began, some ten years after the event, to recover from its effects. It seems evident to me now that there was an extra dimension to my experience which cannot be accounted for by the attractions of a theory of revolution or a doctrine of the state.

Reflection suggests that there had been imprinted on my mind by processes which are not easily explicable – the archetypes of the Judeo-Christian religion. Marxism is primarily anti-religious – 'religion is the opium of the people' – but the fundamental ideas of Marx and Engels follow very closely these archetypal patterns. There is the promise of a better life, the final state towards which humanity is progressing. In Marx the quality and character of life in this final state is no more defined than are heaven and the state of the world after the arrival of the Saviour or after His second coming. There is, however, an element of definition which has nothing to do with the quality or character of life, i.e., in the communist utopia the means of production will belong to everyone. This does not tax the imagination as the Revelation of St John the Divine does. It has a negative concreteness which can have an appeal to minds already enmeshed in the consideration of economic problems, much in the way that an image of living waters must have evoked hope in peoples with problems of low rainfall.

The concept of progress is a Christian not a Marxist notion. Man has not only a history but a destination. But the Christian images of progress from the darkness of paganism to the light of the Christian faith, though they find a concrete expression in social practices and personal behaviour, were, at least to me, abstract moral images which did not altogether serve to illuminate and sanctify the progress which impressed the mind and imagination of ordinary men and women like myself. In our homes and in the community we became familiar with Christian Protestant ideas and rituals, but there we encountered too little of the cultural heritage of the European aristocracy or even of the established upper middle class. Progress in our minds was predominantly associated with the marvels of technology – the steam engine, the motor car, the telephone, the aeroplane, the radio – the growth of population, the spread of western civilization, improvements in standards of living and so on. There were Canadian Christians who argued that Christian progress and the gospel of bigger and better and more and more were not identical, but I am afraid I was repelled by what seemed the woolly-mindedness of, for example, the Student Christian Movement who held less philistine views than mine. The bold assertions of men like my teacher, Fieldhouse, or G.K. Chesterton or Henry Adams to the effect that 'modern progress' was an unmitigated disaster did cause me to waver in my faith in material progress of the kind I have described. Then along came Marx with his positive and enthusiastic reassertion of what I had long believed as a kind of self-evident truth.

There is another central feature of Christian doctrine which finds a material expression in the ideas of Marx. This has to do with the place of suffering in the journey of the human race towards its final goal. The Saviour suffered a terrible death upon the cross and triumphed over His agony on our behalf in order that we may know God and enter the Kingdom of Heaven. There is in the Christian account a recognition of the place of suffering as a creative part of life, although in a plain, simple man's Christianity there is a tendency to regard suffering as something Christ endured on our behalf and all we have to do is believe in Him to achieve the goal of eternal life. Experience, however, indicates that suffering comes in varying doses and to everyone, or at least to the vast majority, and that this suffering is real. Christ can be regarded as an example of how to handle suffering and how to triumph over it. The story of the crucifixion provides us with an archetypal account of human life which contains within it a doctrine of hope that by endurance and faith in the possibility of eternal life one cannot be defeated by suffering but can rise again with new strength.

Although it was not apparent to me at the time, subsequent reflection has led me to the conclusion that the Christian account of suffering as a redemptive agency which turned what is cruel and hateful and much to be feared and avoided into its opposite of triumphant fulfilment had prepared my mind for the reception of Marxism. The doctrines of Marx on the subject of revolution seemed to me a considerable advance on the Christian doctrine because it expressed in terms of social facts the place of suffering as a motor force in the evolution of society. Suffering was certainly present in society. I did not suppose that I had myself ever experienced suffering, and I did not regard my own family's experience of 'hard times' as suffering in any significant sense; but, like any person with half an eye open, I could see that many thousands of people in Canada were suffering hardship, disappointment, and the ruin of their endeavours in the catastrophic depression. If the depression did not plumb the depths of suffering, and I did not suppose that it did, attention had to be paid to the very recent and real suffering that millions had experienced in the World War then only eighteen years in the past. Again, I had no experience of this, nor had my family, but cousins and family friends had perished. Moreover it was by 1936 becoming evident to anyone who could read and think that the death of millions in the Great War in Europe involved terrible suffering which could not be rendered acceptable and then forgotten by draping flags on stones. The dead did cry out and their cries echoed in the mind and demanded answers. But what kind of answers?

Marx seemed to have some answers at least as worthy of consideration as any others. Implicit in Marx's doctrines and analysis of society was the conclusion that suffering is unequally distributed in society. He and Engels argued that there is a class in society which they believed could be defined, identified, and described – the proletariat – which suffered from exploitation and oppression. There was another class – the capitalist – which did not suffer but was the agency of suffering in others. This view seemed to me to coincide with my own experience, not in the sense that my brief experience of work in a packing plant had convinced me that the employees of Roy Calof had been oppressed and exploited by him, but in the sense that I believed, as my family and nearly everyone with whom I was acquainted believed, that it was better to be rich than to be poor because the rich suffered less than the poor. I had never gone as far as some in believing that the possession of riches solved all problems, but I certainly had concluded from observation that the possession of money did help to solve some problems and opened up opportunities which did not exist for those who were poor.

At this time I explained to my own satisfaction that the unequal distribution of wealth, which has a relationship to the unequal distribution of suffering, can be attributed to differences in moral behaviour. While I acknowledged that some fortunes can be attributed to luck and some to ruthless and unscrupulous greed, the rich, the well-to-do, and the economically comfortable people in society were not privileged but simply people who work harder, live prudently, cultivate their intelligence through education, and keep control of their desires and emotions so that they are not disabled in doing their work. Now I was confronted by Marx's argument that the unequal distribution of wealth, and hence of suffering in society, can be explained in terms of economic relations: the exploitation of labour by the purchase of the power to labour at its price of production and the sale of the products of labour at prices not determined by the amount of labour time entering into their production. Marx did not leave the argument there. He then argued that this great suffering class of proletarian wage workers are the agency of salvation and of the transformation of the world into a better place: into the heaven of communism. William Jennings Bryan when he was campaigning for the presidency of the United States had declared that mankind was crucified on a cross of gold. This phrase had always stuck in my mind, even when I laughed at it as a piece of populist idiocy and prejudice. Now I was encountering in Marx an argument of a political and economic kind which fitted the archetype of crucifixion and redemption. I had been looking through a glass darkly, and now the glass seemed suddenly to clear.

The experience of sudden enlightenment was real enough at the time. I felt enlarged and strong and free. I had learned my destination and been told how to get there. I thought I had discovered something new, refreshing, and invigorating. Events and meditation slowly taught me otherwise. Marxism is not a contradiction of the Judeo-Christian religion which had shaped my moral life; it is very like it – a materialist restatement of Judeo-Christian archetypes with the hard bits left out.

Marxism has a great attractive advantage over the Judeo-Christian religion – and not over Christianity alone – inasmuch as it flatters the species *homo sapiens* and makes men and women the centre of everything. Purporting to fit man into the natural world and thus a subject of study like bees or atoms, Marx in fact detaches men from nature by attributing to the species powers which men and even liberated women clearly do not possess. Christianity teaches that part of the power of God resides in man. This is a realistic doctrine. Marx dismisses God from the universe and locates all the power of creation and judgment in man. This is Marx's most profound error, but not one I could perceive in 1936. Indeed, my experience of sudden enlightenment was simply the sensation of escaping from the thraldom of forces encapsulated in the concept of God. Suddenly power belonged to me now that I had the key to its understanding. A new and exhilarating arrogance was born.

I suspect, however, that most of the reborn are not as much transformed as the sensation of rebirth leads them to believe. Rebirth does not so much transform as confuse, and it requires much time and mental effort to straighten out the confusion, to recover one's reason, and to discover how to use new insights, if any.

As our ship approached the shores of Britain it was bathed in mist, but I was bathed in light: not the light which leadeth men unto salvation, but unto revolution when 'tis very bliss to be alive. 'But to be young is very heaven!'

Whether Major Hooper was a communist or simply a Marxist I never discovered, nor was it in my mind to make this distinction. At that time the predominant tendency was to consider Marxism and the Communist International as one and indivisible – one doctrine and one church. Fifteen years passed before I encountered in the flesh a man who was a learned Marxist and a good scholar and at the same time a very strong and life-long anti-communist, a refugee from Germany who was not a Jew.

Major Hooper may have been a Marxist and perhaps he was a com-munist, but he was otherwise an unreconstructed British sahib. I cannot recall that he ever introduced into his discourses anything about the Indian movement for political independence or the more general question of imperialism as the highest stage of capitalism. I asked him once about 'the Jewish question,' then a matter of debate on account of the torrid anti-semitic propaganda of the German Nazis. 'Jews?' Major Hooper said, 'Never liked 'em. One of them did me over a polo pony. Never liked 'em.' This disposed of the Jewish question.

Then there was his advice about how to behave in British society, given just as our voyage was coming to an end.

It was late afternoon, and the ship was making its way slowly up the estuary of the Thames towards Tilbury. I was leaning on the rail gazing at the distant shore and the heavy oily water the surface of which was set in slow movement by the passage of the ship. I was in fact undergoing another bit of enlightenment which had nothing to do with Marx.

At Queen's University, Professor Prince had talked at some length about the English painter Turner about whose work he was very enthu-siastic for its own sake and because, he said, it had greatly influenced other painters to work in a new way. When I had visited the National Gallery in Ottawa there had been a small exhibition of Turner's work, possibly on loan. I had looked at them, but I had felt that they did not live up to the enthusiasm expressed by Professor Prince. They seemed to me just a lot of coloured fog. Where I had lived all of my life the air is clear, the sun brilliant both in summer and winter, mist only an occasional phenomenon, and fog hardly ever known and then usually accompanied by glittering frost. One of the great natural beauties of Manitoba is the wide clear blue sky in which the clouds are distant and changing but definite shapes. One sees things sharply in Manitoba.

Now I was seeing something different. There in the evening mist and setting sun was Turner's world. Suddenly I realized his work was not just a lot of mist and fog but a record and an interpretation of a nature I had never known.

Major Hooper, however, had another kind of message from a different world. Because there was no wind and we were packed up to disembark, I was wearing a top coat and a bowler hat, a common type of headgear among the more prosperous city-dwelling Canadians at that time. He came up to me and said:

'Ferns, I hope you won't think this a personal intrusion, but I am bound to say that a hat like that is unsuitable.'

'Why?' I said. I rather liked my bowler hat.

'You see,' he replied, 'In Britain hats like yours are worn by only three kinds of people: officers of the Guards when in mufti, commercial men, and in Cambridge by college porters and servants. You are not an officer of the Guards; you would not care to be thought a commercial man; and in Cambridge a hat like yours could be very much out of place.' He then suggested that we meet in London in order that he introduce me to his outfitter where I could purchase something suitable to my station. I agreed. We met a day or two later in London. Major Hooper took me to a shop in Golden Square where I purchased a soft felt hat and a macintosh. Then he took me to a book shop in Farringdon Road where I purchased a copy of the *Communist Manifesto* and Lenin's little book on *Imperialism*. So equipped I was ready to face the mysteries of Cambridge University.

Marxist revelation or not, I was excited to be at the centre of a vast empire: to see the monuments of great victories and achievements of the past and the present seats of power. But what struck me most forcibly was the evidence of prosperity and energetic activity so different to the atmosphere of shabby depression which prevailed in the Winnipeg I had left. Here in Willesden, where I was stopping for a few days with a cousin of my mother, a master in a council school, there were street upon street of houses evidently built only recently, new factories along the roads, and in the streets on Friday and Saturday nights swarms of people going to cinemas and public houses, bent, it seemed, on pleasure in a way which could only be seen in Canada when there was a fair or an event like the Calgary Stampede. And on Sunday people flocked to the picture palaces in Harlesden and along the Edgware Road. The sight of this on a Sunday shocked me. I had grown up under a sabbatarian regime in predominantly protestant communities where nothing happened on Sundays, and only the churches were in business. My cousin's wife, a plump, jolly, laughing woman, not only went to the cinema on Sundays; she went twice during the week, and lamented the fact that she had to travel as far as Marble Arch to see 'the best films.' This seemed to me not only a defiance of a taboo but excessive indulgence, and yet Eadie was a woman with no evident moral defects, a warm friendly personality, and without a worry in the world except her son, Jack, who had abandoned his place in an architect's office to join the Royal Air Force, where she feared 'he is going to get himself killed one of these days.' But she was not punished by the loss of what she most loved, for her Jack survived air crashes, shot down German planes when the time came, was himself shot down and parachuted to safety, emerged with the DFC and other decorations, and, endowed with nerves of steel, never seems to have lost a night's sleep or a day's duty; he retired a wing commander without a scratch on him.

The train journey to Cambridge was another revelation for me. There is, of course, much natural beauty in Canada, but where man had been at work, particularly in western Canada, there tended to be squalor, barbed wire, weeds, dusty gravelled roads, flaking paint or no paint at all, roads all at right angles to each other. Few of the towns and villages had anything attractive about them, and even the cities like Winnipeg and Regina were redeemed only by an effort to create a few parks where trees and flowers and green grass flourished. How different was Hertfordshire! It seemed to me a great beautiful garden. Sometimes when I try to analyse why I have lived so long in Britain rather than in my native Canada, I am at times a little bit persuaded that beyond politics and intellectual concerns and opportunities to earn a living there is some deeper attraction – the beauty of Britain in its vast variety, most of it made by man over a thousand years or more.

My first encounter in Cambridge was with Mrs Stubbins, my landlady, whose house overlooked Midsummer Common. Her hair was done up in curl papers and wire clips and she wore a faded apron. Her manner was impersonal, and she seemed to regard my arrival with some relief, as if a problem had been solved. She showed me to my rooms and called my attention to a postcard on the mantelpiece from my tutor, Mr G.S.R. Kitson Clark. It was dated a few days before my arrival and ordered me to see him *as soon as possible*. Although she did not say so, Mrs Stubbins' manner suggested that I was in for trouble. She advised me to go at once to the college, where no doubt it would be her husband, one of the porters, who would direct me to Mr Kitson Clark's rooms.

It was with a vague sense of uneasiness that I made my way down Jesus Lane, and entered a gloomy Victorian gothic portal with a courtyard, which I later learned was the Spitoon, then through an archway to a somewhat larger courtyard, the Billiard Table, where I encountered a servant of some kind who directed me across the street to the Great Gate of Trinity, where, I was told, I would find a porter who would take me to Mr Kitson Clark.

Mr Kitson Clark lived above the Great Gate. One climbed a narrow spiral stone staircase to a long room on the right where one was obliged to wait for an audience. This was Mr Kitson Clark's dining room. The dominant piece of furniture was a highly polished, elegant mahogany dining table. There were framed prints on the walls, and a long white bookcase under the windows opening on what I supposed were stone battlements. There was a rather complicated notice instructing students how they were to inform Mr Kitson Clark of their presence and how to answer his summons by bell. There were two or three young men sitting on chairs against the wall. No one spoke. I sat down. This was all new to me. In Canada university teachers lived in houses like other people, and they saw students in offices just as lawyers and insurance men saw clients in offices.

After fifteen minutes or so it was my turn. At a desk to one side of the large high-ceilinged room with windows looking out on one side (or end, for the room was square or nearly so) on Trinity Street and on the other on Great Court, there sat G.S.R. Kitson Clark. He was a plump red faced man in black horn-rimmed spectacles. He did not get up or greet me in any way.

'You're ...?' he said.

'Ferns,' I said, 'H.S. Ferns.'

He thought for a moment.

'Ah,' he said. 'From Canada.' There was a pause. 'Manitoba.' The syllables came slowly as if the word Manitoba was a barbarous joke.

'Yes,' I said, 'Winnipeg.' He let the possibilities of this pass. He looked at me with some distaste.

'You are not wearing a gown,' he said.

Thus was my relationship with Kitson Clark established. Being put in the wrong was a new experience for me. Thus far university teachers had always treated me politely and kindly. Some even conveyed the impression that they liked me. Not so Kitson Clark. I saw him quite frequently while I was at Cambridge, and off and on from 1949 until he died in 1975. Always there was this effort to put me down in some way or other, even when his tutorial duty required him to visit me in Addenbrooke's Hospital.

But there was one time when he did not. At the end of my first year he advised me to go down saying that he did not think I would get a degree. I ignored his advice, and instead I got a first class with distinction in Part II of the Historical Tripos. The scene in Trinity Street on a June morning in 1938 was quite extraordinary as far as our relations were concerned. I had parked my bicycle in front of the college and was making my way to the Senate House to see how I had done in the examinations. In front of Arthur Roper's tailor shop I encountered Kitson Clark.

'Ferns,' he exclaimed, 'You've done it!' He grasped my hand. 'Congratulations!'

'Oh,' I said, 'What have I done?'

'Go along and see for yourself,' he said. 'You have surprised me. Congratulations.'

His unfeigned pleasure was a great pleasure to me. It made me think that maybe I had got a first. Then a doubt crossed my mind. Maybe he was excited because I had managed to get a degree.

On this occasion Kitson Clark did everything that could be done for me. I was given all the prizes and scholarships I could have wanted, and a quite gratuitous bonus was thrown in the shape of a scholarship from the Goldsmith Company to provide for me during the Long Vacations because I had no home in Britain.

Once the euphoria had exhausted itself, Kitson Clark soon returned to his old style. In the 1950s I saw him from time to time. I ran into him once in the mid 1950s when I was examining for the Oxford and Cambridge Joint Board. He said, 'Hello, how are you?' and then apropos to nothing at all, 'Did you know Guy Burgess?'

I assured him I did not know Guy Burgess. How could I? Burgess had gone down before I arrived in Cambridge.

In 1959 I attended a College Gathering. Again the same question. Again the same answer. In January 1961, I had my last exchange with my tutor. It happened in Oxford. I had finished with an examiners meeting in St Edmund Hall, Oxford, and I was looking in the window of a bookshop in Broad Street, when a voice said:

'Ah, Ferns, I believe.'

It was Kitson Clark standing there with his belly thrust forward, and seeming to lean backward in order to keep his balance. He wore a black wide-awake hat of the kind clergymen affected in Edwardian times.

'I hear you have got something in Birmingham,' he said.

I had just been elected Professor of Political Science at the University of Birmingham.

'Yes,' I said, 'I suppose I have.'

Then came the question about Guy Burgess.

By January 1961, our relative positions in the world of learning had altered. I was not so insensible to the nuances of the academic pecking order to suppose that he would regard a professorship at Birmingham as the equivalent of a readership at Cambridge, but I did have the conviction that I had written and published a book at least as good as anything he had produced, and so I felt I was his equal.

'Is there,' I said, 'any way apart from reiteration that I can persuade you that I did not know Guy Burgess? This is the third time you have asked me this question.'

'But you were a Communist, weren't you?' he replied.

'Yes,' I said, 'I was a Communist. And so was Jack Gallagher, and so was Michael Straight, and so was Dick Synge and so was Hugh Gordon, and so was Reggie Trim and so was Maynard-Smith and so was John Waterlow and so was James Klugman. And so what?' I had named only those who sprang instantly to my mind at that moment, and Kitson Clark could see I was angry.

'James Klugman! I loved him like a son. But what could I do? One had to be fair.'

'Yes,' I said, 'You were fair. You were fair and decent and so was everyone in the college. We thought you were a bloody reactionary, but no one ever thought you were unfair.'

I look back on this episode with sadness. I think Kitson Clark would have liked to talk to me, to explore something which troubled him greatly. But here we were standing in a cold and windy street. And there was a great divide which perhaps both of us were too shy to cross.

'I have to go to lunch in that place.' He pointed in the direction of Balliol College. This was the last time I talked to Kitson Clark.

Back to the beginning in October 1936.

'I am sending you to Mr Kiernan for supervision this term,' Kitson Clark said.

I could not tell from the way he said this whether he considered Mr Kiernan an enemy on whom he was inflicting someone from Manitoba or whether he regarded Mr Kiernan as a man of sufficient experience with difficult cases to undertake an extraordinary burden. 'The porter will tell you where you can find Mr Kiernan. And you must wear a gown.'

So I was dismissed. I bought a gown. I hung it in the cloakroom of the Union while I paid my subscription. Someone stole it. When I drew this to the attention of the porter he said with a faint smile: 'Oh, you should always hang on to your gown, sir. They are not like coats or hats.'

The *aufklärung* which I had experienced on the Atlantic was a mental event which as yet had no effect upon what I hoped to do with myself in Cambridge University. I had been advised and I had resolved to 'get something out of this opportunity' which was not limited to academic study. I was going 'to fit in' and make myself into something which I vaguely conceived of as a gentleman. To this end I was determined to participate in activities which were part of the university life.

I decided for a start to go to the college chapel. I discovered when the chapel service was held on Sundays and further that one was obliged to have a uniform appropriate for this purpose – a surplice. There was no difficulty about this except that I put it on back to front.

There is probably no church of the Anglican communion in Canada so opulently ornamented as the chapel of Trinity College, Cambridge. And none so dead. The congregation consisted of seven young men. The place was cold in every sense. No one spoke to anyone before or after the service. The voice of the priest conducting the divine service was beautiful like the windows and the memorial tablets to the departed. But it seemed a dead voice from the past. Obviously the whole proceeding had nothing in any immediate sense to do with Trinity College, Cambridge, or anywhere else. I went out and never returned. Save when my children were baptised in St John's Cathedral in Winnipeg, I never entered a church for another thirteen years.

Then there was rowing. I had once been a member of the Winnipeg Rowing Club, and I knew something about the sport: not much but something. At the time of my residence there were two rowing clubs in the college: Third Trinity for those who had attended Eton and Westminster schools, and First Trinity for the rest, the broad masses – to use the vocabulary I was about to learn.

I acquired the appropriate uniform which included a truly splendid dark blue scarf which after more than forty years of use looks as good as the day it was purchased. So equipped, I went to the First Trinity Boat House. The secretary spoke to me, but no one else did, and he only to assign me to a group of nine young men. We managed to co-operate together sufficiently to become water-borne, and so we rowed. Then we got the boat out of the water.

We went for a shower. Then we dressed. I found myself talking to a shy handsome young man who spoke slightly accented English. I spoke Canadian English. We were alone together. No one spoke to us. We went to tea together. Another outing on the river and Felix Winter and I found ourselves alone. We went to tea again. I said to myself, 'To hell with First Trinity.' I never rowed again.

I did see Winter from time to time. He was a gentle young man who liked to read German poetry and listen to records on his 'radiogram.' Once he invited me to tea to meet his mother. She was a handsome woman and obviously rich. She spoke with a marked German accent, and she talked of life in Vienna from which she and her son had been sent to England. She was a bewildered woman full of forebodings about the future. She adored her son and he was very tender and kind to her. For years F. Winter has been listed in the Trinity College Annual Record as one of those whose address is unknown. I do not wonder at this.

CHAPTER FIVE

A Marxist Missionary among the Natives in Cambridge

A visit to Mr Kiernan was my first intellectual encounter with Cambridge University. Victor Gordon Kiernan is a man of my own age. I have always thought of him, however, as senior to me. He was my first supervisor and I was in *statu pupillari* for my first term. Although we became friends and companions, this feeling of Victor's superiority endured, and for good reason. He had achieved a first class with distinction in both parts of the Historical Tripos. In 1936 he was in his third year as a research scholar and in 1937 he was elected a Fellow of Trinity College. A list of his academic distinctions does not alone account for his authority in my mind then. He was immensely learned. He had a good knowledge of Latin, Greek, French, German, and Spanish. He knew some Italian and was acquiring a knowledge of Urdu and Chinese. He loved music – particularly that of seventeenth and eighteenth century. He had an intimate knowledge and love of English literature, which, like his taste in music, seemed concentrated on comparatively few artists of the first rank: Shakespeare, Samuel Johnson, and Wordsworth. If his knowledge was limited to men of the past his taste was catholic. I very well remember once going with him to the Arts Theatre to see *The Ascent of F6*, and Victor saying with some astonishment, 'You know, Henry, that man Auden *is* a poet.'

I found Mr Kiernan in a dingy set of rooms at the top of G staircase in Great Court. These were a great contrast to the spacious abode of Mr Kitson Clark. When I entered he was seated in a basket chair by the fire. He put down his book, and stood up, peering at me through round shell-rimmed spectacles. He was clad in a long heavy wool dressing gown and was wearing carpet slippers. I was wearing a gown and a square, which I removed, as I explained who I was and that I had been sent to him by Mr Kitson Clark. Mr Kiernan seemed to blink rather uncertainly and then said 'Oh, from the wilds of Canada, but not a red Indian, I see. Do sit down. Would you like a cup of tea?'

We liked each other from this moment for Victor Kiernan was genuinely interested in me as he was in anyone who came from far parts of the world and might bring him information from beyond the confines of Europe. Victor, of course, knew that Canada was an immense country, but like many Englishmen he assumed also that Canada was a kind of village in which everyone knew everyone else.

Did I know Herbert Norman? I did not. Herbert Norman was a Canadian who had been at Cambridge and Victor admired him greatly because Norman knew a great deal about Japan, and spoke and read the Japanese language. Victor wondered if I might be able to communicate with the Crees in their own tongue. No, I was afraid I knew no Cree Indians, and could only claim to have seen some Sarcees at a distance when a small party of them passed along a dusty road in Strathmore, Alberta. This rather disappointed Victor, but we drank tea and talked while he smoked innumerable cigarettes. This was his only vice. Some years later he yielded to the propaganda of the medical profession and gave up smoking. I met him once by chance in the British Museum, and we went to the tea room. When we were seated Victor said, 'This is a great day for me, Henry. It is my 1,000th day without a cigarette.'

But he was my supervisor, and finally he asked me whether I would care to write an essay for him on Canada and the British Empire.

By this time I had, of course, read Lenin's essay on imperialism which Major Hooper had advised me to purchase. I cannot say that Lenin on imperialism much influenced me except that it put 'imperialism' in a wider context than any which had been part of my thinking. It taught me to think of imperialism as a phenomenon or general development in the world, and not as a particular problem of communities wanting and deserving more self-government. Canadian students of history in the 1930s and those active in politics were ambivalent about the British Empire. We did not regard the British Empire as an oppressive tyranny. There was no evidence of this either in our history or in our experience, and Canadian politics were entirely Canadian. None the less I was aware of the connection with imperial policy which divided Canadians politically into those who were 'for the Empire' like the good ladies who were financing me at Cambridge, and those, like some of my teachers and many French-speaking Canadians, who argued that we should not be drawn into 'Britain's wars,' which, I had just learned from Lenin, were a critical aspect of the highest and last stage of capitalism.

Then there was the imperialism of the United States. Some Canadians like myself had studied the history of the United States and had read books like *The Rise of American Civilization* by Charles and Mary Beard and *Imperialism and World Politics* by Parker T. Moon. These were the works of respected American scholars, and they had taught me to think of Canada's relations with the United States not just in terms of a narrow, xenophobic dislike of the United States, which was a fairly common sentiment among English- and French-speaking Canadians alike, but as a problem for Canada created by political tendencies inside the United States. These political tendencies were not regarded, however, as inevitable. American imperialist adventures, which involved 'sending in the Marines,' seemed to me aberrant departures from American democratic principles, and the work of small selfish interest groups and newspaper proprietors like William Randolph Hearst. If I had been asked my opinion of the United States in the autumn of 1936, I would have said that, although there were imperialists in the United States, the United States was not an imperialist power like Britain, France, Portugal, and Italy and as Germany and Russia had been before the Great War.

My essay seemed to impress Mr Kiernan. He asked to see my M.A. thesis, on the subject of George Brown and the American Civil War. Although I could not bring myself to read it Victor did, and 42 years later he quoted it as an authority in his book *America: The New Imperialism*.

The immediate consequence of my essay was an invitation to tea to meet some friends. These turned out to be Indians, not red Indians, but Indian Indians with the problems of British imperialism well established in their minds. One was Surendra Mohan Kumaramangalam who became my closest friend until he returned to India in 1939.

Mohan Kumaramangalam took his name from the village in the province of Madras where he was born. His father was a wealthy, happy-go-lucky, and charming zemindar, a species of landlord, Dr Subbarayan. His mother was a forceful, intelligent lady, the first woman in India elected to a public body, the Madras Provincial Assembly set up in an endeavour by the British government to introduce a participatory element into the government of India. Mohan had great charm and splendid social talents, refined by education at Eton, but obviously a natural endowment from his father. But he possessed something his father lacked: a strong sense of practical reality, a self-discipline, and an impatience with inefficiency and ineffectiveness equally in others and in himself. In these qualities he was very much his mother's son.

I met Mohan's parents twice when they visited Britain in 1939. One occasion was immediately after a royal garden party at Buckingham Palace. For some reason, probably due to the gathering storm in Europe, a few students from the Commonwealth were invited to this party. Another Canadian student at Cambridge and I, a Communist like myself, were sent invitations. With a sneer on our lips and curiosity and anticipation in our hearts, we decided to go, and to this end we visited Moss Bros. and rigged ourselves out in the appropriate dress. After the party was over we dropped in to Subbarayan's flat in Artillery Mansions, Westminster, and it was then that I had a glimpse of Indian life, values, and ideas which Indian students were unable directly to afford me.

Dr and Mrs Subbarayan were most welcoming and put us quickly at ease. Mrs Subbarayan was very interested to meet Canadians of the same age as her children. She seemed only mildly troubled about the militancy of her three youngest children, but she seemed to want to discover what young people from a 'self-governing dominion' might be like. She had a sharp and inquiring mind and she was well informed. We, of course, presented a picture of earnest, opinionated, and concerned prigs, who thought that the Munich agreement was a fraud and war with Nazi Germany or, more likely, another capitulation to Hitler was not far off.

Mrs Subbarayan did not dissent from what we said, but Dr Subbarayan was too happily engaged in the immediate delights of life and was too optimistic and good-natured to enter into our forebodings. He was much more concerned to share with us the satisfaction he felt with the purchase of three sets of golf clubs and telling us about the problems he faced as steward of the Madras Jockey Club. I was ashamed to admit that I knew nothing at all about the state of horse-racing in Canada and he seemed to have little enthusiasm for the only equestrian spectacle with which I was acquainted, the Calgary Stampede.

When Dr Subbarayan and I had become separated from the rest of the gathering and were looking out of the windows at the street traffic, a glimpse of which we could see through the entrance to the courtyard of the apartment complex, he told me of the satisfaction he felt with the sacrifices he had made to send his three sons to Eton and his daughter to a celebrated Quaker school and to Oxford. He was interested to know whether I thought it better to send a son to Eton and King's College, Cambridge, than to Eton and Christ Church, Oxford. He asked this question with such an innocent and enthusiastic charm that it did not sound either silly or snobbish.

There was never to my knowledge any tension between Mohan and his parents. Mohan had an intense commitment to revolutionary politics, and his father was all easy acceptance of life as it was, but there was no antagonism which I could sense, and father and son had an affectionate regard for each other which it was a pleasure to experience. When independence came to India, Dr Subbarayan became the Indian ambassador in Indonesia and Mohan was put in gaol.

Kiernan, Kumaramangalam, and their friends presented me with a key which opened some of the many mansions of the mind which constituted Cambridge University. The contemplation by the British community in the late 1970s and early 1980s of the possibility that some malign and secret agency is sapping the British spirit of independence and self-respect, and which manifests itself popularly as a preoccupation with spying, has created an impression of Cambridge University in the 1930s which is both false and foolish. In the long perspective of history, Cambridge University in the 1930s will very likely emerge as one of the focal points in the intellectual development of the human race. The achievements in the natural sciences between the great world wars were astonishing, particularly in physics, chemistry, biochemistry, and physiology. Knowledge and understanding in the natural sciences tends, of course, to be cumulative. In the social sciences this is not so readily apparent, and it is therefore harder to judge what of permanent value was accomplished, but it is none the less the case that there was a great surge of creative and critical mental activity in the fields of economics, historical enquiry, philosophical reasoning, and literary criticism without which the human race would probably be poorer.

That intellectual ferment of the kind taking place at Cambridge should be accompanied by political ferment is in no way surprising. Nor should it surprise any but the grossly stupid that this political ferment should have broken through the limits of established political thought and practice. Given the advantage of hindsight, what seems to me our fault in the Cambridge of the 1930s was our failure to break sufficiently or radically enough with the underlying optimistic and complacent assumptions of liberal constitutionalism. We did not sufficiently appreciate the black evil of which human beings are capable particularly in their political relations, and we assumed as natural and took for granted modes of behaviour in the sphere of politics which are only frail and temporary achievements of moral understanding. Bitterly hostile as many of us were to Fascism and Nazism it is fair to say that none of us could imagine Belsen or Auschwitz, and while a large majority in Cambridge were anything but Communists, there can have been very few who were willing to believe that Stalin was a blood-thirsty tyrant. There was so much in the intellectual life of Cambridge which was creative, positive, and satisfying that it required almost superhuman understanding and insight to assert that, for all their achievements, men and women could be and were then in the process of becoming unredeemed brutes.

For a young Canadian like myself the political life of Europe, which found one point of concentration in Cambridge, had an exciting attraction. Canada was not where the action was. Senator Dandurand had described Canada as a fire-proof house far away from the sources of conflagration.

And this was then true, so that living in Canada one tended to know nothing about world politics except through observation at a distance. One could not feel world politics in Canada. In Cambridge one could, and one had to be dull indeed not to become in some way involved.

Victor Kiernan and Mohan Kumaramangalam soon interested me in the Indian nationalist movement and more generally in 'the colonial question.' The struggle against imperialism was not, of course, a central political theme at that time in Cambridge. The Spanish Civil War, which had broken out the previous July, occupied the centre of the political stage, and this was a tremendous force in politicizing a broader and larger body of students and to a lesser extent senior members of the university than any event hitherto. There was an immediacy about the Spanish Civil War, inasmuch as some students had witnessed the outbreak and a few had actually stayed to fight on the side of the republic. The issues seemed very clear. The revolt of the officers and the subversion of an elected government imparted to the arguments about the dangers of fascist authoritarianism to democracy, both liberal and socialist, a concreteness which had been obscured by the political manoeuvring of Hindenburg and Hitler in the case of the Nazi regime in Germany. Not only was the Spanish Civil War a concrete and obvious illustration of the international dangers of fascist authoritarianism but it served to confirm the prediction of the socialists and communists that the triumph of the Nazis in Germany was not a 'on-off' event in a particular community but a world process which would not necessarily stop at the borders of France or the English Channel.

I joined the Cambridge University Socialist Club and the League of Nations Union. Friendship, interest, and knowledge, however, combined to engage most of my attention on the movement for the dissolution of empires. Concern with the phenomenon of imperialism seemed to take me to the heart of world politics in a way which the study of the pros and cons of Spanish politics or German politics or British politics did not. The contemplation of the politics of empires told me something about the why and wherefore of war, and of the likely consequences of what seemed pretty inevitable – the renewal of the First World War. As I rearranged my information and the previous thinking of five years as a student in Canada in the light of Lenin's theory of imperialism, I began to foresee that another world war could very likely become a revolutionary event transforming the structure of the international political order: there would not be another Treaty of Versailles. Of the imperialist character of the Nazi regime in Germany I had no doubt, but somehow I did not believe that the Nazis could win. This was a matter of faith, for I could see no geopolitical reasons why they could not conquer.

This faith was, of course, sorely tried by subsequent events. As I think back, I can, however, see that my faith had some material and political substance in it. As I learned more about Marxism and more about the Russian Revolution and communism I came to the conclusion that the USSR was a strong state which it would be hard for any power to defeat and destroy. In the manner of many others I invested the Soviet regime with human qualities which it did not possess and I could not then grasp that it was an imperialist regime as much as any other great power of that time, but this was not the heart of matter as far as the USSR was concerned. Like my own country it was an immense tract of territory and physically an inhospitable one. Russia had gobbled up and destroyed Napoleon. But this was not all. Under Stalin Russia had industrialized on a massive scale. Above all in the Bolsheviks the Russians had a government which did not compromise. The Bolsheviks were hard, tough, and ruthless in what I conceived to be a good cause. In my mind I equated Stalin with Cromwell, and the communists with the puritans of the English Civil War: men of resolution who changed the world and would not yield in a time of trial.

The outbreak of the Spanish Civil War may have raised the political temperature in Cambridge, but it was the death of John Cornford in a battle outside Cordova in December 1936 which effected a transformation. Until the death of Cornford, left-wing anti-fascism and the United Front line of the communists had been only one of several political tendencies among the students. Thereafter until the Soviet-German Pact of August 1939 anti-fascism and opposition to the appeasement policies of the Chamberlain government became dominant forces. Belonging to CUSC became fashionable.

John Cornford was not the only Cambridge man or Cambridge communist to die fighting in Spain, but it was his death which served as a catalyst. Cornford possessed in his own person all the qualities which a wide variety of young people at that time either had or wished they had in some degree or other. James Harrington observed in *Oceania* that a successful political leader (in Harrington's terminology, a king) is either a great soldier or great lover. John Cornford was both. Perhaps not great; for dying on the day after his 21st birthday, he had had but little time. None the less he was a man who had proved himself both by giving life and taking life and losing his own. Additionally he was a poet of some talent, academically brilliant, and a political leader of subtlety, skill, and ruthlessness. He had a careless grace and he defied all the conventions. He was indifferent to the comfort which was provided in such abundance to teachers and students alike in Cambridge. He was sure of himself, and a single-minded fanatic. In short, John Cornford was a man whom others had too little talent and too much common sense to imitate. But they did admire him, and one did not have to be a fellow believer to do so.

In his book *Cambridge between the Wars*, T.E.B. Howarth has posed 'two most intriguing questions … how and why quite so many intellectually gifted people acquired what can only be described as a salvationist belief in Stalin's Russia and consistently preached pacificism and disarmament, while at the same time urging resistance to armed Fascism.' These questions could equally be asked about intellectually gifted people in respect to the Nazis. The fact is that everyone whose minds were not dulled by games, or social climbing, or self-indulgence, was aware of something portentous happening in European society and was confused by it. Hence the grasping for certainty; hence the fanaticism; and hence in the end the comfort and clarification which came when Churchill took office and declared that there was only one thing to do: to stand up and fight.

My sphere of activity in the larger commotion was 'colonial work.' I was already a Marxist when I arrived at Cambridge, in the sense that my mind was open to Marxist arguments. But I did not know much about Marxism. I sought at once to remedy this defect. Most of my first term was spent in reading Marx, Engels, Lenin, and Stalin. At first I was puzzled by the fact that there was not much visible evidence of the Communist party in Cambridge, but I soon began to realize that there was an organized force which animated and directed CUSC, the biggest political society in Cambridge, was at work in the Majalis, the Indian student society, had an influence in the League of Nations Society, in the Peace Pledge Union, and so on. There were transmission belts everywhere. The Communists aspired to have a line on everything. Within six months I could give an account of the history of the world which carried great conviction to those who knew nothing – a fairly large constituencey.

During my first term I was being sized up. I was a 'contact.' As the Christmas Vacation approached I had to decide where I was going to spend it. Mohan informed me that there was a Nigerian in King's College who had already solved the same problem. Perhaps there was a place in the boarding house in Margate where Louis Mbanefo was going. And so there was.

Louis Mbanefo was a large, handsome Ibo of an amiable, easy-going disposition. He was one of the very few African students then in Cambridge. He came from the town of Onitsha, where his family were market traders in a fairly substantial way. Years later I met a man who had been a district officer in Onitsha. He told me that Louis' mother was the real head of the family and that she had sacrificed a great deal to send her son to Britain to study for the law. Louis was amply supplied with money and lived well in a fine set of rooms in King's. He possessed a splendid radiogram which was much envied by other students and which Mohan acquired along with the rooms when Louis went down at the end of 1937.

Mbanefo was much my age, and he had a law degree from King's College, London. At Cambridge he was, like me, reading an extended Part II of the Historical Tripos with the object of obtaining a degree in two years. Simultaneously he was completing his bar examination and eating his way towards a call to the bar at one of the Inns of Court.

We agreed from the outset that we were going to devote ourselves to academic study, and particularly to work our way through Bosanquet's *Philosophical Theory of the State*, Bentham's *Principles of Morals and Legislation*, and *The Social Contract* of J.-J. Rousseau. This gave us plenty to talk about and argue about, and I found that in order to develop a 'line' on these bourgeois thinkers I had to understand them, an altogether salutary experience.

Naturally Louis and I talked about politics. This was the time when almost the sole topic of political discussion was the abdication of Edward VIII. When we arrived in Margate we found our landlord and his lady together with a daughter and two grandchildren gathered around the radio in a sitting room lit by gas, listening to the King's speech of abdication. All except the youngest grandchild were weeping. We were asked to drop our luggage in the hallway and join the party. We tactfully said nothing, but neither of us could carry tact to the length of tears. Louis and I agreed that the abdication of Edward VIII was an event of no intrinsic importance and hardly worth talking about. And yet we were somehow touched by the tears of our landlord and his family and during our stay in their house we preserved a silence on the topic much as if we felt them bereaved.

At intervals we were voluble enough on other political topics. Louis was no Marxist and was certainly not a Communist. His view was that the politics of national independence, which engaged so much the attention of Kumaramangalam and his friends, had no place in his country. 'In seventy-five years maybe,' Louis said, 'but not now. There is no basis for such a political movement in my country.' He had no idea then that he could and would become Sir Louis Mbanefo, the chief justice of a newly independent Nigeria, chancellor of the University of Ibadan, and one of those who served as an informal go-between in the Biafran War.

Because I came from North America where the index of race relations was the number of lynchings per annum, I was interested to hear Louis' experiences of colour prejudice. He said he had only encountered one instance in his six years in Britain.

'And what did you do?' I inquired.

'I knocked the fellow down. There was no trouble.'

But Louis had a view of the subject, and he gave an interesting account of the making of the film *Sanders of the River* in which Paul Robeson was the star. This film was made in Britain by Alexander Korda. The producer required a substantial number of black Africans as extras, and Louis was invited to play a part, as Jomo Kenyatta was and did. Louis asked to see the script, and then told the recruiter of extras that he would not touch the project with a ten-foot large pole. Later he met Paul Robeson, and lit into him for playing a part in a picture which represented Africans as good or bad in proportion to their acceptance of the white man's leadership. He told Robeson that he ought to have more pride than to participate in the production of political rubbish like *Sanders of the River*. Thereafter Robeson refused to attend the world première of the film, and this seems to have been the beginning of Robeson's slide into communism and his flight during the Cold War to Moscow, where he died.

On New Year's Eve I decked myself in a dinner jacket and Louis in white tie and tails and we took our landlord's daughter to the new year ball in one of the civic buildings in Margate. The daughter was on her way to join her husband, a coal mining engineer, who had emigrated to South Africa. She was quite happy to go. Louis was a popular figure and he had no trouble finding dancing partners among the young ladies of Margate. Indeed they seemed very pleased to be asked to dance with a handsome black man. The only notice taken of Louis' colour was in connection with a local superstition to the effect that it would bring good luck to touch something black as soon as the bells went welcoming the

New Year. A number of people came up to Louis saying, 'May I touch you for luck?' And he laughed and said 'Of course.' (How different from Canada, where blacks were segregated as much as they were in the United States, although less abused!)

Louis seemed to accept the regime in Nigeria in a matter-of-fact way, and there was no apparent bitterness or sense of oppression in him, but one day in a discussion he said to me: 'Back before the First World War my grandfather was obliged by the district officer to live away from our town. You know we don't forget that sort of thing.'

Louis went down from Cambridge in June 1937, and returned to Nigeria where he built up a lucrative legal practice mainly concerned with the establishment of land titles. With the coming of the Biafran War he resigned all his public offices, but he did not associate himself with General Ojukwu. He had some part in bringing about peace, but he refused any appointment under the victorious government. When he died his sole public office was the presidency of the Synod of the Anglican Church in Nigeria.

When I left Margate I had one more encounter with what is nowadays called the 'establishment.' There existed at that time an organization – perhaps there were several such – whose object was to establish personal contact with students in Britain from overseas, and particularly from the dominions. To this end ladies and gentlemen mainly in the shires had volunteered to give hospitality in their homes to students during the university vacations. I was written to and invited to visit a home in Wimbourne, Dorset, for a few days. I accepted the invitation. The lady inviting me wrote to me personally, a polite note expressing the hope that I would enjoy the visit and so on. The organizing office, however, sent me an advice sheet, about what to wear (I must take a dinner jacket) and how to behave (e.g., how much and when to tip the servants). I was not advised about bathing and cleaning my teeth, but I would have felt hardly surprised had this been included. No doubt the advice was well meant and intended to save embarrassment all around, but none the less I resented it. It seemed to suggest that I was unacceptable on my own terms, only on theirs, and that I was an ignorant boor and they alone knew how to behave. Pommy bastards! At this time I had never heard 'strine' talk of this kind, but I would have understood it had I done so.

The visit turned out to be a nothing experience. My hostess was a comparatively young woman who lived alone in a beautiful cottage outside Wimbourne; alone, that is, if one excludes from the reckoning two servants. She appeared to have no profession of any kind and I assumed, probably rightly, that she was one of the rentiers about whom Hobson complained in his book on imperialism. She was polite, impersonal, and neither friendly nor unfriendly. I soon discovered that in her home the same rule obtained as, I understood, governed the art of conversation in an officers' mess. One never talked about politics, women, or shop. What else is there to talk about? Well, there is the countryside, social life, church architecture, sports. The list is endless, but none of these topics was more than something to talk about as an alternative to embarrassed silence.

I proposed that I go for a tramp around the countryside. My hostess seemed to think that this might represent some kind of failure of hospitality on her part. She suggested that we go to the cinema in Bournemouth. I said, 'O.K.;' perhaps we could see a Marx Brothers film, which I thought I had seen advertised on a hoarding in the railway station. No, she had once seen a Marx Brothers film and it was incomprehensible, boring, and unfunny. I suggested that she needed an interpreter and I volunteered to act in this capacity. In the end we went to a very forgettable production full of chorus girls.

The high point of my stay in Wimbourne was tea in a splendid country house in the area. The architecture and the paintings were impressive, but the company exuded the same spirit of uptight conventionality as my hostess. Naval officers predominated in the gathering. I still had a romantic feeling about the Royal Navy, and I could feel a faint twinge of the enthusiasm I had had at the age of 12 or 13 which had provoked the ambition to become a midshipman in the service of Hawke and Nelson. But these naval officers soon put an end to my lingering admiration. No doubt they were brave, competent men and I suppose some at least perished in Arctic seas or off the coast of Malaya, but I could establish not even a fleeting contact with them. Whose fault? I do not know. In fact I liked better than these people my landlord in Margate, a bankrupt Tory baker from Newcastle-on-Tyne, eking out an existence running a seaside boarding house. At least he could weep for his king going over the water. These people, by contrast, seemed dead, and I am sure they only came alive when there was real and unavoidable danger and Churchill put some fire into them.

I tipped the servants at the recommended rate, said thank you in the way my mother on the prairies of Canada had taught me to do, and I returned to Cambridge.

Shortly after the term began Victor Kiernan and Mohan Kumaramangalam invited me to tea. Once we were settled down in front of the fire they told me something which was no surprise to me: there was in Cambridge a student branch of the Communist party and that a section of the party was devoted to 'colonial work.' They invited me to join. I had no hesitation. I said, 'yes, sure, certainly.' It was then explained to me that 'colonial work' required the greatest discretion; that students from overseas who joined the Communist party put themselves at great risk and that the least they could suffer when they returned home would be surveillance by the authorities. For these reasons I could not be an 'open' member of the party, I could not have a party card, nor could I participate in the ordinary meetings of the party.

And so it turned out. John Cornford may have proclaimed that 'all we [have] are our party cards,' but I never had one from first to last. I never paid any party dues, although God knows I subscribed frequently enough to help the *Daily Worker*, provide for Spanish and Chinese relief, and so on. As far as I know my name was in no records of the Communist party in Cambridge. And yet when I went home to Canada during the Long Vacation in 1938 I had a letter of introduction to Tim Buck, the leader of the Canadian Communist party, signed by Harry Pollitt, the general secretary of the British Communist party, and when I returned to North America in December 1939, I carried with me a letter of introduction to the CPUSA, signed by Palme Dutt, Pollitt's successor. My name was in the files of the Communist party. There can be no mistake about that.

This informal, secret relationship with an organization, which was itself a secret freemasonry as much as it was an open political party, had some unusual consequences. For example, I am not able to say when I quit the Communist party. Was it between 2 January 1940, when the party headquarters in New York gave me the name of a comrade in Boston, and April 1940 when I left the United States to work in Ottawa? During that time I did not look up and introduce myself to the comrade in Boston, and thereafter I had no contact with a Communist party officer anywhere. And yet during this time when I had objectively, as the Communists say, dropped out, I was still very much a Marxist and I had no idea of repudiating the Communist party even though I disagreed with its line on the war and supported the war policies of the Canadian government. In a court of law it would be very difficult to prove that I ever was a Communist; but then the law is sometimes an ass.

The celebrated discipline of the Communist party was something I never experienced. I was always a free agent in what I did on its behalf. On only two occasions was I ever 'ordered' to do anything, and these things I would have done without an order. The first might just as well have been a request or a suggestion, to attend a national meeting of Communist students in Birmingham in September 1937, to talk about the importance of the 'colonial question.' The other was an instruction in the spring of 1938 to go to Oxford with the object of forming a society of North American students. The only meeting of a party aggregate in Cambridge which I ever attended was to hear the national student organizer, Jack Cohen, instruct us in the right response to the imposition of conscription for service in the armed forces by the Chamberlain government.

Publicity concerning the activities and character of Burgess, Blunt, *et al*, has tended to suggest that the Communists in Cambridge in the 1930s were a collection of homosexual traitors. As to the homsexuality I can only say that I never once encountered a Communist in Cambridge who was a homosexual. So little homosexuality was there among political activists of all kinds that I hardly knew what the word meant. Even while still at Cambridge I came to the conclusion that part of the popularity of CUSC could be attributed to the impression that the girls who joined CUSC were more willing and the boys less inhibited than elsewhere in the university. With few exceptions the leading Communist students I knew had well established and intimate relations with girls. Indeed the Socialist and Communist students in Cambridge anticipated by thirty years the free and easy heterosexual relations which only became widespread among students generally in the late 1960s. One young woman in Newnham whom I knew quite well only yielded to her suitor when it was put to her that sex was a party duty. There is no evidence, however, that there was a directive from the party headquarters on King Street on this subject. But John Cornford had written a few days before he died to Margot Heinemann:

Heart of the heartless world,
Dear heart, the thought of you
Is the pain at my side,
The shadow that chills my view.

As to treason this is another matter. When one joined the Communist party and if one took seriously what one was doing, one was committing

90

oneself to the overthrow of bourgeois government and the conquest of power. No one in his or her right mind and capable of facing the truth can doubt that Lenin committed treason when he agreed with the German government to cross Germany in a train provided by that government in order to overthrow the government of his native country. No one today thinks of Lenin as a traitor, because he was successful, i.e., he captured sovereign power and became himself a definer of treason and the creator and master of an apparatus for identifying and eliminating traitors. The Communist party of Great Britain prided itself on being a Leninist party, and we held up to ourselves the ideal of Bolshevik hardness and rational ruthlessness in the service of the revolution. The Communist party was not pledged to uphold the parliamentary form of government. Quite the contrary. Of course, the Communist party was not planning a *coup d'état*, or the conquest of power in the immediately foreseeable future. But this is beside the point. The Communist party was the enemy of the British government, and that was part of its appeal. For my part my object in undertaking 'colonial work' was not to 'improve' or democratize the British Raj in India and around the world. My object was to end it, not tomorrow but sooner or later – and the sooner the better.

No one who took all this seriously can complain if the British government and the governments of the empire overseas regarded us as enemies. In fact the British government did not take us seriously; certainly not in Britain itself and only marginally more seriously overseas. There was no prohibition on ideas or organization in Britain. People were free to be as batty as they wished. In Cambridge in particular it was a point of pride that any one could do anything or think anything provided they wore a gown in designated circumstances and did not get involved with the police. In Trinity College there was a deep sense of guilt over the deprivation of Bertrand Russell of his fellowship on account of his pacifist stand during the First World War.

The hard fact is that the Soviet government took the Communist party seriously. They saw in it a means of working their political will. In the international community all sovereign governments are the enemies or potential enemies of each other. Through history the allies of today are frequently the enemies of tomorrow. In this respect the Soviet government was and is no different from other governments. But the Soviet government differed from other governments inasmuch as it regarded all other governments as bourgeois or imperialist regimes which were, by the definitions enshrined in their ideology, enemies. To have friends and adherents in the camp of the enemy was regarded, and rightly regarded, as an advantage. In their own case they went to great lengths – they still do – to ensure that no enemy government had friends in their camp. But they had friends in the British camp, and they knew it and acted upon that knowledge in a variety of ways.

Of course, being a Communist and being a traitor were not one and the same, nor are they today. Treason and offences in this category involve breaking laws designed to enable the government to act as it deems best in international politics, and to prevent such actions being impaired to the advantage of another sovereign government. In the 1930s Communist parties affiliated to the Third Communist International were assemblages of people who had an emotional, intellectual, and political predisposition to assist the Soviet government, but whether any individual Communist would do so depended in the first place on the degree of his or her commitment, and in the second place on whether his or her knowledge, activity, or power of decision in their community could benefit the Soviet government, and finally whether the Soviet government thought it worth while to bring particular individuals under its orders. The evidence shows that some individuals in Britain were thought worthy of being so controlled, and some of the decisions of the British government, particularly decisions involving the repatriation of hundreds of thousands of Soviet citizens after the close of hostilities in May 1945, were of so much political advantage to the Soviet regime that it is possible to suppose that these were the work of people in the British state machine playing on the Soviet side. Not all blunders are accidental.

As a Communist I was a backroom boy. I served on no committees, chaired no meetings, nor made any political speeches. My task as an organizer of the 'colonial group' was that of a missionary: to recruit people to the faith and to instruct them in it. Students from the whole British Empire, from China, and from Latin America were my parish. We had no systematic way of going about our business, but not all was left to chance encounters. Because the Indian students were a comparatively large group in Cambridge, and the Indian student society, the Majalis, was already well established, it was reasonably easy to establish a list of contacts among Indians. Those from Ceylon were few in numbers, and they tended to be shy and lonely, and happy to have overtures made to them. Students from Africa were very few in numbers and they were non-political, not rationally like Louis Mbanefo, but simply incapable of grasping what politics is about. The Aleki of Abakouta was a prince from the Gold Coast, who thought that being a prince was politics enough for him. Chinese students were few in number – forty or so – and all of them were deeply disturbed by events in their country, but none of them wanted to join anything which was not Chinese. I was on terms of friendship with several of them, and CUSC helped them to advertise the plight of China, but to my knowledge no Chinese ever became a Communist. One was, however, a very knowledgeable Marxist economist, but having once been sentenced to death by a warlord in his native city, he preferred to have no political views.

Some Canadians, South Africans, and Australians did become Communists, but they joined the party through other channels, and the colonial group paid little or no attention to students from the self-governing dominions. Another Canadian (a scientist who had become a Communist) and I did pay some attention to the Canadians in Cambridge, but in general the Canadians were indifferent or hostile. My friend and I once spent some time working on a Canadian graduate student who came from my friend's home town in Nova Scotia. Theoretically he should have been a prime subject for conversion. His father was a miner, and to student Communists there were no people of more proletarian virtue than coal miners. But this student resisted with a practical argument.

'Look,' he said to my friend, 'It's O.K. you being a Communist. Your old man's a doctor and you can afford to think what you like. But my old man's a miner, and I can't afford to have fancy ideas.'

Some time in 1938 a group of Canadian students decided to form a Canada Club in the university and my friend and I were invited to attend. What was up? We went along to the meeting filled with curiosity and hope. The first item on the agenda was the club tie. A sharp debate developed about the gold maple leaf on a green ground which was proposed. A maple leaf? Was this the sign of nationalist militancy? Not at all. The objection to the maple leaf was its shape. What would a maple leaf look like on the knot of the tie? It would be 'ass backwards' as one critic put it. The Canadians generally were either so engrossed in their academic studies that they refused to think about anything as unprofitable as politics, or, if they had non-academic interests, these were games or membership in the air squadron. At least these last were doing something practical about fascism.

When I reflect upon my two and a half years as a Marxist missionary I can see that there was a differential in the degree of response of students to my message. The Indians were much the most responsive. None of the Indian princes – and there were several maharajahs and rajkumars at Cambridge – were responsive, although one princeling was a good friend of mine who proposed that I should become his Divan, or prime minister, which from his job description I took to be a sort of business manager of his estate. Those who did respond were the sons and daughters of professional men – mainly lawyers – and civil servants. Most of them were rich; one had to be rich to send a child to Cambridge, but not fabulously rich. The Sarabhai brothers, sons of a very wealthy family of textile manufacturers, were at Cambridge, but although they were indiscriminately generous with money, they would never have anything to do with political activity, nationalist, Communist, or any other.

On our own and without any direction from above, the 'colonial group' refrained from making the objects of our missionary activity Indians who were entrants into the Indian civil service. The program of gradually 'Indianizing' the top levels of the Indian civil service was already underway and there were at Cambridge a small number who had already been selected for appointment and who were undergoing the last stage of their education. One of these whom I came to know quite well was L.K. Jha. He was a large man of great intelligence, wit, and amiability. In addition to his academic work in economics part of his training for the bureaucracy of the Raj consisted of lessons in horsemanship. He had to learn to ride like an officer and a gentleman.

'Cricket I can stand,' he used to say. 'But horses! There are more agreeable creatures one can mount, but only the British would insist on horses. They really like what is difficult and unpleasant.' None the less Lakshmi persisted, and his accounts of his equestrian adventures were exceedingly funny, so much so that some of us used to look forward to the days when 'Jabba' had been out with the horses. He was an accomplished and witty public speaker and became president of the Union in 1937. With Michael Straight, he was one of the two Trinity men to get a first in economics in 1937.

It was this quality in the Indians I knew which reinforced my belief in the legitimacy of Indian political independence. By the standards I respected at this time, the Indians I encountered were intellectually superior to most Canadians of the same age who aspired to run their country and could legitimately expect to do so. If Canadians were capable of exercising authority in Canada, why not Indians in India? I did not need Marxism to lead me to this conclusion.

The Indians who responded to my arguments were in the main Hindus. There were a few Muslims who were well disposed to the nationalist appeal of the Indian National Congress, but the Muslim Indians of my acquaintance were very resistant to Marxist arguments. In fact there was a minority of Muslim students who kept very much to themselves and whom we seldom or never encountered in our contact work. I discovered them by accident away from Cambridge; actually in Berlin.

In the Long Vacation of 1937 I went to Germany for eight weeks for two purposes: to look at Nazi Germany in the flesh and to learn some German in the summer school of the University of Berlin. Students were, if they wished, accommodated in the old home of the philosopher, Hegel, in Am Kupfergraben not far from the centre of the Nazi capital. There I met two Indian students from Cambridge, who were types new to me. They had none of the knowledge or any of the enthusiasm I had begun to regard as normal in Indians. Furthermore, they exhibited none of the revulsion against Nazism which was widespread in Cambridge.

At that time I shared the belief, which featured in all descriptions of British imperialism in India presented by the Communists, that sometime after the Indian Mutiny the British authorities had practised a policy of divide and rule, or better divide to rule, and that this policy's main feature was a persistent discrimination in the public services and the armed forces in favour of Muslims and to the prejudice of Hindus and other Indian linguistic/racial/religious minorities. The Muslim League was regarded as a put-up job of the British. The Indian National Congress was the expression of the natural aspirations and unity of the Indian people. Were there not millions of Muslims supporting the national struggle? Was not the president of the Indian National Congress a Muslim, Abdul Kalim Azad?

In these two Indians resident in the Hegelhaus I encountered a total hostility to this view of Indian affairs. They were English-speaking Indians like the Bengalis, Madrasis, Gujeratis, and Tamils whom I knew. They were studying law like many other Indians, but they were totally different. They aspired to political independence, too, but they were seeking an independent Muslim state. For the first time I heard the word Pakistan, but being a good Marxist and in possession of the truth I dismissed Pakistan as the insubstantial dream of some bemused provincials in the grip of an obscurantist religion.

Sooner or later one is bound to puzzle over one's experience. There occurred at this time an episode of no importance, but one which on reflection illustrated a fundamental problem for Marxist missionaries, and not just for them alone.

One evening Badr el Din and I strolled together in the Spreewald chatting about our respective countries. On the way back to the Hegelhaus I proposed that we have a drink in a *Bierstube* near the Fredrichstrasse station. Badr el Din was a tall, solemn, shy young man of a rather expressionless countenance, but at this suggestion he seemed a bit disturbed. None the less we went into the *Bierstube* and sat down. A waiter appeared at our table. He was a big, fat, baldheaded man with a white apron wrapped tightly around his great belly. He looked remarkably like the gauleiter of Thuringia, Fritz Sauckel, whose picture had appeared in the rotogravure papers on account of some celebration in his part of the Reich. I ordered a 'München' and the waiter turned to Badr el Din. He said timidly that he wanted a glass of milk. The waiter looked at him in astonishment which turned to something approaching rage. '*Milch!*' he roared. '*Milch! Nein! Hier ist ein Hofbrauhaus!*'

Poor Badr el Din! He quailed and said he would have a beer, but only a little one.

We sat in some embarrassment, and I told him to leave the beer if he didn't want it, and we could go to a coffee shop. He seemed frightened as if the German waiter might come back and beat him up, and so he downed the glass of beer slowly and with evident distaste.

When we were out in the street he laid his hand gently on my arm and said very solemnly:

'Can I ask you to do something for me?'

'Sure,' I said. 'What is it?'

'Please promise me you won't tell anyone in Cambridge that I drank that beer. Please.'

And so I promised to keep his secret. He had broken a taboo, and he was deeply upset.

The point of telling about this little incident is to underline something that I only realized after much experience: that there are in the world millions of people like Badr el Din, intelligent, educated, and able, who have moral personalities centred around religion and age-old feelings about things and behaviour which make them impervious to ideas and practices which Europeans and North Americans take for granted. Marxism and/or liberalism are simply incomprehensible to them, and many of the modes of behaviour which flow from them are regarded as loathsome and even sickening. The Marxist missionary only succeeds when for some reason or other a moral vacuum is created in peoples' minds. Then Marxism flows in to fill the emptiness.

When we returned to Cambridge I naturally got in touch with Badr el Din and his friends. I learned many facts from them, but they learned nothing from me. I could influence them in no way, nor could any of the Indians to whom I introduced them. Pretty soon they were written off as nothing. Perhaps I should have analysed the problem more deeply, but I did not. I knew the truth; that was the reason.

But let us not be too ironic. As missionaries the colonial group had considerable success in terms of numbers recruited, the quality of the recruits, and the influence they exercised in the wider community. As a measure of the last – influence in the university as a whole – two presidents of the Union in two years is not bad. As a measure of the second – the only quality we knew, i.e., academic quality – one was elected a fellow of Trinity College, one got a first class with distinction, three got firsts, and only one member got a lower second-class honours degree. Furthermore all but one of us were playing on an 'away ground' – a university outside our countries and our culture. Only one of us was English and only two were white.

It speaks well for the open, international, and genuinely liberal non-racial character of the University of Cambridge that, playing under the university's own rules, a heterogenous selection of outsiders and political dissidents could get so much and do so well and be heard so widely. That is what I meant when I told Kitson Clark he was fair, and I do not think he need have had any guilt on account of Guy Burgess or Anthony Blunt. A liberal regime is a liberal regime, and what comes out of it is the responsibility of the individuals, not of the tutors or the master or the government of the university.

The success of our missionary efforts were not alone due to our techniques of indoctrination. The doctrine sold itself, if one may use such a non-proletarian manner of speaking. Karl Marx devised a doctrine with a dual appeal which flowed naturally from the historical and dialectical mode of reasoning developed by Hegel. Marx had written briefly on India. In articles published in a leading newspaper in the United States in the 1850s before and after the Indian Mutiny, Marx applied to an analysis of British rule in India his general analytical principles. These principles enabled him to argue a dual preposition: 'England has to fulfil a double mission in India: one destructive, the other regenerating – the annihilation of old Asiatic society and the laying of the material foundations of Western society in Asia.'

The apologists for the British Raj did not dissent from this. From Warren Hastings to Lord Halifax the architects of British rule in India believed that they had the task of what we call today 'modernization': order, justice, railways, public works, education, science, and 'European progress.' They were proud of having banished suttee, put down the Thugs, and opened India to the world. The kind of Indians who responded to Marxism were those who had been influenced and moulded by the British Raj: men like Kumaramangalam's father who sent his sons to Eton, or Jawaharlal Nehru (Harrow and Trinity), or his daughter (Somerville College, Oxford). There were hundreds of millions of Indians, but there were a few millions who had learned English in their schools in India, who appreciated Shakespeare, had read Milton, regarded Macaulay as a great historian, had studied Darwin and Mill, and wanted to run railways and build aeroplanes and endow India with steel plants and scientific laboratories. I knew Indians who had a much better appreciation of English literature and European philosophy than any comparable students I ever encountered in Canada. Indeed I befriended and worked on one 'contact' in Trinity who had such a good knowledge of English literature and philosophy and so great a love of the same that he was as impervious to Marxist indoctrination as Rudyard Kipling or my Muslim friend for whom a glass of beer was a traumatic experience.

The antagonism in Marx to the dark part of feudalism in Europe, and to Asiatic stagnation, superstition, and hierarchic exploitation, and his enthusiasm for and faith in progress, technical achievements, and bigger and better productive organizations was particularly attractive to young people who had learned from their masters and more distantly from Europeans and the United States that the future devoted to industrial production was better than the past of peasants with hoes and of kings, courts, and conspicuous waste.

It was attractive for another reason. Marx's dialectical mode of reasoning enabled him to condemn what he elsewhere approved of. Progress was good. Heaven was not far off. What was required was a revolution which would destroy the bourgeoisie and the imperialists, who were the last of the obstacles to unlimited abundance and the expression of the infinite capacity of mankind for human development. Thus it was possible to condemn forcefully the ruling class while at the same time one could approve of nearly everything they had accomplished. What had been achieved was the result of past history. What could be achieved in the future required a breaking of the power structure and the creation of a new order.

To be perfectly fair to the British rulers of India and their masters in Whitehall, they, too, acknowledged the need for change. India was not only being educated but educated for self-government. Kumaramanga-lam's mother had responded to the reforms from above and had been elected to a provincial assembly. But the British had a very slow time-scale for change. Furthermore, they thought that Indian self-government required the creation of a politically conscious governing class which governed as the British government did through the agency of a mandarinate and a parliamentary system linking the governors with the governed.

We acknowledged this aspect of British policy in India and we were opposed to it. In the first place, the time-scale was too slow, and when and if India ever reached a condition of self-government agreeable to the British government India would still be an undemocratic hierarchical state like Britain itself. In this opinion of British society, we shared the views of British socialists of both the Labour party and the Communist persuasion. Capitalist Britain was a failure, and the social and economic structure were obstacles to the realization of the full potential of the British people and we did not want a repetition in India or the colonies. Although we appreciated what the British bourgeoisie had done in the past, there was a root-and-branch aspect to our thinking about the present and the future.

While we developed a considerable understanding of Marxism and were acquainted with the history of the Russian Revolution as it was being told by the victorious Bolsheviks with an increasing bias of advantage to the politicians in office in the Soviet Union, it is questionable whether we knew very much about India or Ceylon, whence our members came. There were two big problems which we never completely or even partly resolved. One was the question of Gandhi and the other was that of the Muslim League. We had to admit that Gandhi commanded more popular support in India than any other leader, and much more than our hero, Jawaharlal Nehru, or the Congress notables like C.R. Das and Subhas Bose. If we did not develop any clear understanding it was not for the want of trying. Much of the activity of the colonial group consisted of self-education not only in the Marxist classics, which we used to call

'Bible reading,' but in the study of the structure and character of Indian society and the Indian economy. We puzzled over the Permanent Settlement, the zemindari system, and the ryotwari systems of land holding. Needless to say, a group of young men and women with academic labours to perform and triposes to prepare for and themselves full of a variety of conflicting impressions of their own country did not achieve the enlightenment they were seeking.

Mahatma Gandhi was regarded as a remote figure, a kind of saint who had aroused the people but a man whose example no one wished to imitate or one into whose hands one wished to commit one's conscience and career. When Mohan returned to India in the Long Vacation of 1937, he brought me back a length of khaddar, the hand-woven cloth whose production was recommended by the Mahatma, and I had an expensive shirtmaker in Cambridge to do it up as a shirt, but this was about as far as we went in paying deference to Gandhi. He was like a force of nature in India, but we did not see much in what he did or the example he set as anything but useful nationalist propaganda. No ashrams for us.

The most serious gap in our knowledge concerned the Indian Muslim communities and their political organization. We simply swallowed whole the view that the Raj encouraged, if it did not create, Muslim-Hindu antagonism, and that a struggle against British imperialism in India would cause the antagonisms of four centuries to melt away and India would emerge as a free, united nation. This was much too simple-minded a view of reality, and one of the early instances of the foolishness of blaming on foreign influences and on foreign imperialism problems that are indigenous. The Indians were ready enough to gloss over the Hindu-Muslim antagonism, and I was ill-qualified at that time to correct the bias because I had roughly the same view of French-English antagonisms in Canada, i.e., they were due to an obscurantist church, politicians and newspapers who made a living out of peddling racial hatred, and to the judgements of the imperial Privy Council which persistently found in favour of divisive provincial governments against the government of the Canadian nation.

Although I can now see that my political analysis at that time and for some years was deficient in relation to the varieties of nationalist opposition to foreign imperialism, I think I had at that time gone to the heart of the most important political problem of the twentieth century, the very heart of the darkness of the world and its tragedy. The British student Communists, however, were not at all interested in the problem. When

100

I spoke to the student party gathering in Birmingham in September 1937, I asserted as forcibly as I could that the problem of imperialism was the most important general problem of politics, and that Fascism and Nazism were but particular manifestations of a general phenomenon the end product of which always had been and always would be war. But the comrades were not interested. Of course, they sympathized with anyone opposed to the British government or any bourgeois government anywhere, but what really engaged their attention and attracted all their energy was the war in Spain and building a 'front against fascism.' What I had to say was academic and peripheral, and so I suppose it was in the circumstances of the moment. But I was profoundly right and history is proving this to be the case. The attractions and impulses of imperialism have ruined or diminished every state which they have afflicted. But enough. I put my thoughts on imperialism in an inaugural lecture delivered in the University of Birmingham in December 1961.

I was the organizer not the leader of the colonial group. I had no power or inclination to order any one to do anything, and I never made any policies. I was not even concerned with the ways in which the right people were manoeuvred into control of this or that society, front, committee etc. Mohan Kumaramanglan and Pieter Keunenan were the 'influentials' in the university at large, in the Union society and with a wide circle of friends among conservatives, liberal socialists, and non-politicals more interested in the arts, the 'Footlights,' and so on. Pieter Keuneman was particularly good in this role.

He was a Eurasian from Ceylon, now Sri Lanka, the son of a high court judge whose forbears were Sinhalese and Dutch. Pieter was a large, handsome, laughing young man educated at an English public school. He was so addicted to the 'good life,' making jokes, spending time with the beautiful and talented Austrian girl he eventually married and divorced that some of the more puritanical and solemn members of the colonial group were suspicious of his Marxist integrity. He wrote daring satirical songs which were much admired in some circles. 'Violate me in violet time in the vilest way you know' was a particular favourite. Oddly enough, of all the colonial group save one, Pieter remained a faithful active member of the Communist party and perhaps still is. He has held several ministerial posts in the government of Sri Lanka.

Apart from recruiting members I concentrated on raising the level of political awareness and understanding. I did this in three ways: weekly

101

session on current politics, the study of the Marxist texts, and spring or summer reading parties lasting three or four days in the vacation away from Cambridge: twice at the county home of the parents of a friend in Trinity at Lakenheath in Suffolk and once in rented accommodation near High Wycombe.

The study of current politics was undertaken by assigning some one each week to read the daily newspapers and journals like the *New Statesman*, the *Labour Monthly*, the *Spectator*, *International Press Correspondence*, etc., and then to report on the leading events and their meaning in terms of the fight against fascism, the class struggle, and so on. This sounds a tendentious program and it was and was intended to be, but at the same time it greatly sharpened perception and developed in the members some sense of the interconnections between politics and economics, and even with the arts and especially the popular arts like the cinema.

In encouraging the study of the Marxist classics I was selective in what I directed the group to apply their minds to. This had a pedagogic not a political purpose. I insisted, for example, that everyone read, learn, and inwardly digest Marx's *Value, Price and Profit* because it is a short, succinct, and clear statement of principles. On the other hand, I discouraged too much study of *Capital* because this might either defeat the neophytes or encourage closet Marxism at the expense of active political work. In my own mind I doubted whether Marx's labour theory of value could ever be made into a tool for the analysis of everyday economic phenomena such as prices, but I did strongly insist on the dogma that the foundation of all wealth is work, that people can possess wealth without working, but that without work there can be no wealth. This seemed to me then, as it still does, the essential and profound truth in the doctrines of Karl Marx.

To the works of Lenin we paid close attention. We even laboured through *Materialism and Empirio-Criticism*. But especially did we study Lenin's doctrines concerning the party: the great engine of revolution. In this I think we got at the heart of the matter, for we learned, as Lenin had demonstrated, that a small body of men and women can overturn a great society if they are organized in a disciplined way and if the society in which they act is sufficiently bewildered and confused by the follies and corruption of a government. Although we talked and argued a lot about 'the class forces,' Lenin inculcated a sense of the importance of will power and calculation in politics. Numbers did not matter as much as determination, intelligence, and hard realism. All very exhilarating, especially to those who are young, innocent, and ambitious to do good!

Our reading parties were organized with two purposes in mind: to enable us to sit at the feet of senior and experienced revolutionaries and to study the history and problems of Indian and other communities in the grip of the imperialist powers. As I recall it we had Page Arnot as a speaker at one of our parties and Ben Bradley at another.

The direction of our activities did not involve much personal contact with the party higher-ups. Such control as there was came from within ourselves, but I did learn of the discipline and how it operated on one occasion. The man who exercised an unseen power was Ben Bradley. He was an amiable, jolly, fat man who had in our eyes great prestige because he was, in the first place, a genuine worker and trade unionist (or he had been at one time) and in the second he had been the centre of the Meerut Conspiracy case and had been sent to prison for attempting to form trade unions in India. I liked Ben Bradley and I think he liked me, but I am bound to say that he was by my lights a stupid man.

Our general source of information about the Party line was *International Press Correspondence* (*Inprecor*). In 1937-38 the line on India was shifting in the direction of less militancy and civil disobedience and this shifting was experienced in the form of statements about the annual gathering of the Indian National Congress and the resolutions to be put before the Congress. Kumaramangalam and I questioned the shift in emphasis and we worked out a rather comprehensive critique of the position of the party in this matter. We asked for an opportunity to put our point of view to Ben Bradley. He very obligingly came to Cambridge. We explained why we thought the line of the party was inappropriate and why a call for more militant action was required in the circumstances. Bradley listened to our arguments and then he told us our views were wrong. The party had decided the line and it was right. I started to argue, but Bradley offered no counter-arguments. He kept repeating himself, declaring there was nothing more to be said. At this point, Kumaramangalam switched over to support Bradley. Everything we had argued about was forgotten. I felt completely let down, and so I shut up. The matter was closed. Whenever I see a particularly slow-witted trade unionist on television stolidly repeating himself and avoiding questions, I am reminded of Ben Bradley. And yet I liked the man and I respected him for the virtue of loyalty and faithfulness. But he was stupid.

The other man at the centre of the party who exercised considerable influence over our deliberations in the colonial group was Michael Carritt. He was quite a different type from Ben Bradley. The son of a professor of philosophy at Oxford, he had retired early from the Indian civil service and lived on his pension in Dolphin Square, London, and drove a snappy little sports car. He had a lively mind and, of course, a very considerable knowledge of India and how the government of India worked. At one stage early in 1939 he toyed with the idea of having me tutor a much younger brother of his, still at Eton, in Marxism-Leninism, but nothing ever came of this.

At the end of the summer term in 1938, Victor Kiernan left Cambridge to go to India where he remained for eight years teaching in an Indian university, and experiencing academic democracy at first hand. Early in 1939 it was decided that we ought to make some changes in our work in the interest of continuity because I, too, would sooner or later move on. To this end we interested a bright, lively, young undergraduate, Jack Gallagher. He attended our reading party that spring, and at the end of the summer term I handed over the colonial work to him. My new sphere of activity was to do for graduate students what I had been doing for the victims of imperialism.

It is possible to make a rough estimate of the outcome of work in the colonial group during the years 1937-39. Two members, Pieter Keuneman and Sonny Gupta were never lost to the Communist party. Both became leaders in the parties of their respective communities: Keuneman in Sri Lanka and Gupta in India. So far as I can discover, none of the other members are still in Soviet-oriented communist parties; at least not in prominent positions. The two Englishmen associated with the group and myself have made use of our interest in imperialism in our academic careers. Jack Gallagher achieved the distinction of being successively a professor of imperial history both in Oxford and in Cambridge and was vice master of Trinity College, Cambridge. Victor Kiernan was for many years a professor of history in the University of Edinburgh. All of us have written books concerned with imperialism. Jack Gallagher in collaboration with R.E. Robinson wrote a famous article in the *Economic History Review* on the imperialism of free trade and a well-known book on *Africa and the Victorians: The Official Mind of Imperialism*. Victor Kiernan's first book was concerned with the British activity in one of the last areas of European expansion, *British Diplomacy in China, 1880-*

1885, and his most recent is *America: The New Imperialism*. My own *Britain and Argentina in the Nineteenth Century* was an attempt to describe and analyse what I once wrongly denominated as a problem of 'informal empire,' and two of my books on Argentina are, among other things, endeavours to examine the lamentable consequences of rhetoric about imperialism used in inappropriate circumstances. Of the three of us only Victor Kiernan has stuck to Marxism as an analytical tool. Although Jack Gallagher was for most of his career anything but a Marxist, his use (or in my view his misuse) of the term 'imperialism' has contributed to the loose rhetoric of anti-imperialism as a means of arousing hostility to all forms of 'western' enterprise.

One member of the group, Arun Bose, was an active leader of the Indian Communist party from 1941 to 1950. For many years he has been an academic. Judging from his writing he is no longer a Communist, but he remains a Marxist in the sense that he is seeking to 'improve' Marxism by directing upon it the light of econometrics. He has entitled his latest book *Political Paradoxes and Puzzles*, which seems to be an admission that the certainties of our youth are something less than truth.

Then there is the career of my dearest and closest collaborator, Mohan Kumaramangalam.

Mohan returned to India in 1939, and I never saw him again for twenty-nine years. I had no communication with him of any description until in February 1966 I was handed by an hotel clerk in Buenos Aires a letter postmarked Madras and inscribed in his familiar handwriting. In May 1968 Mohan and his wife visited England. I met them in Richmond where they were staying and we drove to Cambridge. We stopped overnight. I then drove him and his wife to Saffron Walden and delivered them at the home of his closest boyhood friend at Eton, Viscount Caldecote. There I left him.

What had the years done to Mohan? He greeted me with a punch, 'Henry, you old rascal! It is good to see you.' There were a few streaks of grey in his hair. He had put on a little weight. His English, which my wife has always declared to be the most beautiful English she had ever heard, had now a slight Indian intonation. But he seemed not to have changed: the same charm, the same school-boy jokes, and below the surface the same hard, practical sense; the same impatience with slackers, the same indisposition to indulge in talk once it became apparent that it was just talk.

In the thirty-six hours we were together there was time to review the past: his rather than mine, for I had never been in the eye of any storm. Had he left the Communist party? Yes. Why?

After his return to India Mohan had twice been in jail: once in the jails of the British Raj in the 1940s and again in the jails of independent India. But these experiences had not affected him. Jails for a 'political' in India had been boring, frustrating but not frightening. What in the end had persuaded him to leave the Communist party was very much a 'Mohan reason.' 'We just were not getting anywhere. We had nothing practical to offer the Indian people,' he summed it up. 'I had to find another way.'

He told me that when he left the Communist party he had nothing: no money, no means of making a living. He tried journalism, but that yielded nothing. There remained the bar. 'I was a barrister, but I knew no law,' he said. 'You remember how we cracked International Law at Cambridge. Well, I employed the same methods. I just worked like stink for months, until I knew some law. Then I started to practise in the High Court.'

I had no difficulty in understanding what he said. We had once spent a Christmas vacation together in Bideford, Devon, working for the Historical Tripos. Kumaramangalam could work: hour after hour, day after day, with inflexible self-discipline. On this occasion I cracked before he did. Once Mohan set himself a goal – getting a good degree or practising at the Bar or governing Air India – he never gave up, and he focused his attention on only those matters which were germane to his object.

At the Bar he was willing to take any case referred to him, except one kind. He would never handle a case involving a landlord against a farmer. Everything else was grist to the mill, and he soon found he was making a good income. No golf clubs for Mohan, however. No interest in the Madras Jockey Club. He was dressed in a cheap wind breaker made of some unpleasant artificial fabric.

Shortly after he returned from his visit to Britain in 1968 he became the head of Air India. He called me once when he was in London on his way to the United States. He asked me to get some information about an executive in British Airways who was a relation of a common friend. I got the information and when I called him back he said laconically, 'Thanks, old boy. I just want to find out how they do things in the USA.'

He found out right enough. From what I learned from friends he went to Washington and then on to the west coast where he succeeded in buying several Jumbo jets with no money. When all was over, the Boeing company gave a dinner in Mohan's honour. He made a graceful speech.

I can imagine it: light, witty, charming, and friendly. I am told that when he sat down, the president of Boeing was heard to say, 'I wish I had gone to Cambridge.'

Of course, the Boeing wallah had it wrong; he should have said 'I wish I had gone to Eton,' for that is where Mohan learned to refine and polish his natural talent for social intercourse.

After Air India, Mohan became the minister of Steel and Mines in Mrs Gandhi's emergency government. Then he was killed in an air crash at Delhi Airport on 2 June 1973, and in a very Indian way, which Mohan hated: nobody had bothered for some weeks to put in order the low visibility landing guidance system and there was this day a heavy dust storm. Had he not died the history of India might have been different from what it has been since.

When he moved from Madras to Delhi and after he became a minister, I wrote to him a joking letter in which I said: 'Biff! Bang! Kumar comes to town and Governments fall!' Some time later I was chatting with a politically knowledgeable Indian and told him about my letter to Mohan. He said solemnly, 'That is no joke. That is how it was. Biff! Bang! Kumar did come to town.'

During my drive to Cambridge and then to Saffron Walden we went over the ideas which had guided us in the colonial group. I argued that our big mistake was in believing that the Muslim League was a by-product of the favour shown to Muslims, especially in north-western India by the Raj. The Raj did not create religious/regional differences in India. They were there as a fact of life and we had insufficiently appreciated this. Mohan would have nothing of this. He still believed that Pakistan was not a 'natural' development but one which had been called into being by politicians who did not want to see a strong, united India.

When we got on to Marxism in general, Mohan did not respond to some of my fundamental criticisms. Part of my comment, of course, involved a positive appreciation of Marxist analysis: the importance, for example, of socio-economic analysis as a key to understanding political forces; the dogmas about work as the only source of wealth; the general relevance of the concept of change being brought about by quantitative increases, and so on. These positive facts Mohan consented to, but he had little sympathy with my criticisms of the psychological consequences of making man and then a party of men into gods.

In the course of our discussions I ventured to suggest that more attention ought to be given to Gandhi's ideas; that perhaps Gandhian non-violence as a means of rallying the mass of the people against otherwise impermeable bureaucracies had a very real importance, and one which we had insufficiently appreciated. Mohan's reply to this was very interesting. He said that, of course, Gandhi's ideas and the movement he had created were important in India. But his ideas had no general relevance. Gandhi was up against the British in particular and not against the Nazis. The British were not brutes. There were very severe limits to what the British would do. Yes, there was a massacre at Amritsar. Yes, there were atrocities after the Indian Mutiny. But the British were not Nazis and that is why a movement like Gandhi's could exist and grow.

Mohan and his wife had come from India via Moscow where their son was a post-graduate student in physiology. And so I said, 'Yes, the Nazis. Would you say the same thing about the Soviet Communists?'

Mohan smiled and turned on the charm. 'Henry,' he said, 'We were Bolsheviks once, weren't we? We know they are tough. Let's leave it at that.'

Once during our trip Mohan became angry with me. He had been urging me to come to India. Oddly enough, India is not a country I have ever felt a desire to visit, but I said, 'I'm a poor man. I couldn't afford to visit India. But you can do something. Get me invited to India to advise about something. You know, air fare there and back. A month in expensive hotels. Then a report for file.'

Mohan became quite angry. 'No! No!' he barked with some intensity. 'I could never do that! There are far too many people in India just like that. Slackers! Parasites!'

'For God's sake, Mohan,' I replied. 'I'm only joking. I despise academic free-loaders as much as you do. When I've made my fortune I'll come to see you.'

One hesitates to comment on one's friend's wife. There was, however, one episode during our trip which made me unhappy on Mohan's account. This occurred at breakfast in Cambridge. Because they had just come from Moscow and had been describing the advantages which they believed were accruing to their son in his graduate studies there, I asked them to comment on the reports that ordinary Russians had been displaying hostility towards black Africans studying in the Soviet Union. Was there anything in these reports?

I was surprised indeed by Mohan's wife's reply. I supposed that there was probably little substance in the reports. Not at all. Mohan's wife launched upon a denunciation of black Africans: the Russians are right; these people are lecherous, ill-mannered barbarians, and so on.

I could see Mohan was deeply embarrassed. I said as mildly as I could, 'What you say surprises me. We have thousands of black Africans in Britain and a few hundred in Birmingham but I have never noticed they are any different to the rest of us, except that they are black and better behaved on the whole than some of the whites I have to deal with.' But this did not silence the woman, and Mohan managed to change the subject without making any comment.

What a sad and sorry contrast was the wife Mohan had married to the attractive, amusing, and wryly ironic Scottish girl he had loved at Cambridge!

I was never much acquainted with the 'rank file party cadres' in Cambridge, but my own activities and my connections both with Kumanamangalam and Keuneman brought me into contact with the student party leaders during the years 1937-39. From sometime early in 1938 until I left Cambridge just before Christmas 1939, I was quite a close friend of the secretary of the student party in Cambridge, Ram Nahum, and I spent Christmas 1938 with Ram at his home in Manchester.

Ephraim Nahum was the most intelligent and forceful man I have ever known personally. I have known men and women who are probably more intelligent, sensitive, and creative than Ram, but none who combined mental ability and force in such a degree. He was a stocky young man of medium height, bursting with great energy. His clothes always seemed too tight as if there was in him such great muscular and nervous energy that mere clothing could not contain him. Had he not despised organized sports of all kinds I am quite sure he could have become a blue at rugger or some other strenuous, battling kind of game. With his energy he had a splendid brain and a great imaginative talent in the natural sciences. He never displayed much interest in music, literature, or the arts, but off-hand remarks which he made from time to time indicated that he knew more about music and literature than he ever let on. One had the impression that he had tried out music and literature and the visual arts and found them all wanting. He lived in semisqualor in Pembroke College, but he had odd little *objets d'art* in his possession which suggested that had he wanted to do so he could have furnished his rooms like the most elegant of undergraduates. He had, too, tastes in food and amusements which ran counter to the accepted 'proletarian puritanism' so predominant a sentiment among the party faithful.

For example, Ram was inordinately fond of playing bridge, and, because his rooms were more like a public office than a place of private study and entertainment, he used to borrow my rooms in Great Court in Trinity for the purpose 'holing up' for two or three hours with friends to play bridge. Also he loved sports cars, and he and Kumaramangalam pooled their resources to purchase an M.G. which they took turns driving hither and yon on business. When I knew him he was thwarted in love: the object of his desire was a plump, placid, sleepy girl in Newnham who unfortunately was in the possession of a man in Trinity. Ram could never understand how his beloved allowed herself to be attached to a man like Michael. In a less civilized age, I am sure he would have picked a quarrel with his rival, run him through with a sword or shot him in a duel, and carried Kay off whether she liked it or not.

Young men like Ram had not in fact shed altogether their public school characters. Several episodes illustrate this. On one occasion Ram, Mohan, and I were in London, and we put up in the flat of two school teachers in Belsize Park. We were obliged to sleep three to a room, and so we had to undress together before going to bed. I put on my pyjamas. Unfortunately my pyjamas were not like their pyjamas. My mother had made mine, and she had designed them on the very sensible assumption that her beloved son, being destined to live in foreign parts and away from her ministrations, would appreciate having pyjamas without buttons which come off and have to be replaced. They were beautifully made, sensible pyjamas, but they were different from the pyjamas one could buy in the shops. Ram and Mohan began to rag me about my pyjamas. This went on for some minutes and it looked to me as if they intended to debag me or throw me in the bath. And so I became angry.

'You're just two goddamned public school boys,' I shouted. 'Straight out of the *Boys Own Annual*. In the Lower Fifth at St Georges. Bullying poor little Gig Lamps from the colonies. Why in the hell don't you sew leather patches on your pyjamas like the ones on your jackets so that you can be phony proletarians 24 hours a day? To hell with you.'

This stopped them in their tracks. Mohan became at once conciliatory and charming. We were getting on to dangerous ground. If one questioned the authenticity of one's uniform where might we not end up? And so to bed and to sleep.

The then leader of the student party in Cambridge was a young man named David Spenser; an inoffensive, moderately competent organizer whose main claim to fame was his beautiful girl friend and the fact that he was able to boast about having once had a bath in Newnham College. He had been educated in a grammar school in London. Having inherited £1,000 from his grandmother he financed himself at Cambridge. Unlike the public school members of the party, he was a 'snappy dresser' and sported a well-trimmed moustache. He had a pork pie hat. This caused Ram and Mohan to sneer at David Spenser. This made me realize how wise I had been to follow the advice of Major Hooper in the matter of headgear.

Ram's father was a successful Manchester textile merchant. He had a great reputation in Lancashire as the only business man who had made profits every year during the depression. Like his eldest son Alphonse Nahum was a man of tremendous energy and twice his son's girth. He ate and drank hugely and had a great passion for bridge. When I knew him he had just been invited on account of his business acumen to take over the direction of a large hire-purchase company.

He was a man with few inhibitions, if any. Once Ram had brought David Spenser home for dinner. In the course of the meal the student leader of the Cambridge Communists started arguing about politics and, according to Ram, this enraged his old man so much that he threatened to run Spenser through with the carving knife. On another occasion while I was staying in the Nahum household in Didsbury, we were having coffee in the library. There was present a gentle, cultivated, and shy German woman, a refugee from Germany, who was serving as a governess for the younger Nahums. Alphonse Nahum disliked her intensely. When she excused herself after coffee, Nahum launched into a great attack on the *Fräulein*. He accused her of every fault one can imagine. Finally Ram's mother said, 'You know very well, Phonsey, that every word you say is untrue. The *Fräulein* is a good woman, and you know it.'

Phonsey exploded. 'I don't know what she does. Maybe she pees on the carpet. But I know I hate her.'

Nobody said anything. As calm as could be, he then turned to the telephone and asked the operator to get him a number in Paris and he spent the rest of the evening calling business colleagues around the world ordering them to do this or to get clued up about that.

For some reason or other – probably because I avoided discussion of politics – Ram's father seemed to like me. At any rate he sought me as an ally to induce Ram to do what Alphonse wanted, i.e., to become a patent lawyer. After dinner on Christmas Day he asked me to join him in a walk in a nearby park. He explained his intentions for Ram.

'Why did I send him to a good school eh? So he could amount to something. He's got brains. He's got education. He could be a good patent lawyer. There are not many good patent lawyers, I can tell you. He could make real money.' And so on.

I did not think it prudent to say that at the moment Ram was planning to bring down the European bourgeoisie. Instead, I said that Ram was bent on being a great physicist. 'So what's a physicist? You can do better than that. I want Ram to do better than that.' I timidly mentioned the name of Einstein, as an example of a physicist who was not so bad, but Alphonse Nahum dismissed Einstein as not relevant to the argument. The problem was Ram.

Finally Ram's father made an offer which maybe Ram would not refuse. A few weeks previously Alphonse had purchased a large, Elizabethan timbered house in the country to which he intended to move his family. And so he said, 'You tell Ram that if he is willing to become a patent lawyer, I'll build him a squash court at our new place.' I did not laugh. I said I could put the proposition to Ram, but I could not guarantee acceptance.

'I know my son. He's stubborn. But maybe also he has sense. Maybe from you he will take advice.'

Alphonse was not very interested in politics except that he approved heartily of Neville Chamberlain and Zionism. That Christmas Moshe Shertok, one of the big Zionist leaders, was in Manchester and the local Zionists had organized a gathering of Jewish youth to meet the great man. Alphonse wanted Ram to go to this meeting. So did Ram's mother. There was a great argument. Here was a matter on which I could influence Ram. I persuaded him that we ought to go to this meeting, not because it meant giving in to his father or pleasing his mother, but because I would like to go. After all, I had my responsibilities as a colonial organizer and I needed to know what went on in the Middle East. And so we went.

There were sixty or seventy young Jews gathered together in the home of one of Ram's parents' friends. I was the only goy present. Although I was going deaf at this time and one of my purposes for being in Manchester was to learn lip reading from Professor and Mrs Ewing in Manchester University, I managed to overhear one of those present say to another, 'Look who's here, Alphonse Nahum's son.' And she put her nose in the air to suggest what she thought of Ram.

Moshe Shertok's discourse was designed to bring tears to the eyes. It must be remembered that in December 1938, the world only knew of Hitler's anti-semitism and nothing of what was in store for the Jews of Europe. For this reason what Shertok had to say was repellent to Ram and me. He told a tale of a young Jewish boy who had been rescued from Germany and had been transported to Palestine. At night he heard distant gun fire just as he had heard it in Germany, but he slept soundly and without fear because it was the gun fire of heroic Jews conquering land for the foundation of Zion.

When we left Ram was in a rage. The Zionists are as much Nazis as the Nazis, he declared. For him, as for me at that time, the solution for the Jews was not Zionism, but revolution; revolution brought about by a united front of all progressive forces and the destruction of Nazism and reaction everywhere.

The following Easter vacation I was able to learn a little more of Zionism. I was in Paris, and, of course, I looked in on the headquarters of the Rassemblement Mondial des Etudiants in Cité Paradis, where James Klugman was at work. Early in April Mussolini invaded Albania and incorporated it in his fascist empire. James quickly decided that this attack by a fascist power on an Islamic state offered an opportunity for bringing together Jews and Arabs in a common front against fascism. I was enlisted in this enterprise along with Eric Hobsbawm from Cambridge who was in Paris then. A meeting of Jewish and Arab students was hastily summoned, and about forty or fifty young people assembled to hear arguments and pass resolutions.

What struck me most forcibly was the disparity in the intellectual accomplishments and capacity for argument between the Jews and the Arabs. The Jews always had something intelligent to say even when one did not agree with what they said. The Arabs had no arguments and simply abused the Jews with slogans. It was plain that the Jews knew more about and cared more about the Moslem inheritance in Palestine than the Arabs. Both parties to the assembly decided to invite the whole assembly to cultural evenings. The Jewish cultural evening turned out to be a concert of high quality; the Arab to be a session in a club featuring belly dancing. Up to that point I was a staunch critic of Zionism and a supporter of the Arabs. This experience turned me around, and when, after the war, Begin and his friends blew up the King David Hotel in Jerusalem I felt a surge of hope that maybe the desert would bloom again, as it has done. The Jews make the best possible use of the meagre gifts God has given them, and that is their claim to anything they have. By comparison the well-endowed are contemptible. Anti-Semitism is not an assertion of superiority, but an expression of inferiority, a jealous acknowledgement that God has chosen the right people.

When David Spenser went down from Cambridge in June 1938, he was succeeded in the secretaryship of the student party by Eric Hobsbawm of King's College. Eric was and is an exceptional man of splendid talents: an exact reading and speaking knowledge of several languages, an excellent memory, a very quick understanding, and wide-ranging interests. As an academic historian there are few in his class. Furthermore, he has never allowed himself to become bogged down in the minutiae of scholarship. Whether he is still a party member I do not know, but he is still very much a Marxist. His books have gone around the world, and I have found that in discussion with Indians or Argentines or Japanese or even Americans as often as not it emerges that if they know the name of an English historian it is Hobsbawm, just as it used to be that of Toynbee: not A.J.P. Taylor, Christopher Hill, Trevor-Roper, but Hobsbawm. His service to the diffusion of Marxist ways of thinking have obviously been very great.

But was he a leader? Eric knew everything but he seldom knew what to do. Ram spotted this weakness very early. More than once he said to me, 'Damn it, Eric is making the party into a debating society.' Of course, in Marxist circles the last thing the party should ever be is a debating society. Bolsheviks are men of decision and action. Be that as it may be, indecision was not congenial to Ram. If one was going to fight Hitler one had to prepare to fight him. He did not care whether the pacifists approved of the CUSC's policies or not. Ram always saw the main point clearly. Just as his father was an excellent business man, so Ram could have been an excellent soldier, but only as general officer commanding. And so he did become the commanding officer of the Communists in Cambridge.

After the war broke out in September 1939, the political movement in Cambridge seemed to fragment. It was not a matter of great arguments among people of differing values and points of view. The great calamity all of us had concerned ourselves with since coming to Cambridge was now on us, and I think it silenced us. I saw little of Ram after the end

114

of the summer term in 1939. I never learned whether he turned to physics because he disagreed with the party line or whether in the final analysis physics was where his greatest interest lay. Because he was such a talented man and such a strong character I would like to know more of the last few years of his life. One of the few bombs dropped on Cambridge got him. He was dining in the Blue Barn near the Round Church with a girl we both knew, Winnifred Lambert. Freddie's legs were blown off but Ram was killed.

By the time I returned for the Michaelmas term 1939, Britain had declared war on Germany. So much had happened during the Long Vacation that few people had thought out the meaning of the Soviet-German Pact and the Allied declaration of war on Germany. Nothing was clear except that all the assumptions of the past years since the outbreak of the Spanish Civil War had dissolved. About the Nazi-Soviet Pact my reaction was quite simple. Chamberlain and Daladier had appeased Hitler, now Stalin was having a go at the same policy, but with a difference. Stalin was gaining something, whereas Chamberlain and Daladier had done nothing but lose: part of Czechoslovakia, then all of it. Certainly the danger to Britain and France had greatly increased and we were now in a war and were obliged to do what for three years at least we had been advocating. We were fighting Hitler or would be soon. The first thing I did on arriving back in Cambridge was to put my name down at the Joint Recruiting Board with the proviso that I be enlisted in the Canadian army. I believed that the time had passed for talk, and what political feeling I had, as distinct from analytical understanding, was bitterness that Chamberlain and Daladier had got us into a war without an alliance with the Soviet Union. Without that alliance the war was going to be a very tough proposition and one which we might very well be unable to resolve. What I feared more than war was another round of appeasement which would do to Britain what had been done to Czechoslovakia.

My party job was to organize the graduates group, i.e., those members of the university who were neither undergraduates nor dons – people like myself who were engaged in research and were working for higher degrees or towards fellowships in the several colleges. Altogether I rounded up ten or twelve people who were already party members. Now that I was no longer under the need to work semi-secretly with students from overseas, I should, I suppose, have regularized my formal position in the party, but I did not, and no one asked me to do so. Our group met a few times, but what we discussed or what line of action we resolved to take, remains a blank in my mind. I only remember Eric Hobsbawm coming back from London with word on the grapevine that Harry Pollitt was out as general secretary and that the war had become an imperialist war. I had never thought that the war was anything but an imperialist war. None the less it was a war which the British people ought not to lose. It was alright for Kiernan, Kumaramangalam, and Ferns to take apart the British Empire, but I did not relish Hitler doing it.

My behaviour and the decisions I made concerning myself between September and November 1939 ceased to be political. My ideas did not change nor did my political allegiance, but I began to find myself governed in my actions by non-political or at best semi-political considerations.

I was examined by the Joint Recruiting Board, and was found medically unfit on account of deafness. It was stated that I was good only for guard duties! I was advised that my name had been reported to a central registry for employment at tasks of national importance suitable to my experience and training. When it became abundantly clear to me that I was going to have no active combatant part in the war, something died in me and something new took its place. I wanted to go home and establish a family.

Before I left Winnipeg to go to Queen's University I had become engaged to be married. I loved my fiancée, but it is plain from my actions that marriage was not as important for me as reading books, seeing the world, playing around with ideas, and enjoying the excitement both intellectual and political of Cambridge University. Now all of this went dead. The college agreed to let me go to Harvard University and to pay me my scholarship so long as I continued my studies but not beyond June 1940.

Much has been written about Cambridge University in the 1930s, and much of what has been written in so far as it concerns communism in Cambridge is unsystematic and often wildly wrong. Who became Communists and why? Sociological or semi-sociological, psychological or semi-psychological theories have been advanced in attempts to explain the phenomenon, to explain why the right-inclined and predominantly apolitical Cambridge of the 1920s became the politicized and left-leaning Cambridge of the 1930s.

The only element common to all the Communists I encountered was high intelligence. All the people of high intelligence in Cambridge did not become Communists. Far from it. But those who did were nearly all people of high intelligence measured in terms of academic achievement.

They were not all predominantly public school boys and the female equivalent. Nor were they predominantly grammar school boys and girls. Some came from humble homes and some from upper-middle-class and aristocratic backgrounds. Two I knew very well were the sons of Liverpool dockers. Two others, one a very close friend, were from the highest ranges of the aristocracy. Some came from the public schools – Eton, Westminster, Winchester, Stowe, Clifton, and so on; others from the great grammar schools in Manchester, Bristol, Birmingham; others from schools so obscure they had to explain where they were. The percentage of Jews and Quakers in the party was probably higher than the percentage of the university as a whole, but not markedly so. Schooling and social background do not explain membership in the Communist party in Cambridge at that time.

One explanation which seems to me particularly silly and baseless depends upon the alleged existence in the minds of young men and women of the traditional ruling class of a sense of loss associated with the decline and fall of the British Empire and jealousy and envy of the United States. Attitudes to the United States in the years I was a student at Cambridge hardly existed. Apart from a taste for American jazz and American films, Cambridge students knew very little about the United States and cared less. There were a few exceptions, but these students were interested to know something about the American New Deal. During my first term at Cambridge some students in the League of Nations Union, hearing my North American accent and some of my views about state action to remedy unemployment and revive business activity, asked me to give some talks on the United States. I delivered what I suppose were the first lectures ever given in Cambridge University on American history. There had been a time in the past when a special subject – the American Civil War – had been offered in Part II of the Historical Tripos, but in the late thirties the United States was less a subject of study than Borneo or the Trobriand Islands.

As for responses to the decline of the British Empire, there was no sense of this. Quite the opposite. Such concern with the Empire as existed was directed to criticizing it as a powerful, repressive, political force. I never found the left as a whole and the student members of the Communist party particularly concerned about imperialism or the British Empire, certainly not about its decline. There was, however, a vigorous strand of anti-imperialism in British politics which manifested itself in Cambridge. This anti-imperialism dated back to the Boer War and was to be found in the Liberal party and then the Labour party. The Gillets and the Clarkes – Quaker bankers and shoe manufacturers and represented at Cambridge by many progeny at one time or another – were very active anti-imperialists. All the Kumaramangalam children were guarded, protected, and helped by the Gillets to the extent that in the Gillet household they found a second home. The suggestions made in popular TV spy thrillers that one reason why Englishmen spied for the Soviet Union was their sense of loss of empire and jealousy of the United States is a particularly foolish anachronism if their authors have in mind Cambridge men who really were Soviet spies before, during, and immediately after the Second World War.

The politicization of Cambridge in the 1930s is in fact quite easy to explain. Politics at that time was simply the most thrilling, fascinating, and important of human activities. One had to be stupid and insensitive indeed not to take some notice of what was going on in the world and to feel at least some degree of involvement. Those who today claim some kind of wisdom because they stood aside and kept quiet were not always the virtuous ones. Quite otherwise. Many of those who abstained from politics have turned out to be what we believed they were in the 1930s: clever, self-indulgent careerists given to compromise and half-truths, the sort of men and women who have helped to shackle and misgovern Britain for a quarter of a century.

What became of the Cambridge Communists? They certainly did not all become spies for the Soviet Union. In my last term at Cambridge I was the organizer of the graduate group. Before I left Cambridge in December 1939, the group had a small party and presented me with a two-volume work by Louis Fischer, *The Soviets in World Affairs* published by Jonathan Cape. Eight of the group, i.e., 80 per cent of the members, signed their names on the fly leaf. What has happened to them? What have they done in the world since December 1939? One has helped to transform the science of chemistry and biochemistry and has won a Nobel prize. One has become the head of a college in Cambridge and another the head of a college in Oxford. One has served as a dean of science for many years in a Canadian university. One has had a long and creative career in research related to medical science. One has had a career in the city of London. Eric Hobsbawm is the only one who has made a career having some relationship to Marxism and communism, and what is wrong with that in a free society? Of one man's career I have no knowledge. In assessing the contribution of people to the life of the world it is hard

118

to quantify in order to make comparisons, but I am satisfied that the eight graduate communists who gathered to present me with a book have contributed as richly to civilization and the work of the world as any eight men anywhere. And one who did not sign the flyleaf of my book and was not present contributed fundamentally to the development of the use of radio impulses in the detection of oil deposits in the earth's mantle. A rather important contribution I would have thought, but this did not prevent him from being jailed in Canada in 1940 when the party was suppressed.

Somehow or other word of my departure seems to have reached the party headquarters in London. I received a letter from my sometime superior, Ben Bradley, asking me to see him before leaving Britain. Accordingly I travelled to London and groped my way through the black-out to the spot in north-eastern London where he lived. Ben was a plump man and he had a plump wife. (Some years later one of my children was given a picture book about a plump man and plump woman and their plump children and plump pets. It always reminded me of Ben and his wife.) My memory of the visit is much more dominated by the cosy domesticity I encountered in the Bradley household than by the political discussion we then had.

But the visit was not a social call. We did discuss politics and my future. Ben hoped I would make contact with the American comrades, and to this end he proposed that he get for me a letter of introduction from Palme Dutt. I agreed to this. As to the political line at that moment and the opposition to the war we seemed to avoid a frank exchange of views on this subject. Instead we talked more generally about imperialism, and we agreed that the great events in progress meant the end of empire in the not too distant future. Then our time would come. We did not discuss the Russian seizure of 70,000 or so square miles of Poland or the Soviet attack on Finland which had just begun. These were not, of course, the sort of questions Ben Bradley would ever discuss, but candour obliges me to say that I did not try to discuss them. I did not regard Soviet policy at that time as an example of imperialist power politics. The Soviet Union found itself in a nasty military situation and was doing what was necessary to secure its survival against the Nazis. I had no sympathy at all with the view that the Nazi-Soviet Pact, the attack on Poland, and the invasion of Finland revealed what 'communism is really like.' Rather, these actions confirmed my belief that the Bolshevik leaders were tough, realistic men who had the intelligence and will to survive, qualities which I thought were lacking in Chamberlain and Daladier and in the people who wrote editorials in *The Times* and the *Daily Express* and composed idiotic songs like 'We'll hang out our washing on the Siegfried Line.' This was a time for Bolsheviks, and it was this reaction in me which, I think, accounts for the unintellectual but profound enthusiasm I felt when the crusty old imperialist, Winston Churchill, summoned the British people to fight on the beaches, to fight in the hills, and to fight on, etc.

And so with a letter from Palme Dutt hidden in the lining of my hat (the very one Major Hooper had recommended) and Dostoevsky's *The Brothers Karamazov* for light reading I embarked on the S.S. *Georgic* in Liverpool bound for New York. I did not know it then, but my connection with the Communist party was at an end.

CHAPTER SIX

The Other Half of the Cambridge Experience: John Saltmarsh and the study of history

It would be quite wrong to suppose that politics was the only concern of students in Cambridge in the years between the outbreak of the Spanish Civil War and the commencement of the Second World War. Not only were a great number of students – probably a majority – in no way interested, but those so concerned had also many other interests, not the least of which were academic studies. Academically, Cambridge University was a serious institution which set very high standards. There were, of course, a minority who came to the university primarily for fun and games or to make the right friends and to lay the foundation for reputations in the higher ranges of society, but the place was none the worse for their presence. The Pitt Club and the Hawks Club by no means dominated the university. It was possible for some to spend more time at Newmarket than in Cambridge, but these students commanded no special respect or attention. The one sure avenue to respect at Cambridge was success in its competitive system of examinations. These were open to all and required of all. Once one had passed the hurdle of the Triposes and was allowed to stay on for further work, respect depended upon one's ability to ask questions significant in the world of science, of the humanities, and of intellectual enquiry generally and then upon one's ability to find answers which commanded interest and assent in the world at large.

The rewards for achievement were prestige and further opportunities. If one wished to pursue a career in research or scholarship, one wanted to become a fellow of one's college or gain a place as a demonstrator or lecturer. This was not only an honour and a mark of distinction but also a provision of income and an opportunity to find answers to the questions one set oneself and to do so freely in one's own way.

Before 1939 no one – least of all the left-wing students – challenged the system of competitive examination in Cambridge or the right and duty of the senior members of the university to judge the abilities and suitability of entrants into the university and of undergraduates. The intellectuality of the Marxists tended to reinforce the system of selection because the Marxist students not only attached great importance to knowledge and analytical expertise as such but were eager to demonstrate that they were better than anyone else. The anti-intellectualism, the seeking after exotic religious experience, the resort to drugs, the hankering after astrology or vegetarianism, the preoccupation with sexual 'liberation' which characterized student activism thirty years later would have been rejected by the student activists of the 1930s as evidence of decay and disease. One had only to read *Mein Kampf* and the intellectual garbage published in *Der Stürmer* and the *Völkischer Beobachter* to be confirmed in one's enthusiasm for intellectual enlightenment, the pursuit of truth as practised in Cambridge University, and indeed for most manifestations of academic life as it had developed in Cambridge since the Reformation. We did not even criticize the existence of more professors of theology in Cambridge than of any of the more recent sciences. We only laughed.

I never doubted at any time the desirability of achieving the highest I could in the academic life of Cambridge. I did not, however, spend too much time working on the formal requirements of the university during the session 1936-37, and there probably were some grounds for Kitson Clark's doubt about my capacity to get a degree. Partly this was due to my preoccupation with mastering the works of Marx, Engels, Lenin, and Stalin and partly it was due to my disenchantment with the lectures offered by the university. Some of the lecturers may have been good scholars but they were poor lecturers. Others seemed to offer nothing which I did not feel I could get for myself from reading and discussion with fellow students. Indeed, for me the principal advantage of Cambridge as an educational institution was the presence of many students of high intelligence, academic zeal, and wide and vigorous interests. Teachers were not so important. Nor did I find the tutorial system everything it was supposed to be. Aside from Victor Kiernan no tutor I ever encountered had any effect on me or helped me in any way towards higher standards of scholarship or anything else.

But there was one great exception. This was John Saltmarsh of King's College. I chose as my special subject in Part II of the Historical Tripos, the economic and social history of England, 1540-1560. One sat two examinations for this course. John Saltmarsh was the lecturer, and he was more than a lecturer inasmuch as he required each student to write for him several essays which he marked and criticized with the greatest care. Often his commentary on what one wrote in an essay was half as long as the essay itself. John Saltmarsh was the greatest teacher I have ever encountered.

He was a shy, awkward man with spiky hair and he peered at his audience through shell-rimmed spectacles. His trousers always appeared to be too short for his legs. He was not a flashy lecturer and he had no capacity or inclination to entertain an audience. There were faint flashes of wit in his discourse, but in the main his lectures were dry. But what lectures! Every sentence contained a well-documented fact or an acute piece of analysis. There were no books which could give one what Saltmarsh gave in his lectures. He never published very much. It seemed as if almost everything he did as a scholar went into his lectures, and the only audience that mattered for him were the dozen or so students who had elected to read his course.

He was totally impersonal as far as I was concerned. He may have been different with members of King's College, but I have no evidence of this. I cannot recall ever exchanging more than a dozen or so words with him face to face or in private circumstances. The powerful influence he exercised came entirely from the quality of his lectures and the rigorous standards he maintained in criticizing one's work.

The economic and social history of England from 1540 to 1560 was concerned with a period of great change, when inflation was disorganizing society and generating antagonisms expressed in a variety of ways. It was a happy hunting ground for those seeking to illustrate with historical facts great generalizations about religion and the rise of capitalism, the emergence of the bourgoisie, the destruction of the peasantry, the management of the economy by the state, and so on. There was not much in the social and economic history of England between 1540 and 1560 which could not be used to prove some great truth about society provided one made the right selection. Saltmarsh made it his business to see that students did not select facts in the service of theories.

For Saltmarsh the truth was not something one already knew. Truth was what one did not know. I am not sure that Saltmarsh would have ever cared to define truth. That was not his style. If there is any truth, it is something which emerges from the contemplation of verifiable facts or evidence and from the ascertainable relationships among bits of evidence. Something had happened in English society during the years under scrutiny. That made it worth studying. But what was happening so far as Saltmarsh could see did not substantiate any of the grand theories of Marx or Weber or any of the other artists in intellectual speculation. As far as I personally was concerned, Saltmarsh was challenging me to affirm or deny why I had said in July 1936 that we did not know enough about history to generalize in the way Marx had done.

Unconsciously and without deliberate intent I sought to justify the truths Major Hooper had helped me to embrace. My first essay came back loaded with criticism and marked 'beta minus minus.' I admired Saltmarsh's pains-taking lectures so much that I responded to his criticism. I gathered more evidence and scrutinized it more carefully. When finally I produced an essay which was not covered with critical comments and was marked 'alpha minus' I felt great satisfaction. I was finally getting somewhere with the course.

Here I was, simultaneously expounding the great truths of Marxism to the colonial group and other assorted students, and undergoing an intellectual experience of a quite different kind. I did not then fully appreciate this contradiction. In fact, however, Saltmarsh was reinforcing the first lessons I had learned in St John's Technical High School in Winnipeg and in the University of Manitoba. What I would make of this only time would tell.

The scholarships I was given by Trinity College in June 1938 provided me with the opportunity to ask my own questions and find my own answers. My first inclination was to ask a question about my own country, Canada. I consulted the great Innis in Toronto, but nothing emerged which attracted me. In Cambridge, suggestions were made to me about the economic and social development of various English regions or various English industries, but these seemed to me pedestrian proposals. Finally I went to see C.R. Fay, a reader in economic history. He said to me, 'You know Argentina is a country of immense importance to Britain economically and financially and yet no one knows anything about this except those who do business there.' I hardly knew where Argentina was. I could have confused it with Chile. I knew no Spanish. And yet I replied at once, 'Yes, that is what I want to study.'

Why did I reply in this way and so quickly? There flashed through my mind the great theses on imperialism of Hobson, Lenin, and Rosa Luxemburg. What could be proved and disproved from the Anglo-Argentine experience? Here was no pedestrian theme. Here was fresh untrodden territory to explore.

I soon discovered how true this was. Nobody in Cambridge, indeed nobody in Britain at that time, knew anything about Argentina. Presumably there were people in the Foreign Office and the Board of Trade who had information, but that was not readily accessible. There were businessmen who knew what they were themselves doing, but this information was equally inaccessible. Where to begin? A distinguished scholar, Sir John Clapham, was appointed to supervise my work, but he knew nothing about Argentina. I used to see him from time to time, but the only advice he gave me, repeated several times, was: 'Ferns, do not write like an American.'

In going about my self-imposed task I imitated Victor Kiernan and the way he studied China. Learn the language and read everything. I bought a Spanish grammar book and a dictionary, and I went to the university library and started to read, beginning with Charles Darwin's *The Voyage of the Beagle*.

At first, the facts seemed to fit the theory of imperialism. In 1806 a naval commander with experience in India and close connections with business interests in the City of London, Sir Home Popham, decided on his own to use the ships under his command and soldiers employed to capture Cape Town from the Dutch for the purpose of liberating Buenos Aires from the yoke of Spain and of 'opening up markets' for British enterprise. The ideas, the socio-economic connections, and the rhetoric of Sir Home Popham, of whom I had hitherto known absolutely nothing, so completely fitted the theory which I had been expounding to the colonial group that I was more than enchanted. To add to my delight, Sir Home Popham seized Buenos Aires, was recalled by the government in London for acting without orders, was brought before a court martial, was acclaimed in the city of London, and was presented with a jewelled sword, whereupon the government turned about-face and assembled an armada and an expeditionary force of many thousands to break up and 'liberate' the Spanish Empire. How right were Hobson, Lenin, and Luxemburg! This was like being hit on the head by Newton's apple.

But then the facts began to go wrong. The advanced, capitalist, industrializing power of Britain was defeated in the Rio de la Plata. The invading armies surrendered. Then the Spaniards of the Rio de la Plata kicked out their own imperialist masters. Liberal enlightenment and free trade prevailed for a few years. The revolutionaries wrote to Bentham and borrowed money from Barings. A very bourgeois state of affairs came to pass, but only briefly. Tyranny and bloodshed supervened. Something akin to the dark ages which followed the break up of the Roman Empire descended on Latin America.

When I left Cambridge I had not got very far with the study of British activity in the Rio de la Plata as a case study in imperialism. Nine years passed before I took it up again: for four months at the University of Chicago and for another year at Cambridge, 1949-50. When the study was completed early in the summer of 1950 I had found that the Argentines had managed to create some sort of order for themselves and that a fruitful, free-trading connection had developed between Britain and the River Plate; so fruitful indeed that in terms of trade and investment Argentina was, after the United States and India, the most important economic partner of Britain. But the factor of political power which is the essential fact in an imperialist relationship was lacking. In the 1840s both the French and the British had attempted by force to enlighten the Argentines, but these attempts had failed. Lord Palmerston had formally acknowledged this failure and had agreed that the ships of the Royal Navy in the River Plate should salute the Argentine flag as an acknowledgement of Argentine sovereignty. No Argentine marched in the parade celebrating Queen Victoria's golden jubilee.

Shortly after that jubilee, however, there was an event which served to test the generality of the theory of imperialism: the Baring crisis of 1889-92. Britain had capital claims in Argentina amounting to an enormous sum measured in the currency of that time, at least £300,000,000, and Anglo-Argentine trade was correspondingly large. In 1889-90 signs began to emerge that the Argentine government's policies involved a default on its debts and prejudice to the claims of the investors, mainly British, or investors who had bought Argentine bonds and equities through British banks and the London stock exchange.

Would there be a resort to political action, i.e., force or a threat of force to oblige the Argentine government to pay? Hobson had taught us to expect such an outcome. So had Lenin. Had it not happened in Egypt, in China?

As if illustrating the theory, a delegation of bankers waited on the Foreign Office. They requested the British government to intervene or, if they thought prudent, to ask the United States government to intervene with the object of obliging the Argentine government to appoint a 'sound' minister of finance, i.e., one who would impose policies necessary to pay profits on investments. The under-secretary of state reported the request to the Marquis of Salisbury, who was both prime minister and foreign secretary.

The answer of Salisbury was stated in one word scrawled in red ink in the margin of the memo from the under-secretary: 'Dreams!' A few days later he spoke in the Mansion House to the dignitaries of the City of London. He declared that the British government did not propose to set itself up as providence in South America. Loud cheers!

This episode did not, of course, dispose of the theory of imperialism, but it did make a dent in it. Obviously the theory did not fit all cases.

And the sequel was interesting. Barings were going bankrupt. How was this to be avoided? Contrary to law and custom, the chancellor of the exchequer and the governor of the Bank of England got together and the chancellor of the exchequer agreed secretly to underwrite the bankers if they would put up the money to enable Barings to keep going. The first lame duck was hatched. The British government and tax payers lost no money on this occasion, but the principle was established that if an enterprise is big enough, badly enough run, and its proprietors well enough connected, it will be rescued in the 'public interest.' When the proprietors of hopelessly worn out or technically backward enterprises began surrendering their properties to the government, this became known as socialism.

The purpose of relating briefly this experience of testing the theory of imperialism is not to discredit the theory, for the Argentine case does not do so, but to show how one used Saltmarsh's principle that evidence comes first and theory second. In this instance a study of the facts led to a new view of the theory of imperialism, one not widely shared but none the less worthy of consideration.

Unfortunately I have misspent my intellectual life since my study of the Argentine case. The theory of imperialism has become a very big academic industry, but I withdrew from the argument and never contributed what light I had discovered to the development of the subject. This development has had disastrous consequences in the sphere of practical politics, particularly in Latin America. Marxist theories of imperialism and variants of the same have flourished greatly, but always as assumptions which it is the business of scholarships and research to illustrate, not to prove or disprove. The spin-off in politics has been a vast volume of anti-imperialist rhetoric which has established in the minds of intellectuals and politicians in Latin America, in Africa, and in Asia, that they and their societies are the victims of the great industrial nations; that what is wrong in their societies is the product of malign foreign forces and owes nothing to themselves or their own political processes. The saddest aspect of all this is the inculcation of the belief that the political independence of the new nations – and many not so new (the Latin American nations, except Cuba; have been independent states for more than 150 years) – is a sham and not a tool, which used with courage and intelligence, can be the means of a life at least as satisfactory as life is supposed to be in the so-called imperialist states. Theories of imperialism improperly and unscientifically used have become as much a plague and as harmful to human life as malaria or hookworm. They have provided rationalization for several varieties of political con men from Perón to Castro. In fact, theories of imperialism, originally intended as a means of understanding the underlying forces of politics, have been turned into their opposite. They have become the bases of the propaganda of the great imperialist states of the contemporary world and the means of deluding innocents everywhere. Some achievement!

As an institution of learning the influence of Cambridge University upon those who were its members during the 1930s was overwhelmingly liberal and scientific. The anti-liberal intellectual influences, of which the Marxist and communist were the most marked, was not primarily an outside influence. It was mainly self-generated, very largely by the students themselves as a means of understanding and participating in the political life of Europe and the larger world. Apart from Victor Kiernan, who was

a graduate student when I first knew him as a supervisor, I never encountered a teacher who was a Marxist or a communist. There were some
dons who were Marxists and communists, but these were very few in
number and what they studied and had to say ahd no more or less an
influence on thinking than the lucubrations of Michael Oakeshott, Kenneth
Pickthorne, or Ernest Barker.

In spite of the attempts of J.D. Bernal and J.B.S. Haldane (not at
Cambridge in my time but voices heard there above the intellectual din)
to establish a link between Marxism and the natural sciences, Marxism
had no effect whatsoever upon the professional thinking and work of the
Cambridge scientists. Some party scientists paid some attention to the
ideas of Lysenko, then beginning to come out of the Soviet Union with
Stalin's imprimatur, but no one took them seriously or allowed them to
influence their conception of problems. Somewhat later, one chap did
write an essay in a party-sponsored symposium on Lysenko which examined these ideas critically. The publisher put the title, *Lysenko Is Right*,
on the volume, and this ruined the unfortunate man's reputation.

In the social sciences, in history, and in literary studies Marxism did
have influence, but not as much as some suppose. Although it did have
some effect on the conception of problems, and the framing of questions
for study, it had little effect on methods of study. After the war a group
of historians and social scientists with strong Marxist sympathies, several
of them Cambridge men, founded a learned journal, *Past and Present*.
Anyone who reads *Past and Present* over the thirty years of its publication
cannot but recognize, however, that the editors and writers of *Past and
Present* have been more concerned with evidence and information than
with ideology.

Party strictures coming out of the Soviet Union in art, architecture,
music, and literature were counter-productive, if anything, in Cambridge.
The first niggling doubts I had abour the faith were provoked by examples
of Soviet art. In 1937 there was a great international exhibition in Paris.
One of the features of this were the two great pavilions facing each other:
the Soviet and the German. In the first there was an enormous mural
painting of Stalin with his generals. In its obtrusive vulgarity it reminded
one on a large scale of the portrait of Col. Stanley Jones which adorned
the central hall of my old school in Calgary. I asked myself how a great
nation could produce and wish to exhibit to the world as an example of
the best that it could do something so crass and cheap. But I crushed
down my revulsion and rationalized what I saw as the result of the

proletarian innocence. My reaction resembled that of many comrades in Cambridge in the presence of Soviet productions and pronouncements. 'How can one expect,' we said, 'a newly liberated class of peasants and workers to equal in a few years the civilization of a thousand years?' We made excuses, but not many were taken in by what came out of Moscow concerning the arts.

There still remains the big question: why were we taken in by the Soviet regime? How could we have faith in a monster like Stalin? Why did we not hearken to the messages to the world of men like André Gide, Malcolm Muggeridge, W.H. Chamberlain and Bertrand Russell? We were being nourished in an intellectual environment (and most of us were responding positively) which attached supreme importance to scientific objectivity and which defined truth not as what one knows but what one does not know. And yet we believed – and believed – in a regime which exhibited contemporary evidence of a savage character and was in fact much more senselessly brutal than Malcolm Muggeridge and André Gide even suspected. Most of us had I.Q.s from 40 to 80 per cent higher than the average population. And yet?

It can be said at once that intelligence is no proof against foolishness, and this was true then as it is always. Furthermore there is a strong propensity in people to believe what they want to believe and to reject evidence which contradicts their faith. Undergraduates at Cambridge were as susceptible to this propensity as the editor of *The Times* or the prime minister of the United Kingdom. Although the most essential function of Cambridge University was to overcome this propensity, it did not always succeed.

But there is more to the matter than these generalities. Those of us who were Marxists and pretended to be Bolsheviks did not regard the spilling of blood in a good cause as wicked and forbidden. We subscribed to Napoleon's proposition that one cannot make an omelette without breaking eggs. Arguments against spilling blood and crushing capitalist and feudal opposition as obstacles to the support of revolution we rejected as hypocrisy and nonsense. The very worth of Bolshevism lay in the fact that the Bolsheviks were men of strong will, courage, and determination in the service of what they and we conceived to be ordained by history. In this respect they differed not at all from the men who had brought to birth the British capitalist state: Henry VIII, Oliver Cromwell, the Earl of Chatham, and his son William Pitt the Younger. All these men and many others had used violence when it was necessary to ensure the survival and growth of British power. Oliver Cromwell had been thorough in Ireland, and so had William III: imperialists, of course, but examples of success in politics and of a terrible beauty.

As far as the Soviet regime was concerned, we were taken in by the argument worn threadbare in the purge trials that the revolution was being protected and strengthened against the last remnants of the old regime and enemies of the Soviet State. These arguments about the revolutionary nature of the trials and the liquidation of the kulaks were much more convincing to the communist students and to me personally than the testimony about the merits of Soviet communism presented by Beatrice and Sydney Webb and the Red Dean of Canterbury. The contrived enthusiasm of prestigious visitors to the new civilization helped to allay the doubts and hesitations of Labour party supporters who were troubled by the smell of blood and the echoes of firing squads, but we prided ourselves on the realism which enabled us not to shrink from the stern dictates of history.

How many of us would have shrunk from real bloodshed I do not know. Many years later I had a colleague, Alexander Baykov, who founded the Centre of Russian and East European Studies in the University of Birmingham. He once told me how, when he was about to finish secondary school in his native city in South Russia, he became a Bolshevik, and how, with the outbreak of the revolution, he, being one of the few Bolshevik enthusiasts in his part of the world, was appointed to a position of authority. This was wonderful until the party adopted a policy of terror. When he was ordered to take action, he could not bring himself to participate in killing a selection of his fellow citizens. He deserted to the White Guards, and according to his testimony there were more of his kind of White Guards than there were outright enemies of Bolshevism in the ranks of the counter-revolution. I rather suspect many of the Cambridge Bolsheviks of the 1930s would have behaved as Alexander Baykov did.

The most important factor in the obliteration from our minds of the inconvenient evidence of Stalin's thirst for blood was, I think, the well-founded animosity we felt for fascism. The Soviet Union was the strongest ally we could find against Hitler, Mussolini, and Franco. In the presence of the expanding power of the Nazis we regarded soul-searching about the behaviour and motives of our strongest and most completely committed ally as foolish. At the moment when Franco and his backers were winning the Spanish Civil War, we considered it treachery and worse for

130

Orwell and Koestler to start dismantling the engine of anti-fascism and seeking to redesign its parts.

There were two aspects of the Soviet regime about which we had little or no evidence. Subsequently these aspects were revealed by the royal commission of enquiry into Soviet espionage in Canada, the revelations of Khrushchev, and the writings of Alexander Solzhenitsyn. Perhaps we should have known about these aspects of Soviet power, but we did not, nor did very many others.

The first aspect concerns the dimensions of political murder and repression in the USSR. This we could not conceive of. It was not a matter of breaking eggs to make an omelette; of speeding up the necessary process of industrialization and the locating of the new heavy industries as far away as possible from the marauders from western Europe. We did not repudiate ruthlessness, but what was revealed and what we knew nothing about was brutality and bloodshed which was neither necessary nor capable of justification in any way. Some of it can only be explained as insanity.

The second aspect of the Soviet regime of which we were ignorant was the nature of its political methods. As we conceived of political methods these involved missionary work and the mobilization of the faithful to vote, to demonstrate, to strike, and to take power. Missionary work was essentially argument and explanation. We believed that revolution required understanding. Of course, we believed as Marx and Engels did, that there was a social force called class consciousness, but we also accepted the teachings of Lenin that the class-conscious workers need leadership and that leadership depends upon understanding and organization. We knew very well that the Standard Oil Company did not organize itself; Rockefeller did. The British Conservative party did not naturally exist in spite of the cloudy nonsense talked by Conservatives about the autogenesis of the Tory party. It was the work of men and women. No one knew just who they were, but it was the business of the Labour Research Department, sponsored by the CPGB, to find out.

But when all this is said, we believed that revolutions, like parliamentary party victories, are made by people who understand society and believe in what their reason tells them is true and possible. Political work means convincing people about what to do and how to do it. In this we differed in no way from Conservatives, Liberals, or Social Demoncrats. On the other hand, we assumed we knew better than any of them what history had in store for mankind. We did not subscribe to the parliamentary conception of democracy, but we did believe in the dependence of political success upon the open support of more and more people. We were in that respect democrats. As we saw it, we differed from the bourgeois parties only in that we did not think of party contests as ding-dong struggles which are a part of a cyclical or reversible political process. We conceived of party activity as a linear process leading to the conquest of power and the transformation of society into a community free of class struggle and political antagonisms.

All this may have been very naive, but none the less our conceptions of political activity were democratic and open. The discretion we practised in 'colonial work' was dictated by a regard for the personal interest and freedom of people who lived in circumstances where the authorities kept a watch on 'politicals' and jailed them when the government believed this to be necessary. There was nothing fanciful in this inasmuch as Jawaharlal Nehru (Harrow and Trinity), to mention only one man, had been in and out of prison in the 1920s and 1930s, and we confidently expected that S.M. Kumaramangalam (Eton and King's) would go to jail, too, if he were not careful.

As to political work through 'front' organizations, we had no qualms. Taking the initiative in forming organizations or joining existing organizations to 'put across the line' was a legitimate means of engaging in missionary work and achieving limited political results. Was not this the mode of work of the Fabian Society or some of the churches or the suffragettes and so on? The Evangelicals had formed organizations and filtered into organizations with the object of abolishing slavery and they had succeeded. We were sometimes taxed with our tactics of infiltration and the formation of fronts, but my answer to this charge was always: 'Look at history! There is nothing new in what Communists do. Infiltration is as British as the Carlton Club or the Masonic Lodge in Trinity College.'

What we did not realize and what we had no evidence of was the extent to which the Soviet regime had in practice relegated open political methods to a secondary role in politics. When Ben Bradley urged me to keep in touch with the American comrades, this seemed to me a natural enough expression of the internationalism which I admired. If I concealed Palme Dutt's letter of introduction to the American comrades in the lining of my hat, this was only because there was an anti-Red witch hunt in progress in North America at that time. What I did not know was that Ben Bradley, or more likely an unknown person in King Street, passed my name back to Moscow as a possible recruit to the service of the Soviet regime. I did not know and I do not think many people of my views knew that the Soviet regime had become an enclosed bureaucracy which regarded open political methods as a secondary factor in politics, and that the disruption and infiltration of rival bureaucracies had become the primary method of politics. For all our self-satisfied realism, there was one real fact we did not appreciate: that revolution in the interest of the Soviet regime was something in the baggage train of the Red army, not a force for the liberation of peoples but an up-to-date technique of imperialism. Unfortunately, the truth is something one discovers only slowly and by experience and not by sudden flashes of inspiration.

There is an aspect of the development of the left in Cambridge deserving of some remembrance. Students found in left politics – not just in the Communist party – an escape from the inward-looking caste system which flourished in British society. I do not know whether Britain is more caste-ridden than other societies. The only societies I know much about from personal experience, apart from Britain, are Canada, Argentina, and, to a lesser extent, the United States of America. These all have their own caste systems. In the Canadian and American cases they are less complicated than they are in Britain, but they are there none the less and often harsher, as minorities know very well. One belongs or one does not belong. So long as the units of such caste systems admit people on merit or manners there is no harm in the formation of in-groups. Indeed this seems a natural development in any society. Too much preoccupation, however, with in-groups and especially with those which have little or no relationship with personal character and capacity and depend only upon accents, mannerisms, and dress generates self-satisfaction and complacency in many, but also boredom and discontent in others. Those who were bored with the artificiality of little loyalties – and these were numerous in Cambridge – found an escape into the open society of the left.

The left, of course, had its own forms of snobbery and its own kind of self-righteous complacency, but it did provide an alternative where school and sex and family background were matters of little or no concern, where indeed one could sneer at one's parents, if so disposed, hold in contempt the ordinary manners of polite society, and enjoy the experience of returning to what was fondly imagined to be a more natural order of living. This escape into circumstances of a new kind of human solidarity and comradeship was an attractive and exciting experience for many. It broke down barriers and liberated young people from shyness and inhibitions with which many felt they had lived too long. On a small scale this experience anticipated the general experience of the British people when the war came and, willy-nilly, all felt they belonged to a great open community.

CHAPTER SEVEN

In and Out of the Canadian Bureaucracy: 1940-44

Early in the morning of 3 January 1940, our ship entered New York harbour. The towers of Manhattan were bathed in mist, delicately coloured by the watery sun. I was standing at the rail of the boat deck with a stocky, bald-headed Austrian refugee, an art historian by profession. 'Ah,' he said, 'Pure Impressionist!' Then he turned to his blond son, a lad of 13 or 14 years, and explained to him in German what he meant.

After lunch we disembarked, and I remained in New York for three days. At my hotel I found a telegram from my father informing me that the Civil Service Commission of Canada wanted me to attend an interview for a secretaryship in the Department of External Affairs on 8 January. Would I go or not? It is a measure of the uncertainty of my mind at that time that I decided to do three things: to go to Ottawa for an interview, to return to Harvard, and to present my letter of introduction to the Communist party of the USA.

The last of these decisions I executed the next day. The address given me by Ben Bradley in London was a dismal building in lower Manhattan which had been, and perhaps still was, a warehouse. I rang a bell and the door was opened by a surly young man of dark complexion, who asked me what I wanted. He ushered me into a large room which judging by an expanse of counter must have been at one time a place where wholesale customers took delivery of large parcels. Beyond the counter were offices panelled with grimy ground glass. The young man said nothing but took my letter and disappeared into one of the offices. After an interval of perhaps fifteen or twenty minutes, during which time I had nothing to do except stand staring at the blankness around me, he returned with a piece of paper and my letter.

'That's the name of a guy in Boston you ought to see.' He said nothing else. He did not even say goodbye. There was an anti-Red witch hunt in progress in North America which could explain the impersonality, the bareness, even the nothingness, but the whole proceeding seemed to me excessive in the absence of even a hint of that comradeship which was one attractive feature of party life in Britain.

For the rest of my time in New York, I just enjoyed being there. Then it seemed to me the best city I had ever encountered: beautiful, energetic, free, a triumph of human achievement, a place outside the mess of mankind. (In January 1971 I spent another few days in New York. It seemed, then, the very epitome of the mess of mankind – a place full of fear, dirt, and nastiness. Progress?)

My appearance before a selection committee concerned with appointments to the Canadian Department of External Affairs was not my first experience of this proceeding. In 1937 I had written the entry examinations in London, and had been called for an interview at the Dorchester Hotel by a board comprised of officials attending the Commonwealth Conference and numbering among them Dr O.D. Skelton, the Under-Secretary of State, and Norman A. Robertson. It was a beautiful spring day when I went for the interview. I felt happy and free and the last thing I wanted then was to work for a 'bourgeois government.' At the interview I was asked whether I thought the British government 'had a peace policy.'

'Oh yes,' I replied airily, 'in so far as peace is compatible with the protection of 4,000 million pounds invested around the world.'

One cannot suppose that this answer appalled an anti-British bureaucrat like O.D. Skelton or an ex-leftist like Norman Robertson, but it did suggest that I was not cut out for diplomacy. Although I was placed near the top of the list in the written examination and the assessment of my academic record, I was placed thirteenth in the interview; and that was that as far as an offer of employment was concerned, in 1937.

But now I wanted a job and the means of establishing a family of my own in my own country. What attracted me most was the pay. At this time the prestige factor weighed not at all in my mind. I had no clear idea of what work in External Affairs entailed, but I was anxious enough to try my hand. The interviewing board was friendly enough, but when I could not hear one of the questions I said straight-out that I was hard of hearing and I would appreciate it if the members of the board could speak up. Nothing was said at the time, but subsequently it was explained to me that deafness was an obstacle to my appointment. One of the Civil Service Commissioners present probably came to this conclusion at the time, for he asked to see me after the interview, said he remembered me from 1936, and kindly suggested that he could arrange for me to sit an examination for an administrative post the next day. I agreed to do this, wrote the examination papers the next day, and departed for Harvard.

During my last term in Cambridge, I had found it extremely difficult to settle down to academic work. At Harvard this restlessness disappeared, and I found myself working steadily seven days a week with a power of concentration which I had not known for three years or more. Harvard was a splendid place to be. C.H. Haring, the professor of Latin American history, to whom I came with an introduction from Sir John Clapham, could not have been more kind and helpful. I liked him and I think he liked me. He arranged for me to have a desk in the Widener Library and he introduced me to the lady in charge of the books on Latin America, the first person I had so far encountered who really could guide me intelligently in reading, particularly in the literature of Argentina written by Argentines. The Widener Library was a wonderful place to work. The books were there in abundance. They were close at hand and well arranged. There was a comfortable desk, and one could work any hours one wished. When I turned on my reading lamp and took down Coni on the gauchos I was in another world, no less savage than Europe, but more explicable and in some respects more attractive. I forgot about the 'guy in Boston.' I made no decision about the Communist party of the USA. I simply forgot. For three months my mind and imagination worked on only two topics: Argentina and the prospect of establishing a home somewhere with Maureen when she had finished her year as a school teacher in Manitoba.

I not only read books on Argentina; I met a real live Argentine who worked at the next desk in the Widener Library. Thus far I had encountered only one Argentine: a student in Corpus College, Cambridge, named Verstreten-Anchorena. He came of the highest level of the Argentine oligarchy, a member of the Anchorena family, so rich that the phrase *rico como un Anchorena* means in the River Plate what rich as Rockefeller means in the United States. There was nothing mealy-mouthed about Verstreten-Anchorena. Naturally we discussed politics and he soon learned where I stood. With a refreshing and unoffensive realism he let me know where he stood. He could understand why a person like me would support the Spanish republic. He, on the other hand, was rich, and he intended to stay that way. The Spaniards, he argued, are a lazy, disorganized, and individualistic lot, and nothing can be done with them except by thrashing them into obedience and order. Franco, he said, was just the man for this, and he predicted that the Caudillo would make something of the Spaniards. When I remarked that Franco would probably have to shoot half the Spaniards to do this, Verstreten-Anchorena replied in a matter of fact way, 'What's wrong with that?'

Having introduced myself to Argentina by reading Darwin, Sarmiento, *et al.*, and by meeting Verstreten-Anchorena, it was with some surprise and relief that I became friends with Raimundo Lida. He was a quiet, gentle philologist in the United States on a Guggenhein scholarship and engaged in the study of the language of the Iberian peninsula a thousand years ago. His only complaint about life in Argentina was connected with the fact that he was obliged to work half days as a bank clerk to enable him to support himself, his wife, and son as a teacher at the University of La Plata. Otherwise he regarded the Argentine as an almost perfect community, free, liberal and agreeable. For Lida the fact that in *La Prensa* Argentine had a newspaper of Liberal views and high standards was proof that all was right with his country. He was in fact as apolitical as one could be without making an effort to close one's mind to the world.

It was otherwise with his wife. She was an intense, small, dark woman of a fanatically nationalist disposition. She hated the United States. She refused to learn any English. Everything was wrong with the United States, and particularly the price of beef. But her dislike of the United States was a feeling without any clear or well-developed intellectual content. When she and her husband and her little son visited Maureen and me in Ottawa in August 1940, she found Canada an agreeable place largely because it was not the United States.

But poor Raimundo Lida, who wanted no part in politics, was none the less affected by events in his beloved country. When Perón came to power he migrated to Mexico. His wife went mad. Eventually he established himself in the United States, divorced and re-married, and ended his life as a highly respected professor of Romance languages at Harvard.

By an odd coincidence his son Fernando, who had visited us in Ottawa, a dark-eyed lively little boy, introduced himself to me in Buenos Aires in 1971. He was engaged in translating a book of mine for Editorial Sud Americana. He was learned in a miscellaneous sort of way. He was full of ideas, all of them gloomy. He scratched a living as a journalist and translator. He had two sons, Fidel and Ernesto, dark-eyed little boys as he had been in 1940. When I returned to Britain I sent him some stories about Argentina to translate into Spanish, and I sent him a few hundred Canadian dollars for his work. These came back beautifully translated. I sent a fourth. By this time Argentina had become a chaos of violence. I wrote repeatedly to him, but no reply ever came back to me. Fernando Lida Garcia, where are you?

In April 1940, a letter came from the Canadian Civil Service Commission offering me a junior administrative post. I was nearly penniless, and so I did not hesitate. I would go to Ottawa! Perhaps the biggest mistake I ever made in my life, but almost an inevitable one. I needed a job, and somehow I could not think in terms either of carrying on with my academic work or staying in the United States when Canada was at war. I had no large ideas about my contribution to what the public relations men described as the Canadian war effort. I did not think in such terms, but nevertheless I did not want to remain outside the collision of powers which had taken up so much of my thought and energy since leaving Canada in 1936. Once at Harvard I had a chance encounter with an English research student of Trinity College, Cambridge. We had a drink and a chat. From this it emerged that in spite of his anti-fascism and his democratic and socialist enthusiasm for which he was well known in Cambridge, he had got out, and was pretty pleased with the wisdom of his action. Put down in black and white his position and his behaviour differed very little from my own, and in spite of this I felt a surge of contempt for this man, who in his own telling was saving himself when his country was in peril. I felt this way in spite of the fact that anyone in North America in 1940 was as much out of harm's way as anyone else, and I no less than others.

I arrived in Ottawa on 14 April 1940. Already the 'phoney war' was at an end, and the Germans had invaded Norway. The Anglo-French forces had attacked Narvik on 13 April and were in the process of seizing the town. The commotion in Scandinavia seemed to have communicated itself to the Naval Department in Ottawa where I was sent to work. There may have been some sort of order and direction at the top of the department, but at the bottom, where I was, there was chaos. No one seemed to have any use for me, and I could not find anyone to assign me a task of any kind. After a day or so I found someone who was happy to have me put cards in a file which he was assembling. The purpose of the enterprise I never discovered, but I occupied my time none the less. This went on for ten days, until there was a telephone call for me. Would I come around to the Office of the Prime Minister, where the principal secretary, W.A. Turnbull, wished to see me?

I was a member of the secretarial staff of the Rt. Hon. W.L. Mackenzie King from the end of April 1940 until the spring of 1943. Then I moved down a flight of stairs to the Department of External Affairs where I remained until I resigned from the public service at the end of November 1944. These four years and seven months in the East Block were an almost total waste: of my time, the taxpayers' money, office space, stenographic services, everything. Save for six weeks in April/May/June 1944 when I helped to superintend an exchange of prisoners-of-war in Spain, I contributed nothing to the war against the Nazis and the Fascists. The one public cause which commanded my greatest concern was the one in which I had the least share. Why this should have been so remains something I do not completely understand.

The fault cannot have been wholly mine. I was but one of many who passed through the Prime Minister's Office between 1939 and 1945, entering with high hopes of doing something significant and leaving with nothing to show for the experience. The examples are numerous of men of talent, good will, and good intentions who came and left: L.W. Brockington, E.K. Brown, Sydney Wheelock, W.F. Blissett, and my closest and dearest friend, William Paterson. And there were others whom I did not know so well, but whom I suspect could tell a tale not unlike my own.

The nothingness of the Prime Minister's Office for some, perhaps the majority, who passed through it can be explained in terms of the circumstances of the time and the character of the Prime Minister himself. For at least two years previous to the spring of 1940, Mr King had known that war was inevitable or nearly so, and he had made some personal preparations, one aspect of which was to expand his secretarial staff and to improve its quality. The expansion and improvement which he considered adequate were very modest. When I arrived there were altogether ten members of the secretarial staff together with a supporting body of stenographers, file clerks, and messengers. Mr King was, of course, Secretary of State for External Affairs as well as Prime Minister and in that capacity he could rely on a small body of civil servants to assist him in his work. But it must be remembered that the staff of the department of External Affairs was very small: not more than a dozen of the rank of third secretary and higher. Additionally he could rely on help from the Clerk of the Privy Council, A.D.P. Heeney, who had not long before been his principal secretary.

This entourage of the Prime Minister in the spring of 1940 would appear very limited by modern bureaucratic standards, but it seemed then adequate and perhaps more than adequate. Mr King himself felt rather guilty about the size of his staff and feared that he was wasting public money and, what was worse, might be seen to be wasting public money. Neither he nor anyone else could at that time conceive of the volume of work and the rush of events which the war would entail.

Fortunately for Mr King and for Canada, his conception of ministerial government and its application stood him in good stead. He believed that his business was to recommend the appointment of ministers who really did run their departments. Although he sometimes counselled the less able of his ministers, he refused to interfere in the work of his cabinet colleagues and he always supported them. He judged the worth of ministers by two criteria: the extent to which they got on with the job they were appointed to do and the extent to which they stuck to their briefs and refrained from interfering in the political leadership of the government and the country, which he rightly in the Canadian context considered to be his business and his responsibility.

If one reads the celebrated Mackenzie King diaries for the years 1939-45 one forms the impression that Canada was governed by a superstitious lunatic. This is not at all the impression that members of his secretarial staff, observers in the Parliamentary Press Gallery, or members of Parliament had of the Prime Minister at that time. He appeared to us and to them as he appeared in his diaries when recording or turning over in his mind his encounters with president Roosevelt, Winston Churchill, J.L. Ralston, the British High commissioner Malcolm MacDonald, or the Leader of the Opposition: a sensitive, clear-headed, political technician with an unrivalled sense of the nuances of Canadian politics. One did not need to agree with Mackenzie King about everything he said or did to acknowledge that he was an extremely able politician. Even his worst enemies paid him the compliment of saying 'Willy is always too clever by half,' and many of them considered it grossly unfair that the Prime Minister had been endowed with better brains, quicker responses, and more guile than themselves. In terms of understanding the political problems of Canada and in knowing what the Canadian people as a whole

140

were willing to accept from a government, Mackenzie King was miles ahead of any of the active participants in politics.

Undoubtedly, however, the public availability of his voluminous diaries has diminished the man, in much the same way that 'his tapes' have done for President Nixon. Those portions of the diaries which I have read shocked me, not on account of any strange quirks that are there exhibited, but because they reveal a foolish and childish immaturity of private personality in contradiction to his great ability as a public man. It appears that he realized in some degree that his diaries were too personal for any eyes but his own. He intended in his retirement to cull from the immense mountain of his literary remains what required concealment and destruction. But he was old and tired and lonely. L.W. Brockington used to visit him. 'I had seen Mr King in recent weeks,' Brockington told me in a letter written in April 1950. 'In his sadness, illness and old age he appears to find some comfort in my company and advice. Strange to say, this pleases me. Our old associates continue to flourish like the green bay tree on the Mount of Olives, and the skunk cabbage in the swamps of British Columbia ...'. Obviously, the former Prime Minister was unequal to the task of preserving his privacy, and he had no one to help him to do so. It will take a long time to rescue the reputation of Mackenzie King from the psychologists and the pornographers, and to leave it to the judgment of those interested in what is truly relevant in the man: his activity as a Canadian politician in a period of extreme political disturbance.

Without engaging in amateur psychoanalysis it is possible to find a commonsense explanation of why, for me and for others, working in the Prime Minister's Office was an unsatisfying experience and equally why Mr King always felt he was ill-served by his staff. Like most human beings Mackenzie King had a need for love and loyalty freely given by others. As a politician he would have liked to enjoy the love and devotion of all Canadians and even a wider constituency of people elsewhere. But he lived in a democracy, he lacked a charismatic personality, and he had neither the desire nor the opportunity to create loyalty through terror or the stimulation of public hysteria. His long life in politics in Canada, which in a sense went back to the days before he was born when his grandfather William Lyon Mackenzie was a public figure, had taught him that in Canadian politics one trades in opportunities. The power of the state and of the politicians who control it is used to buy the support of individuals and interests. Loyalty is a two-way proposition: you do something for me and I'll do something for you. Loyalty and devotion are never unconditional as they are ideally in a marriage, in a monastic order, in a love affair, in a divinely ordained monarchy, or in a well-organized army. By 1940 Mackenzie King had so long been a Canadian politician, had calculated the odds in human relations so many times that he was in fact almost alone in the world; his immediate family was dead, no wife, no children, many political friends but very few friends who expected nothing of him and were willing to give him everything he wanted and needed in the way of affection, respect, and uncritical love.

When the war broke out Mackenzie King did, however, have two real friends who, although in a formal sense subordinate to him, were his equals in their knowledge of politics, in their devotion to his interest, and in the absence of self-seeking in so far as office and power were concerned. These were O.D. Skelton, the Under-Secretary of State for External Affairs, and the Rt. Hon. Ernest Lapointe, the Minister of Justice. With these men Mackenzie King did not need to be wary or calculating. Although each had his own understanding of politics and point of view, both thought along similar lines to the Prime Minister. He could thus be easy and familiar with them. Furthermore they were of a similar age and generation. One has to attain the age Mackenzie King then was to imagine what life can be like without real friends as old as oneself. And it is necessary to do so in Mackenzie King's case for in 1941 both Skelton and Lapointe died. Henceforward Mackenzie King was condemned to live the daily life of politics and administration almost exclusively among the young people from thirty to forty years younger than himself. Even the principal secretary, Turnbull, was twenty years younger than the Prime Minister, and J.W. Pickersgill was only marginally more than half the Prime Minister's age.

In the wider life of politics Mackenzie King was well able to handle his relations with his party, Parliament, opposition, foreign politicians, and various interests in the Canadian community. A less tractable problem was the more intimate relations with his immediate entourage of civil servants, where contact was closer, personality more uninhibitedly revealed, and emotions more evident.

It is pretty clear from his diary that the only completely satisfactory creature in Mackenzie King's life from 1935 onward was his dog Pat and Pat's successor also called Pat. Pat I and Pat II gave him the uncritical affection he needed, and the extravagance of his grief when Pat I died only underlined the emotional impoverishment of the Prime Minister. Further up the evolutionary scale was his stenographer, Edouard Handy. Handy was, too, utterly devoted to the Prime Minister, always present and totally without a critical response to anything that Mackenzie King said or did. Handy and Pat I or Pat II went for walks with the Prime Minister. Handy ate meals with the Prime Minister. Unlike the little Irish terriers, Handy accompanied Mackenzie King to the movies. And uncomplainingly and without comment to anyone Handy took down in shorthand Mackenzie King's daily reports on his night's sleep, the state of the Prime Ministerial bowels, his visions of his mother and occasionally of his father, sisters, brothers, and grandfather, and the number of times the hands of the clock were seen in propitious positions indicating a good day, a good week, or even a victory over Nazi Germany. Furthermore Handy typed all this nonsense together with the more serious parts of the diary accurately and quickly. And he said nothing. It can be assumed, likewise, that he thought nothing.

Still further up the evolutionary scale was J.W. Pickersgill. He too was devoted to the Prime Minister. He was always available. He never answered back. But Jack could think. Indeed, within certain limits he was an able and ingenious man. An aspect of his ability was a chameleon character. When he came back from Oxford he had adopted the accents and mannerisms of the English academic upper-middle class. A short exposure to A.R.M. Lower in United College in Winnipeg turned him into a Canadian nationalist. Ottawa turned him into a Liberal partisan and a man functioning as nearly as one could on the mental wavelength of Mackenzie King. When the time came he adjusted himself to Louis St Laurent's frequency, distanced himself from Mackenzie King and his reputation, declared Mr St Laurent the nearest thing to perfection on earth, rose as far as his talents would take him, made a sinecure for himself, and retired to the dignity of literary labour in the service of Liberal truth.

Pickersgill came as near to serving the Prime Minister in his public capacity as the first minister of the Crown in Canada as anyone in the office ever did. He could understand what the Prime Minister wanted when he had to speak in Parliament or over the radio, and he could provide information and drafts of speeches that bore some relationship both in style and content to what Mackenzie King wanted to say. Even so, Mr King was never satisfied with what was sent to him. His mania for consistency, where there was or could be no consistency, drove him to refine and alter what Pickersgill provided so that the preparation of speeches was often as exhausting a labour as if no one did anything for him. None the less it is fair to say that Pickersgill was the only member of the office who did help the Prime Minister, was allowed to help the Prime Minister, and was felt by the Prime Minister to be helpful.

Apart from his good knowledge of Canadian affairs and his quick way of working, there was another factor in Pickersgill's comparative success in serving Mackenzie King. Although he was formally a third secretary in the Department of External Affairs seconded to the Prime Minister secretarial staff, Pickersgill forgot his career in External Affairs and committed himself wholly to the service of Mackenzie King both in terms of time, of making a career, and as a whole-hearted political supporter. No nonsense about civil service impartiality for Jack! Mackenzie King had made his start in politics as a civil servant, and in the presence of Pickersgill like spoke to like.

By contrast one has to consider the experience of another third secretary seconded from External Affairs to the Prime Minister's staff, James A. Gibson. Gibson thought of his career in terms of the department to which he had been appointed. He took seriously the ethics of civil service neutrality. For this he served a five-year sentence in the Prime Minister's residence in Ottawa, Laurier House, where, on the evidence of the diary, he became a whipping boy. Mackenzie King resented Gibson's attempts to define his responsibilities, to maintain his interest in the Department of External Affairs, and to keep clear of domestic politics. On the day of Pearl Harbour Mackenzie King, in recording the excitement of the day, found space to express his annoyance at Gibson's absence from Laurier House because he was dining with his mother. One gains the impression that Mackenzie King resented that Gibson had a real mother while he was obliged to rely on visions and dreams of *his* mother.

The principal secretary, Walter Turnbull, was a civil servant of considerable experience who had been a public relations officer in the Post Office. He had come to the Prime Minister's notice on account of some rather expert organizing during the royal visit to Canada in 1939. Experience in dealing with irate customers of the Post Office was a suitable preparation for running the Prime Minister's office. Walter Turnbull was a cool, calm, and polite man but a tough one. For him the Prime Minister and the people who wanted to intrude on the Prime Minister and waste his time were equally problems which he had to solve. It was to Turnbull that Mackenzie King expressed his dissatisfaction with his staff and complained about the overburden of work which, he alleged, was left to him to do by others whose responsibility it was. For the most part Turnbull mothered the Prime Minister, recognizing that the complaints were evidence of nervous exhaustion in a man going on for seventy who had a really heavy burden to bear. But when Mackenzie King became unreasonable and went a bit too far, Turnbull could be as firm with the Prime Minister as he was with the people from whom he protected the Prime Minister. On more than one occasion Turnbull answered Mr King's complaints by offering him his resignation. Confronted with the prospect of Turnbull's departure the Prime Minister quickly recognized the truth of the matter. That he was on the whole satisfied with Walter Turnbull's services was signalled by Turnbull's appointment as Deputy Postmaster-General of Canada in June 1945.

A factor, partly political and partly emotional, in the problem of the Prime Minister with his staff was his well-established preference for working at home and not in his office in the East Block – either at Laurier House about two miles from Parliament Hill or at Kingsmere, his country place about thirty miles away across the Ottawa River in the province of Quebec. The logistics of this practice were considerable and his personal contact with the majority of his staff was minimal. Those of us who functioned in the East Block hardly saw the Prime Minister more frequently than members of the public. Although I had brief telephone communication with Mr King on numerous occasions I never had a face-to-face discussion with him during my three years on his staff, and in this I do not think my experience differed substantially from that of L.W. Brockington or Jules Léger or W.F. Blissett or E.K. Brown. Memoranda for the Prime Minister on various questions, prepared often with care and thought, were simply cast into the void. One never knew whether Mr King liked them or disliked them or even that he read them. I recognized words and phrases of my own in his tribute to the Rt. Hon. Ernest Lapointe, but that is the only evidence I ever had that anything I did reached him.

For Mr King his office in the East Block was no more than a place where he stopped off on his way to the House of Commons or to meetings of the cabinet in the Privy Council office a few steps down a corridor from his office. In his office he did hold meetings of the War Committee of the Cabinet and there he received foreign visitors or Canadians who had some legitimate claim to see him or whom he wanted to see. But he never worked in his office in the East Block. He visited it. Nothing more.

Indeed, his knowledge of the geography of the East Block was limited. I discovered this one evening when I was on the late shift which ended at 10.30 pm when the telephone switchboard was closed and everything was locked up. It had been the usual evening of gentle quiet, and I was happily reading Hickey's *Memoirs* of his life in India in the late eighteenth century. A few minutes before 10 the switchboard operator rang me to say the Prime Minister had come in and was in his office. I dropped my book and hurried to the outer chamber of the Prime Minister's office, very apprehensive because I had dismissed the duty stenographer at 9 o'clock. There was, however, nothing but silence for twenty minutes or so. Then Mr King emerged through the red baize door.

'Oh, Ferns,' he said. I am not sure that he recognized me, but I knew that he had asked who was on duty. I asked the Prime Minister whether there was anything he needed.

Now this evening was a time shortly before Mackenzie King achieved one of his cherished records. In fact only a few days previously I had been engaged in the task of determining the exact day and the hour when Mackenzie King's tenure of the office as first minister would exceed that of Sir Wilfrid Laurier. It is therefore easy to see why the Prime Minister's request for advice at this time surprised me. When we were out of earshot of the girl on the switchboard, Mr King said in a half whisper, 'Can you tell me where there is a lavatory?'

I could see that the Prime Minister's usual path from his office to the Privy Council office and the cabinet room, along which lay a lavatory, was barred by locked doors. As I directed him to the right and down a flight of stairs I could see that he was exploring new territory. The atmosphere of adventure was reinforced by the beat of wings.

'What is that?' said the Prime Minister.

'Bats, sir,' I replied. 'It might be prudent to put on your hat. A bat entangled in one's hair can be unpleasant.'

'Oh!' said the Prime Minister putting on his hat. 'Bats! Tell Turnbull to inform Public Works. We shouldn't have bats in the East Block.'

'Yes, sir' I said.

Another difficulty in working for the Prime Minister is one perhaps to be found in most bureaucracies and instruments of political power. This is the difficulty of making information credible and operational. There is a tendency in bureaucracies to establish the credibility of messages not from their content and their likely reliability as information but from the position in the hierarchy of the messengers. This can be illustrated by the sequence of events on 7 December 1941, the day when the Japanese attacked Pearl Harbour.

In his diary Mackenzie King set down his account of what happened that day in Ottawa and at Kingsmere where he went after working at Laurier House during the morning. According to the diary the Prime Minister first heard the rumour of an attack on Pearl Harbour at 3.30 pm from Norman A. Robertson, the Under Secretary of State. This is probably true, but the information about the rumours and an estimate of their worth was reported by me to Kingsmere at least one hour earlier.

The circumstances were these. Walter Turnbull was on duty in the East Block during the Sunday morning shift. I came in to relieve him about 1.30 pm. We chatted briefly about what was happening in Washington, and we more or less agreed that the United States government would likely consent to let the Japanese government have more strategic raw materials than hitherto. The Prime Minister had gone to Kingsmere and Turnbull went home. I settled down to some reading. I had no sooner put my feet up on my desk than the phone rang. It was a United Press reporter inquiring whether we had any news of a Japanese assault on the United States. I replied, 'No, we had not.' The United Press reporter declared that we had better damned well find out, because the rumours were really ominous and far from vague. I suggested he try to reach the Under-Secretary of State for External Affairs, and I assured him I would alert the Prime Minister. This was at approximately 2 pm.

I at once rang Kingsmere and said I wanted to speak to the Prime Minister immediately. He was out walking. Well, have him call his office in the East Block as soon as he comes in. Then I instructed the switchboard operator to call the secretaries of all the ministers warning them that there might have to be a meeting of the cabinet before evening. No call came from Kingsmere to the East Block. Even a message from the Under-Secretary of State for External Affairs could not keep Mackenzie King from going to bed for his afternoon rest. It must be borne in mind that Robertson had only recently become Under-Secretary, and in Mackenzie King's mind was still only two or three stages up from office boy. He would take a call from Robertson, but he would not effectively accept his message. An hour later Robertson called again. This time he was able to say that President Roosevelt had told the British ambassador that the rumours had substance. At last the Prime Minister was willing to think about what was happening. What was happening only became real in his mind when the information came, not from an obscure secretary or a UP reporter or a young and newly appointed under-secretary, but from the British ambassador. Even so Canada was officially at war with Japan before the United States.

The fact is that the Prime Minister's much maligned staff had provided him with information about a catastrophe sooner than any other agency of the government and had alerted the members of the government before anyone else, and yet the Prime Minister's only reference to his staff that day was a denunciation of one member who was having Sunday dinner with his mother while the Prime Minister himself was walking with his dear little dog and having his afternoon rest.

If some of the meaninglessness of work in the Prime Minister's office can be attributed to the character of the Prime Minister, much can be explained by the politics of the Canadian community at large and by the politics of the Canadian bureaucracy. This factor can best be illustrated by the case of L.W. Brockington.

Leonard Brockington was born in Britain of English and Welsh stock. Educated in the University of Wales, he was for a short time a classics and English master in a grammar school before migrating to western Canada. In Calgary he entered the offices of Lougheed and Bennett as an articled clerk and upon becoming a fully fledged lawyer was appointed solicitor of the city of Calgary. Possessed of considerable wit and rhetorical powers he soon developed a reputation as an urbane and entertaining speaker at dinners and public functions. People liked to listen to Brockington on account of what he had to say and how he said it.

Brockington can best be described politically as an undogmatic, unideological, social democrat, a man of good will who fitted into none of the rigid categories of European political analysis. I once asked Brockington, having regard for the fact that he had worked for two Canadian prime ministers, Bennett and King, how they compared. 'Six of one and half a dozen of the other,' Brockington replied, 'Except that King has a few gentlemanly instincts totally absent in Bennett.'

This reply in fact encapsulated Brockington's political views. He tended to judge men and women by their character rather than by their policies. As to policy he subscribed to no school or party. He did not regard it as the whole duty of man to make as much money as possible in any way possible. He had a strong but pragmatic disposition to work for the public good. He once told me of the occasion when he was visited in his office in Calgary by a famous and wealthy bootlegger, who specialized in supplying 'good stuff' from Scotland and France to American bootleggers during the prohibition era which had only ended in the early 1930s. This man put a cheque for $100,000 on his desk and said, 'Get me a licence to build a liquor warehouse on the Milk River. That is yours.' Brockington flatly refused, although this man was then wealthy and went on to become one of the wealthiest men in North America. On the other hand Brockington became the legal councillor of an association of private grain merchants, who were regarded by some of the farming community and by socialist politicians as wicked exploiters. When I asked him about this, he replied that human salvation does not depend upon compulsory, co-operative grain marketing as some people suppose. Anyone could believe what they liked about grain marketing. The people he worked for were on the whole honest businessmen who succeeded and could only succeed if they gave their customers as square a deal as the pools or the government itself.

This was the man who was appointed to the chairmanship of the Canadian Broadcasting Corporation, modelled on the British Broadcasting Corporation and set up by Parliament in 1936. Brockington thus became the spokesman for a public enterprise the immense potentiality of which was fully recognized and which he emphasized in his evidence to the parliamentary committee set up in 1939 to consider the development of the corporation at that time. But Brockington was not alone in recognizing the potentiality of radio, television, and facsimile systems of information. So did the Canadian newspaper proprietors, and they were against a publicly owned system which would compete with them, bar them from what they saw to be rich pickings from advertising, and permit the free expression of opinions not controlled by them. Brockington handled himself with consummate skill when confronting these interests before the parliamentary committee, and the CBC went its way – or so it seemed.

When the war came Mackenzie King at once thought of Brockington as the man best suited to head the wartime information service of the government. He was so invited. He gave up his employment in Winnipeg and came at once to Ottawa. In slid a delegation of newspaper proprietors. They told the Prime Minister that, war or no war, they would not support the government if Brockington were appointed to run the information services. Mackenzie King gave way, and asked Brockington to go back to Winnipeg. Then he compromised and invited Brockington to become his information counsellor. When the election of March 1940 was called, Brockington provided the Prime Minister with some effectively barbed prose directed at Mitchell Hepburn and the Toronto Tories.

Then Brockington was put on the shelf and that is where I found him in May 1940. Very shortly after I arrived in the office he sent for me. Like most people educated in Britain he attached considerable importance to the academic prestige system based on university examinations. I think he simply wanted to see what a Cambridge starred first, born in Calgary and educated in Winnipeg, looked like. I found him in a small office on the ground floor of the East Block to the left of the door where the Prime Minister and the Ministers entered on their way upstairs to the Cabinet room. He was a handsome man with a splendid head covered with yellow hair, but he was terribly crippled by arthritis and obliged to walk slowly with a very pronounced stoop. He was a prodigious smoker of tobacco in all its forms: expensive cigars, cigarettes, and pipes, and equally a prodigious reader of books, newspapers, magazines, anything in print. He usually sat slumped in an easy chair in a haze of smoke amid a litter of literature. It is hard to imagine a greater contrast than that between the Prime Minister of Canada and his information counsellor, and this was only emphasized by his discourse: joking, witty, satiric, laced with quotations and uninhibited both as to topics and to people. No cautious, close-lipped Canadian was Leonard Brockington.

Although there was a disparity of twenty-five years in age, and as persons we were very unlike in our interests, understanding, and modes of expressing ourselves, we soon became very good friends. I sensed very early on that Brockington was deeply unhappy about his situation, baffled and incapable of explaining what had gone wrong. And why not? He was a man of exceptional talent with wide experience of public life and endowed with a great gift of charm. If he could not do something for his country and for liberty who could?

For a time we joined forces in an endeavour to do something significant. We produced a weekly appreciation of international political developments condensed to the prescribed one page which the Prime Minister would read. This generation of 'information' and pieces of paper, a common device in bureaucracies for justifying one's place on the payroll, was a futile proceeding, and we soon realized its absurdity. For a period in 1941 Brockington and John Grierson of the National Film Board worked together to get established a ministry of information (called something else) under the direction of a Liberal politician, but Mackenzie King blocked this, realizing that, if Brockington alone was *persona non grata* to the press lords of Canada, what might be their reaction to so talented a combination as Brockington and Grierson?

Brockington had a wide network of influential contacts in Canada and in Britain, and he began to use them to find a way out of his uselessness. Through friends in Britain, where his talents were more admired than they were in Canada, or, put another way, where he had no enemies who had an interest in excluding him from the power game, Brockington found opportunities for radio work of his own in the BBC in speech-writing for others. One of the most moving passages in one of King George VI's Christmas broadcasts had its origin in a suggestion made by Brockington.

Finally Brockington concluded that he could no longer stand the meaninglessness of his position and he wrote to the Prime Minister to say that he could not justify to himself or anyone else a salary of $9,000 a year (then the near equivalent of a ministerial stipend), and that he wanted something significant to do; otherwise he would be obliged to resign. King's response to Brockington was an instructive example of his political skill in dealing with an awkward development.

His first step was to phone Brockington personally inviting him to come to Kingsmere, for tea. 'And do bring Mrs Brockington. You must bring Mrs Brockington.' A car was sent for Brockington and his wife. The Prime Minister was out on the drive to welcome them. He opened the door of the car and assisted Brockington, who did not move easily, to get out of the vehicle. He ushered the couple into the sitting room and seated them comfortably. All the while he praised Brockington to the skies, addressing his eulogy to Mrs Brockington. He owed a great debt to her husband; he is indispensable, a comfort, etc.

'He covered me with whipped cream and bullshit,' Brockington told me afterwards. 'And all this to my wife.'

When tea was over, Mackenzie King then said to Mrs Brockington, 'Now, you'll excuse us, won't you? Brockington and I have something to discuss.' They then went into the library. As he was sitting down Brockington dropped his pencil and it rolled under the Prime Minister's desk. In an instant Mackenzie King was on his knees retrieving the pencil.

'My God, Henry,' Brockington told me, 'here was the Prime Minister of Canada down on his knees getting me a ten-cent pencil.'

Once the pencil was retrieved, Mackenzie King launched himself into an almost tearful recital of his own troubles. Hepburn was attacking him. Drew and Meighen were out to get him. Everything he did was misrepresented. He had no one to help him. He did not know how he could carry on, and on and on.

'How could I say anything? I had come with my problem, and here he was nearly in tears telling me about his problems,' Brockington told me. 'I came away with absolutely nothing.'

Brockington then resigned, and became the 'legislative counsel' in a large Ottawa firm. Shortly before he left the East Block he took me to lunch in the Rideau Club. At the bar he introduced me to a smooth man in a beautifully tailored suit. We exchanged a few words, and then we went into lunch.

'That chap,' Brockington said, 'sent me a barrel of Malpeque oysters last week. I am sure they are the last oysters he ever sends me when he learns I am in the same business as he is: lobbying.'

Brockington went on to become the head of the Rank Organization in Canada, and for many years he was elected and re-elected Rector of Queen's University by the students. But in fact the newspaper and media interests in Canada destroyed Brockington as a force in shaping public broadcasting, and Mackenzie King allowed them to do so.

None of this shows up in Mackenzie King's diaries. There Brockington is depicted as a man who bit the hand that fed him. Fed him! Before he had anything to do with Mackenzie King, Brockington was an independent professional man who earned a respectable living. At Mackenzie King's invitation he took on the chairmanship of the Canadian Broadcasting Corporation, a public office which paid him a small fee plus expenses and involved an enormous amount of time and energy to the prejudice of his obligations to his employers. At Mackenzie King's request he undertook war work and was let down by the Prime Minister. He accepted this betrayal and the compromise offer of a place in the Prime Minister's office. The hand that fed him! Here we see Mackenzie King in the grip of the delusion common in politicians from Herod and Nero to Stalin and Kennedy: they are the gods who feed the flock. Mackenzie King did not feed Brockington, he fed off him. He was jealous of him. Brockington's mistake was in believing he could serve Mackenzie King and his country at the same time. Had Brockington come to Ottawa with votes behind him or the spokesman of an interest group with some power to damage the Prime Minister, he would have got along nicely with Mackenzie King. As it was he came as a talented individual qualified and able to work at the top in the bureaucracy, and this was fatal. To me there is something very touching in the knowledge that in the last lonely months of Mackenzie King's old age, Brockington used to visit him and comfort him, and likewise a terrible irony that Mackenzie King was too ill and tired to cut from his diaries the mean and petty things he had had to say about Brockington.

There was once made to me an observation which explains the hazards of working in a bureaucracy, as Brockington tried to do, and the nature of civil service politics, as distinct from the politics of the community as a whole. The time was the late evening of the 3 June 1944. I was standing at the rail of the *Gripsholm* in the bright lights which illuminated the Swedish flags and the Red Cross painted on the sides of the great vessel. My companion was George Magann, the senior Canadian officer in charge of the prisoners-of-war exchange in which we had been engaged for some six weeks. The ship was moving slowly in a calm sea. The lights on the shores of New Jersey were faintly visible. The captain was waiting orders to enter the port of New York and journey's end. We had had just enough to drink to be friends and to forget the hierarchical relation between us as civil servants and between an older man and a younger one. We were reflecting on our experiences.

'You know, Harry,' Magann said, 'when I left Toronto to come to Ottawa I thought I was leaving behind profit-making and self-seeking to join a companionship of men and women devoted to serving the country and serving a good cause. But it isn't like that. In Toronto I had only one competitor in my line of business. I know that Bill *X* would never say about me, and I would certainly never say about him, what one civil servant will say about another to gain an advantage of a hundred dollars a year more salary.'

This was the sort of thing Brockington was up against. To his face the Prime Minister's staff were all admiration for Brockington. 'He was a wit, he was a card.' 'Where did you hear that, Brock?' Smiles and laughter all the way, so long as Brockington was present. When he was absent, however, Brockington was seldom mentioned without some deprecatory qualification echoing what can be read in Mackenzie King's diary. You know what Brock is like. Brock has no judgment. Brock's style is too over-heated, etc.

One day Turnbull made some slighting remark about Brockington. I asked him, 'Why do people say the things they do about Mr Brockington? He is a man of great ability, more able in fact than half of Mr King's cabinet. Why doesn't Mr King make him a minister in place of one or two of the clowns whose names you know as well as I do? Mr. King would do himself some good and the country too, if he would make some use of Mr. Brockington.'

Turnbull replied that there was more to it than just making him a minister, and anyway Brock probably did not want to have anything to do with politics. After that I never heard any further disparagement of Brockington, but I had probably done him more harm than good.

There was nothing subtle about the way Canadian civil servants conducted their competitive warfare with one another. At first I found the vulgarity and nastiness quite incredible. Pickersgill was one of the boldest and crudest of these warriors, and I had an instance of his technique within a few days of entering the office. To appreciate the quality of his first performance one needs to know the circumstances, which were these.

The Principal Secretary asked me to share an office with X who would instruct me in an art rather more recondite than it sounds, – opening the Prime Minister's mail. X had entered the civil service at the same time as Pickersgill and they were both on the same level of the hierarchy. Academically X had rather the edge on Pickersgill inasmuch as he was an ex-Rhodes scholar who had earned a D.Phil. from Oxford. But in the civil service they were equals and colleagues. I was, on the other hand, junior to both of them, a stranger to both of them,and one of them had been assigned the task of teaching me my job.

A few days after I commenced work, X's wife was delivered of a child. The day this happened I was summoned to Pickersgill's office for the purpose of being asked to perform some small job. I had at that time encountered Pickersgill twice in my life, and had exchanged at most one hundred words with him. By way of making conversation on this occasion I remarked how nice it was that X had a child.

'I'm surprised he was capable of it,' was Pickersgill's comment.

I was appalled by the crude insensitivity of this remark. I said nothing. In my innocence I did not recognize that Pickersgill was early seizing an opportunity to let me know who one of his enemies was and was giving me the chance to play on his team if I knew what was good for me.

Another example of the Pickersgill style in this aspect of bureaucratic politics was exhibited at a little gift ceremony for a stenographer who was leaving the Prime Minister's service. When anyone resigned or left the office Turnbull used to invite a small contribution of 50 cents or so from members of the staff towards a modest gift, and when the day of final departure came he would have the switchboard operator ring around inviting those who wished to assemble in his office for a farewell presentation.

On this occasion we were assembled to say good-bye to Miss Sugrue, a pleasant and competent little girl rather more endowed with feminine charm than her colleagues in the stenographic service, who were somewhat on the severe and efficient side. The Principal Secretary said a few kind words of appreciation for Miss Sugrue's work and he wished her well in her new job. Miss Sugrue then stood up and thanked Mr Turnbull and everyone who had worked with her. She said she was sorry to leave, but she thought the time had come when she ought to employ her talents elsewhere.

'What talents?' said Pickersgill in a hoarse whisper which, if it was loud enough for me to hear, was surely audible to everyone. There was an appalled but momentary silence. A look of real annoyance passed across Turnbull's face, but he quickly grasped Miss Sugrue's hand and repeated his words of gratitude.

If anyone but Pickersgill had done something like this, Turnbull would have fired him or her on the spot or had them transferred out of the office. But Pickersgill was secure in the regard of the Prime Minister, and Turnbull could do nothing. Jack for his part was completely unperturbed.

If Leonard Brockington illustrated one kind of difficulty of people in the Prime Minister's office, William Paterson illustrated a totally different aspect of the problem. Theoretically he should have had no difficulties at all. When he joined the staff late in 1939 the Prime Minister noticed his arrival favourably in his diary. He came from Winnipeg, a protégé and admirer of A.R.M. Lower and Pickersgill, who was still teaching at United College when Paterson entered the university. He was a grandson of one of Laurier's ministers. He had a great interest in politics and he was a committed Canadian nationalist and a Liberal.

William Paterson became my closest and dearest friend. He was universally known as Bill Paterson, but to me and Maureen and to his wife and widow he was always known as Pat. This came about by an odd set of circumstances created by my old-fashioned reluctance ever to use a Christian name until I had achieved a degree of trust and intimacy with a person. I did not know Paterson very well when I invited him to dinner shortly after Maureen arrived in Ottawa late in June 1940. When I in-

155

troduced our guest, Maureen was a bit non-plussed about how to address him. I called him Paterson, and she thought it a bit much to address him as Mr. Paterson. She said, "What do I call you?"

'Pat,' he said, and that is what we always called him and what we have always called his namesake, our second son, William Paterson Ferns.

Ours was in many ways a stormy friendship. Paterson was a highly intelligent man – when he joined the RCAF in Montreal the officer in charge told him they had never encountered so high an I.Q. as his – and he was a very amusing and witty one. I was a dogmatic Marxist and he was an equally dogmatic liberal. Our favourite occupation was to engage in energetic polemical exchanges about ideological and political questions. There was nothing quiet or academic about our controversy. Sometimes Maureen feared we would come to blows. Pat could be corrosively sarcastic and also extremely funny, and against this kind of opposition my three years of experience in the mission field in Cambridge stood me in good stead. Neither of us yielded to the other on general ideological questions, but we began to develop a common ground in our understanding of the great political events in progress in Europe.

When I first met Pat in May 1940, he still retained something of an isolationist view of European politics. Canada's declaration of war on Germany was in his opinion necessary not so much for reasons of foreign policy as a necessity of Canadian internal politics. The English-speaking majority would never have consented to neutrality when Britain was at war, and therefore Mackenzie King's policy was right. But as the Nazi power increased and the evidence of pusilanimity and incapacity on the part of the western European political leaders became more evident everyday, Pat's views rapidly began to change. If anything he became more anti-Nazi and more critical of Chamberlain than I was, and his passionate Canadian nationalism prompted him to see flaws in the policies of the Canadian government which, in his view, too much resembled the policies of Chamberlain and Daladier. At the same time we both shared the same detestation of the strident antics of the enemies of Mackenzie King: Drew, Hepburn, and the Toronto Tories. We agreed that the cry for a national government in Canada was foolish and dangerous to the war effort Canada was then making. But Pat thought the war effort we were making was not enough and that it was limited by too much calculation about political consequences in Canada and too little concern about the prospect of Nazi triumph in Europe.

Pat had no patience with my analysis which attributed the disasters in Europe to the failure of the British and French governments to come to an agreement with the Soviet Union. In his view the Soviet government was as incompetent as the British and French governments had demonstrated themselves to be. He always pointed to the war in Finland as a proof of Soviet incapacity. I countered this by arguing that, so long as Stalin thought he could overthrow Marshal Mannerheim by playing the Internationale on a tin whistle, the Red army was, as he said, incompetent, but once it was evident that the Finns would and could fight, Stalin 'turned it on' and the Finns capitulated. I added for good measure that Stalin had displayed statesmanlike prudence in taking from the Finns only what was necessary to protect the security of Leningrad. Pat's answer was simply, 'Nuts to you!'

In the evening of 21 June 1941, we heard rumours that the Germans were moving against the USSR. This was a piece of idiocy on the part of Hitler which I found it hard to credit. In the office the next morning, this was not how the firm news of an attack on the Soviet Union was viewed. Some declared that at last Hitler was doing something useful. Others predicted that the Reds could last three weeks. The optimists said three months. I was alone in predicting that Hitler had committed political suicide and that the USSR would win. Pat did not say much, but when we were having lunch he said, 'You have laid it on the line, and I will too. If Stalin is still fighting in 1942 I'll agree you are right. By that time, whatever the outcome, the Germans will have sustained so much damage that we are going to win. But we have to make a greater effort than we are doing.'

It was not, however, political events in Europe and the Canadian response to them that decided Pat to quit the Prime Minister's Office. The major factor in his decision to get out was the failure of the dominion-provincial conference in January 1941. In our fierce controversies I always took a very high line about the very limited capacity of a capitalist society to reform itself and overcome the problems of depression and international anarchy. Pat, on the other hand, had a great faith in pragmatic reform and in the capacity of democratic governments to find solutions bit by bit. While I agreed with him that the dramatic attempt of R.B. Bennett to reform Canadian society and the Canadian economy had been an instance of trying too much too quickly, I argued that the Rowell-Sirois commission's enquiry into Canadian problems was only an attempt to avoid essential change through talk and more talk. Pat, however, believed both in the honest intentions of the commission and in a general way in the solutions proposed. In the end he persuaded me that the Rowell-Sirois proposals were a radically new and workable program which would endow Canada with a stronger and better national government capable of implementing a new deal. This really would work in the sense that depression could be overcome and sane management of the economy inaugurated. By the autumn of 1940 our high ideological disputes had somewhat subsided, and we were to a considerable degree at one in our enthusiasm for a dominion-provincial conference designed to create for Canada a new kind of government of intelligent action in the interest of the whole of Canada.

Brockington was the one man above us in the hierarchy of the office who shared our enthusiasm. We were humble labourers in the vineyard and did we labour under Brockington's guidance! We assembled information, prepared press material, and worked with a will. Came the day of the conference, 14 January 1941. Our knowledge of what the Prime Minister intended to say filled us with hope. Mr Ilsley would weigh in with great authority. The logic of the federal government would carry all before it. Mr King made a good start and our spirits rose. Then began the disillusionment. Hepburn was crude and rude. Little Godbout said only a few words which meant nothing. Patullo of British Columbia was stupid. Aberhart of Alberta was ridiculous. The Maritime premiers seemed sympathetic enough, but they were woolly and confused. Bracken of Manitoba alone seemed to understand what was needed, but even he was boring.

While Pat and I were full of contempt for what we had heard from eight of the nine provincial premiers, in our immaturity and innocence we inferred from their performances that the Prime Minister would prevail because he simply had a better case. But Mr King did not fight. He wound up the conference. To him it was a mistake to start quarrelling with eight or nine provincial politicians when the world was in flames. For me this was a disappointment. For Pat it was heart-breaking. The qualities in Daladier and the French leaders which had brought France to ruin and the qualities of Chamberlain and the British Tories which had brought Britain to the brink seemed to Pat the essential qualities of Mackenzie King. He began then to want out. The littleness of the men assembled at the conference and their crabbed and mean provincialism was a humiliation to the proud and intelligent man that Pat was.

He concealed his disquiet better from me than he did from Brockington.

Brockington responded to Pat's need by asking his friend William Stephenson whether he could use Pat in the British office of information he had set up in New York. Pat judged the offer made to him in terms of its real contribution to winning the war against the Nazis, and he decided that as the job was described to him it would mean the best employment of his capacities in fighing Germany and Italy.

Pat never used the term 'fighting fascism.' His principal concept in so far as international politics was concerned was the nation state, and it was the Canadian nation state and nation states allied to Canada which he was concerned to defend and two nation states, Germany and Italy, were the political entities which had to be destroyed.

As to fascism Pat took a quite doctrinaire, liberal view of the Nazis and the Fascists. Hitler and Mussolini were populist demagogues like Huey Long in the United States and like Mitch Hepburn, Maurice Duplessis,and William Aberhart in Canada. These last were parish-pump politicians compared with Hitler and Mussolini, but they had the essential characteristics of the fascist dictators. They only lacked genius and opportunity.

I think Pat would have put Stalin in the same category as Hitler and Mussolini had it not been for the fact that long arguments about Marxism on my part and my description of Stalin as a Bolshevik and Marxist had persuaded him, not to accept my arguments, but to recognize that Marxism is a serious intellectual kind of analysis like liberalism and not on a par with the turgid prejudices of *Mein Kampf* or the editorial pages of the *Toronto Telegram* or the *Chicago Tribune*.

Shortly after the invasion of the USSR Pat departed for New York. We maintained a lively correspondence mainly about Canadian politics. As time passed I became more a supporter of Mackenzie King's line in domestic affairs and Pat less so. I developed the view, to which I still hold, that Mackenzie King was a great war leader for Canada because he so handled the conscription issue that Canadians did not dissipate their energies fighting one another, and delivered at the enemy the maximum of men and materials which the Canadian political system would permit. This maximum was below the theoretical maximum as far as manpower was concerned, but it was the practical maximum which involved no waste of manpower or the coercion of those who refused to go overseas. Pat on the other hand was inclined to sympathize with Colonel Ralston and the Liberal conscriptionists. What distressed him most was the evident falsity of the 'national unity' peddled by the Liberals. A letter written a

159

few months before he was killed in action summed up his views as the war was approaching its end:

August 15/44

Dear Harry,

After August 8th, the results [of the election in Quebec] of which I have just learned from the Canadian Press weekly, I imagine that any letter addressed to the East Block should bear a somewhat funereal tone. However, as this is going to your home, and to Ferns the Man rather than to Ferns the flute player on the party band-wagon, I can be natural. I was not surprised that Godbout ended up with a minority, but for some reason I had expected the majority to be much more evenly divided between the UN and the Bloc Populaire. Two points on which I would like you to comment: (1) Who had the support of St. James Street, Duplessis or Godbout? If I knew how my brother (a business man in Montreal) thought it would give me a good indication. I'm fairly sure he was for Godbout despite his damnable interference with M.L.H.& P. [Montreal Light, Heat & Power, nationalized by Godbout]. I don't think even the Quebec English could quite swallow Duplessis' disloyalty with his reaction. (2) What prospects are there of Bracken getting into the same bed with Duplessis? If John, Maurice and Drew all get under the sheets together something in the nature of a political Jukes family should result. I was surprised at the Alberta election. Either we shall have to cease thinking of the Social Credit party as rather comic or else start thinking of the whole province in the same way. I can foresee nothing but a deadlock in the next federal election, with each party enjoying a largely sectionalized support. It is depressing to think that after all the soul-searching of the Rowell-Sirois period and after five years of 'unification' produced by a so-called common war effort, we face only a future of further sectionalism in the federal and provincial fields with what I predict will be a new high in bitterness. I should think it likely that we shall see ever more young men turning to radical solutions of our country's problems. What remains to be said for the conventional formulae applied in discussion of Quebec? By the way, why did none of the Liberal ministers stake their political lives on this election? Surely they are not men who only bet on a sure thing. Yet Duplessis and Laurendeau were surely more provocative now than in 1939 ...'

Pat never talked about his work in the British intelligence service. At first his duties fully absorbed him, but after a year it seemed evident to me that the job was not living up to his expectations as a means of 'doing something.' He spoke of enlisting in the armed forces, and his superiors offered to put him in uniform if he would stay with them. More and more he found the intelligence service loaded with passengers, upper-class British twits bent on avoiding active service and enjoying the delights of life in New York. When the kennel fees of two aristocratic cats were passed as expenses chargeable to the British government, Pat handed in his notice, went to Montreal, and walked into an RCAF recruiting office.

Because by the summer of 1943 I had had some small experience of intelligence reporting from Latin America as it filtered into the Department of External Affairs I was curious to know what Pat thought of the value of intelligence work now that he was out of it. He told me that that part of it based on the postal censorship and involving the patient piecing together of bits of information relating to enemy economic activity was very useful both in identifying and closing off sources of critical materials and machines. But a lot of intelligence reporting was nothing more than passing on bar-room gossip of no value to anyone. This last part of his evaluation squared with my experience. Of the romantic exploits of the man called Intrepid, Pat gave not the slightest hint.

It has always seemed to me that the integrity of Paterson's character was the force which drove him ultimately to express his political faith by fighting in a personal capacity. He could have contributed more to the defeat of the enemy by the employment of his excellent brain and orderly and efficient capacity for administration, but he never found an opportunity to use his talents in a way which measured up to his conception of the urgent needs of the moment. In the air force he had two opportunities to escape the ultimate test and he refused to exploit them. First, he had a tendency to air sickness which could have meant transfer to administrative duties. But he conquered air sickness, qualified as a navigator, and was assigned to active service overseas. Second, before he left Canada Pickersgill, acting on behalf of Brooke Claxton, offered him a post as an administrative assistant in a new ministry. Paterson replied that he would consider this *after* he had done the duty he had enlisted to perform. When he was overseas and already on active service this offer was renewed with the prospect of immediate release from the air force. Paterson replied that he would accept, but only after he had completed a tour of duty with the crew of which he was a member.

The tour of duty was never completed. Over the Ruhr on the night of 23 December 1944 the bomber of which he was the navigating officer was caught in the flak and raked from end to end by a German night-fighter. The plane being on fire the pilot gave the order to abandon. The last man to speak with Pat was a Scottish tail-gunner, Harry Yardley. Pat put his hand on Yardley's shoulder and said, 'Jump, Harry.' Pat himself went down with the plane which disintegrated on impact.

This in a sense was a mercy. The two gunners who parachuted were injured on landing, were severely beaten up by the Germans who found them, and were carried to a hospital in a wheelbarrow, one with an eye hanging out of its socket. Doctors refused to attend to them for some days. Both men were crippled for life, dependent for years on the attentions of their wives. Harry Yardley died in Edinburgh in 1978, a victim of what had happened to him 33 years previously.

When William Paterson died, Canada lost a young man who had all the talents necessary to become a prime minister. Had he completed his tour of duty he would have returned to the life of politics. I am sure he would have risen to the top, for he had a splendid mind, good rhetorical talent, firm character, and the guile and subtlety necessary for political success. My only doubt about Paterson centres on his lack of self-seeking. Perhaps he was too disinterested, too straightforward. In this he resembled no politician I ever encountered in Ottawa.

The statement that the Prime Minister's Office was a nugatory experience prompts the question: why did you stay there for three years? Why did you not get out as Brockington did? As Paterson did? As E.K. Brown did? At first I was mesmerized by the thought that I was at the centre of the political world in Canada and at least on the edge of world politics at a decisive historical crisis, I had encountered unparalleled good luck which had located me not just in a grandstand seat but right in the arena. Maybe I was only a ball-boy, but what a game!

Familiarity did not breed contempt, but it did soon produce in me a sense that I was doing nothing of any significance. I argued with myself that a humble task like opening the Prime Minister's mail, distributing it to the proper persons inside or outside the office, and drafting answers to the left-overs, was ennobled and rendered significant by the fact that it was a labour performed for the Prime Minister of Canada. More than once I reflected on Milton's thought, 'They also serve who only stand and wait.'

As time wore on and particularly so after the failure of the dominion-provincial conference in January 1941, I began to want out of the office. There was nothing political in this. On the whole I thought Mackenzie King was doing his job in the right way on all the big issues. Even on the question of constitutional reform I soon began to see that the Prime Minister was probably right in avoiding an occasion for domestic dispute in time of war. The real reasons for my discontent were personal.

The first was poverty. I earned $135.00 a month. Rent for a furnished flat was $55.00 a month. I had a wife to support and a child was on the way. In those far-off days young married women did not work in paid employment. The social logic of the depression was still so present that marriage was regarded as a socially beneficial act because it removed one more person from the labour market and correspondingly improved the chances of those seeking work. In any case Maureen was qualified as a teacher in Manitoba, not Ottawa. We really were poor. Gone were the easy circumstances I had known at Cambridge. No more sherry! No more cigars! No more entertaining! When our first son was born Maureen had to cash her insurance policy to pay the hospital and doctor bills, and when she came home from the hospital she had no clothes which would fit her. I had only one shabby overcoat purchased in a sale at Eatons in Winnipeg in 1932.

Mackenzie King believed, and rightly so, that no one should benefit materially from the war. In this he wanted to set an example, and the best way he could do this was in seeing that those around him did not have their snouts in the trough. I did not really object to this. I thought then, as I still think, that leaders ought to set the example to their followers which circumstances require. On the other hand, I could see that there were people in Ottawa doing less prestigious but more remunerative jobs, and that if I worked elsewhere, say in the newly organized Unemployment Insurance Commission or the National Film Board, I might earn maybe another $50.00 a month.

Leaving the Prime Minister's Office was no simple matter. In a sense one was caught in a 'poverty trap.' Enlisting in the armed forces was not a solution for me on medical grounds, and in Ottawa almost all employment opportunities were in the civil service. One might seek another job, but other departments were reluctant to take anyone already employed. Seeking to have someone transferred out of the Prime Minister's Office was not a politic thing to do. I had several discussions with John Grierson about transferring to the film board, but in the end Grierson decided that it would be unwise, considering his many political problems in the bureaucracy and his need for the goodwill of the Prime Minister, to take me out of the Prime Minister's Office.

In the summer of 1941 the principal secretary decided to do something on my behalf. After a lengthy discussion with the Treasury Board it was decided to pay me an additional $600.00 a year, and, wonder of wonders, the increase was back dated to May 1941. $200.00 in one chunk on top of $185 a month less tax was like the pay-off on a $2.00 ticket on a 100-1 shot at Tijuana.

While this piece of good fortune was in the process of gestation I was assigned a new task: that of briefing the Prime Minister on parliamentary questions either asked or likely to be asked. This sounds an important task, but it was like carrying coals to Newcastle. The Prime Minister had a preternatural sense of what was up in the House of Commons and could anticipate a question before the opposition had even thought of it. None the less the need to scrutinize the unrevised Hansard hot off the press and to size up the flow of debate had a fascination not entirely dulled by the need to wade through the turgid rhetoric of the Tories and the repetitive drivel of the Social Credit members. The CCF members, however, required close watching. They were in general more intelligent than the rest of the opposition and, indeed, of most of the Liberals, and their line of approach was one with certain danger for the Prime Minister, of which he had a lifetime of awareness. Scrutinizing the utterances of the *Bloc populaire* was equally necessary, and I found that the best way to anticipate what they were up to was to read carefully everything which Leopold Richer wrote in *Le Devoir*.

I do not suppose there was any journalist in Canada with whom I was more in disagreement than Leopold Richer and one whom I more respected. There was always an intellectual substance in what Richer wrote, almost totally lacking in the stuff turned out by men like Grant Dexter and Charlie Bishop. Dexter and Bishop were always full of information about the here and now, but Richer wrote of events *sub specie aeternitatis* with a hard realism which suggested he had some knowledge of the mind of God. And sometimes Maxime Raymond, the member for Beauharnois-Laprairie, would ask that kind of question.

For the most part my duties in this matter were not onerous. Most questions directed to the Prime Minister concerned external politics or events outside Canada, and these were the responsibility of the Department of External Affairs. I had, however, an autonomous responsibility

164

as a member of the Prime Minister's staff, and I did alert him to an 'external policy' question which in the end caused my resignation from the public service. And the irony of it all is that I resigned not because there was a difference between the Prime Minister and me, but because we agreed.

The circumstances were these. When the mission of Sir Stafford Cripps to India failed in April 1942, the Indian government jailed M.K. Gandhi, Jawaharlal Nehru, and Abdul Kalam Azad of the Indian National Congress in August. While this was happening the Japanese were enjoying great military and political success. Politically they were playing the nationalist card with great skill, and their sympathy for national movements of liberation in French Indo-China, the Dutch East Indies, and in Malaya was beginning to blot out the effect of their assaults on China. The Japanese were emerging as a liberating force directed at white imperialism. Thailand had allied itself with Japan. A section of the Indian National Congress under the leadership of Subhas Bose had fled to the Japanese and were organizing any army of Indian independence under Japanese auspices.

In my view the answer to all this was Indian independence *now*. However, this was none of my official business, but I did have the duty of alerting the Prime Minister to possible questions he might be asked on this topic. Both the CCF in Canada and the politicians and newspapers in the USA were making noises about imperialism in India. And so on 29 October 1942, I sent Mr King a memorandum which serves as an example of the kind of work I was doing at that time.

Memorandum for the Prime Minister.
Re. India
I do not know what may be the motive of Mr. Coldwell's statement on India, coming as it does so soon after Mr. Willkie's speech, but I have reason to believe that it may become for many, a public expression of a hitherto inarticulate current of uneasiness that is running strongly in Canada and has to do with the conduct of the British Government in its dealing with India.

My own study of Indian politics leads me to believe that there are a number of competent widely respected Indian politicians, both Hindu and Muslim who could form a strong gov't committed to as vigorous a war against Japan as that being carried on by China.

Today there is not a single authentic Indian political organization supporting the Indian Gov't.

From the public statements of the various Indian leaders, it seems clear that a transfer of power would not involve a dictatorship by the Indian National Congress. While this organization is itself the most representative political organization in India it is prepared to share power with representatives of sectarian Muslim and Hindu organizations.

Mr. Churchill's statement that there are more white troops in India than at any time in history is likely to become a source of political controversy and particularly in Quebec. People like Maxime Raymond may very soon be saying that Canadians are being sent to India to keep under and defend people who only ask for the right and power to govern and defend themselves.

The purely negative attitude disclosed in speeches by Mr. Churchill and Mr. Amery seems to have undone the good effect on American opinion which undoubtedly resulted from Sir Stafford Cripps mission. While opinion in Canada is less articulate than in the United States, it is probable that the reaction in this country is very similar. The fact that Mr. Coldwell has made a statement might serve as an occasion to bring this aspect of the Indian question once more to the attention of the British Government.

H.S.F.

By the time I wrote this memorandum Mackenzie King had long since made up his mind about what needed to be done in India. As early as March 1942, when the Cripps mission was headed for failure, the Prime Minister had talks with the Chinese foreign minister, T.V. Soong, and they were agreed that the British government should be urged to grant India real independence at once along the lines of the Cripps proposals, but implemented at once and guaranteed by the great-power members of the United Nations alliance. In this policy Mackenzie King had knowledge of the sympathetic, informal support of the wife of the governor-general, Princess Alice of Athlone. On 6 March 1942, Mackenzie King had recorded in his diary that HRH had told him that 'she did not like them having to give in to blackmail, but felt it important that no time should be lost in giving India self-government ...'

When the Prime Minister drafted his cable to Churchill after consultation with the Chinese foreign minister he showed it to Norman Robertson. Mackenzie King recorded in his diary (15 March 1942) that Robertson agreed with the policy, but persuaded him to cut out a friendly reference to Nehru on the grounds that Churchill particularly disliked Nehru.

166

In fact Robertson and his cronies in External Affairs were opposed to independence for India. It seems that the only people in the Canadian political community who recognized the need for Indian independence were the Prime Minister of Canada, the granddaughter of Queen Victoria, and H.S. Ferns. When my memorandum of 29 October 1942 went to the Prime Minister, he evidently read it with care, judging from the pencil marks in the margin (Public Archives of Canada, ME 26 J4 vol. 27 81).

External Affairs on the other hand, in the person of Professor Henry F. Angus, tried their hand at policy-making, and this was completely negative. Angus' draft of a letter dated 31 October 1942 to M.J. Coldwell, the CCF leader, stated that 'it would ... be a negative contribution to a settlement in India to suggest in any way that British promises require re-inforcement by undertakings from China, the U.S.S.R. and the United States, or from others of the United Nations, and it would be utterly unrealistic to assume that Canadians have a knowledge of the complex political scene in India which would qualify them to render advice as to the content of negotiations there.' The letter seems never to have been sent.

Ignorance as a justification for neutrality and inaction was evident enough in the case of the staff of External Affairs. Soon they discovered another reason for doing nothing: the racial discrimination against Indians in British Columbia. A thousand or so East Indians in British Columbia were denied the right to vote. This, therefore, disqualified anyone in Canada from talking common sense on the question of political independence for 440,000,000 people.

Once I had transferred to the Department of External Affairs (in June 1943), my opportunities for independent advice to the Prime Minister ceased. In December 1942 I had a complicated and experimental operation on one of my ears performed in St Michael's Hospital, Toronto, by Dr (later Senator) J.A. Sullivan. The object was to reconstruct one of my ears by micro-surgery in order to restore my hearing. I was extraordinarily lucky inasmuch as the object was partially achieved and the restoration effected lasted for several years. Thus was the obstacle to my employment in External Affairs removed.

Why I was transferred I never knew. I did not ask for the move. When I enquired of the Principal Secretary whether he was getting rid of me, he replied, 'No, on the contrary, We want to make a better opportunity for you.' This may have been so in Turnbull's mind, but I do not think it was so in that of the high command in External Affairs. In External Affairs I was under closer control than in the Prime Minister's Office. In 1980 a brief glimpse at the Prime Mininster's file from Laurier House on the subject of India revealed to me how the filtering operation conducted by Norman Robertson as the under-secretary closed the channel of communication with the Prime Minister which I unknowingly had had when I was one of his secretaries.

I was assigned to the American and Far Eastern division of the department, the head of which was Dr H.L. Keenleyside. Theoretically I should have now been in closer touch with policy-making and with the Prime Minister as far as India was concerned. Nothing of the kind.

In the first place I was lumbered with the task of assisting the man in charge of Latin American affairs, an academic named F.W. Soward. India was very much a side-line. None the less I kept in touch with the subject as best I could. But this was not the real difficulty. Now what went to the Prime Minister on India passed across the desk of the Under-Secretary of State, and he sent forward what he wanted to send and put aside the rest. An inspection of the Prime Minister's file on India kept at Laurier House shows that only two of my memoranda on India ever reached the Prime Minister: one analysing and condensing a speech of Lord Wavell which called attention to what was not said and another on a ten-year plan advanced by some Indian businessmen designed to raise Indian productivity and life expectancy to the then modest levels of Japan. What did not go forward was a memorandum of mine written in March 1944 in which I reviewed the policy vis-à-vis India and endeavoured to supply the Prime Minister with facts and arguments in support of his policy. The head of the division sent me a personal memo saying he had read the 'paper on India with great interest and profit to myself,' but he gently suggested that I bow to the line of the department – that the war against Japan must take precedence over independence, that Roosevelt had more or less accepted Churchill's policy, and that Canada had no standing on account of the discrimination against East Indians in British Columbia. He added in long hand that he thought that opinion in Britain and events in India could bring about independence in the not very distant future.

The memorandum reached Robertson and lay on his desk as evidence that I was unsuitable for employment in the Department of External Affairs. Nothing was said at the time but by the end of November 1944 I had resigned from the department.

My resignation came about in this way. In September 1944, an invitation came to me from David Bowes-Lyon of the British embassy in Washington to join a British political warfare mission in India. Who had ever suggested me for political warfare work in India remains a mystery. Was it Mackenzie King? This is not impossible but it is unlikely. Was it Princess Alice of Athlone? There is no evidence that she knew I existed. Was it someone in Moscow? There is evidence that people in the Kremlin had their eye on me, but, the Soviet party line being what it then was, it is most unlikely that anyone in the Comintern-that-was would wish to promote political warfare against the Japanese in mid-1944. Probably it was some old friend in Cambridge, but I cannot think who it might have been. Most of my Indian pals were in jail. My English friends were either scientists in places like the Wool Research Institute or the Medical Research Council or were in the armed forces. It might conceivably have been James Klugman, who was engaged in political warfare in connection with Yugoslavia, but I doubt it. When I saw him once in 1951 he told me that he had no idea of what I had been doing during the war.

Mystery or no mystery, here was the King's brother-in-law inviting me to join the British political warfare mission and, according to L.B. Pearson in the Canadian embassy in London, 'apparently the United Kingdom are anxious to have Ferns for the work in question' (Pearson to Keenleyside 12 September 1944).

By this time in my life family interest was uppermost in my mind. I was willing to go to India and fight the Japanese with my tongue, but I wanted to ensure the welfare of Maureen, our son John, and a second child then on the way. The British were willing to pay me what they paid their own people, and to provide for my family in the event of my death. But what about the future? I insisted as part of the arrangement that I be given a permanent post in the Department of External Affairs and be then seconded to the British authorities. It was at this juncture that I went to see the Under-Secretary about my future.

What happened is set down in a memorandum I wrote a few hours after the interview. I sent Robertson a copy. He never acknowledged the memorandum nor did he make any comment on it, and so presumably it is a true record of what was said.

Compared with subsequent encounters with Canadian bureaucrats in matters concerning myself, my interview with Norman A. Robertson on 6 November 1944 revealed certain imperfections of technique. Robertson, for example, was open and honest and he was willing to give me information. He exhibited no disposition to bring down the shutters, to feign ignorance, or to lie. Because what he said denied my hopes and aspirations I reacted with hatred, and this endured for some years. But reflection and encounters with the average well-trained bureaucratic operator has persuaded me that I was childish and unjust to react to Robertson as I did and that he was both an intellectual and a gentleman with whom I had a political difference of some magnitude.

According to my memorandum, 'Mr. Robertson stated that the question of making me a third secretary was a difficult one, inasmuch as an appointment could only be recommended if an officer was regarded as indispensable ... he did not think I was in that category ... and there had long been some question in his mind concerning my personal suitability as a permanent employee of the Department of External Affairs ...'

Did Robertson share the view that I lacked those social graces which made A.D.P. Heeney such a success? Did he not recall the time only a few weeks in the past when I had two Chilean generals dumped on my doorstep with instructions to 'look after these people,' and no help from anyone? Was it not the case that in a matter of twelve hours I laid on a dinner at the Country Club, arranged for the richest and stupidest member of the cabinet to invite them to lunch in the parliamentary restaurant, fixed for them a meeting with the Prime Minister, which, when the press of business in the House caused him to cancel, obliged him to send the generals personal messages? That these Chilean generals went away with an impression not only of Canada's military might but the warmth of the Canadian heart?

Actually Mr. Robertson 'did not have this in mind. The unsuitability to which he referred was rather of a temperamental and intellectual character?' For example, I asked?

He had in mind a draft letter I had written for his signature addressed to the Argentine ambassador to Canada. It should be explained that Argentina had but recently opened a legation in Ottawa, and Canada one in Buenos Aires. It is further necessary to keep in mind that Argentina was in deep trouble with the USA on account of its neutrality in the war against Nazi Germany. Bad judgement, eh? What was wrong with telling the Argentine that Canada's information about Argentina is gathered in Argentina by Canadians and that we do not rely on US hand-outs for information about Argentina. And what was so wrong with inviting Señor Gaucho to consider the fact that Canada is more exposed to American power than any nation on earth, that we have been invaded by US armed

170

forces twice in our history; that the US Congress has no compunction about screwing up Canadian economic interests if American vested interests dictate congressional decisions; that on the whole we don't like Americans very much; but that we get along with them just fine. Four thousand miles of undefended frontier is a cliché, but it is also a fact. The Argentines ought to stop crying in their maté and get along with the Americans like we do. I never expected Robertson to put this so plainly, but the letter was written in good faith as a means of stimulating discussion. Why be so damned mealy-mouthed about facts?

On this one Robertson backed down and suggested that my draft letter to the Argentine ambassador was perhaps not as good an illustration of what he had in mind, namely a memorandum written for the Prime Minister in March 1944. He stated that this memorandum 'expressed a point of view that was wholly unacceptable in language which was too adjectival ...' We had come to the crunch – my views on Indian independence *now*. My style and my line, I said, was probably influenced by the knowledge that 'my views on India more closely co-incided with those of the Prime Minister than with those of other members of the Department. I suggested that Mr. Robertson consult the file and he could see there an example of what I meant. I referred particularly to Mr. King's disposition of a public statement made by Mr. M.J. Coldwell on India in October 1942.'

Robertson then acknowledged that he was aware that on India and Palestine Mr King did not generally follow the advice of the Department. He added that he was speaking to me more frankly than was generally his practice. This appears to have been a step in the direction of his final answer to me. He did not want me in External Affairs because I was a red.

He asked me if I was familiar with the novels of Arthur Koestler. I said I had read *Darkness at Noon*; otherwise I did not know his work. Robertson then said I ought to read *Arrival and Departure*, 'which deals in a very penetrating way with the problems of a disaffected red.'

I kept calm, and even denied that I was a 'disaffected red,' but I imploded violently. Nothing so distresses a communist as to discover that the bourgeois state is really what he says it is. I was still sufficiently a communist to have this experience. The interview then came to an end. Robertson said he hoped there would be an opportunity for further discussion.

There never was. That afternoon I wrote to my old teacher Fieldhouse in Winnipeg to ask whether there were any university teaching posts available. There was one in United College, an affiliated institution of the University of Manitoba. On 28 November 1944, I resigned from the Department of External Affairs determined never again to work for any government, Canadian, British, or other.

I was livid with anger and chagrin, and Robertson became a demon in my life. How to get back at him? Years later I asked myself why I had not had the sense to go to Leopold Richer with my story of the Prime Minister of Canada hemmed in by imperialist blackguards. Richer would have understood and would have had no inhibitions about making the most of the information. Such a thought never crossed my mind in December 1944, for the simple reason that I supported the war, and Richer and his friends did not.

One idea tempted me at the time: to go to M.J. Coldwell who had Cripps' view of Indian questions. But I was not sure wht Coldwell would do; perhaps do no more than thank me for the information.

Finally, I decided to write to the Prime Minister a flattering good-bye in the hope that he might himself investigate why so warm a supporter was leaving the government services. His response was otherwise than expected. On my last day in the East Block, Walter Turnbull came to my office with a package. He said, 'Mr King asked me to give you this.' I pulled off the paper. It was a photo of the Prime Minister by Karsh, something he did not freely give. It was inscribed 'To Henry Ferns with all good wishes W.L. Mackenzie King, Ottawa, Christmas 1944.' Not Robertson's scalp, alas!

My memorandum on India of March 1944 was a mistake. It could have no effect on events for the simple reason that the time for decision about independence for India by then had passed. Churchill had paid no attention to Mackenzie King's intervention in 1942 when the active involvement of Indian political leaders in the war with Japan would have had a real meaning and would have changed the political character of the war. Roosevelt accepted Churchill's judgement, and the political initiative in Asia was left to the Japanese. Having jailed the Indian political leaders instead of involving them creatively and on their own terms in the war against Japan, Churchill went to Yalta under the imputation of being an imperialist. He was thus isolated and could do nothing except participate in a fresh carve-up of the world not on his terms, but on the terms laid down by the practitioners of the 'new imperialism' disguised in the rhetorical garments of democracy and socialism. The failure to involve the Indian leaders in the war on their own terms had the future effect of destroying the one great benefit conferred on the Indian subcontinent by the British – its political unification. God himself could not stem the tide of political sentiment in India, in support of national independence. In denying the opportunity of the Indian leaders to work together with the British against a common enemy, threatening the Hindus and the Muslims alike, as the Japanese were in 1942, Churchill opened the way for the Hindus and Muslims to start fighting one another – his own self-fulfilling prophecy.

It was in the presence of problems and possibilities of this kind that the second-rate men in External Affairs deserted and obstructed the Prime Minister of Canada. Mackenzie King frequently lamented that Canadians never gave him enough credit for what he did and that Churchill, Roosevelt, and King George VI never gave Canada credit for what the nation as a whole did. All this might have been different had he not been surrounded and penned in by a second-rate bodyguard better at advertising their reputation as 'the best civil service in the world' than at understanding what the welfare of mankind demanded.

After my interview with Robertson I talked with several friends about what had happened, but none of these discussions added anything to what I already knew. In one or two instances I was chagrined by the suggestion that maybe Robertson was right; maybe I was not cut out for External Affairs. Finally one friend said, 'Why not have a talk with Alex Skelton? Alex knows more about Ottawa than anyone else.'

I had never met Alex Skelton, the research director of the Bank of Canada, face to face, although I had talked to him in the way of business over the telephone and I had once been introduced to his second wife. I rang him up. He said he had long wanted to have a talk with me, and why don't you and your family come out to the farm on Sunday?

Maureen being very pregnant, the weather being what is was and the bus journey down the Ottawa valley being uncomfortable, only John (our son aged $3^1/_2$) and I went to see Alex and Janet Skelton.

Divorced from a rich American woman who had wrung out of him every cent she did not need, Alex was poor, but he had managed to keep a splendid old stone farmhouse. At a distance from the house were some barns obviously in use. I said to Alex as we walked from the road towards the house.

'What do you *do* with the farm?'

'I produce horse piss. Bull shit during the week. Horse piss on the week ends. That's how I get a living.'

I said I could understand the bull-shit part, but what about his weekend activities. He explained that the pharmaceutical industry bought the urine of pregnant mares from which hormones were extracted for various purposes. In fact the business was a serious and complicated matter, and he drew a rent for the use of his land and barns.

By any manner of reckoning Alex Skelton was an unusual Canadian. His father had been O.D. Skelton, the Under-Secretary of State for External Affairs, who until his death in 1941 was the most important civil servant in Ottawa. Both his father and his mother had written, among other books, biographies of Canadian politicians. Alex himself had made a reputation at Queen's University as a football player as well as a scholar, and he went to Oxford as a Rhodes scholar. At Oxford he paid little attention to academic matters, but he won a boxing blue and enjoyed himself immensely. In 1937 he was appointed secretary of the royal commission set up to enquire into and make recommendations on dominion-provincial relations. This was an immense task inasmuch as Alex was obliged to organize an intellectual as well as political enterprise of very great complexity and to ensure that the commissioners heard not only political views but also the expert opinions of lawyers and social scientists in Canada, United States, Britain and Europe.

Alex was very much equal to his task, and sometimes he resorted to unusual methods to expedite the work of the commission. Some Canadian politicians were willing to co-operate with the commission. Some boycotted it. Some were rude, and many were boring. Among the most boring were the Social Crediters. Although their leader, William Aberhart, refused to give evidence, a very large number of his followers applied for an opportunity to air their views. When one had heard one, one had heard them all.

In Winnipeg a local Social Credit leader asked Alex to be heard by the commission. In the course of conversation it emerged that this man, who was Scandinavian-Canadian and a lumberjack by profession, had once been a wrestler. Alex decided to make him a proposition. Why not he and Alex try three falls? If the Social Crediter could win two out of three falls, he could present his brief, otherwise no. The man agreed that this was a pretty fair deal, and so they shoved back the furniture in Alex's room in the Fort Garry Hotel to make a ring in the centre of the room. Alex threw the Social Crediter once. Then the Social Creditor threw Alex.

'I remembered the length of that brief,' Alex said, 'and I put something into that last fall.' He won, and so the royal commissioners were spared.

My purpose in visiting Alex Skelton was to discuss with someone who was knowledgeable and possibly sympathetic what had gone wrong with my career in Ottawa. Historians understand, or think they understand, the past, but some of them do not understand the present very well, and I could then be numbered among those who grasp what has happened better than what is happening, particularly to themselves.

I explained to Alex that I felt I could not stay a day longer in External Affairs than was absolutely necessary, and that within a few days I was leaving Ottawa, I hoped for ever. But why?

Alex attempted an answer, and it surprised me. Canada, he said, is run (he did not say governed) by a few hundred people who spend most of their time gossiping about one another and the Canadians who do the work of producing the wherewithal for Canada to exist and sometimes to prosper.

'You say you are an obscure little guy who never did anything good or bad as far as others are concerned. Maybe. But I have heard you talked about more than once,' Alex said. I replied that I found this hard to credit. Perhaps he could give me an instance of what was said and why.

He asked me to recall an occasion, which I had all but forgotten, when I had had a discussion in a room in the Chateau Laurier with a certain lawyer about the possibility of me becoming the organizer of the federal Liberal party. I remembered the meeting but I could not remember the lawyer's name. The meeting had grown out of an idea in the mind of a friend in the Prime Minister's office, Florence Adamson, that I would make a good organizer of the Liberal party. She was always making suggestions about what people might do to get on in the world, and this was one of them. I told her she was crazy, but none the less she set up the meeting. I went along to please her but with no intention of taking the matter seriously. There I met a man whom I had never heard of before; a well-barbered and well-dressed gentleman from Toronto. He said very little, but he was quite handy at asking questions. I was not off-hand or rude, but I also was not interested, and I declared that I knew for a fact that the Prime Minister was very opposed to activating the National Liberal Federation while the war was on. And so I shook hands and left.

'You puzzled him,' Alex said. 'You puzzle everybody. They don't know where you stand. They can't understand what makes you tick.'

'I'm not sure I know myself, but who cares? Why should anyone care?

The only thing I have been interested in is fighting the war. I can't fight in the army, but I can do other things, and I have tried to do other things, apparently without success. Robertson says I am a disaffected red. What the hell does that mean?'

'Just that you don't fit in. Do you want to hear about another occasion when you were discussed? I've heard Arnold Heeney (Clerk of the Privy Council) talk about you. He asked you to interest yourself in post-war administrative organization. Did you interest yourself? No. People cannot understand a guy who doesn't jump at a chance like that. I can understand it, but others can't.'

I suggested to Alex that maybe Robertson *et al.* did not like my interest in Marxism.

'Do you know something?' Alex replied. 'My father got his start from an interest in Marxism. He wasn't a Marxist, but he understood Marxism. Did you ever read his book on socialism? It's a good book. I'll show you something.'

Alex led John and me to his library. It was a truly splendid private library: the books his father and mother had accumulated over forty years and those he had acquired himself. He took down a book, and handed it to me. It was *Socialism: A Critical Analysis* by O.D. Skelton published in Boston in 1911 and it was described as a Hart Schaffner and Marx Prize Essay. Then he took the book back, and shook from the leaves a letter. 'Read that,' he said.

The letter was a single sheet of good-quality paper, written in English, and dated 1915 from an address in Switzerland. The handwriting was in black ink in a kind of scratchy straight up and down script. As far as I can remember the letter read:

Dear Mr. Skelton,
I have read your book on socialism with much interest. It is the best book on socialism by a bourgeois scholar which I have ever read. Congratulations and greetings.
    Yours faithfully,
    V.I. Lenin

When I read the book later I could see why Lenin felt impelled to write to Dr Skelton. After surveying various pre-Marxist ideas about socialism, Skelton wrote: 'The chief contribution of Karl Marx to socialist theory and practice ... was to represent socialism as no longer an individual fantasy, as a sect's Utopia, but as the inevitable next step in the development of human society. He put socialism in the main current of the world's history. He attained a new conception of the forces which had shaped society in the past and that will shape it in the future, a conception which changed the point of view of the analysis of the capitalistic system, conditioned the ideal commonwealth which was to develop out of capitalism and shaped the tactics of the movement ... ' (p. 95).

Skelton, of course, went on to explain why, in his view, socialism could never prevail, at least in democratic capitalist society. Capitalism produced popular abundance not poverty, and he assembled a great array of statistical material which contradicted the Marxist arguments about the impoverishment of wage workers. This was one argument. The other was focused on democratic institutions. In societies where everyone can vote and governments are controlled electorally by the people as a whole, socialist movements and socialist arguments can never command a sufficiency of support to prevail and to implement their ideas. Lenin obviously learned from Skelton, for he never allowed democracy to establish itself.

After this we started to drink whisky. I had never had to keep pace with a drinker like Alex, and I was soon morose and stupid. Alex on the other hand grew merry after lunch. He wanted to sing. I cannot sing a note, and so he turned to John. Could he sing?

'Come on John. You must be better than your old man.'

John could in fact sing, and urged on by Alex he sang a few nursery songs.

'You ought to sing real songs. Not that sissy stuff your old man teaches you.' Whereupon he launched into 'Joe Hill' and a succession of Wobbly classics. John had a great facility for picking up rhymes, and soon he and Alex were singing together about the unions and the blacklegs, John sitting on the head of tiger, part of a tigerskin rug in front of the fireplace, and Alex on a sofa keeping time with a whisky bottle.

The sky was leaden with snow clouds when John and I caught our bus back to Ottawa. I was drunk and gloomy and John was enchanted, both of us, I suppose, much enlightened each in our own way. That evening, I am ashamed to remember, I spoiled the farewell party Irene and Herbert Norman had arranged for us by refusing to play word games and finally going home by myself leaving Maureen and John to get home as best they could. This they did with the assistance of the brother of a Trinity man who had been killed in Spain, Haden Guest. I encountered them in the snow, now sober and appalled at my bad behaviour.

I never saw Alex Skelton again. In the course of the next five years he had a crushing run of bad luck. The man who had been his No. 2 in the research department of the Bank of Canada, Eric Adams was arrested and questioned by the royal commission on espionage, but found not guilty when tried in open court. Whether this was the reason for Alex leaving the Bank of Canada I do not know. He transferred to the Department of Trade and Commerce. Then his house burnt down and his library was destroyed. In 1950 he went to Nigeria on an advisory mission connected with commercial matters. While he was waiting for a plane to return to Ottawa he went sailing by himself in the harbour of Lagos. There alone on the water he died.

It was a strange run of bad luck. I have often wondered whether someone did not fix the roulette wheel.

CHAPTER EIGHT

What Is a Red, and Who Was? Me? Herbert Norman?

So Robertson thought I was a 'disaffected red.' There was nothing very perceptive about one word in this observation. I had never concealed my Marxism, nor did I particularly parade it. As to the adjective disaffected, this was another matter. Robertson would have been hard put to point to any instance of my disaffection. I never once in the depths of my own mind followed the Communist party line to the effect that the war against Hitler's Germany was an imperialist war which should be opposed as a means of bringing down the bourgeoisie. When Hitler attacked the USSR I rejoiced because I thought he had made a fatal mistake. I rejoiced when Churchill announced his determination on behalf of the United Kingdom to ally with the Soviet Union and to fight on to victory. This seemed to me the only intelligent course of action to take in the circumstances. The war in my mind was not 'legitimized' by the participation of the Soviet Union. To me it was a just war because it was a war for the survival, not only of Canada and Britain, but for the survival of the possibility of life on terms other than those proposed and put into practice by the Nazis, the Fascists, and the Spanish regime of General Franco. I believed throughout the war, as I believed before the war, that the defeat of the German Nazis required the participation of the USSR. I was over-optimistic about what victory would mean with the USSR on the winning side, but I was not alone in this. Indeed, I thought that the *Toronto Star*, the most enthusiastic supporter of the Liberal party and of Mackenzie King personally, rather gilded the lily too much, and that life in the USSR and the Soviet leaders were both tougher than the 'Red Star of King Street' led its readers to believe. Robertson's allegation of disaffection was simply untrue.

Calling a person a red was not, in 1944, what it became a few years later. In his diary (7 December 1944) Mackenzie King recorded how he attempted to joke with his chauffeur, Lay, after returning from the House of Commons following the victorious vote on his conscription policy. He said to Lay as they entered Laurier House, 'Well, it looks as if we don't have to leave Laurier House for a while.' Lay only muttered a response and Mackenzie King then recorded, 'Lay is sullen about the vote in support of the Government. He is, of course, for out and out conscription ... Being an Englishman, he has a characteristic attitude the Englishmen of the upper and lower classes have towards Canada. In addition he is increasingly becoming a Red.'

In calling me a red, Robertson was not as unintelligent as this. Unlike the other senior members of the Department of External Affairs, Robertson had at one time entertained a sympathetic understanding of left-wing materialism, and he was, I think, troubled at times by the contradiction between his past and his present views on political questions. He had, however, been so long a bureaucrat that the over-all interest of the civil service department of which he was the head was more important to him than a right judgement on questions of high politics. He was a comparatively young man. He had not been long Under-Secretary of State. Mackenzie King was not an easy man to work with and for. And then there were several persons of Robertson's own age and degree of ability at hand to take his place should he make any serious mistakes. He was, therefore, cautious, and one could see then the foreshadow of the 'middle-power ideology' which developed later. Being a middle-range

179

person makes one important enough to enjoy some profit and prestige but not important enough to have any real responsibility. That is what Robertson wanted and that is what Canada got.

I think he was right in regarding me as unsuitable for the Department of External Affairs he was building. Just as horses have to be broken to do the jobs their masters require of them, so men and women have to be broken to fit into the organization from which they derive their livelihood. I had too long enjoyed the uninhibited freedom of Cambridge University easily to be broken. At the same time there was another factor to be considered. There was only one thing I really cared about as distinct from what I thought about. This was my family. The concern for my family in turn translated into the economic question of earning a living. Now, it may be asked, if you cared so much about your family, why did you not accept the fact that you had to adapt to the circumstances in which you found yourself, to study what was necessary to do to advance your interest and to do it? I saw the dilemma but I wanted to have it both ways. I am sure if I had never experienced the freedom of Cambridge University and had never left Canada I would have adapted well enough. As it was, I had bitten into the apple and the garden was no longer for me.

But what about this matter of being a red in Canada in the 1940s? Objectively, as the Communists say, I had ceased to be a Communist by virtue of the fact that I had not followed the instruction 'to see this guy in Boston.' Nor did I think of seeking out 'a guy in Canada' who could lead me into the party. Save with one exception, which I shall explain, two years passed before I even encountered anyone in Ottawa or in Canada who could conceivably have been a Communist, openly or underground. I never encountered anyone who even vaguely sympathized with the Communists. And this was not suprising. Nobody in Ottawa I ever met took the Communists seriously or thought communism worth discussing.

The government did, however, take the Communists seriously enough to ban the party under the Defence of Canada Regulations. Those Communist party leaders on whom the authorities could lay their hands had been interned. Harry Binder, his brother, and a civil servant in Ottawa named Saunders had been fined $1000.00 and sentenced to two and a half years in jail for organizing the banned party. I never encountered anyone who thought these sentences objectionable or worth discussing or who shared the fear, I was later told about, among party sympathizers.

For my part I felt no fear, and in private conversations with friends like William Paterson I argued without reservation or concealment about Marxism and political and social problems as I understood them. In September 1940 Sammy Levine, who had been a member of the graduate group in Cambridge, was arrested along with two Communist apparatchiks who lived in his house in Toronto. When this happened I had no compunction about coming to his assistance in the way I thought best. I wrote a memorandum for the Principal Secretary saying that I had known Levine well at Cambridge; that he was a scientist of distinction whose work on geophysics had been financed for some years by the Royal Society; and that he was in politics a naive and simple-minded man incapable of doing the government any harm. I added that a Communist official in Cambridge had expressed the view that Levine was so innocent and simple-minded that he should not be a member of the Communist party. I did not, however, tell Turnbull that I was the Communist party official who had expressed this opinion. I was being jesuitical in two senses. I did not tell the whole truth, only the expedient part of the truth, and I had behaved like a seventeenth-century papal official who thought that all men could and should be Catholics but not that all men could or should be members of the Society of Jesus.

Then there was the matter of my books. In July 1940, I received a letter from a firm of forwarding agents in Boston informing me that my books sent from Cambridge, England, had been held up by agents of the FBI and US Customs special service. I immediately wrote to J. Edgar Hoover on the stationery of the Prime Minister's Office informing him as politely as possible that I am a Canadian citizen, that I did not reside in the United States, and that I did not see what could be his concern with my library. A courteous correspondence ensued in which Hoover said he had nothing to do with the matter, but that perhaps I might write to the US Customs. A further courteous correspondence ensued and the books were released. Then they were stopped by the Canadian Customs. More correspondence in which I suggested that they remove the books thought dangerous to the government and let me have the rest. This was agreed.

My books were delivered to me minus thirty or so books on the USSR and Marxism. On the other hand, my small collection of books by Nazis, nearly all purchased in and bearing the label of the main Nazi book shop in Berlin, were released. These included a pamphlet *Das Programm* by Godfried Feder decorated with a large swastika, Alfred Rosenberg's *Der Mythus des XX Jahrhunderts*, Haushofer's *Weltpolitik von Heute*, Joseph

181

Goebbels' *Kampf am Berlin* and *Signal der neuen Zeit* and, of course, *Mein Kampf* in English by Adolf himself.

When it had become an established fact that the USSR was the ally of Canada I wrote to the Customs asking whether my books still in their possession could now be released. They were released. Only one was missing: J.S. Mill *On Liberty*. I supposed they had lost it, but I hoped that some customs officer had stolen it and read it. It might have got him into trouble if he had taken it seriously.

Political intelligence in the Canadian government was characterized by boneheaded stupidity. I was not alone in this opinion. A few weeks after I entered the Prime Minister's Office, an RCMP constable came to my room bearing a large brown envelope marked SECRET. He saluted and asked me to sign a receipt. This I did. With some awe I carried the envelope to Pickersgill and asked him what I did with this. Jack gave one of his loud guffaws, waved his hand with a flourish and said, 'That's *The Perils of Pauline*. Throw it in the file, but read it if you want a laugh.'

I went back to my room and opened the envelope. Inside was another envelope together with a receipt returnable at once to the RCMP attesting to the fact that I was about to open the second envelope. Inside this envelope I found a mimeographed pamphlet bound in a green cover bearing the arms of the RCMP. About 80 per cent of the items were extracts from Canadian newspapers concerning the movements and utterances of Communists, supposed Communists, and various trade union officials. Some of the items I had already seen among the daily circulation of the Prime Minister's clipping service. There were a few items on various priests and pacifists, and nothing at all about splinter groups in Quebec opposed to Canada's entry into the war. It was something of a mystery to me how the RCMP ever found the home-grown Führer, Adrien Arcand, let alone arrested him. After reading this intelligence bulletin a few times I began to follow Pickersgill's advice. I simply 'threw it in the file.' It never surprised me that a large Soviet espionage organization was established in Ottawa without the knowledge of the RCMP and that its discovery owed nothing to Canadian 'intelligence experts' but was the work of the Russian opposition to the Soviet regime.

And yet one cannot be too harsh about the intelligence work of the RCMP. The little evidence I saw suggested that their intelligence officers were simply 'dumb cops,' ill-educated and of limited knowledge and mental capacity. But even if they had all been honours graduates of the University of Toronto, this would not necessarily have enabled them to understand the nature of the Soviet regime as an indispensable means of knowing what to look for and to understand the *modus operandi* of the Soviet government. They would very likely have made the same mistake which I and thousands of European Marxists had made, and were making, in supposing that the Soviet regime was something new and 'progressive,' an agency of human liberation and not the old Tsarist bureaucracy equipped with a bemusing new rhetoric, strengthened by more comprehensive techniques of political control, and veiled in much more impenetrable secrecy than the Tsarist regime had ever devised. The RCMP were taught to see Communists at work wherever men and women assembled to talk about civil rights, trade union problems, poverty, and peace. This they could grasp but they no more understood the Stalinist regime than any but a very small band of men and women who had direct experience of its tyranny. Those who had first-hand experience of building the White Sea canal and the OGPU always had a 'credibility problem.' Ordinary people found it hard to believe what they had to say, and this difficulty was mightily reinforced by the thought that Uncle Joe with his friendly tobacco pipe was a necessary ally in the fight against the Nazis.

My first personal acquaintance with the Soviet regime dates from the autumn of 1943. When the embassy of the USSR was established in Ottawa and a 'diplomatic list' was made available giving the names and rank of the embassy staff, a few of us in the Department of External Affairs thought we ought to make ourselves acquainted with the newcomers by entertainment somewhat more personal and intimate than formal receptions and occasions of that sort. I selected one name of a man from the list whose rank was, like my own, at the bottom of the heap; he had a Georgian name which might have been suitable for the marketing of perfume in the pages of the *New Yorker*. I wrote to him at the embassy inviting him and his wife to dinner. Some weeks passed without any response. Then one day there was a call for me, not at my home, from which I had written to the embassy, but at my office in the East Block. It was from the Soviet embassy enquiring whether I was the person who had written to Mr Fragrance. I said yes, and it was then explained that Mr Fragrance had not in fact come to Canada, and perhaps I might call at the embassy some time to introduce myself to Mr Koudrieatsev. I replied that I would, of course, do this, and a time was fixed which would enable me to drop into the embassy on my way back to the office after lunch.

The Soviet embassy was established in what had been the mansion of

183

an Ottawa valley lumber tycoon, a house larger and more luxurious than Laurier House where the Prime Minister of Canada lived, but nothing like the palace in Moscow which a Russian lumber king would have been obliged by revolution to vacate. When I had identified myself I was taken upstairs to the office of the counsellor of embassy, Sergei Koudrieatsev.

Koudrieatsev was a large fat man of the proportions of Orson Welles. He had a sallow, Slavic face and dull blond hair. He was carefully dressed, but in a way which seemed old-fashioned and at the same time a little overdone: the lapels on his jacket too wide, the buttons too numerous, and the finish of the cloth a little too shiny. He spoke good English with a slight accent.

We exchanged compliments and I made some admiring comments about the Red army and so on. Koudrieatsev repeated what I had been already told over the telephone, and then added that, of course, other members of the embassy would be happy to become acquainted with members of the Department of External Affairs. I felt then obliged to invite someone else to dinner, and inquired whether there was anyone else he could suggest who was of a similar status to myself. He replied that there was a man whom I might like to invite, Mr Pavlov, who unfortunately was at that time not in Ottawa. I said that I would keep Mr Pavlov's name in mind and, perhaps, there might be a time when my wife and I would be able to entertain the Pavlovs. That ended the interview.

During the conversation with Koudrieatsev there was a small episode which intrigued me. Koudrieatsev appeared to have a cold, and at one point in our conversation he searched in his pockets and found he had no handkerchief. He said something in Russian on the telephone, and a few minutes later a large, handsome man in a dark suit entered bearing a silver tray on which reposed a snowy white handkerchief. Koudrieatsev took the handkerchief without looking at the man or saying a word, shook the handkerchief open and blew his nose. The man bowed and backed away to the door.

An odd kind of comradely solidarity, I thought. I could not conceive of any one bringing our Under-Secretary of State a handkerchief on a silver tray. And this man was *only* a counsellor of embassy! There flashed through my mind an incident in the East Block when I was one of Mr King's secretaries. One of our messengers was a young man, Charlie, who wore 'snappy' suits, plastered his hair down with hair cream, and in his spare time played the drums in a jazz band. One day the War

Committee of the Cabinet was meeting in the prime minister's room in the East Block, and at one point the committee wanted the views of the Chief of the General Staff. He was summoned, and he appeared in the outer office all polish and red tabs and service ribbons. Charlie opened the red baize door of Mr King's room, pushed open the inner door, leaned around the door post and bellowed, 'Mr King, your man's here!'

But I rationalized the incident of the silver tray. The Soviet diplomats in bourgeois countries wanted to be like their hosts. They were too innocent and everything was too strange and so they overdid what they conceived to be bourgeois manners.

We invited the Pavlovs to dinner. Again I had to rationalize about their behaviour. Mrs Pavlov was dressed in a long gown adorned with sequins and fringes. Maureen and our other lady guest wore simple knee-length dresses. Pavlov, a stocky man with a smooth sallow Slavic face, was dressed in a suit which aimed at formality, but was too shiny and too light in colour. Horror of horrors! He wore yellowish brown shoes with a blue suit. But my powers of rationalization were equal even to this dreadful breach of the canons of male taste as they then existed at the confluence of the Ottawa and Rideau rivers.

My first social contact with a Soviet citizen turned out to be a dull experience. During the crisis in the Soviet embassy in September 1945 when the cipher clerk, Igor Gouzenko, defected with a selection of Soviet intelligence files, Pavlov showed himself to be a sharp, quick-witted, and determined operator, and a man ready to use a gun if he had to. But he was intellectually a very dull man. Here I was in all my innocence expecting to encounter a knowledgeable Marxist from the homeland of socialism, a man able to speak from experience of the great insights of Marx, Engels, Lenin, and Stalin applied in a real society. Pavlov worshipped Marx, no doubt, but he did not know anything about Marxism. It was not so much that he refused to talk about Marx and Lenin. He just knew nothing about them except that they were 'right,' great expositors of self-evident truths which no one could discuss. At that time I was particularly interested to know something about the problems of industrial growth in a classless society. According to Pavlov there were no problems. Maybe there were no problems, but perhaps he could tell us something about the way in which science and technology had a much more direct and beneficial effect in industrial development than it did in capitalist economies. This was the case according to the great English scientist, J.D. Bernal. How did this come about?

185

Pavlov did not know, but of course it was true. I offered to lend him J.D. Bernal's book *The Social Function of Science*. This would interest him a great deal. Pavlov seemed doubtful about learning anything from a book, particularly a book written in a capitalist country. However, he agreed to borrow the book from me.

After this the conversation ran steadily downhill until we were talking in order to ward off silence. The difficulty was that Pavlov was not really interested in anything he saw or we did in Canada. He seemed curious about nothing and he could only assert that this or that was better in the USSR. Finally we got around to discussing flowers. Maureen had a book of colour photos of flowers and she was asking whether this one or that one flourished in the USSR. She came to a photo of a lily of the valley and she said, 'Oh! I do think that is the most beautiful name!' Pavlov exchanged some words in Russian with his wife. Then he said, 'Not as beautiful as the name in Russian.' Then he repeated the Russian name several times in order, I supposed, that we could savour the aesthetic superiority of the word.

Dinner with the Pavlovs was a disappointment. There had been no interchange between them and the Canadians around the dinner table. In his wife's case this was understandable because her knowledge of English was not good. Ever willing to rationalize and make allowances I decided that, although Pavlov spoke reasonably good English, he perhaps did not understand it as easily as he spoke it; that he was like a deaf person who does not understand conversation as quickly as persons with normal hearing and who, to keep up appearances, talks about what he knows and not about what others are saying.

Many months passed, and the Pavlovs and the Soviet embassy passed out of my consciousness. Then in December 1944 about ten days before our departure from Ottawa for ever there came an invitation to dinner with the Pavlovs. Maureen was in an advanced state of pregancy, there was much ice and snow underfoot, she was tired, and I think she had little enthusiasm for a further discussion of flowers, and so she asked to be excused. I went alone.

Pavlov returned Bernal's book. He showed no evidence of having read it, and I did not wish to embarrass him with further talk. He did, however, ask me what I was doing in External Affairs. I told him I had resigned. The idea of resigning from the government service seemed to puzzle him, almost to shock him. I could not at the time understand this. I imagined that he would approve an action like resigning from a bourgeois govern-

186

ment. Why had I resigned? Because the Under-Secretary thinks I am a red like you. This puzzled him. Could I explain? I told him that I disagreed with the policies of the Canadian government, the British government and the US government about national independence for India. As far as I knew the only government which wanted independence for India *now* was the Chinese government and I hoped the Soviet government did, too. Pavlov said the policy of the Soviet government was well known. The Soviet government wanted a firm alliance to beat the Germans, and beyond that he could not discuss the matter. We smoked a number of black Russian cigarettes, and finally I said I thought I ought to get home to be with my wife. Before leaving I gave him the address of Maureen's parents with whom we would be living in Winnipeg. If he was ever in Winnipeg we would be happy to see him ...

Blow me, if three weeks or so later did I not have a telephone call from the Royal Alexandra Hotel in Winnipeg. Pavlov was in town, and he would like to see me. That evening there was a very heavy snow storm in Winnipeg, but he came to Maureen's parents' house in a taxi. Maureen's father was an Anglo-Irish country gentleman, and he really did like talking about flowers, and hunting. This seemed to please Pavlov, and they spent a happy evening around the Christmas tree. When the time came for him to go there were no taxis willing to come out to the edge of Winnipeg. But the trams were still running, and so I accompanied him to the tram stop observing that I guessed the snow in Winnipeg was as good as anything in Moscow.

Eighteen months later (in the summer of 1946) I was on the sand at Victoria Beach on Lake Winnipeg. There I encountered a colleague in United College, the Rev. Professor David Owen. After a bit of chat he said, 'How do you feel about being mentioned in the spy scandal?'

I was flabbergasted. I had followed the exploits of Pavlov in the press. I had met two of the people taken into custody by the royal commission, Kathleen Wilshire and Fred Poland, but the whole episode was as much a surprise to me as it was to any Canadian. Immediately I wrote to friends in Ottawa for information. There was a dead silence. People really were frightened, it seemed. I could get no facts.

Finally, however, I did. Earlier in 1946 I had been endeavouring to organize a co-operatively owned daily newspaper, the *Winnipeg Citizen*. I had in mind as an organizer of the enterprise Frank Park whom I had met in the autumn of 1944 when he was an executive in the Canadian Information Service. In February 1946, a few days before the spy scandal broke, I had written to Park asking him whether he would be interested in the project which I described to him. He replied that he was leaving the Information Service and had been appointed national director of the Canadian-Soviet Friendship Council. He seemed to me a man with the guts and the understanding to supply me with the information I was now looking for.

Park was a lawyer by profession and a handsome, self-confident man of a family of United Empire Loyalists in New Brunswick. Like another famous Canadian communist, Stanley Ryerson, he had been educated at Upper Canada College. In short Frank Park was more like the men I had known in Cambridge than he was like any Canadian I had encountered, and certainly unlike the frightened little rabbits in Ottawa to whom I had unavailingly written.

Park dug around in the trial records in Ottawa and Montreal and he examined the record of evidence taken by the royal commission but which was not printed in the *Report* of the commission published in June 1946. He examined the pages taken from the notebook of the head of the Soviet spy network, Col. Zabotin. One of these pages devoted to Dr Alan Nunn May, the Cambridge scientist sentenced to ten years for espionage, is in part reprinted in the *Report* of the commission on page 48. Item two, in a list of points about Nunn May, read: '2. Characteristic of the work of the laboratories and of the people. Friend of Henry —.' Park found, however, that in the page offered in evidence in one of the trials in Montreal, that the 'Henry —' in the printed report was Henry Ferns and that there was a further item numbered 88 which read, 'To think about develop [sic] Henry F.'

Further Park discovered in a transcript of evidence (p. 285) taken from Gouzenko the following:

By Mr William (counsel for the Commission)
Q. On the front there, there is a reference to Henry Ferns. Does this mean anything to you?
A. (Gouzenko) Yes, I know him.
Q. You know him?
A. I know what the subject is that is being spoken of. Moscow sent a telegram to the effect that in the research laboratory in Montreal there is a friend of Allan Nunn May, one Henry Ferns, and that contact should be made through Allan Nunn May.'

I let the matter rest. Obviously I was not in a laboratory in Montreal.

188

But Henry Ferns is not a very common name. It is unlikely there are two Henry Ferns. All I know is this: I never knew Alan Nunn May, and I have never been able to discover any friend in Cambridge who knew him. Nunn May had left Cambridge before I arrived there and before many of my friends had arrived there. Victor Kernan who was in Cambridge from 1931 to 1938 had never heard of Nunn May until he saw his name in the newspapers.

One can only speculate about why Moscow supposed that Alan Nunn May could contact Henry Ferns. Assuming that the intelligence bureaucracy in Moscow is no more intelligent and efficient than bureaucracies of which we have direct experience, what could be more natural for them than to make a number of mistakes and false hypotheses? My guess is that someone in the Communist party headquarters in London passed my name back to Moscow as a likely prospect. Nunn May had been at Cambridge. Henry Ferns had been at Cambridge. *Ergo*, they must be friends or would soon become friends if they were brought together. Inasmuch as my immediate superior in the Communist party had been Ben Bradley it may very well be the case that Bradley did not know that I was an historian and not a natural scientist. He was not a curious or well-informed man, and to him students were students and historians and chemists were all one as far as he was concerned. This is as likely an explanation as any why Gouzenko and his bosses in Moscow thought Henry Ferns could be found in a laboratory in Montreal. And then, of course, they did not know Henry Ferns.

In his history of the Communist party in Canada, Ivan Avakumovic has brought together much evidence of the development in the 1930s of a circle of intellectuals, mainly in Toronto and Montreal, who acquired an understanding of Marxism and were attracted to the Communist party. The disclosures by Igor Gouzenko indicated likewise that there were in Ottawa during the war years a number of people in the public service, mostly of my own generation, who shared these enthusiasms and some of whom the intelligence agents of the Soviet government had been able to influence. Intellectually at that time I could have been classified as part of this political tendency. On the other hand I was for much of my time in Ottawa an isolated individual who had no contact with these people. It was only during my last six months in Ottawa that I began to meet some of them.

This was very much a bit-by-bit process. They never sought me out, nor I them. The process was initiated by Florence Adamson, the stenographer/secretary of L.W. Brockington and then of E.K. Brown and others in the Prime Minister's office. Florence Adamson had an avid interest in politics, but not in politics as I understood the term. She had no interest in ideologies or principles of any description. Hers was an interest in people and their relations with one another: who had done what for whom; who hated whom; who was on the way up and who on the way down. She was not just interested in gossip. She had an active interest in bringing people together, of seeing what she could promote. She never seemed to have any ambition of her own, and she seemed only mildly concerned in promoting the interest of her husband, a journalist, who was before the war's end an executive assistant to a member of the cabinet. I think Florence just liked being 'in the know' and enjoyed the sense of power which came from befriending and advising a variety of people.

Some of Brockington's liking for me seems to have rubbed off on Florence for she entertained an exaggerated opinion of my merits and capacities. She seemed to think I had some high destiny, and she was disappointed that I did not seem sufficiently interested in 'getting ahead.' She once declared that I ought to spend less time with my wife and son and more time in the Chateau cafeteria and beverage room meeting people and making myself known.

Some of her interest had been genuinely helpful. One day I told her about a clever surgeon in Toronto, one of two in North America, who was having some success with an operation called fenestration designed to remedy the otiosclerosis which impaired my hearing.

'Why don't you go and see this man?' she asked.

I said I had no money: not enough to pay a return train fare to Toronto and put up in a hotel there.

'I'll do something,' said Florence. 'You won't have to spend any money.'

A few days later she reported that she had discovered the existence of a daily air service between Ottawa and Toronto run by the RCAF for officers, scientists, and business men in a hurry. She had spoken to Turnbull, and he would see that I was transported from Ottawa to Toronto and back in a day whenever there was a vacant seat in the plane. Within forty-eight hours an RCAF driver called for me at 6.30 am. I boarded an amphibian plane at Uplands Airport. The plane landed in Toronto Harbour. A ten-minute taxi ride brought me to the office of Dr J.A. Sullivan, and I was home in Ottawa for dinner.

Some months before this in the summer of 1942 Florence had also suggested to me that there was a friend of hers whom I ought to meet. 'She's Janet Skelton. She's a red hot socialist like you.'

And so a meeting was arranged. (Janet was the second wife of Alex Skelton, the research director of the Bank of Canada.) She may have been a red-hot socialist, but I did not find her to be a driving political force of any kind. She was a pretty, warm-hearted, and unpretentious Scottish girl who had she lived in Fife would have voted for Willie Gallacher, but equally had she lived in Glasgow for Jimmy Maxton or Jock MacGovern. She might even have voted for Hector McNeil. In short, she was a lowland Scottish radical, and no Communist party liner. She had no political connexions of any kind so far as I ever discovered. She lived a very private life with her husband on their farm on the banks of the Ottawa River and never appeared much in Ottawa.

Janet Skelton and Florence Adamson did, however, introduce me to one of their friends, Bessie Touzel. Bessie came out of the Marxist ferment in the University of Toronto. She is one of the great Canadian women of the twentieth century. There was no political purpose in my introduction to her. Bessie Touzel had been commissioned by the federal government to undertake a study of manpower: who did what, where they could be found, and what needed to be done to make manpower and womanpower more effective in the productive life of the nation. Bessie was naturally concerned that some use be made of her study, and to this end she was advised that I might be the means of ensuring that the Prime Minister heard the essence of what she had discovered.

This was not the first time people interested in contributing ideas and understanding had approached me for help in making their proposals known to the government. In 1940-41 I spent a considerable amount of time on behalf of some engineers, introduced to me by a totally unpolitical Cambridge friend, who were enthusiastic about the use of resin-bonded plywood as a structural material for aircraft.

Bessie's study impressed me and I set to work boiling down her work and extracting the essentials so that the Prime Minister could digest them in ten minutes. Of course, I never learned whether he ever looked at my memorandum, but eventually 'policy outputs' began to suggest that some-one somewhere had taken Bessie's work seriously. Inasmuch as she had brought her work to the attention of others beside myself, there is no reason to suppose that I had served her any better than they.

None the less Bessie was kind enough to visit me in St Michael's

Hospital in Toronto after J.A. Sullivan had reorganized one of my ears. We became friends and she invited me to a party in January 1943. There I met some of the left intelligentsia of Toronto. It was a novel experience to encounter people who did not shudder when one made a remark implying that there actually are classes in Canada, or who unflinchingly encountered the thought that national independence in the British Commonwealth and Empire was not just for whites or who found nothing exceptional in the notion that we were fighting Nazism not Germans.

Bessie Touzel never believed that an acquaintance with and respect for communists was a dirty little secret that one had to conceal in order to do positive and creative work in society. She laughingly told how she was asleep in Joe Salsberg's pyjamas when the RCMP raided his home in Toronto to intern him under the Defence of Canada Regulations. Joe had wisely gone to Cuba and Bessie was keeping Joe's wife company. She told the Mounties they could have Joe's pyjamas if they wanted.

I cannot recall any occasion when Bessie Touzel and I discussed ideological questions or the general principles and tendencies of Marxist thought. We just seemed to understand each other. What I liked, and always have liked about Bessie, is the practical and creative character of her mind which is for ever critically alert to what is wrong now and can be put right in six months or six years. This raises a point for speculation. How much can be attributed to Marxism in energizing the mind and setting goals of social and political action of people like Bessie Touzel? The connection may be there, but it is not obvious. Bessie, for example, fought the Roman Catholic Church and Church-dependant politicians and lawyers over the right of women to obtain information about and the means of practising birth control. Then there were family allowances. A great many people claimed after the event that they invented the policy of federal family allowances. If there was any first begetter of this policy it was Bessie Touzel, and it was a major factor in Mackenzie King's electoral victory in 1945. But Bessie was no more a Mackenzie King Liberal than I was. We just voted for him.

Bessie Touzel was a pioneer of social work in Canada when this term meant a fight to dispel ignorance, and to create programs of social action adequately financed by public funds and addressed to helping and developing people for whom the task of self-support was too great. She was concerned with people in need, and not with the creation of a 'caring profession' concerned with expanding its clientele and *pari passu* with opportunities for its practitioners. After her retirement from the directorship of the Canadian Council of Social Agencies Bessie was invited to advise the Tanzanian government on the development of social agencies. Far from recommending agencies for child care modelled on the Canadian pattern, Bessie told the Tanzanians that they already possessed a better child care agency than any in North America – the extended family. This they should preserve and develop.

If there is any conclusion to be drawn from knowing Bessie Touzel and from considering her career it is this: the Marxist intellectual ferment of the 1930s in Canada produced people who were radical but not mindlessly radical. If one judges this ferment exclusively in terms of those who became apparatchiks of the Communist party, one can come to one kind of conclusion; if one judges the outcome in terms of those who did not, one comes to another and a more positive conclusion.

As a result of meeting some of the left intelligentsia in Toronto I began to meet similar people in Ottawa. I added to the number of my acquaintance, but not all to my number of friends. Late in the summer of 1944 Frank Park and Brough Macpherson of the Information Service discussed with me the desirability of establishing a society devoted to the study of political issues likely to emerge during the election which was bound to be held within a year. It is a measure of my frivolity and cynicism at that time that I proposed that the society be named the Parliamentary Issues Study Society. This was agreed before it was recognized that the name yielded a satirical acronym. My home was chosen as the venue for the first meeting of the society. Thirty or so people turned up. The man who dominated the proceedings on account of his capacity for relentless talk was dressed in the uniform of an RCAF squadron leader, Fred Poland. When, sixteen months later he was taken into custody by the Royal Commission on Soviet Espionage, he absolutely refused to say anything with the result that, although the commissioners alleged much about Poland, they could prove nothing.

I never learned what happened to PISS. My attention was soon taken up with the offer of employment as a political warrior in India with the consequences I have already described. In fact I had become so habituated to political isolation that I had ceased to have, if I had ever had, a disposition to join organizations or to act collectively. I had already become an individualist, not ideologically, but operationally.

The anonymity of the civil service irked me, and I longed to speak out in an endeavour to influence opinion. An opportunity to do so presented

193

itself early in 1942. There used to come to the Prime Minister's Office a journal, *Free World*. It was published in New York. Beautifully but soberly produced, *Free World* had a very European flavour. The editor was a man of whom I had never heard, Louis Dolivet. The editorial board included several little-known French savants. The tone of the journal was drily intellectual, and the general line seemed to be sympathetic to nationalism of a non-fascist sort. It was Gaullist in its stance but not stridently so. As far as I could judge *Free World* owed nothing to Marxist inspiration, and it was obviously respectable in its presentation of its material. Ah, I thought, this is a journal in which something constructive could be said on behalf of Indian independence.

I put together an article, and despatched it to Louis Dolivet, explaining that as a civil servant I would be obliged to use a pseudonym. He replied enthusiastically and agreed to publish the article, dropping my surname.

The case for Indian independence by Henry Stanley duly appeared. This was the first time I had blossomed into print, and I was tremendously excited and satisfied with myself. At that time I shared an office in the East Block with Jules Léger. The copy of *Free World* containing the article by Henry Stanley was put in circulation and it came to Léger's in-tray. He leafed over the journal, and then he began to read it. After a time, he said: 'There's an article here on India that should interest you.'

Pride of authorship was too much for me, and I said, 'I wrote it.'

'You didn't!'

'Yes, I did. Here's a carbon of the original,' I said producing it from a drawer. Jules liked the article so much that he translated an edited version into French and had it published in *La Revue Dominicaine*. A pseudonym like Henry Stanley did not seem appropriate for a French journal, and so another was chosen, Jean Pierre Henry. This had an amusing consequence. It was reported to Léger that some readers thought the author was Henry-Haye, the Vichy ambassador to the United States!

My second excursion into journalism took place in 1944. My work in External Affairs being boring and inconsequential and being poor, I decided to look around once more for alternative employment. To this end I wrote to Charles Bowman, the editor of the *Ottawa Citizen*, asking whether he had a place on his paper for an editorial writer. He invited me to visit him. He explained that he needed help, but that some of his staff would want their jobs back when they returned from the war. He made me a proposition. Why not write for the *Citizen* on a piece-work basis? I could have a free hand to write about anything I liked, and he would have a free hand to print anything he liked. He would pay me at least $10.00 a piece for anything he printed. He asked me never to call his office because his telephone was tapped.

'Just put your stuff through the slot in the mail box marked for me.'

Between April and the end of September 1944 I wrote forty-five pieces for the *Citizen*. Everything I wrote was printed, and I was paid approximately $500.00 for my work.

The second piece I wrote nearly got me into trouble. In the course of my duties in the Latin American and Far Eastern division, there came to my desk a despatch from the Canadian embassy in Chungking, telling a shocking tale of how armaments given by Canada to China and transported at great expense across the Hindu Kush were being sold to the Japanese by Chinese warlords.

I wrote a piece on China drawing attention to the fact that China seemed to be fighting the Japanese only in Burma and in Changteh. Elsewhere the Chinese seemed to be fighting one another. Furthermore the Chinese government had allowed a vast inflation to develop and that this was the means by which the US government was being milched of millions, perhaps billions, of dollars. I then concluded by drawing attention to Canada's provision of supplies and armaments to China. Are these being used to fight the Japanese? This is something about which the Canadian House of Commons ought to seek reassurance.

Of course, everyone in External Affairs concerned with China was shocked by the despatch from Chungking. But enquiry of the kind the *Citizen* was demanding was the last thing the department wanted. Hume Wrong, the assistant secretary, was on the warpath. Was there a leak? The man on the Chinese desk hinted to me that he thought I was the source. I told him to go to hell, and the matter of the Canadian artillery batteries sold to the Japanese died a natural death. Nobody cared enough. Efficiently fighting the war was the last thing that interested the opposition in the Canadian House of Commons at that time. They could talk of nothing but conscription as a means of beating Mackenzie King.

After this episode I avoided writing about matters of which I had knowledge by reason of my work in External Affairs. The best articles I wrote were, in my view, three longish pieces on Mackenzie King published at the time when he was celebrating his twenty-fifth year as leader of the Liberal party. Re-reading them after almost forty years I think they are the most perceptive and fairest short studies of Mackenzie King as a politician that have ever been written.

195

Mackenzie King's response to these articles revealed in his diary is amusing. He did not, of course, know who wrote them. They were attributed laconically to a young Canadian and described as a preface to the volumes which could be written about the Prime Minister. The first article, published on 2 August 1944, was concerned with Mackenzie King as a social reformer. He was sitting up in bed when he read it. He liked it, but he seems to have missed the mild sarcasm in two of the last sentences of the article: 'Given his outlook and character there is good reason to believe that Mackenzie King will survive another fifteen years of active political life. He may, like Clemenceau, accomplish more after his seventieth year than he ever did before.'

Instead, the Prime Minister was astonished and somewhat dismayed by the prospect of fifteen more years on the treadmill. No, he couldn't do it. But maybe, if he were asked. Yes, if he were asked. Then with an outburst about his staff, he declared he could only do it if he had a thoroughly reorganized staff which would enable him to be a Prime Minister instead of a maid of all work. The next day he recorded how he was tempting Charlie Bishop, the Canadian Press' most thorough political reporter, with the prospect of the clerkship of the House of Commons. How silly I was to keep *my* light under a bushel! Who knows? Maybe I could have become Canada's youngest senator or the first Canadian ambassador to Paraguay. What glory had I denied myself?

The only person in Ottawa apart from Maureen and the editor of the *Citizen* who knew of my secret career as a journalist was Herbert Norman. During 1943 he had become my closest friend in Ottawa, and he remained so until my departure at the end of 1944.

Who nowadays remembers Herbert Norman and how and for what? As one of the architects of the peace treaty which ended the war with Japan? As a great scholar of Japanese history? As a successful Canadian diplomat? As a Soviet spy?

This last allegation was made in 1968 by an American, William Rusher, sometime counsel of the United States Senate's committee of investigation into security in a book entitled *Special Counsel* (pp. 231 and 234). It was made again in 1981 by an Englishman, Chapman Pincher in *Their Trade Is Treachery* (p. 139).

In 1956-57 Herbert Norman was the Canadian ambassador to Egypt. He played a most important role in negotiating with General Nasser Canadian participation in the United Nations peacekeeping force on the

196

Suez Canal following the failure of the Anglo-French-Israeli assault on Egypt. Simultaneously it was alleged in an investigating committee of the United States Senate that he was a Communist. In April 1957, he killed himself by jumping from a tall building in Cairo.

In a sense I knew Herbert Norman before I ever met him. Although he had gone down from Trinity College, Cambridge, in 1935, a year before my arrival, he was remembered with much affection and respect, and both of us, being Canadians and Marxists, were somehow bracketed in a few minds as nearly similar people. More than one person has said to me, 'You remember when you and Herbert Norman were in Cambridge ...' But we were not.

In the summer of 1937 I was introduced at a distance to Herbert Norman by the visit to Cambridge of a Japanese professor of economics named Shibata and his wife. Shibata came to Cambridge with an introduction to Victor Kiernan from Herbert Norman. I was drawn into the entertainment of the Shibatas and from this into a connection which has more than anecdotal interest. Shibata was examining the theoretical foundations of the American New Deal, and, economic theory being what it then was, I was able to engage in discussion with Shibata, which he, at least, seemed to think profitable. This led on to him showing me an article he was writing in English and enlisting my help with the language and the formulation of some of his ideas. What I found surprising in Shibata was his easy acceptance and familiarity with Marxist economic concepts and the absence in him of contempt for them, so present in English, American, and Canadian economists, excepting, of course, men like Maurice Dobb, Piero Sraffa, and Paul Sweezey. Indeed, he introduced me to Japanese learned journals in English such as the *Kyoto Journal of Economics* in which Marxist concepts were commonplace, expressed in the ordinary language of discourse, unconnected with political programs, and cohabiting, as it were, with articles devoid of any taint of Marxism. The Japanese 'fascist imperialists' were obviously not as intellectually narrow-minded as I had been led to believe. Indeed, and at least in their intellectual discussion, they did not seem to be as narrow-minded as the Americans and Europeans.

A few weeks after the visit of the Shibatas to Cambridge, Victor Kiernan and I were in London working at the British Museum. We received an invitation to dinner from the Shibatas in their place of residence in Hampstead. On the day appointed we had been working from the opening of the Reading Room until about 4.30 pm, having shared a sixpenny bar of chocolate as our lunch. Hungry and full of expectation of a novelty in the shape of a Japanese meal we set out for Hampstead. When we arrived at the address given us we found Madame Shibata laden with groceries letting herself in to her residence with a key. Her husband came to the door and explained that his wife was about to prepare dinner. Was not Karl Marx buried in a cemetery near by? Could not we visit the grave of this famous man while his wife got on with dinner?

Victor and I had to admit that Karl Marx was indeed buried in Highgate Cemetery – about two miles away across Hampstead Heath. And so we agreed with Professor Shibata's proposal, stoically refraining from disclosing our lack of nourishment. There is nothing like a walk across Hampstead Heath on a hot evening to improve the appetite especially when one is already craving for food.

Finally after two hours we returned to the Shibata's residence. It seemed to be an official Japanese guest house of some kind. We were ushered into a dining room, scrupulously clean, painted in a uniform simple light colour and adorned with only one ornament, a plum-coloured plaque of the imperial chrysanthemum. In the centre of the room was a table of an austere Japanese design but of conventional European height around which were four chairs of a matching simplicity. In the centre of the table was a gas ring and over the gas ring was a heavy iron vessel, perhaps four inches deep in which bubbled a pallid watery stew a prominent ingredient of which was a vegetable resembling cabbage. At each place was a bowl containing a raw egg, another empty bowl, and a pair of chopsticks. There was a large bowl of rice with a porcelain spoon on the table.

I looked apprehensively at the chopsticks. Obviously I could not eat with my hands as Indians did. Was I to perish of starvation in the sight of food?

Madame Shibata explained that this was the student's dish. With our chopsticks we were to extract fragments from the bubbling cauldron, dip them in the egg, and either pop them into our mouths or mix them with our rice. There was a further rule. Unlike the greedy Chinese, the Japanese never handled their rice bowls or picked them up the better to shovel food into their mouths.

Hunger is a good educator. I quickly acquired the art of eating with chopsticks. When the cauldron was nearly empty Madame Shibata broke several eggs into the remaining liquid. A kind of omelette was formed, and with our chopsticks we demolished the remainder of the student's meal.

As a sequel Victor and I pooled our resources to entertain the Shibatas to dinner. We met them at their home in Hampstead. Professor Shibata was clad in an ordinary western suit, but Mrs Shibata was magnificently attired in an obi, silk slippers, her hair done with ivory pins, and so on. On the tube train she commanded great attention. Victor and I had reserved a table at a Chinese restaurant in Wardour Street. When we entered there was some hesitation on the part of the head waiter, a brief discussion in Chinese, and we were conducted to our table. We were politely served, and politely bade goodnight. But when I passed their restaurant a day or two later there was a notice on the door: 'No Japanese served in this establishment.'

Subsequently Shibata became an economic adviser to the imperial general staff. Apparently he regarded the Japanese army as a great instrument of revolution, and he was one of the authors of the Japanese Co-prosperity Sphere. As such he was purged by the victorious allies. But he understood what he was doing. Once the war against the United States and the British was joined, the Japanese were able to mobilize millions against white imperialism, and they were able safely to stimulate nationalism among communities not large enough or strong enough to offer them any serious political opposition in the forseeable future. Shibata had just the right kind of understanding to help formulate such a policy. On the other side of the world I thought I had the answer to Japanese policy, but the provincial dimwits in Ottawa, Washington, and London with their contempt for anyone who did not wear their mental blinkers were incapable of a creative political initiative. Einstein once remarked that politics is a much more difficult subject than physics. The Americans and the British leadership, incapable of constructive political thought, were obliged to rely on physics for victory. This generated in the American and British communites a disabling sense of guilt and in the rest of the world moral revulsion. Now that physics is not enough, the Americans and their allies are losing all along the line, and this does not surprise me. They were then and remain unprincipled, uncreative, political numbskulls.

But to Herbert Norman. Not Herb or Bert! Herbert. I do not remember him being called nor did I ever call him anything but Herbert, a dignified English name appropriate to the character of the man.

His full name was Egerton Herbert Norman. Egerton called to mind and was intended by his parents to remember Egerton Ryerson, the Methodist divine who fought for and won religious equality and firmly established public education for all in Upper Canada. Herbert's father was for many years a missionary of the United Church of Canada in Japan. Herbert was born there, and he was schooled in the Canadian Academy in Kobe, an institution maintained by the United Church.

In order to understand, if it is possible to do so, a political tragedy of a kind unparalleled in Canadian history, one must always bear in mind the religious and moral circumstances of Herbert Norman's origins. He once remarked to me, speaking of his family, that, unlike his elder brother, he had left religion behind. I supposed that I had too, and this was something we shared. But for all that, Herbert was a natural protestant, individualist. Some seeking to praise his learning have reported him as quoting Baudelaire. I never heard him quote Baudelaire, but I did hear him quote Milton's sonnet to the Lord General Cromwell, and I remember particularly these last three and a half lines:

> new foes arise
> Threatening to bind our souls with secular chains:
> Help us to save free conscience from the paw
> Of hireling wolves, whose gospel is their maw.

He once related to me an incident which happened in Tokyo shortly before Pearl Harbour. He told it in a way which expressed what he hated most in political life, and what concerned him most: the freedom and dignity of the individual.

That day he had to catch a train, and there was little time to spare. He hailed a taxi, explained his problem, and urged the driver to get him to the station as quickly as possible. The driver agreed and drove off at a great rate. Unfortunately he jumped a traffic light. A police whistle shrilled, and a policeman came running with his sword clatter-banging on the pavement. The driver had stopped the instant he heard the police whistle. The policeman came up to the cab. He said nothing. He simply clouted the driver several times on the head with his fist and then he said 'Now drive on!' The taximan said nothing. He drove on.

Herbert hated this display of arbitrary authority and equally the help-lessness of the taxi driver, and even more the knowledge that no protest on his part could remedy what had happened. Evil was there in the system. No one could do anything about it as matters stood and what had happened was an offence against decency, dignity, and freedom.

Herbert's indignation in this instance was not, however, a product of a western liberal sense of moral superiority. He often quoted examples of kindness and understanding in social intercourse in Japan which it would be hard to encounter in North America and Europe. He pointed, for example, to the Japanese understanding of homesickness. In the imperial armed forces there was a fixed rule that new recruits were always given a week's leave at home after the second or third week of their service. Inasmuch as the cure for homesickness is going home, no Japanese soldier was obliged to suffer a malady which in western society is often an unrecognized but agonizing experience for young men. He cited, too, the example of how Japanese officers accepted it as a compelling obligation to assist their men in writing home. They laboured often for hours every day helping illiterates or men who knew insufficient characters to compose adequate letters to write satisfactory understandable letters to their families. And yet, Herbert would point out, these same officers would beat these same recruits with the flat of a sword should they infringe the regulations or fail in their obedience and their duties.

A favourite description of the Japanese which he used often was 'Janus-faced.' They were a peaceful, gentle, intelligent race of flower-arrangers, and they were capable at times of diabolical savagery.

Herbert told me, too, of an incident from his boyhood which affected him deeply and is worth relating because it touches upon some of his general ideas about the mass of the people in the political processes of history. It occurred in the immediate aftermath of the great earthquake of 1923. He was walking with his father surveying the devastation, when a crowd of excited people approached them shouting and screaming for vengeance. Herbert's father was able to calm them sufficiently to enquire what it was they wanted. There were shouts about them being Koreans. Herbert's father was able to assure them that he and his son were not Koreans, and someone in the crowd shouted out that he knew them. They were Christians. This information was conveyed in a neutral way, which suggested that these strangers were not in the same category as Koreans. The episode ended there, but later there was news of the massacre of Koreans by mobs in several Japanese centres.

Herbert very naturally was concerned with manifestations of this sort of behaviour. One of our favourite topics of conversation was calling to mind examples of mass hysteria in other communities and other ages: the first crusade, *la grande peur* during the French Revolution, pogroms in Russia, the Gordon riots, the Taiping movement in China. I had some vague knowledge of an instance in Brazil recounted by Euclides da Cunha in his book *Os Sertões*, and we eagerly read Samuel Putnam's translation published in 1944 under the title *Revolt in the Badlands*. In his *Feudal Background of Japanese Politics* Herbert brought together a great body of information about mass outbursts of enthusiasm and anger in Japanese society, and showed pretty conclusively that the excitement of mass festivals in several Japanese centres in 1867 was an important factor in the physical breakdown of the Tokugawa control system which contributed to the revolutionary restoration of the Emperor's authority.

The evidence concerning the role of the masses, as distinct from the political élite, was very much Janus-faced, but Herbert held firmly to an optimistic view of the potentiality of the masses for good. And so did I. In this we owed little or nothing to the inspiration of Marxism. On the contrary, we shared, perhaps uncritically, one of the common underlying moral prejudices of North American democracy, the belief amounting to an article of faith, that the people *en masse*, the great majority, are a good, creative force with heaven for a destination. The outburst of vile, unreasoning rancour against Koreans which had nearly cost him his life at the age of 14 was in Herbert's view the product of manipulation of malignant political elements in the community. They were institutionally created and not a natural manifestation of wickedness. Herbert had a very great faith in the capacity of free people to use their freedom for good and noble purposes.

From early in the spring of 1943 until the end of 1944, I was more in the company of Herbert Norman than anyone outside my family. In January 1953, when he was sent to the Canadian embassy in Chile, Jules Léger arranged for me to take over his house in Chapel Street in the Sandy Hill district of Ottawa. Almost simultaneously Herbert and Irene Norman secured a small, new flat in an apartment building in Friel Street in the same area. We were not neighbours but we lived close at hand. Herbert and I both worked in the East Block, and we customarily walked home for lunch together, a matter of about two miles. Herbert was very fond of playing tennis, in the late afternoon at the Rideau tennis club, and we lived between the club and his apartment. On his way home from playing, he frequently dropped in for a chat and a drink. Fortunately Irene and Maureen liked each other very much, with the result that we often ate meals together without any formality of arranged invitations or any sense of social occasion. We were, in fact, good friends who in our relations with one another created a kind of domesticity into which others were not invited to intrude.

The reasons for this were several. Although Herbert and I had been separately at Cambridge, we had shared an experience. We had lived in a little world of large ideas and lively feelings inhabited by exceptional and strongly differentiated characters like Victor Kiernan and G.S.R. Kitson Clark, the eccentric and learned clergyman-historian F.A. Simpson, the amiably tolerant and famous master Sir J.J. Thompson, and the cold American snob Gaillard Lapsley. Herbert had the advantage of friendship with the Trinity heroes who had died in the Spanish Civil War, John Cornford and Haden Guest. He had, too, participated in the great demonstration in 1933 on Parker's Piece and the march to the Cenotaph, the event more than any other which turned Cambridge University around from right to left. Herbert always remembered, when he described this student *émeute*, that it was a Canadian tory tough who perpetrated the one piece of serious violence which hospitalized a demonstrator and caused a wave of revulsion against the 'fascists.'

Reliving our own personal past had, however, a very small part in our friendship. We had very similar tastes and interests. Unlike my friendship with William Paterson with whom I spent approximately half my time agreeing about Canadian politics and the other half disagreeing with him about the meaning and movement of history, my friendship with Herbert Norman was founded on ideological and philosophic agreement. Hence we were both free to engage our main intellectual energies in considering human history in the widest way. In a sense our friendship was one long history seminar. I was given a prolonged and fascinating course in the history and politics of Japan of such scope and understanding that, although I have never visited Japan, have talked for more than ten minutes with only two Japanese in my whole life, and have forgotten most of the facts, I still after nearly forty years *feel* I know Japan and sympathetically understand its people.

We ranged around in our discussions from China to Peru. Especially China. Herbert had some knowledge of the great Chinese novel, *Ching Ping Mei*, translated by Clement Egerton under the title *The Golden Lotus*. I had a good relationship with F.A. Hardy, the Parliamentary Librarian, and he let me have the four volumes, which were kept separately in his collection of 'dirty books.' He was able to do this because *Ching Ping Mei* was not in such demand by senators and MPs as was, for example,

Fanny Hill, published in Madras. The reason is simple. *The Golden Lotus* was very long, was not always easy to read, and the scatological passages, to use Herbert's terminology, were all translated from Chinese into Latin.

The reading of *The Golden Lotus* and its analysis with Herbert's help was a great intellectual experience, for the story of the anti-hero Hsi Men Ching is one of the great works of art on a political theme. *The Golden Lotus* depicts what happens to a great empire when family morality is dissolved by sexual libertinism and anarchy, commercial and economic relations by greed and irresponsibility, and political life by corruption and failure to perform public duties honestly. The journey of Hsi Men Ching across the wintry plains to the Imperial City to bribe the officers of the government is one of the most moving passages in literature presaging, as the author intended it to presage, the destruction of authority and civilization.

Sometimes I would read a book; sometimes Herbert would read a book, and this would set off a discussion of why this and why that. I once read Mungo Park's *Travels in the Interior of Africa*, and this led to an extensive discussion of slavery, of the place of women in primitive society, of the impact of the slave trade on traditional African industrial development, and so on. We worked through Lord Hailey's *African Survey*, which I had been given as a college prize in 1938, and asked ourselves whether my friend Mbanefo was right in supposing that 'there is no politics in my country, not for 75 years.'

As far as Herbert was concerned discussions of this kind were only one of his pastimes. In addition to political intelligence work relating to Japan and Japanese-occupied territories in Asia, which was his official job, he was then writing his book, *The Feudal Background of Japanese Politics*. His earlier book, *Japan's Emergence as a Modern State*, published in 1940, was a splendid achievement for a man not long turned thirty years of age. *The Feudal Background*, however, was a great step forward as an historical work, for in it Herbert got down to the details without losing sight of the great movements and conflicts of which the details were a part.

While he presented himself in social intercourse as an easy-going, spontaneous, and charming man, Herbert was in fact powerfully driven to achieve the perfection he prescribed for himself. He wanted to become the greatest scholar ever. Had he ordered his life differently and disengaged himself from the bureaucracy in which I encountered him, he might very well have accomplished his purpose. As it was he did not do badly. Scarcely 10 per cent of academics achieve as much as he did.

Additional to a good intelligence, a refined imagination, and a relentless interest in history and politics, Herbert had a wonderful capacity for disciplined work. In this he was partly an Ontario protestant and partly Japanese. This is illustrated by his acquisition of the Japanese language. He had learned to converse in Japanese through his contact as a child and youth with servants, tradespeople, and childhood friends in Japan, and to that extent he 'knew Japanese,' but as he explained to me, he felt he needed to know and wanted to know Japanese as a Japanese scholar knows Japanese – i.e., to be able to read and write the language using the ideographs which the Japanese had borrowed from the Chinese as a means of written communication. This meant learning at least 2,500 ideographs with a goal of knowing up to 4,000 or more. A Japanese embarks on the task of learning ideographs at the age of three or four years, and under a regime of severe discipline over a varying number of years will make himself or herself literate at a low level or high level depending on time spent, capacity, and so on. Herbert used to argue that the Japanese are a talented people on account of their language. In order 'to know it' thoroughly, the Japanese have to undergo from an early age the rigid mental discipline necessary to learn their ideographs and the intense handicraft training necessary to construct them with accuracy and clarity. Ideographs have to be carefully and clearly constructed or else they are incomprehensible. No Japanese, according to Herbert, can achieve literacy without rigorous self-discipline which is both mental and physical, and this makes the Japanese capable of great achievements in anything they undertake which requires orderly concentration and handicraft skill. What was once upon a time imposed on the European upper classes in the shape of compulsory instruction in the languages of Greece and Rome for the purpose of disciplining the mind and improving the knowledge of working European languages is imposed on the whole Japanese people by the character of their own working language. As Herbert explained it, the introduction of syllabary based on sounds as a means of assisting the recognition of ideography was a requirement for the achievement of universal literacy, but was such a small concession to the mass of the people that it did not in fact bar the common people from the improving discipline of learning their own language.

To achieve a scholarly knowledge of Japanese was the task Herbert set himself when he went to Harvard in 1936. At that time, he told me, he knew only as many ideographs as a marginally literate Japanese. Within two years he could read scholarly journals, manuscripts, and classical Japanese texts.

'Boy, oh, boy, did I have to work,' he said. 'After that everything else has seemed easy.' I can well imagine this.

A third factor in our friendship was the freedom of discussion which Herbert would allow himself in my presence. Unlike me, who was at that time too innocent and perhaps too stupid to appreciate that my enthusiasm for the liberating experience of discovering Marxism generated hostility and disapproval in others, Herbert had already had several encounters that made him cautious and close-lipped about his underlying ideas in the presence of the generality of society. These experiences had affected him so much that he feared what he called 'proletarianization,' i.e., denial of opportunities for intellectual work which would oblige him to become a casual labourer. Thus, we, who were colleagues at work and Marxist historians in private, formed a little island of freedom in an intellectually hostile environment.

Herbert's first experience of working for a living in Canada made him understandably cautious and fearful. When he graduated from Cambridge in 1935 postgraduate scholarships in Canada were not easy to come by, and jobs of a kind which attracted him were not readily available. Before leaving Trinity, he asked Kitson Clark for a reference. With his usual condescension towards anyone from 'the colonies,' Kitson Clark wrote a reference in which he described Herbert as having some knowledge of classics. Inasmuch as Herbert had a good degree in classics from the University of Toronto, Herbert resented this suggestion that he had little Latin and less Greek. He invited Kitson Clark to test him in Latin and Greek. Kitson Clark backed down and wrote him a reasonable testimonial. Herbert discovered, as I did later, that Kitson Clark was a fair-minded man if one demonstrated to him that one was good on his terms: otherwise he judged one by the canons of contemporary snobbery.

Armed with this reference, Herbert obtained a teaching post in classics at Upper Canada College, in Toronto. At that time Upper Canada College rather prided itself on the employment of individualistic and even eccentric masters, and to be quite fair Upper Canada College was in some respects educationally well in advance of state schools, e.g., in its insistence that every boy must learn French and that bilingualism was a goal which Canadians should seek to achieve. The encouragement of individualism, eccentricity, and French did not, however, extend to Marxism. Indeed, some of the masters admired the Nazis. This was not unusual at the time. Pickersgill's brother Frank, who fought the Nazis and died a horrible death at their hands, expressed some enthusiasm for the Nazis when he first visited Europe in 1934.

Be that as it may, Herbert's views were not popular with his fellow masters. When he came down to breakfast on 7 March 1936, the day Hitler moved his army into the Rhineland, demilitarized under the terms of the Treaty of Versailles, some of the masters began to rag him in a nasty way. Herbert lost his temper, denounced this enthusiasm for fascism, and declared that they were stupid fools who were betraying their country and civilization. A few days later Herbert was summoned to the headmaster's office and told that his services were no longer required because he could not keep discipline in his class. Herbert believed that this was only a pretext for dismissal on political grounds. This could very well have been the case, because 'keeping discipline' was a fetish in Upper Canada College at that time. Herbert said that his classes were just as orderly as any other and the students did as well under his teaching as under other masters. There had been one incident some months previously when he had left his classroom during which absence a window had been broken in the course of a fight with chalk brushes. This incident had come to the headmaster's attention at the time, and all that Herbert encountered in that quarter was a few words of sympathy. As far as Herbert was concerned he was completely convinced that he had been deprived of his livelihood by political prejudice, that he had been unjustly treated, and that there was no remedy open to him. As it was Herbert got himself a scholarship at Harvard. Upper Canada College lost a good classics master, and the world gained a high-quality scholar.

Herbert had come to Ottawa in July 1939, to work as a language officer in the Department of External Affairs. After the Soviet-German Pact of August 1939 and the outbreak of war in September, the Communist party of Canada had been banned and the leaders of the party were rounded up and interned. Herbert confessed that he was really frightened at that time, and that he and his friend from schooldays, Charlie Holmes, who worked in the Civil Service Commission, thought they might be seized at any time, not because they were leaders or even members of the party, but because of their past associations. When I told him of my attempt to help Sammy Levine by writing a memorandum to the principal secretary of the Prime Minister, Herbert was quite incredulous, half-admiring my boldness and half-regarding me as a madman. He warned me that active political prejudice against Marxists was a lot stronger than I supposed no matter how much contemporary enthusiasm there was for the glorious Red army fighting the Nazis.

Some of this realism in the matter of keeping one's thoughts to oneself was a product of Herbert's personal experience, but much of it was a consequence of his observation of the repression which operated in Japan. I used to subscribe to *New Masses*, the weekly journal of opinion and cultural comment sponsored by the Communist party of the USA. We used to read this each week and often shared our disappointment with the poor quality and thin content of the paper. At one period in 1943 *New Masses* ran a series of exposures of the red-baiting activities of the Dies Committee, then the major agency in the US Congress engaged in revealing the Communist connections of preachers, movie stars, and academics. What struck us as odd and contradictory was the way in which the *New Masses* reporter seemed able to meet members of the Dies Committee and the staff of the Committee to extract information of a discreditable kind from them. I remember very well Herbert's comment, which ran something like this:

'They ought to live in Japan. Then they would know what anti-communism can be like. The United States is a comparatively free society. The Americans have not yet developed a comprehensive system of political police. The FBI are trying to get into the act, but in the main anti-communism is a kind of private enterprise undertaken by politicians seeking issues to obscure what they are really up to which is probably robbing the public treasury.' Inasmuch as a few well-known witch-hunters later went to jail for just such offences, Herbert was very right.

The real confusion in Herbert's mind, which seems to me to have been a central fact in his tragic end, was a duality of goals. Above all he wanted to be a great scholar and he valued prestige as a scholar more than anything else. He attached little importance to money or riches, and there was no snobbery in him. Unlike many of the people in External Affairs he derived no satisfaction from the knowledge that he was a member of the social élite of Ottawa and that, abroad as a representative of Canada, he would be part of a charmed circle of privileged people. On the other hand he liked to be 'on the inside of the inside' and close to the centres of power and authority. I am not sure that he had any taste for power and authority in his own hands, but he did have an insatiable interest in people who had power: how they behaved, what motivated them, how skilful they were, and so on. I can well imagine the tremendous satisfaction he must have derived from his close connection with General Douglas MacArthur and his relationship with the Japanese imperial family. That he influenced their thinking and their actions must have been an exhilarating bonus. But I do not think he had any ambition to be like them or to supplant them. I am sure he thought of them as living documents, the flavour and bouquet of which could be directly experienced.

Early in 1944 Herbert was offered a professorship in Japanese in Yale University. This seemed to me a wonderful opportunity for a man just turned thirty-five. Appointment to a full professorship at that age in those days was an exceptional event, but in Herbert's case quite explicable. I envied him greatly this splendid chance, which had to be measured not just in terms of the post itself but of the resources for scholarship which he could command. I argued with all my powers of persuasion and logic that he should seize this opportunity, that he should give up the bureaucracy and all the restrictions upon one's freedom that were inevitable in a place like External Affairs.

No. Herbert havered, but there was no doubt that the attractions of being 'in the know' were too great. He then committed himself to the bureaucracy, and, although he had several subsequent opportunities to leave, he remained *en poste* to his bitter end.

In general Herbert and I never discussed Marxism as such, nor were we concerned to analyse critically the general propositions of Marxism-Leninism. There was, however, a general point which worried me, and the source of this worry was 'the letter from Schlesinger.' Herbert and I did discuss this.

Arthur Schlesinger, Jr, had been in Trinity College, Cambridge, during the year 1938-39. I met him, liked him, and respected him as a lively and intelligent young man in his own right but also as the son of the American historian who had written a very good book on the colonial merchants in the American Revolution. When I was in Harvard early in 1940 I bumped into Schlesinger by chance, and we had a drink and a chat on a couple of occasions. Late in 1941 he wrote an article in the *Nation* attacking Marxists of all kinds and particularly the Communist party of the USA. I challenged him in a long polemical personal letter, and he replied in an equally long letter.

At the heart of the letter was an argument about the nature of fascism which contradicted the standard Marxist analysis of fascism as a creation of monopoly capitalism.

A general weakness of Marxist thought seems to me to be its assumption that force can be ignored, except as an accompaniment of economic power. This was true in the 19th century, but not often before, and certainly not now. Power and property have been frequently separated in history. When this happens, it is as likely that power will take over property, as that property will capture power. This seems to me what is happening in Germany. A revolutionary party fully as authentic as the Communist, though even less desirable, has appeared in response to the breakdown of capitalism, and has seized the state. Its rise to power has been expressed in terms of the German tradition, and has enlisted the general consent of the German people, especially the business and military classes. But the business class have lost control, just as so often before decadent governing groups, which invited barbarians into the empire as a means of bolstering their own rule, found themselves the captives of their own protectors. The difference between Nazism and liberal capitalism seems to me far greater than between Nazism and Communism; obviously there are continuities among all of them, as of course there must be; but the basic issue is the location of power; and it seems to me to be simply disingenuous to talk of Nazism as the last resort of entrenched capitalism.

At first I refused to think about Schlesinger's argument because in my heart of hearts I knew I had no answer. I was not so much shaken by his argument about Nazism, as I was by the more general point on which his particular argument was based – that force and political mobilization are autonomous factors in historical development. If one admitted this general proposition, what significance were the Marxist laws of history and the comforting certainty that everything will be put right by the triumph of the working class and the construction of a socialist and finally a communist order?

I put his letter aside. I could hardly bear to read it, but I felt I had to and that I had to talk to someone about it; someone of Herbert's intellectual calibre who agreed with me. Perhaps he had an answer. The letter from Schlesinger had reposed in a drawer for two and a half years. Finally, I took it out, presented it to Herbert, and asked for his views.

He read the letter slowly, and then he re-read it. He pushed his glasses up his nose and then said, 'this *is* interesting. But what worries you?' I called attention to Schlesinger's central underlying generalization about the autonomy of force and techniques of political mobilization: the gaping hole in Marxist theory.

Herbert allowed that he had certainly felt when working on the Meiji restoration that there was no easy Marxist explanation of why the decadent feudal class of Japan had been able to generate from the ranks of feudal society a band of political leaders who had created a modern industrial society. There were numerous factors in the Japanese situation – remoteness from Europe and the first areas of European penetration in Asia, for example – which assisted the Japanese in the preservation of their independence, and that these had little or nothing to do with class forces as agencies of revolutionary success. History presents the historian with more mysteries than certainties, and Marx and Engels had only insights to offer.

We left the argument there, but the letter from Schlesinger remained in the back of my mind; remained there, in fact, for twenty years until I found that I could no longer endure the mental confusion and inadequacy of Marxism and had to find for the sake of sanity a more satisfying general set of propositions concerning history.

What immediate effect my departure from External Affairs and the reasons for my doing so had on Herbert I do not know. Certainly it affected his estimation of Robertson, but not in the sense that he became hostile. My first reaction to my interview with Robertson had been chagrin and hostility towards the man personally. It upset me, but not for long, to discover that Herbert seemed more interested in a revelation of an unsuspected aspect of Robertson's mind than in my fate. I very vividly remember the circumstances in which I experienced what seemed then Herbert's cold objectivity and detachment.

This was immediately after the interview with Robertson, and we were setting out home for lunch. He was, of course, all ears about what had been said. When we reached the entrance facing Wellington Street I was recounting Robertson's enquiry about whether or not I was familiar with the novel of Koestler. This stopped Herbert completely. We stood on the steps. He turned to me and said: 'Now that *is* very interesting. Robertson has read *Darkness at Noon* and *Arrival and Departure*. Well, well! I wonder how and why he made the time to do so. I've always been given to understand he's too busy to read anything but despatches and memoranda.'

Obviously Herbert was not so disturbed by what had happened to me that he thought he ought to dissociate himself from me or people like me. When I returned to a historical conference in Kingston, Ontario, in May 1945, he invited me to stop off in Ottawa and stay with him and Irene for a day or two. When the order came for him to depart to the

Phillipine Islands in the summer of 1945 he and Irene were spending a summer holiday with Bessie Touzel, politically someone like myself.

After his departure for the Far East I never had any further contact with Herbert Norman. When he was in New Zealand, as Canadian high commissioner, I sent him photostats of two letters of his father to Rodolphe Lemieux which had come to my attention during the writing of *The Age of Mackenzie King*. I received a friendly, civil acknowledgement, and Irene wrote to Maureen at the same time. There was a vague mention of the possibility of meeting when they were passing through Britain, but this never happened.

As Herbert became more and more involved in high policy-making in the Supreme Command for the Allied Powers in Tokyo, he was obliged more and more to cut himself off from his past associations. He found himself in the real-life politics of a military and civil bureaucracy in which necessarily the US military had the final authority.

No Canadian and few people anywhere on the Allied side had greater assets than Herbert for the role in which history had cast him. His knowledge of the Japanese language and society was all but unique at a time when there were few 'experts' in the field of Japanese politics, and fewer still with the capacity to evoke a sympathetic response from the Japanese themselves. He had a constructive insight into what needed to be done to make Japanese political life not just acceptable to the conquerors but the Japanese themselves. His book, *Japan's Emergence as a Modern State*, became the bible of the American policy-makers, and because this is so, there are few men in history to whom more is owed for a decent and stable peace after a terrible war.

It is no surprise that Herbert soon emerged as the confidant and adviser of the new 'emperor' of Japan, General Douglas MacArthur, and that MacArthur deputed him to tutor the heir of the Japanese emperor. Herbert was more at the centre of high policy-making and peacemaking than any Canadian had ever been, and the part he played derived not from power but from knowledge.

This was in an important sense the source of his tragic end. Knowledge without power. Formally he had not risen out of the Canadian bureaucracy. He was a member of the Department of External Affairs so important and prestigious that no one had any motive to cause his career to wither on the vine. He was outside or above the bureaucratic politics of Canada. But not so in the case of the American military and civil bureaucracy. Here he was in a sense too successful and at the same time he had no established body of bureaucratic associates and subordinates whose fate was bound up with his fate. He was a target for every jealous rival who came along, and once he differed with General MacArthur he found himself in much the same position as Cardinal Wolsey when Henry VIII learned that he could not get from the Pope an annulment of his marriage.

Herbert seems very early on in his post-war career to have recognized his vulnerability in the circumstances in which he found himself. The strategy he employed, and it is one in which he was assisted by the Department of External Affairs, was to depict his past as an innocent adventure of youth. This was a mistake. Innocent enough it was, but when does youth end and maturity begin? Herbert Norman was 34/35 years old when I knew him, and I was 29/30. We were serious about our ideas, but we had given up using them to bring on a revolution in our society. Being a communist is a matter of activity in an organized political party, and in the context of the 1940s and 1950s this meant activity in a party accepting the line and the discipline of Moscow, Comintern or no Comintern. In this operational sense, and there is no other meaningful sense, I was not a Communist and I am sure that Herbert Norman was not one either. Herbert seems never to have made the effort to separate communism as a political activity from Marxism as a body of ideas and historical insights, but had he done so he would not have been so vulnerable to people like Robert Morris and William Rusher, the counsellors of the US Senate. As it was they could make him look like a liar by telescoping Communism and Marxism, and mixing up activity in 1936 with activity in 1946 or 1956.

In 1947 Herbert attended a Commonwealth conference in London concerned with the projected Japanese peace treaty. While in Britain he visited Cambridge and dropped in on Victor Kiernan, back from eight years in India and completing his time as a Prize Fellow of Trinity College. Victor was then still a member of the Communist party. After some pleasant and lively talk Victor formed the opinion that Herbert's heart was still in the right place but that he had no organized contact with the Communist party – exactly the same view I had formed of Herbert four years earlier. All this I learned from Victor many years after the event, and I further learned that at that time Herbert requested that Victor not mention him to others and especially to 'HSF who had had to resign from the department because he was too indiscreet.'

As part of a strategy of dissociation with the past, I recognize the wisdom of this. When Bessie Touzel talked to him on the telephone in

1951 she encountered the same distancing. She, too, understood it, and refused to be bitter or to criticize. But I wish Herbert had got the facts straight about my departure from External Affairs, because had he done so he might well have come to different and wiser conclusions about his own position. In the first place I was not obliged to resign. I had a job, but not a permanent job. In the second place Robertson did not say that I was indiscreet or talked too much and about the wrong things. I differed with Robertson about policy. I said this was the case and Robertson agreed. In one area of disagreement, – India – Robertson even agreed that I advocated the same policy as the Prime Minister of Canada and that this policy was not the policy of the Department of External Affairs. When, however, Robertson began to use the red ploy I resolved to resign. This was my decision. Indeed, I began to look for alternative employment three hours after my interview with Robertson and I resigned of my own will twenty-two days later. It seems to be the case that Herbert was so interested in Robertson's mind that he failed accurately to observe the facts about what was happening to me and how I was responding.

Herbert never had any policy differences with the Department of External Affairs – at least not when I knew him. No one ever called him a red. He was just as much a Marxist as I was, and one with about 100 per cent more experience than me. But no one in External Affairs had any motive to call him a red, and so he was not called one. As he rose in the department he was soon making policy by himself simply because the area of his responsibility was Japan and no one in Canada knew as much about Japan as Herbert, nor did anyone have as imaginative conceptions of what was involved in the reconstruction of Japanese political processes. Furthermore it must be borne in mind that the Canadian government had no power in Japan and were only there by courtesy of the US government.

Once Herbert began to encounter people who possessed real power, he was in a different set of political circumstances from those he had been in Ottawa. At first all went swimmingly for him in Japan. Without power himself he had the ear of authority much like an intelligent confessor might have in the court of an absolute monarch. Then came the Gouzenko spy scandal in Ottawa. One of the accused was a man Israel Halperin, whom Herbert had known at Harvard. Halperin handled himself with great skill when in the custody of the royal commission and again at his trial, with the result that the Crown's case failed, and Halperin was found not guilty. But much had come out, and it is reasonable to suppose that Major-General Charles Willoughby, the head of MacArthur's intelligence staff, came to know of the association of Halperin and Norman at Harvard. What a lovely piece of ammunition for use in the wars within the bureaucracy! 'Who is a friend of that red, commie bastard?' 'Who works with a guy like that?' 'Who admires Norman, eh?' Poisonous fruit for the grapevine. Willoughby had a portrait of General Franco in his office and he took up residence in Spain after his retirement.

From that time forward Herbert Norman became a useful weapon in the factional fights in the United States. He could be wheeled out almost at will when one faction in the State Department and their allies in the US Congress was engaged in blasting their opponents. The use of Herbert Norman as a piece of high explosive in 1957 had little or nothing to do with Herbert himself, but was part of an attack on John K. Emmerson of the State Department with whom Herbert had worked in Tokyo. And the ironic fact which could be observed and which illustrates the vulnerability of Herbert as an outsider vis-à-vis the Americans, is this. Herbert was crucified, but it was John K. Emmerson who rose from the dead. He survived and flourished. Not by a miracle but because he was part of a faction in the State Department which, benefitting from the overkill (how literal is this word!), on the part of the Senate Committee, was able to conquer. In counting the damage done in the war in which Herbert Norman lost his life, one right-wing warrior counted it as a major disaster that one of his boys in the State Department, Scott MacLeod, almost failed to have his appointment as US ambassador to Ireland ratified by the Senate. What an awful thing to happen! Those damned commies! And to think that Emmerson was counsellor in the US embassy in Tokyo in 1969 AD! Twelve years after Norman's death! It makes you wish we'd lost the Civil War. Maybe even the American Revolution! (Read William Rusher, *Special Counsel*, pp. 231 and 234.)

When the news came of Herbert's death in 1957, my instant reaction was a furious indignation directed at the United States. I was in London when an evening newspaper told me of the tragedy, and I am quite sure that had I had a pistol I would have gone to the US embassy and murdered someone as a protest against what had happened. Reason, however, soon reasserted itself, and I wrote to a friend in Winnipeg, an historian and student of Canadian politics, to ask for information. His first response was negative. 'There is nothing I can say to you about the death of Herbert Norman, but the thought has been growing in my mind that we should all be as spineless as our Liberal government if we did not do

215

something privately to venerate his name and commemorate his service to this country.' On 2 June 1957, only five days before the election which ended twenty-two years of Liberal rule in Canada, my friend replied from Ottawa:

The word I had in Winnipeg was that civil service circles were buzzing with the rumour that Norman had committed suicide because he had revealed to the USSR that the Anglo-French invasion [of the Suez Canal Zone] was coming, and because the net was closing on him. While this was palpably false, I wondered, as you did, what the country was coming to, and wanted to talk about down here before I replied.

'Well, I have learned nothing; Norman has not been an overt – or, so far as I know, a covert – election issue, and except for passing reference, has passed out of public discussion.

'What happened, as I guess, was this. There were in fact two issues. One was, what business was it of a Congressional Committee who the Canadian government employed? That would have been clean fighting ground for the Conservatives, and that is what many were eager to exploit. The other was, was Norman a red? This was domestic, and to have made it an election issue, I am convinced, would have played right into the hands of the crypto, and unconscious fascists, of whom this country has a frightening number. The former could not be fought without raising the latter; hence the only possible thing to do was leave it alone.

'That at least is what has been done. The one man damaged, and it is a pity, has been Pearson. Diefenbaker is, I think, sound. I judge his question in the House was a genuine attempt to end the matter ...

But the matter did not end there. Herbert Norman has become one of the focal points in a continuing factional war in the United States with an intellectual as well as a political dimension. For a long period in the late 1950s and through the 1960s his scholarship was attacked and then ignored in the United States. In 1968 William Rusher, one of the counsel of the Senate committee whose disclosures were the immediate factor in Herbert's death, published a book *Special Counsel*. One of the objects of this book was to justify the works of the committee, and central to this justification was a re-examination of the 'Norman Case.' Rusher pulled no punches (pp. 213-14): 'By any objective standard,' he wrote, 'and despite any degree of personal idealism one chose to credit him with, Norman had been an enemy, and the enemy of all who love freedom.

In the name of a perverted world view, he had placed his great gifts – his natural charm, his native intelligence, his profound learning at the disposal of a murderous dictatorship ... as a Communist, Norman might (for all we know at the moment) have had a dozen reasons to commit suicide – blackmail, for instance, or imminent danger of exposure as a spy.'

In the 1970s the opinion about Herbert Norman in the US began to shift, or rather, the fortunes of the liberals in the factional fight focused in the universities and the State Department began to improve. Virtues were discovered in Herbert's scholarship which had either been denied or ignored. *Selected Writings of E.H. Norman* under the title *Origins of the Modern Japanese State* were published with a long appreciative critical introduction by John W. Dower of the University of Wisconsin. A biography of Herbert Norman has been undertaken by an American scholar and to this end a conference on 'E.H. Norman: His Life and Scholarship' was organized in October 1979. This conference was held in Canada. An effort is being made by the American liberals to enlist the Canadians in their policy disputes. The reason is obvious. The Canadian community is pretty generally united in believing that Herbert Norman was done to death by American witchhunters and that in their presence President Eisenhower washed his hands like Pontius Pilate.

What will emerge from this continued attention to the tragedy of Herbert Norman on the part of the American academic and political communities is hard to estimate. It seems pretty certain that he will not be left in peace. A changed political climate in the United States may very well produce a spate of right-wing charges that Herbert Norman was not only a Communist but a Soviet spy. All the ingredients for such charges are there. The only element lacking is proof, but as the past has so amply demonstrated proof of truth is not a matter of very great importance in political life. Nor is the judgment about policy prescriptions. Being in agreement with the Prime Minister of Canada over India did me no good in the Department of External Affairs. Being in agreement with the President of the United States over the dangers of attacking China did Herbert Norman no good either. Indeed, being right in the bureaucracy is extremely dangerous as Herbert Norman's experience abundantly demonstrates.

Rusher's attack on Herbert Norman depended for its ammunition on evidence elicited from various people by the Senate committee investigating Communist influence in the United States. His objective was to discredit members of the State Department and various 'advisory' intellectual bodies like the Institute of Pacific Relations. Inasmuch as Herbert had had in the late 1940s great influence on American policy formation and was highly respected in various intellectual advisory bodies, it was important to prove, not that Herbert had been a commie in his youth, which everyone concerned with the matter including Herbert himself admitted, but that he was a commie in the 1940s and was still one.

One of the main foundations of Rusher's case against Herbert was the 'Tsuru affair.' According to Rusher's account based upon unsupported testimony by the FBI, Herbert Norman visited the apartment in Cambridge, Massachusetts, once inhabited by Shigeto Tsuru late in 1942, after Herbert had returned from his internment in Japan. The object of the visit was to obtain some books and papers left by Tsuru in the keeping of the apartment house janitor when he was repatriated to Japan in the summer of 1942. According to the FBI, Herbert represented himself as a representative of the Canadian government and attempted to bluff them into handing over Tsuru's books and papers. According to Rusher, Herbert Norman lied about his intentions and that his real purpose was to get into his keeping papers which would prove that Tsuru was a Communist and one of the men who established in the United States a Communist journal *Science and Society*.

The Tsuru affair demonstrates how important it is in the establishment of an approximation to the truth to examine the testimony, even of FBI agents, in an open court and in accordance with procedures designed to elicit facts. All I can do at this late date is to recount Herbert's own account of the Tsuru affair as he told it to me long before the US Senate or anyone else thought fit to consider it. This is Herbert's account told to me in the autumn of 1943, approximately one year after the event.

Tsuru was a friend of his at Harvard, where both were graduate students. Tsuru was an economist with a strong interest in Japanese economic history. He was a Marxist in the same sense and to the same degree that Herbert and I were.

In the summer of 1942 an exchange of allied personnel interned in Japan for Japanese interned in the United States was arranged to take place at Lourenço Marques in Portuguese East Africa. There the Americans *et al.* disembarked from the ship from Japan, and the Japanese disembarked from the *Gripsholm*. On the quayside Herbert encountered Tsuru. Needless to say there was not much opportunity for conversation. It was night, and in the glare of the lights on the quay they were able to exchange a greeting and Tsuru told Herbert that he had left a number of books and papers in his apartment, as well as a number of historical works, which he wanted Herbert to have as a gift. If Herbert went to the apartment in Cambridge, Tsuru was sure the janitor would give Herbert the stuff left for him.

Accordingly Herbert went to Cambridge, Massachusetts, and called on the janitor of Tsuru's apartment. Quite understandably the man wanted to know who Herbert was and what authority he had to take Tsuru's belongings. Herbert identified himself as an employee of the Canadian government and showed the man his passport and his identity card. The man asked him if he had anything from Tsuru to say he should give him his belongings. Herbert said he had nothing in writing, but suggested that if the janitor wanted to check up he ought to consult the Cambridge police and the authorities of Harvard University of which he was a graduate. The janitor thought this was a reasonable suggestion, and it was agreed that Herbert would come again after the man had had a chance to check upon Herbert. He left his telephone number with the janitor, who said he could give him a call 'maybe next day.'

A call came and Herbert went to the apartment house where he found the janitor in the company of two men who identified themselves as agents of the FBI. From the outset one of the agents was hostile and aggressive. 'Who the hell are you and what the hell do you want?' Herbert identified himself and explained that he was a friend of Tsuru, that he was an employee of the Canadian government, and so on. This sparked off abuse about him being an alien, and what hell right had aliens to get stuff belonging to Japs. Herbert explained that Canada was at war with Japan in the same way as the United States was, and that he had no intention of harming the United States. The other FBI agent had to explain to his colleague that Canada was indeed at war with Japan. This calmed the man down a little, but Herbert got nowhere as far as the object of his mission was concerned.

Herbert's conclusion from the experience did not suggest to me then nor does it suggest to me now in the light of what was proven to be in Tsuru's papers that Herbert was worried by his failure to get possession of Tsuru's papers. What did annoy him was his failure to obtain Tsuru's books. Rusher dismissed Herbert's interest in Tsuru's books on the Meiji restoration as a blind to a cover up his attempt to conceal Tsuru's communist connections. Who would come all the way from Canada to Cambridge, Massachusetts, to get some books on Japanese economic history?

Rusher, in effect, asks. The answer is simple: Herbert Norman would. His interest in Japanese books was little short of an obsession. He liked just to feel them as well as read them.

The total impression Herbert gained from the episode was similar to my impression from reading a few issues of the RCMP intelligence bulletin – that intelligence work was too much in the hands of 'dumb cops.' More than once Herbert remarked that the chief interrogating officer of the Japanese political police had a Ph.D. from Harvard on a theme connected with Marxism. 'At least in Japan there is intelligence in intelligence,' he used to say.

Tsuru, however, did Herbert no good at all when he was called before the Senate committee. It was obvious from his papers that in the 1930s he was a Marxist and a communist. This he attributed to youthful indiscretion and he declared himself ashamed of what he had done. Ashamed of what? Ashamed of being opposed to the men who perpetrated Pearl Harbour? Even Admiral Yamamoto thought Pearl Harbour was a mistake. Surely Tsuru should have been proud, not ashamed, of the political thinking which made him an opponent of the Japanese governments of the 1930s.

The only thing the Rusher attack on Herbert Norman did was to bring forward into the 1940s the date when Herbert was still a communist. Unfortunately, from his point of view, his evidence for this is unconvincing. Evidence, however, is not very important in a matter of this kind. Indeed, it is a positive embarrassment, because the *modus operandi* of political partisans like Rusher is to force their opponents into the difficult position of having to prove a negative.

In his book, Rusher has left hanging in the air the suggestion that Herbert Norman was, maybe, a Soviet spy. In his essay in *Six Journeys: A Canadian Pattern*, the Canadian journalist, Charles Taylor, has attempted to scotch this allegation by quoting from a letter Herbert wrote to his brother just before his suicide. Arguing that he had lived under illusions too long, and realizing that Christianity is the only true way, Herbert went on to assert (p. 149): 'But I have never betrayed my oath of secrecy. But guilt by association as now developed has crushed me.'

An alteration in the political climate in the United States and a consequent change in the relevant positions of the warring bureaucratic factions there may once again disturb the rest which Herbert Norman deserves. The exigencies of politics and the demands of the entertainment industry in Britain may likewise do so. It is not difficult to imagine a new William

Rusher or a Chapman Pincher coming forth to re-examine the evidence that Herbert Norman was a post-graduate communist, i.e., a Soviet agent. All the ingredients are there. Consider them.

Herbert Norman was a communist in Trinity College, Cambridge, at the very time when Guy Burgess and Anthony Blunt were in the College with Donald MacLean next door in Trinity Hall. And we all know about Kim Philby. Point 1.

Point 2. It is an acknowledged and attested fact that Soviet intelligence agencies were recruiting in Cambridge in the 1930s. They aimed high – at the recruitment of men of Herbert Norman's quality. And we know that they succeeded in the case of Alan Nunn May, to mention only a physicist.

Then there was the sequence of events in 1956. Point 3: Suez and the Soviet invasion of Hungary, when the Americans found themselves playing on the same side as the USSR. The smoothness of the Soviet operation in Hungary suggests that the Kremlin had prior knowledge of the disarray in the western alliance and the operational determination of the British and the French to go their own way without the support of the USA.

Put all this together and it is easy to give substance to the rumours buzzing around Ottawa in April and May 1957. One can be quite certain that no one in Canada will try putting all this together, but in the United States? In Britain? There are very many reasons there why such an attempt will be made. The old ploy of forcing one's opponents to prove a negative will very likely be resorted to. It is not hard to imagine reviews of the projected biography of Herbert Norman or the embroidery on the career of Anthony Blunt.

As matters stand we have only Herbert's dying denial that he ever broke his oath of secrecy. For many this is a sufficient proof that he was not a Soviet agent. Unfortunately proof satisfying to the public and to reasonable men and women requires more evidence than uncorroborated assertion, and this is where the difficulty of proving a negative arises.

I do not think Herbert Norman was a Soviet agent. This statement means nothing in itself. Obviously if Herbert Norman *was* a Soviet agent he was not going to discuss the matter with me. In fact, if Herbert Norman had been a Soviet agent he would not have wanted to know me, and it is extremely unlikely that he would have passed some of his time drinking whisky with me and reading *New Masses*.

Well-attested evidence of the *modus operandi* of Soviet spymasters in the 1930s supports this supposition. When agents were recruited, Soviet intelligence at once began to re-make the *personae* of those they employed. Philby was converted into a pro-Franco journalist in the employ of *The Times* of London. Burgess suffered a metamorphosis incredible to his friends: he became a semi-fascist. Blunt dropped out of politics and into art history.

Nothing like this happened to Herbert Norman. When I knew him he was a free man responding freely to events as he saw them. There were no discernible quirks or traumas in him. If there was any guilt in him it was the ordinary guilt of an Ontario Methodist: that he was not working hard enough or that maybe he was too self-indulgent when he bought half a pound of pipe tobacco in New York mixed especially for himself. There was nothing prurient in his contemplation or his comments on the 'scatological passages' in *The Golden Lotus*. He understood them as the author intended they be understood; as descriptions of loathesome sexual behaviour destructive of family life and the bonds necessary for social integrity. Herbert Norman had as few defects of character and personality as any man I have ever known.

There is another point which has to be considered. Herbert Norman was not the kind of student in a British university in whom Soviet intelligence was interested. Burgess, MacLean, Philby, and Blunt were all young men whom Soviet intelligence could reasonably expect to seek and to succeed in careers in the British civil, diplomatic, or armed services and so become part of the power structure of the British state. Herbert Norman was not a public school man. He was a 'colonial.' Furthermore he was an academic and the first job he sought was that of a schoolmaster. There is no evidence that Soviet intelligence was interested in this kind of student.

A few weeks before he died I discussed this matter of the recruiting activities of Soviet intelligence with Professor Roy Pascal. He told me that when he was a fellow in Pembroke College, Cambridge, he had been approached by Soviet intelligence, not to work for them, but to recommend young people whom they might approach. Roy refused to do this on the grounds that he believed that young people should make their own decisions and should not be influenced by teachers or friends. In such a serious matter as treason, individuals must decide for themselves. Roy was much delighted when I remarked: 'Well, Roy, your basic Protestant individualism saved *you* from treason.' But he added, 'They were not interested in me. I was merely a scholar and knew nothing, nor would I ever know anything of interest to them.' And so was Herbert Norman a scholar and he remained one for five years after leaving Cambridge and returning to North America.

There is one piece of information which to my mind puts beyond doubt the fact that Herbert was not a Soviet agent. This concerns the famous Soviet spy, Richard Sorge. The story of Sorge is now well known: how he penetrated the German embassy in Tokyo, established sources of reliable information in the Japanese government and the imperial household, and then communicated to the Soviet government the essential information concerning Japanese troop movements prior to Pearl Harbour which enabled the Soviet high command confidently to remove troops from the Far East for the defence of Moscow in the winter of 1941-42.

But the story was not known except to the allied intelligence community in 1944. Even then what Sorge had done could only be guessed. Herbert was in charge of intelligence work relating to Japan. He learned of Sorge's capture and execution, and he told me about this. Herbert admired very much the bravery and resourcefulness of Sorge even though he could only guess about what this agent had accomplished. It must be remembered that Canada, the USA and Britain were on the same side as the USSR at that time. It was possible then to admire someone who had outwitted the enemy and to honour someone who had died in doing so. Herbert admired Sorge particularly because he had a great respect for the competence of the Japanese police and therefore knew what Sorge was up against.

Herbert talked a great deal about Sorge and speculated at considerable length about how he had gone about his business. I cannot conceive of Herbert talking about Sorge or speculating about his methods, if Herbert were himself a Soviet agent. By late 1944 Herbert knew too much about me and about my free way of discussing everything with anybody who wanted to listen to have talked as he did to me if he himself were in the business of spying on behalf of Soviet intelligence. And Herbert did not talk just to me about Sorge. The man on the China desk heard as much about Sorge from Herbert as I did, and I presume, although I do not know, that the high command of External Affairs did too.

No. Herbert Norman was not a Soviet spy. If a well-briefed Soviet government was able to act swiftly and confidently in Hungary, information about the Anglo-French-Israeli assault on Egypt did not come from Herbert Norman. And, in any case, how could he have possibly known? Even members of the British cabinet were kept in the dark about the Suez operation. It is very unlikely that a Canadian official newly arrived in Egypt knew what was about to happen, and even less likely that he informed the Kremlin.

If any one tries to make further political capital out of Herbert Norman, he or she is going to have to work pretty hard. *Requiescat in pace.*

CHAPTER NINE

The Academic as Newspaper Proprietor: the rise and fall of the *Winnipeg Citizen*

One might suppose that the return to a university could have given me an opportunity to think about the intellectual foundation of my life to consider, for example, the 'letter from Schlesinger' which troubled me, to break some new ground in historical study, to embark seriously on a career. Not at all. I found myself overwhelmed with the day-to-day work necessary for earning a living. United College, then an affiliated institution of the University of Manitoba, was a poor institution in a financial sense. Its first purpose was to educate and to train the clergy of the United Church of Canada and to do this at the least possible expense to the Church. This object was achieved by generating a cash flow from fees from a large body of students seeking a general higher education for non-clerical purposes. This required the recruitment of a staff at the least cost possible and their employment to teach the maximum number of students which could be attracted to the institution.

During the depression and throughout the war, the enterprise had been just viable. By 1945, however, the number of students began to increase as men and women were released from the armed forces and the wartime prosperity enabled more and more young people to find the means for attending university. The consequence for the teachers was an enormous increase in the volume of work. Few teachers in any Canadian university could expect to teach less than three courses. In United College this was always exceeded. In normal circumstances one was encouraged by the thought that at least there was a long vacation lasting from mid-April to mid-September when one might read, write or, better still, just do nothing

224

but this prospect disappeared as the college organized courses for veterans, all of whom had government grants to cover this and more than cover their costs.

The head of the history department, A.R.M. Lower, who was the only member of the staff of United College known and respected outside of Winnipeg, attempted to resist the college authorities by insisting on the sanctity of the long vacation as necessary for the preservation of the sanity and development of the staff, but to no avail. In fact, I did not support him in this because I, like all the young teachers, needed the extra money to be earned by teaching veterans and by teaching in the University of Manitoba summer school. I taught an introductory course on world history, the modern history of Europe, a course on the medieval constitutional history of England, a course on British imperial history and a course on comparative government. There were never fewer than twenty-five students in a class, most classes exceeded fifty and a few exceeded a hundred students. All students sat through a three-hour examination twice a year and all wrote two essays a term. There was some assistance in marking essays, but the lecturers were responsible both for the essays and the examinations and one had to share in the invigilation of the examinations. A John Saltmarsh lecturing twice a week to fifteen students was inconceivable in United College. Needless to say, no one gave lectures of the quality of John Saltmarsh's. We were engaged in a mass-production operation.

And yet I think it was, on the whole, worthwhile. The worst aspect of the experience from the teacher's point of view was the lack of interchange with the students. One never learned much from the students and there were so many of them that one never had the time and opportunity to learn from anyone or anything else.

At first I was rather excited by the encounter with youth. In lecturing on world history, I decided to begin at the beginning – with Genesis and the Garden of Eden story. After this first lecture, a youngster of probably sixteen or seventeen came to me. His glasses were so dirty I doubted whether he could see me, but it was soon clear that he had heard me. He challenged my views about the ambiguous advantages of knowledge; the difficulties which had flown from the abandonment of conformity with the natural laws of the animal kingdom and the problems which had arisen from challenging the authority of the Creator. We had a lively discussion and I thought that this business of teaching had its rewards.

Unfortunately, this student left United College after a year. He went

225

to the University of California where he won all the prizes. Then to Harvard where he won all the prizes. Then to Oxford where he won all the prizes and became a fellow of Walham College. Shortly after he was appointed Under-Secretary of State for External Affairs in Ottawa, I encountered a young Canadian diplomat.

'What is Alan Gotlieb doing these days?' I asked.

'Oh,' he replied, 'he's reorganizing the department.'

A sad fate for the most intelligent student I ever encountered. Too bad we did not achieve a clearer understanding of Genesis.

I did initiate one course for honours undergraduates in the final year open to students of history, economics and politics in the University of Manitoba as a whole. This was built around a theme or topic such as the concept of 'capitalism.' This attracted some good students, was small enough to permit debate and controversial interchanges and was, at least to me, a stimulating experience. Had I been able to stay in Manitoba, this seminar might very well have developed into something worthwhile to the students and to me personally. Unfortunately, I was not allowed to live in Manitoba – at least not as an academic.

What prevented me from making a career as a university teacher in Manitoba and why I gave up trying to live in Canada is now the question to be considered.

It would be easy to depict me as a victim of political antagonism and to argue that Ferns was 'driven out' of Canada by McCarthyism imported from the United States after the Second World War. And this would be wrong. The difficulties I encountered between 1945 and 1949 which caused me to leave Canada, were much more complicated and much less 'political' than can be summed up and encapsulated in the notion of McCarthyism.

Before I arrived at United College, A.R.M. Lower wrote me a frank letter on the subject of the political conduct of a teacher in the circumstances which then obtained.

We naturally have been trying to find out something about you and so far the only point that I think could make a Board hesitate is the report which comes from several sources of your rather advanced left-wing political position ... I can be perfectly frank with you about conditions here. You can also consult Gerald Riddell (an official in External Affairs and the son of a former Principal of United College) and Jack Pickersgill, both of whom know the College thoroughly. I can say for myself that I have always found the College atmosphere

226

quite unconstrained and completely liberal. I have never had the slightest interference with my freedom of thought or speech. Of course, per contra, I have
tried to keep from embarrassing the College in its public relations. I have never
identified myself with a party and I think I have had a good deal more political
influence just because of that. I have never regarded my chair as a medium of
propaganda. The convictions a man arrives at upon which he is prepared to
stand, everyone will respect, but we are in agreement here that in the class-room
the tradition of free inquiry and objectivity must prevail.

While the College is an institution of the United Church, its religious attitudes
are broad, and I personally have never found any difficulty arising from this
source. Since I have been here I have gradually acquired a healthy respect for
this institution, for it seems to me to have a more dynamic quality about it than
any other institution of which I have experience. I am not sure where that comes
from, whether staff, students or traditions – all three probably. At any rate, I
am quite sure you would find us all firm in defence of a tolerant, liberal outlook
which, after a good deal of experience, I find one of the most powerful solvents
of both personal and social difficulties.

I found this an encouraging statement which was completely acceptable
to me. Curiously, though, the only political *contretemps* I had during my
time in Winnipeg was with Lower himself. He was well known as a
Canadian nationalist and as an amusing, caustic scourge of Canadian
Tory imperialists. I thought it safe enough to talk to him about the case
for Indian national independence. One night, I was at his home where I
had been reading to him while he was convalescing from an operation
for a fallen retina. After the reading was over, I began to talk about India
and the nationalist movement there. To my complete surprise, he responded just as Winston Churchill might have done on the subject. India
was not a nation. It was a geographical expression. Peace, order, civilization, all depended on the British raj, etc. Finally, I said, 'You are a
great Canadian nationalist. If independence is good for Canada, why can
it not be good for India? After all, Canada is not exactly a united nation,
but we seem to hold together without dependence on the British raj.'
This caused Lower to explode. His wife intervened, saying, 'Now, Arthur, other people are entitled to their own opinions.'

The next day I received a letter from Lower saying that, 'I have been
thinking over our conversation of yesterday and it seems obvious to me
that if we are to maintain amicable relations these political altercations
will have to stop. I trust you will join with me in attempting to avoid

them in the future.' The long and short of it was that Lower could not tolerate in a younger person any relation but discipleship. He was a natural-born preacher and although he enjoyed and throve on controversy with other churches, he could not endure a difference in his own congregation.

While I was popularly believed, by colleagues and students alike, to be left-wing, I disconcerted some of the former on an occasion in 1946. By that time I had learned enough about the Yalta agreement strongly to suspect that it characterized the sort of carve-up among the Great Powers which had characterized the Versailles settlement in 1918-19. A tiny newpaper item had had a disproportionate effect on my thinking about what was going on in world politics. This had to do with the denunciation by the Soviet government of the Soviet-Turkish Treaty of 1925, accompanied by a demand for the revision of the Montreux Convention on the grounds that the convention fixing Turkey's boundaries had been signed when the Soviet Union was weak. Now there was a new situation – the Soviet Union was strong. From that moment when I encountered a few lines of newsprint, the Soviet Union seemed no longer an anti-imperialist power. A late discovery, no doubt, but a discovery none the less, and an odd one because I had never thought of Turkey as a nation deserving of great sympathy.

Thinking along these lines, I was confronted by a party of my colleagues requesting me to sign a petition protesting against the conduct of the British government vis-à-vis Greece. The *Winnipeg Free Press* had lately published an editorial disassociating Canada from British policy in Greece and these academics were following the party line of the *Free Press*. I reasoned that if the world was being carved up, then the British ought to do what the Yalta agreement permitted and so I refused to sign the petition. No one could see why not. The British were helping the Greek monarchy to suppress democracy and so on. Some years later, I learned from a colleague in Birmingham how right I had been. He had been an officer of the British army in Athens when the ELAS delivered one of their armed assaults on the Greek government. The British forces were under heavy artillery fire, but the Americans draped their tanks in the Stars and Stripes to avoid becoming targets and to encourage the revolutionary forces attacking the monarchy. No solidarity with allies when the 'people' are acting up!

My only excursion into politics in public was at the invitation of the dean of theology of United College. He was an enthusiastic supporter of the United Nations Association, which was planning a large rally in the Playhouse Theatre. Would I be one of the speakers? It seemed to me safe enough to respond to an invitation from a dean of theology.

My line was a simple enough one. I said that Canada now occupied the same position in world politics as Poland had between the two great wars of the twentieth century – we are located between the two greatest military powers on earth. Unless these two powers can keep the peace between them, Canada is in for a rough time. We will be put under terrible pressure and may very well become the same sort of battlefield as Poland had lately been. Therefore Canada's interest is to build up agencies of conciliation, disarmament, and peaceful negotiation. Long live the United Nations! Long live the small powers of the world, etc.

The message was received ecstatically by the audience and I was half-persuaded that politics might be worth while after all. But I do not think my message was so well received by the anonymous gossips who, Alex Skelton had alleged, run Canada. One senior colleague said to me, 'I see you have been sounding off in public,' and I took the implication. I had made a mistake. Do not have opinions in public. Do not get yourself approved by the people. Those are safe rules for academics. In 1946 this was probably so.

At the meeting in the Playhouse Theatre I met a number of people of a kind I had not hitherto known in Winnipeg: businessmen, trade union leaders, and practising politicians. Among these was Dave Simkin. This turned out to be a great misfortune for me. No fault attached to Dave, only to me.

My mistake was to have an idea – that Winnipeg needed and ought to have a third daily newspaper. This idea occurred to me one day in November 1945, while I was walking from my home in St David Road, St Vital, to catch a tram on St Mary's Road. What fired the idea in my brain was a strike which had occurred in the two daily newspapers, the *Winnipeg Free Press* and *Winnipeg Tribune*.

The cause of the strike assumed no importance in my mind, but it is necessary to understand the cause if one wants fully to grasp the event and its consequences. If one talked to the strikers, one was told that the strike was about 'the exchange of mattes.' The managements of the two newspapers had hit upon a method of reducing their labour costs by the device of exchanging the *papier mâché* impressions taken from the type set by the members of the International Typographical Union, Local 191.

There were certain pages of both newspapers which were identical and these were pages of advertising bought each day by the large department stores in Winnipeg. The newspaper publishers proposed to have the type-setter in one of the newspapers set the type for one or more of the pages of advertising mattes and then draw two mattes instead of one. The typesetters in the other paper would likewise set the type for one or more pages and two mattes would be drawn. Then the mattes would be ex-changed. Plates would then be cast and printing undertaken. In this way the number of man-hours of typesetting would be reduced by one half of the time taken to set those pages which were identical in the two newspapers.

To hear the typographical men talk one would have thought that the proposal of the employers was a plot to reduce the work force, which of course it was. The typesetters, however, said nothing about their will-ingness to accept the exchange of mattes provided they were paid for 46 hours of work per week although they would in fact only work 40 hours. In short, the members of the ITU wanted for themselves the entire benefits which would accrue from the economy of man-hours as a result of the exchange of mattes. The other printing tradesmen – the electroplaters, the pressmen and the men, called mailers who handled the final product – would all work as long as they had ever done, and would benefit in no way. Nor would the employers.

None of this was discussed in public statements. The officers of the ITU and the publishers were quarreling about something different and more important. They both agreed that they were quarrelling about the contract between them, but not about its terms. Nor were they quarreling about the interpretation of its terms. They were quarrelling about who should adjudicate interpretations of their contract. The union officers demanded that the interpretation of union contracts should be in accord with the rule book of the International Typographical Union and that the final pronouncement on the interpretation of the rule book should rest with the international officers of the ITU in their headquarters in Indian-apolis, USA.

For some reason never very clear, the publishers did not argue on the grounds of natural justice. It was evidently unjust for one party to claim the sole right to interpret the meaning of a contract in terms of a rule book which that party made in its own interest and for its own purposes. The publishers, however, chose to fight on other grounds which were partly legal and partly political. They declared that they were bound by the terms of an order-in-council made by the government of Canada under the terms of Canadian legislation and that this order-in-council required that all contracts of employment be referred to the War Labour Relations Board. The publishers proposed to obey the laws of Canada and not the dictates of union officials in the United States.

Plainly, the dispute was about economizing the use of manpower and who should benefit, but beyond that it was a power struggle between the newspaper proprietors and the union about which party would control the industry, determine the course of its development and the proportions of income which went to the wage workers and to the managers and owners.

When the idea came to me about the need for a third newspaper in Winnipeg, I knew nothing about the ins and outs of the dispute. My paternal grandfather had been a printer and I was a Marxist and so there was no question in my mind about who had right on their side. But this question of the rights and wrongs from the workers' point of view did not concern me nearly as much as the notion that the people of Winnipeg needed an opportunity to hear another point of view, one different from that of the *Free Press* and the *Tribune*. In both New York and Chicago new newspapers had been founded which provided a voice for progressive, democratic opinion. *PM* and the *Chicago Sun* seemed to portend a wave of the future and one which ought to start surging in Canada. L.W. Brockington's experiences at the hands of the newspaper interests and Mackenzie King's pusillanimity in the presence of men like Henry Luce and his Canadian counterparts powerfully influenced me to believe that 'something ought to be done' and that the strike in the *Winnipeg Free Press* and the *Winnipeg Tribune* was a God-given opportunity.

So I rang up David Simkin. Dave and his father, whom I always knew as 'old Mr Simkin,' ran two interdependent firms, Universal Printers and the Israelite Press, which among other lines of business produced the *Israelite News*, an English-language weekly circulating in the Jewish community in western Canada. Old Mr Simkin had come to Canada from Tsarist Russia before the First World War. He had been an activist in the Jewish Bund, a radical socialist movement against the autocracy. Revolution in Russia had not greatly changed his views of the character of the government there. His wife, however, was sympathetic to the Bolsheviks and this produced from time to time great family quarrels, which, by the time I knew the Simkins, had subsided into sniping amongst the members and had become but dying echoes of a Russian past.

231

Dave had lived his life in an atmosphere full of political discussion and he was acquainted with socialist arguments, several varieties of communism, Zionism, the politics of the Ukrainians and Poles, not forgetting the ordinary political controversies of the Liberals, the Conversatives, and the Progressives, the co-operators and the trade unions. But he took very little of this seriously. It was merely data concerning people with whom he was doing business. It was his talent for business affairs which fascinated me and for which I most admired Dave.

He said to me, 'Harry, you've got to figure all the angles. And I mean all the angles. You can't just have an idea. Ideas are a dime a dozen.' And that was Dave's attitude. He had a kind of unspoken reverence and regard for academics and he was proud of the fact that one of his brothers was doing well at the university, but he had a strong predisposition to doubt the practical good sense of anyone with an academic background. He used to figure the angles on the back of a cigarette box. This meant translating an idea into money costs and profits. Suggest something to Dave and he used to take out his box of Sweet Caporals, which I think he used to buy because the box had a fair amount of blank white and presented a hard writing surface. Then he would make some calculations and say, 'Nah! It'll never work,' or 'Yeah, maybe. But you have to add, say, 20 per cent to cover bad debts.'

Dave was a graduate of the depression. Figuring the angles had been essential for survival. He and his father ran a union shop, partly because they 'believed in unions' and partly because they considered union contracts ensuring their labour supply was good business. I once made a remark to Dave which indicated some sentimental sympathy for the members of the International Typographical Union.

'Okay, okay,' Dave said. 'But there's another side of this you've got to consider. In 1933/34 my Dad and I paid ourselves $10.00 a week to live on. I'm telling you: ten bucks a week! Do you know what the ITU men in the plant were taking home? Thirty-five, forty dollars a week. The guys with the headaches were getting 10 bucks. The guys who sat on their asses at a linotype were getting 35-40 bucks and not a care in the world unless Universal Printers went broke, which it nearly did.'

Dave eventually became a very rich man. Some years later, I was talking to old Mr Simkin. I asked after Dave. 'Dave?' his father said. 'Dave's got problems. Real problems. He can't stop making money.'

When he sold Universal Printers to some Americans in search of a tax haven, Dave could not endure retirement. He took over some businesses in the printing trades, built them up, sold them and finally financed a professional hockey team, in the offices of which he dropped dead while attending to its affairs.

Dave taught me my first lesson about newspapers. At that time I thought of newspapers as agencies for informing the public and for the expression of opinion about public affairs. I had never asked myself, why do people buy newspapers? I simply assumed that they bought them for information about people and events. I had not figured all the angles, not by a long shot.

Dave did not know a great deal about newspapers, but he understood their production. He explained to me a fact which was perfectly obvious, but of which I had taken no account. A daily newspaper requires for its production a high-speed rotary press capable of turning out thousands of copies an hour. A high percentage of the contents of a daily newspaper has to be put into print and run off machines within a very few hours, and this has to happen every day, six days a week.

'There are no high speed presses in Winnipeg except those owned by the *Free Press* and the *Tribune*. There are a few rotary presses in town but they are not fast enough,' Dave explained, 'and anyway they are already in use producing papers like the *Grain Growers Guide*. And so, anybody starting a third paper has to buy high-speed presses. And, boy, do they cost money.' No, Dave argued, to start a third newspaper would cost at least a quarter of a million dollars. And who has that kind of money? And who would put it into a newspaper?

There were many angles to consider. Fundamentally, success in publishing a newspaper would depend on how many newspapers would be sold every day, not on what the newspaper might say or stand for. But in Winnipeg, as Dave explained, a fairly large percentage of people bought newspapers on account of the advertisements which contained information about the prices of goods, particularly those of the two large department stores, Eaton's and the Hudson's Bay.

Dave recalled an episode from the past when there was a dispute between one of the newspapers and the large advertisers. The advertisers withdrew all their advertising. 'What do you suppose happened?' Dave asked me. He did not stay for an answer. 'The paper lost 30 per cent of its circulation in a week. The housewife controls home circulation in this town and if she doesn't find what she is looking for in a newspaper she won't buy it. And don't let us kid ourselves she buys newspapers to read the lonely hearts column. She buys it for the ads, so that she can know what she has to pay for steak and underwear for the kids. Well, the newspaper had to cave in to the department stores and that shows what you're up against. If you don't have the ads, you don't get the circulation and if you haven't got the circulation, you don't get the ads. And if you don't have both you go broke. Okay?'

I began to see that starting a third newspaper in Winnipeg involved more than I had reckoned. If Dave Simkin was not interested maybe someone else might be. Then I had another idea. Marshall Field II (or maybe the III) of Chicago was rich. He had launched the *Sun* in Chicago. He was an old Etonian, and a member of Trinity College, Cambridge. I, too, was a member of Trinity. Why not write to him, and explain the circumstances in Winnipeg and ask his advice?

Marshall Field replied. He thought that the situation in Winnipeg seemed very favourable for the establishment of a new newspaper: that he was so heavily committed in Chicago that he couldn't himself do anything: that a determined effort by others would be worth while; and that if I wished to come to Chicago, his executives would be happy to give me the benefit of their experience.

I showed Marshall Field's letter to Dave Simkin. Its effect was magical. It was as if the heavens had opened and God Almighty had entered into direct communication with Winnipeg. If *Marshall Field* thought the situation was ripe, then somebody ought to do something! Dave began to think positively; not about the difficulties, but about the possibilities.

Dave had a number of business connections with the co-operative movement. The co-operatives – of which the Manitoba Wheat Pool was the most important – were then a very considerable force in business and politics in Manitoba. Although a very strong lobby in the Manitoba Legislature and in the offices of the provincial government, the co-operatives still retained something of an 'oppositionist' character in the community and were anything but the darlings of the *Winnipeg Free Press* and the *Tribune*. The leading co-operators were farmers, temperamentally and emotionally very conservative, but heavily committed to the notion that farmers are a uniquely valuable element in the community and much put upon by other interests such as the Grain Exchange, the railroads, and in fact everyone with whom they are obliged to do business.

Dave had done some printing for the Canadian Co-operative Farm Implements, a new organization which sold farm equipment to its members at going prices, but distributed, or promised to distribute, the profits to the purchasers. The founder and mainspring of Canadian Co-operative

Farm Implements was J.B. Brown, a farmer with a Scottish accent and traces of Scottish radicalism of the ILP kind. But at heart and in essence Jock Brown was a canny Scot with an eye to the main chance. In many respects he resembled Dave Simkin, except that socially and morally he was more conservative than Dave and less adventurous.

Dave Simkin, Jock Brown and I had several talks. The main problem was to raise sufficient capital. We decided that the solution was to raise a lot of money in little bits from a lot of people. The formation of a co-operative company would be the means to this end. Interesting people in the co-operative and inducing them to invest five or ten dollars and not more than fifty dollars would be the first stage in inducing them to buy the newspaper, which we proposed to call the *Citizen*. We needed a readership of from 15,000 to 20,000 at least and, if we were to raise sufficient capital in small individual amounts, we would have to induce approximately 10,000 people to invest. In our minds, selling the *Citizen* as a business proposition meant selling the newspaper we hoped to publish.

Co-operative ownership would, we believed, solve a second problem – ownership and control. 'Ownership and control by 10,000 or more citizens,' we argued in the prospectus we eventually produced, 'is the best guarantee the *Citizen* will serve no narrow political, class or sectional interest. The members of the company will have the final control of the paper's editorial policy.'

Of course, the 10,000 or more people we aimed at enlisting in the company would not provide all the capital needed. To solve this problem we decided on two policies. The first was to commit ourselves to invest nothing in plant, to use the whole capital to cover costs until a break-even point was reached and to rent plant. Little or nothing was to be tied up in fixed capital. The second policy was to invite shareholders to lend money to the *Citizen* through the purchase of loan units of fifty dollars bearing interest at 5 per cent. No shareholders would be allowed to buy more than two loan units without permission of the directors and the possession of loan units would in no way increase a holder's voting right in the company.

According to co-operative practice, no shareholder could have more than one vote in the company and dividends on shares would be proportional purchases of the company's product. Inasmuch as it was expected that few would ever buy more than one newspaper, dividends, if there ever were any, would all be equal.

Who was going to acquire the high-speed press? This is where Dave Simkin and his father came into the picture. If we raised enough capital, Universal Printers would sign a contract with the *Citizen* to print the *Citizen* for a rental/fee and provide space for editorial offices. Universal Printers would purchase a new high-speed press and ancillary equipment and to do this the *Citizen* would advance Universal Printers the printing charges for a fixed number of months. This advance would, of course, not cover the cost of the presses, but would enable Dave and his father to make a substantial down-payment to the Goss Company of Chicago, the manufacturers of the machine.

The plan involved some serious risks for Dave and his father. The public on the other hand could not lose much if the enterprise failed. It was to prevent anyone from losing any serious sum of money that we limited investment in shares to fifty dollars and loans to one hundred dollars. It is a measure of Dave's business genius that, as soon as the contract with the *Citizen* and the contract for the supply of the machines were signed, Dave turned all his attention to drumming up business sufficient to keep the machines running sixteen to eighteen hours a day and not just for the few hours necessary to print the *Citizen*. The concept of a cash flow had not yet been invented, but Dave understood its importance well enough and acted accordingly.

In order to get the project off the ground, we had to assemble a board of directors and to secure a charter under the co-operative section of the companies act of the province of Manitoba. We believed that to sell shares on the necessary scale we would have to enlist the support of the co-operative and trade union movements. Jock Brown was willing to join the board and he persuaded Fawcett Ransome, the secretary of Manitoba Pool Elevators, to join. Dave and I persuaded Robert Holmes of the Trades and Labour Council, W.T. White of the Canadian Congress of Labour, and Reginald Schmok of the International Typographical Union to join. Then we enlisted people representative of education, women, youth and war veterans. I persuaded an energetic, handsome and charming friend of my brother, lately returned from the war, to become our organizer. Unfortunately, I was wrong in supposing that this young man possessed gifts as an entrepreneur and a salesman. What he wanted and in the end he got, was a 'good job' in an established and prosperous business. The novelty, the uncertainty, and absence of any experienced authority simply defeated this young man and I can only say that in persuading him to become the first paid employee of the *Citizen* I wasted a year of his life.

At the initial meeting of the board in Jock Brown's office, I was offered the presidency of the Winnipeg Citizen Co-operative Publishing Company Ltd. Vanity and a sincere interest in my brain child prompted me to accept this office. But this was a serious mistake. Just as I had no proper conception of what a newspaper is, I had no operational idea of what being the president of the organization involved. I conceived of myself as presiding over an idea about to materialize itself in society. The people in Winnipeg needed a third newspaper. They would create it themselves. The trade unions and the co-operative organizations would immediately spring into action. The shares in the *Citizen* would more or less sell themselves and the heart and mind of democracy in Winnipeg would supply itself with the newspaper it needed and wanted. Any benefits accruing to myself would be psychological: the consciousness of having thought of something of benefit to the people. I never for a moment thought of myself as a potential Hearst or a Beaverbrook or an Atkinson or a McCullagh. Indeed, my intention was that the age of the press barons should cease and a new age of the people's press would dawn. What rubbish!

Within a fortnight I discovered that the shares in the *Citizen* did not sell themselves, nor did our organizer, nor did the trade unions, nor did the co-operatives. Only individuals sold shares. The problem was to find the individuals to do the job. In the finding of salesmen the trade unions alone were of some use, but all they did was to introduce the subject of the *Citizen* to the members of the unions and to ask for volunteers. Many volunteered, but few worked at the job. But at least volunteers usually sold themselves a share, which was something. If they went further and persuaded a neighbour or a friend to buy a share, this was marvellous. In the end 12,000 shares were sold to approximately 8,000 people, but this achievement represented hard work by comparatively few people. Who were they?

Not surprisingly the best salesmen were members of the ITU, but surprisingly the ITU membership in Winnipeg was not very sympathetic. I addressed the chapel on two occasions and encountered indifference and even hostility. Some even thought the *Citizen* was prejudicing the jobs they did not have with the *Free Press* and the *Tribune*. On the other hand, there was a minority who could foresee what did actually transpire

– that their jobs in the two established newspapers were gone forever and that the best strategy was to help a newspaper which would employ members of the ITU. Reg Schmok, who was a director of the *Citizen*, and Jack Simons were the principal leaders of the minority devoted to the new enterprise. There was a third ITU man, however, who outdid everyone else as a salesman. He was Nathaniel Insch, a retired printer of 72 for whom his union was his religion. He felt that the *Free Press* and the *Tribune* had behaved unjustly to their printers and the best answer to injustice was to sell shares. He sold over 700 shares during my time as president and one can see why. He was a tubby, white-haired, little man with an occupational squint in his eyes, a laconic manner, and the appearance of a guileless benevolent dwarf which concealed his quality of persistence. Every day, sun or snow, he tramped the streets of Winnipeg house to house. On several occasions, I induced Nate Insch to explain his methods to other volunteer salesmen. He was no rhetorician. All he used to say was, 'If you make the calls, you can sell the shares. If you don't, you don't.'

The headquarters of the *Citizen* comprised two rooms in an old office building, the Donalda Block, in downtown Winnipeg, made available without charge by Sam Herbst, the regional director of the International Ladies Garment Workers Union, AFL. I found it necessary to drop into the headquarters every day after my last class at United College. Soon I was obliged to give two or three evenings a week addressing union meetings and various clubs explaining the *Citizen* and seeking support and volunteers. Sometimes I hoped Hegel or Marx were looking down from their heavenly abode to see just what is involved in an idea materializing itself or the great proletariat making their future.

The person who did more than anyone else to keep the *Citizen* going, who knew what was happening, who answered all the questions and whose constant presence in the Donalda Block gave reality to the enterprise was Jeanette Grosney. She had been a student in United College and was the best in my course on the constitutional history of England before 1485. When she graduated in the spring of 1946, I persuaded her to become a general office worker at a low weekly wage. Because she had a first-class mind, a large fund of energy and idealism and an unobtrusive but firm character, she presided over the prenatal period of the *Citizen* and no one ever noticed her or gave her a word of thanks. But one day, not long before I stepped down from the presidency, I was chatting with Sam Herbst of the International Ladies Garment Workers and he said to me: 'You know something, professor, that Grosney she's the best you got. Dubinsky could use her in New York. Maybe I should speak to her, eh?'

'Like hell you should speak to her. You call yourself my friend, and you want to take the best person I've got.'

When I ceased to be the president, Jeanette left the *Citizen*, not out of loyalty to me, but because her hard sense of realism indicated to her that there was something wrong in the *Citizen* and that she might be wasting valuable years of her youth. She studied to become a social worker, married, had some children and rose to the top of her profession.

What was wrong? Naturally the two established newspapers did not relish the prospect of competition. They preached freedom – and free enterprise – particularly the *Free Press*, but free competition was for others, not themselves. This was especially so in the case of the *Tribune*, the weaker of the two papers. A few days after the announcement the names of the *Citizen* board, the Principal of United College, Dr W.C. Graham, summoned me to his office. After some preliminary courtesies, he told me that he was disturbed by the fact that I was the president of this new and worthy enterprise. Why? I asked. Because, Dr Graham explained, my being president of the *Citizen* might prejudice the fund-raising activity of the College. I was so innocent that I replied, 'We won't be getting money from the same people you will be.'

This very innocence stumped Graham. He said nothing more. When I told Dave Simkin about the incident he said, 'My God, Harry, don't you know that Wesley McCurdy, the publisher of the *Tribune*, is the chairman of United College's fund-raising committee? It's obvious they're twisting your arm. But it's a good sign. They are taking the *Citizen* seriously.'

And so they were. Nothing more was said to me. During the summer, autumn, and early winter of 1946, over 7,000 shares were sold and pledges of loans were made amounting to $30,000. I may have been discouraged by the slowness of the operation, but of course I was still young and arrogant enough to think that I could recreate the world in seven days. In fact, the project was making progress.

In January 1947, we held our first annual general meeting. Before this happened, I was confronted by a situation which required me to make a judgement about the internal politics of the organization. Shortly after New Year's Day, Reg Schmok and Jack Simons, the most effective and enthusiastic members of the International Typographicial Union, made an appointment to see me alone. They came armed with the record of share sales and they asked me to look at them carefully. How many shares, they asked, had been sold by members of the co-operatives in the province? How many members of co-operatives had bought shares? Very few, they pointed out. How many trade unionists had sold shares? How many trade unionists had bought shares? The record showed that trade unionists and city people in Winnipeg had bought 90 per cent of the shares sold in 1946.

Schmok and Simons came straight to the point. J.B. Brown and Fawcett Ransome, the co-operators on the board, were not pulling their weight. Brown was long on talk and short on action. The farmers were doing nothing, and they were a force for conservatism. I remember very clearly the word Simons used to indicate what he wanted me to do. 'Let us,' he said, 'you, Reg and I, form a phalanx, throw these damned useless co-operators off the Board and make the *Citizen* into a paper for working city people.'

I acknowledged that the response to the *Citizen* by the farmers and the co-operators had been disappointing in terms of shares sold, but I argued that we had all gone into the project together and that we ought to stick together. Brown had developed the idea of a co-operative which seemed to me on the right lines and he had used his influence with the big people in the co-operative movement to sponsor our incorporation, which might otherwise have been a much longer drawn-out affair. I agreed that Brown did treat ITU men in a patronizing way as if they had no brains or understanding, but I said that he treated me in that way, too. We had to keep in mind that he did have business experience, which we lacked. No, I would not agree to form a phalanx and purge the board of directors.

There was more to the arguments of Schmok and Simons than I was willing to concede. To an extent which I was as yet unwilling to admit to myself, I had become involved in something more difficult than I had anticipated. I was faced with a personal crisis the dimensions and character of which I only dimly discerned. Was I to go on carrying a busy program of teaching or was I going to give my heart and mind fully to the *Citizen*? Up to this point I had been co-operating with Dave Simkin and Jock Brown. In fact, I was leaning on them and now I needed to stand on my own feet, to take hold of the enterprise and to make it work. And this I was reluctant to do.

To tell the truth, I was already a little bored with the *Citizen*. In the summer of 1946, Dave Simkin and I travelled by car to Chicago, Dave to explore the market for high-speed presses and I to see the people in the *Chicago Sun*. Marshall Field was away from Chicago at the time, but I had two sessions with executives of the *Sun*. What they had to tell me about the problems of running a mass-circulation newspaper did not exactly enchant me. For example, we discussed syndicated features such as columns and comic strips. These, I learned, were absolutely indispensable elements in the sale of newspapers. The *Sun* features editor told me with great emphasis and complete conviction that if he could get the comic strip 'Little Orphan Annie' from the *Chicago Tribune* he could take 20 per cent of the *Tribune's* circulation and if he could get 'Dick Tracy' as well he might be able to take 30 per cent. As it was, he was searching desperately for a skilled myth-maker who could capture the interest and loyalty of the great army of people involved in the adventures of Daddy Warbucks, Annie and her dog. What were we in the *Citizen* to do? The *Free Press* had 'Little Orphan Annie' and the *Tribune* 'Dick Tracy.' Waiting for 'Superman' and being dependent on him for success seemed to me a strange situation to be in. Was it for this that John Saltmarsh had devoted hours criticizing my work on the history of England between 1540 and 1560?

And I was beginning to have some other doubts about this little bastard, my brain child. Did people like Jock Brown and Fawcett Ransome need any bigger voice in the community than they already had? And the trade unions? In their case my feelings were more positive, but none the less mixed. I had a real sense of comradely solidarity with some of the ITU men like Reg Schmok, Jack Simons and old Nate Insch. I still thought that the trade unions in general and the wage workers as a whole were inadequately and sometimes unfairly noticed in the established press. The movement to establish the *Citizen* was already having some effect – and some of the trade union leaders remarked on this to me – viz, that the *Free Press* and the *Tribune* were improving their coverage and the objectivity in the reporting of trades union affairs. This persuaded me that, 'Little Orphan Annie' notwithstanding, the project was worthwhile and that I owed it to those who came forward to support the *Citizen* not to desert or abandon my post.

On the other hand, there were one or two experiences with the trade unions which somewhat disenchanted me. One of these was a superficial triumph when, as a result of a twenty-minute speech of mine, 130 or so shares in the *Citizen* were sold in a matter of minutes. This happened at a meeting of the United Packinghouse Workers, to which the district organizer, Adam Borg, invited me to speak about the *Citizen*. Borg was a CIO militant, an able organizer and a big, tough man. Like many of the members of the his union he called to mind the raw material of the slaughter houses: beefy or bovine men of meaty weight and bulk and rather intimidating when encountered in a mass, like a herd which might run wild.

I said my piece and Borg took over the microphone. He told his members that, having heard the professor, they were now going to buy shares. They were five bucks each and the stewards would collect the money, take the names and the shares would be sent to the purchasers. He did not want to hear about anybody turning down this offer; in fact, it was an offer no one could refuse.

I did not interfere with the proceedings, but afterwards I told Borg that I would have preferred that each worker made up his own mind and bought a share because he believed in what he was doing. Borg replied that not many shares would be sold if one left it to each man to make up his mind. The *Citizen* would be a paper in their own interest, but they did not know this. 'But I know it, and that's why I invited you here,' he concluded.

Episodes like this were beginning to make me see dimly through the myth that the people *en masse* do things; there is no such thing as democratic action. On the contrary, the mass of the people have things done to them and they do nothing. The problem, if one has a taste for such things, is to find an effective way of manipulating them, like inventing 'Little Orphan Annie', or getting them into closed shops where they can be forced by the union bosses to do things like buying shares in the *Citizen*.

The modest success of the campaign to establish the *Citizen* seems to have had some effect upon the attitude of the controllers of United College. A new kind of approach was made to me shortly after the first annual general meeting of the co-operative publishing company. Principal Graham summoned me to his office. There he told me that Lower, who had taken leave to teach history at Queen's University, was not likely to return to the college. I seemed to him qualified to take Lower's place as head of the history department. Furthermore, the influx of students required, and had made financially possible, the expansion of the staff. Headship of the department of history would require my whole attention.

Indeed, my career as an historian required my whole attention. What about that Ph.D. which I had not completed at Cambridge?

These 'great expectations' presented me with a real problem of making up my mind about myself and my future. The experience of the previous nine months had demonstrated that I could not go on being a part-time amateur executive and I recognized the force of Graham's argument that being a scholar and an officer of a university institution required my full-time attention. What to do?

Graham had made me a proposition which had some attractions. What would the *Citizen* do? I decided to test the water. On 3 February 1947 I wrote to the principal of my old school, G.J. Reeve, who was the vice-president of the *Citizen*, resigning the presidency.

The disadvantages of having a board of directors which was largely cosmetic soon became evident. The effective board was not the whole board but only myself, J.B. Brown, Reg Schmok, and Fawcett Ransome. In the backbround and with no formal position was Dave Simkin. Even G.J. Reeve was not very involved in the affairs of the company. No action was immediately taken and I carried on.

Several weeks passed. Principal Graham, obviously under pressure from the financial supporters of United College, complained that I had not severed my connections with the *Citizen*. I explained that my resignation was before the board but that it was not easy to replace me at once. I wrote again to the vice-president in March 1947, saying that 'further complaints have been lodged with my employers concerning my connection with the *Winnipeg Citizen*' and that I would appreciate an early reply to my letter.

This was, of course, formal stuff. I had had several long discussions with Jock Brown, Dave Simkin, Reg Schmok and G.J. Reeve. I put it to them that I either became the paid chief executive of the *Citizen* or I had to get out. In the presence of this alternative Dave Simkin was neutral. This worried me because Dave was the only man whose judgement I really respected. Was he saying he thought me unequal to the job? For a number of reasons I thought this myself and Dave's neutrality reinforced my own doubts. Schmok and Simons and several of the trade unionists who, although not board members, were interested observers, were quite strongly in favour of me becoming the chief executive. Jock Brown was definitely opposed. If I became a paid officer, I would willy-nilly have real power and responsibility and he would cease being what he fancied

243

himself to be – the source of all wisdom in the organization. G.J. Reeve, who had known me as a boy in his school and as a member of his bible class, said he thought my heart was not really set on becoming a news-paper publisher. He thought I could succeed if my heart was in the project, but he did not think it was. And he was right.

I then decided on a compromise. I would cease to be president. I would no longer be the spokesman of the *Citizen*, but I would continue as a director. United College could not surely complain about me being a director of the *Citizen* any more than the Winnipeg school board would or could complain about G.J. Reeve being one.

And so my presidency came to an end. But that is not the end of the story. During the evening of 17 May 1947, Principal Graham rang me up at my home. He said he was about to depart for eastern Canada for the purpose of recruiting new staff for the history department and other departments of the College. He wanted to know where I stood with respect to the *Citizen*. I said I had resigned from the presidency, but that I was still a director and would remain one so long as the by-laws of the company permitted.

'But you can't do that,' Graham declared. 'And I am informed that you are still signing cheques for the *Citizen*.'

I replied that I was authorized to sign cheques until the new president, G.J. Reeve, was free to familiarize himself with the affairs of the office. This would happen in the school vacation which began in six weeks time. But, I added, 'How do you know that I am signing cheques?'

Principal Graham replied that he had had this information from a member of the Board of Regents of the college.

'Who?' I asked.

'I am not at liberty to say,' he replied, 'but he knows the facts because he is the counsel of the Royal Bank.' The Royal Bank handled the accounts of the *Citizen*.

I suddenly became enraged.

'Who is this man?' I shouted. 'I am going to report him to the Law Society for a breach of confidence. Who the hell do the Board of Regents think they are? God Almighty who makes His own rules of behaviour!'

Graham said he did not want to discuss the matter further. He repeated the assertion that I could not be a director of the *Citizen* and continue to teach in United College.

'Then you had better fire me. Good night.'

This is what he did. Two days later I received a registered letter which read: 'Further with reference to our conversation of the 17th inst. I beg to refer you to my letter of February 1st 1947 informing you that your appointment had been extended another year to cover the session 1946-47. Under instruction from the Executive Committee of the Board of Regents, I now advise you that this appointment will not be renewed and therefore terminates as of August 31st, 1947.'

Legally I did not have a leg to stand on. Politically, however, I had a potentially strong case if I chose to exploit it. Six years later, a friend of mine, then a student, Harry Crowe, who was an active worker on behalf of the *Citizen* had his appointment as a teacher at United College similarly terminated on account of his endeavours to build up the Canadian Association of University Teachers. He fought the Board of Regents and he won and ironically the two teachers appointed to fill my place and that of Lower in 1947, Stuart Reid and Kenneth McNaught, both resigned from United College in support of Harry Crowe and the right of teachers to belong to a trade union. Stuart Reid became the executive secretary of the Canadian Association of University Teachers.

In my case there was a different outcome. While I was discussing what to do with the board of the *Citizen*, I tried to get something in writing from the authorities of United College. In this I had no success. Principal Graham replied to my question about my dismissal by saying that I had not been dismissed. I had simply not been reappointed. We fenced around for a few weeks and finally L.J. Reycraft, the chairman of the Board of Regents and the counsel of the Canadian Pacific Railway in Winnipeg, wrote to me. He said, 'You are already aware of the reasons why you have not been re-engaged. The Board of the College is under no obligation to re-appoint you or re-engage you. We wish you every success and feel confident you will find other and profitable employment.'

A delegation of students tackled Graham on the subject, but he stood firm in his refusal to discuss the matter. They said I was an excellent teacher, that I had been elected honorary president of the graduating class and so on, but the principal refused to talk.

In the *Citizen* there was a split about what to do. The trade union men wanted to take up the challenge and fight on the principle of the right of people to do as I had done without being coerced by their employers. Brown and the co-operators thought otherwise. They had no stomach for a fight.

As for myself, I was faced once again with the dilemma either of taking up the fight and so committing myself completely to the *Citizen* or seeking another academic appointment and so carrying on with a career as a teacher. There was an opening available in the University of Manitoba. The department there wanted me to join them. In fact they had wanted me to come in 1946, but a gentlemens' agreement between the administrators of the University and United College designed to prevent competitive bidding for staff stood in the way of making me an offer so long as I was employed by United College. Now this obstacle was removed and I had the prospect of a better paid and less burdensome job in the University of Manitoba.

I decided in favour of university work and so I said nothing more. But there were wheels within wheels. The recommendation to appoint me in the University of Manitoba ran into difficulties. The president of the university wavered. Weeks passed and I began to feel that I was faced with the 'proletarianization' Herbert Norman had feared. I had a wife and two children, a mortgage, no money in the bank and I would have no income after 31 August 1947.

It seemed pretty apparent that those who wanted me out of United College did not want me in the University of Manitoba either. Sometime later it was reported to me that one of the newspaper proprietors of Winnipeg had declared to his friends that he intended 'to run that son of a bitch Ferns out of town.' Having regard for the action taken against Brockington, this report did not seem at all improbable.

However, this was only round 2. I was down but not yet out. The political complexion of the Board of Governors of the University of Manitoba differed from that of the Board of Regents of United College. The chairman of the Board of Governors of the university at that time was W.J. Parker. In real life he was a well-to-do farmer and the president of Manitoba Pool Elevators, the largest and most powerful co-operative in the province. One of my friends, I have never been able to discover whom, had a happy idea. If the dean of the Faculty of Arts and Science could not approve of my appointment and the president of the university feared to approve of me, could my appointment not be referred to the chairman of the Governors? W.J. Parker was the president of a co-operative. Ferns had until a few months previously been the president of a co-operative and was a fellow director with Fawcett Ransome, the secretary of Manitoba Pool Elevators. Surely he would approve of Ferns' appointment at least to a temporary post? This is what happened.

I was invited to a man-to-man interview with the chairman of the board. Parker seemed interested in satisfying himself I was not a red. Up to this point no one had injected into the battle the accusation of communism, although undoubtedly it was a *sub rosa* issue. It was part of the folk culture of the time to suppose that anyone who thought differently from anyone else must be a communist. Jock Brown, for example, was supposed to be a communist. Dave Simkin was sometimes described as one and one of the features about the *Citizen* which worried members of the CCF who otherwise welcomed the *Citizen* was the question of 'communist influences.'

I rather expected something like the kind of questions the chairman of the governors would ask and I came armed with an answer – the text of a speech I had made at a conference of the Institute of Canadian-American Relations in St Paul, Minnesota, in November 1946. This institute was nothing grand. It was a joint enterprise of the students and staff of United College and Macalister College, a liberal-arts college in Minnesota. The speech was in print along with several others, and had been distributed in Winnipeg as well as in Minnesota as evidence of an uplifting spirit of citizenship, international good will and the like which animated United College, its staff and its students. I invited Mr Parker to read this speech and I particularly directed his attention to two paragraphs:

You will recall that at one stage Jesus was asked by one of His followers: 'What shall we do to inherit eternal life?' And Jesus, compelled to give a short and essential answer, replied, 'Love God and love one another.' There is the root of the matter. There is the solution for the problem of inner motivation which is, in my opinion, very practical and valuable in the circumstances of our world.

If we accept this Christian guide as the directing force of our lives, we shall, I think, address ourselves to our complex political problems in a satisfactory way because then we will not frame our politics in terms of what is good for me alone, or my family alone, or my class alone or my country alone. We shall frame our policy in answer to the question, What is good for mankind? What can increase eternal life? What can lead us away from the hell of our own making?

W.J. Parker was somewhat taken aback by this. Here was an utterance of H.S. Ferns in print, published by United College.

'But why are you in trouble with United College?' he asked.

'Because the Board of Regents of United College do not like co-operatives and the chairman of the Board of Regents is your friend, L.J. Reycraft of the CPR.'

This was sufficient to bring the interview to a successful conclusion. The CPR occupied a prime position in the demonology of the co-operative movement and so the head of the Wheat Pool had nothing more to say. And yet I had scored only a partial triumph. I was to be employed on a temporary basis, year to year, as I had been at United College.

After this my part in the affairs of the *Citizen* began to diminish. Although G.J. Reeve was the president, the real power was in the hands of Jock Brown. When the contract with Universal Printers was signed it became necessary immediately to find a chief executive. Brown discovered the man he thought could do the job. This was Jack Sweeney. Sweeney was an experienced newspaper executive, but he had many shortcomings as far as supporters of the *Citizen* were concerned. In the first place he had worked most of his life for the proprietors of the *Winnipeg Free Press*. He had been a Liberal candidate in the federal election of 1945. He was in his sixties and was supposed to be unsympathetic to trade unions.

Because there was much opposition to the appointment of Sweeney, Brown turned to me to help put the appointment across to the membership. I was invited to meet him. I was persuaded to invite Sweeney and some of the leading people in the *Citizen* to my home. The one thing about Sweeney, apart from his pleasant personality, which led me to support him, was his real knowledge of the Canadian newspaper industry and his connections in the business. I had a number of reservations about the man, but I could suggest no alternative.

In order to win me around, Brown suggested that if Sweeney were appointed, I'd write a set of policy guidelines for the paper. I agreed to do this. I laboured at the job of setting forth briefly a policy which would ensure a politicial disposition of equal friendliness to all elements in the community not in the grip of the Liberal and Conservative politicians and the kind of people who had attacked Brockington and were trying to destroy me.

Came the evening when I was to seek the board's approval of the guidelines. As I entered the board room, I noticed Brown and Ransome *tête-à-tête*. When they saw me, they broke up awkwardly and greeted me with false jocularity. It crossed my mind that something must be up, but on picking up the agenda I saw that my guidelines was the fourth item; this seemed to ensure an opportunity for a good discussion and a decision.

248

Understandably with the chief executive officer present and a lot to report and discuss, the meeting moved slowly. It seemed to me, however, that Brown and Ransome were spinning things out a bit. G.J. Reeve in the chair was a great believer in letting everyone have their say and in their own way. Time passed and when 10.15 pm was reached, I appealed to the chairman to speed the proceedings in order to discuss the important question of policy guidelines. Jock Brown intervened to say that inasmuch as it was now after ten o'clock we ought to leave the question of policy for another meeting. Fair enough. Then he added that he had discussed policy with Mr Sweeney. He thought that Mr Sweeney knew what was wanted and that it would be imprudent to seem to shackle the general manager in any way. After this I never had anything further to do with the *Citizen* or with J.B. Brown.

The *Citizen* commenced publication as a morning daily newspaper on 1 March 1948 and ceased to appear on 13 April 1949.

An explanation for the failure of the enterprise is not easy to determine. At one time I had the impression that so many wrong turnings were taken under J.F. Sweeney's direction that Sweeney was rendering a service to his previous employers, the Sifton family who owned the *Winnipeg Free Press*. The theory of sabotage by the established newspapers is, however, quite untenable. In fact, the evidence suggests that Jack Sweeney was in the end the only person at the top of the organization who committed everything to the *Citizen* and that he wore himself out trying to make it work.

One trouble was that Sweeney could only conceive of a newspaper in terms of what he knew – in terms of a daily paper as nearly like the *Winnipeg Free Press* or the *Regina Leader Post* as his resources would permit. The result was evident. The *Citizen* was not a very good news-paper by conventional standards and Sweeney and the people he employed did not have the imagination and daring to create something different, dramatic, and new. They avoided smut, scandal, and the exploitation of personalities. They tried to be totally apolitical. About the only feature of the paper capable of attracting attention was the sports reporting. Even some of the good things in the *Citizen* were an editorial misjudgement. For example, they published an account of the great depression by Jimmy Gray, which eventually became his best-selling book *The Winter Years*. Published in the prosperous and optimistic 1960s this material was immensely popular with readers who had forgotten or had never known what a depression is like. In 1948-49, the depression was not just a memory; it was an active fear. Reminding people of misery is not something a Beaverbrook or a Hearst would have allowed.

One thing about the *Citizen's* failure centres on the inadequacy of its capital. There is something in this explanation, but only something. The *Citizen* could have done with more capital, but only a truly vast amount of capital supplied by someone or some institution with no interest in profit or even in balancing the books could have surmounted the obstacles placed in the path of the *Citizen* by the established newspaper interests. There was, for example, the problem of getting news about Canada as a whole. No newspaper in Canada can long endure unless it gives its readers continuously information about Canada as a whole and the job of reporting an immense and scattered country like Canada is very costly. The established newspapers had solved this problem by a co-operative of proprietors, the Candian Press Association. The established interests refused to give the *Citizen* access to the CP wire service. The only alternative was the impossibly costly task of reporting Canada itself or rewriting what was picked up from already published material or news broadcast on the radio networks. The *Citizen* was able to buy other wire services, but these, except the British United Press, were American services with an international and American coverage. The *Citizen* had the *New York Times* service, but this was not a source of Canadian news and certainly not of Canadian trivia, which is often the news of the greatest interest.

Then there was the matter of newsprint. Ten years of prosperity in North America had greatly altered the commercial position of the newsprint manufacturers. Their productive facilities were overtaxed, as a result of low levels of investment in plant during six years of war. The existing newspapers in the United States and Canada had solved their newsprint problems in a sellers' market by signing long-term contracts with newsprint producers so that there were no sure sources of supply in the open market. The *Citizen* had difficulty in getting newsprint and some of what they did get was very dear compared with the prices paid by newspapers with long-term volume contracts.

Then there was a mistake for which I was as much responsible as anyone else: the decision to publish a morning newspaper. The structure and character of Winnipeg as a community, the habits of the people, the climate, and even the time zone in which Winnipeg is located in North America were obstacles to the success of a morning newspaper. Experience shows that we should not have been frightened by the fact that the

Free Press and the *Tribune* occupied the evening field. We should have set about evicting one or both from this field and this could have been done by concentrating on attracting the big advertisers by low-page rates and by demonstrating to them that their message was getting to the housewife who did *not* read the *Free Press* or the *Tribune*. As it was the *Citizen* was not a good medium of advertising as far as the housewife was concerned. Her day had started by the time the *Citizen* arrived and she had made her shopping decisions before she went to bed the previous evening on the basis of information obtained from an evening newspaper.

One consequence, but not the only one, of being a morning paper was a restricted circulation. The *Citizen* started with 21,000 copies a day. Its best circulation figure in its fifteen months of life was 27,000. This, compared with a circulation of 90,000 plus for the *Winnipeg Free Press* and 50,000 plus for the *Tribune*, suggests some of the problems which faced those selling advertising to both the big department stores and to the individual in the market for classified advertising.

The most fundamental reason why the *Citizen* failed was not, however, economic, financial, or journalistic. The *Citizen* failed because no one cared enought about it. Perhaps only Jack Sweeney cared and he came too late and was too old and too conservative. Dave Simkin and I cared when the project was still but a gleam in our eyes and we had a great many ideas about how to get about establishing a new daily newspaper. But we were baffled by the problem of raising capital and this caused us to be sidetracked into the idea of co-operative ownership. Once this had happened Dave was committed to looking after his own interest, and I was confused about mine.

Falling in love with an idea, as I did, is a harmless enough thing to do as long as one merely puts the idea into a book or an article. Attempting to translate an idea into an instrument for social action is quite another matter – immensely more difficult, demanding from the individual much more than brains and imagination and having consequences for others which are incalculable. Any profit and loss account in this case is hard to establish. Certainly the *Citizen* was a critical event in the fortunes of Dave Simkin and his father. They went on to greater things as printers, employing high-speed machines in the production of advertising 'flyers' on a mass scale and cheap paperback books. The trade unions as a whole benefitted from the brief but sobering effects of competition on the character of labour reporting by the two established newspapers. The ITU, whose dispute with the Winnipeg newspapers sparked off the *Citizen*,

251

benefitted not at all. Ten years after the *Citizen* closed, the ITU men were still forlornly picketing the *Tribune* and the ITU lost their role in the newspaper industry in Winnipeg once the *Citizen* went bankrupt. The rising tide of prosperity in Canada in the 1950s offered opportunities to those who lost their livelihood and the *Citizen* was soon forgotten.

Among the reasons advanced for the failure of the *Citizen* was its political colour. From the outset Dave Simkin, Jock Brown, and I had agreed about one point: that the *Citizen* could not develop and prosper if it tied itself to any political party or dogmatically plugged any party line. Dave knew from experience and I learned as I went along from men like the executives of the *Chicago Sun* that explicit political agitation in the columns of newspapers, no matter what political party is being supported, is counter-productive as far as reader recruitment is concerned. Newspapers can be used to manipulate and form public opinion, but this is a much more subtle operation than nailing a partisan slogan to the mast head. In a volatile, leftish community as Winnipeg then was, any identification with a political party would have been a recipe for disaster. As it was J.F. Sweeney's known identification with the federal Liberal party was a cause for criticism, although it would be hard to prove that any substantial body of people refused to buy the *Citizen* because Sweeney ran for Parliament as a Liberal in the election of 1945. In my endeavour to frame policy guidelines, I aimed at establishing an editorial position which can best be described as centre-leftish non-partisanship with an emphasis on positive and friendly comment and reporting of the activities of trade unions and minority organizations of a non-Anglo-Saxon provenance.

What I did not recognize at that time and which the presence and activity of Jock Brown and Fawcett Ransome obscured from me was the essential socio-political split in Manitoba between town and country. The constituency boundaries and all the political arrangements of Manitoba were designed to assure the dominance of rural interest over popular city interest and to facilitate the recruitment of the rural population as a voting support for a government of hard-line financial interests who attached more importance to public debt service than anything else in the community.

Had I responded to the advice of Reg Schmok and Jack Simons to ditch Brown and Ransome at the first annual meeting, a policy of making the *Citizen* a paper expressive of the interest and ambitions of the majority of Winnipeg's people might have emerged. The attempt to preserve unity between the trade unions and the co-operatives meant that the *Citizen* could never develop as a voice of the real majority in Winnipeg which was politically neutered by a provincial government based on a system of semi-rotten boroughs in the countryside. In 1952, for example, 228,280 registered voters in the urban areas of Manitoba (and this means principally the city of Winnipeg) returned seventeen members of the Legislature and a lesser number of registered rural voters (i.e., 224,083) returned forty members to the Legislature. An endeavour to advertise this discrimination and to build on it might very well have benefitted the *Citizen*.

Although the city of Winnipeg had a tradition of leftism dating from the general strike of 1919 and the ethnic minorities had little direct access to positions of prestige and authority, the non-establishment (not anti-establishment) majority was much divided along racial and ideological lines. For this reason alone, a policy of sympathetic non-partisanship was essential. But this kind of non-partisanship was hard to practise. If one adopted a neutral tone vis-à-vis the Labour Progressive party, the CCF tended to assume that communists ran the *Citizen*. If one took an anti-red line, it was assumed that the *Citizen* was no different from the *Winnipeg Free Press*. Socialists and communists were not the only people who had to be considered. I was approached by the Social Credit movement with promises of support if we would commit the *Citizen* to their policies. A venerable, white-haired, French-speaking cleric, who ran the Credit Union movement among French-speaking Manitobans, came to see me and I warmed to him to the extent of joining him in a dialogue in French over the radio in which I promised that if there was sufficient support for the *Citizen* we would consider favourably the publication in French of articles of interest to French readers.

After the publication of the *Citizen* was underway there was a knocking campaign mounted to smear the *Citizen* as a pinko rag run by the communists. According to one employee, Robert Picken, the RCMP interviewed employees of the *Citizen* after its closure to determine the extent of communist penetration (see Noelle Broughton, 'The Fall of the Winnipeg Citizen,' MA thesis, Carleton University, p. 35). It is, therefore, worthwhile to discuss this aspect of the *Citizen's* affairs.

It was alleged that Jock Brown and Dave Simkin were communists and I am sure that the same was said of me, but never to my face. As far as Jock Brown is concerned, I could never detect any sign in him of being a communist. The only thing he had in common with party members was a complacent omniscience. Otherwise, he seemed to me a somewhat more literate than average Scottish radical with a dogmatic enthusiasm for co-operatives. If he had ever been a communist he must have been a very troublesome and ill-disciplined one. The impression that he was a communist can probably be attributed to the fact that he had, as far as I know, never belonged to the CCF and was inclined to dismiss CCFers as academic dreamers, much as he considered me to be. He always emphasized that he was a 'practical man,' which he was up to a point, that point being where he read the balance sheet of the Canadian Co-operative Farm Implements Co. Ltd.

Dave Simkin was no communist. He only knew communists. Dave illustrated the great truth that there is nothing like making money to make men tolerant. The nature of his business and the time and energy it required ensured, apart from a profound and cynical scepticism, that he was anything but a communist. As for me, that is for the reader to make up his or her mind and that is what this book is about.

As to the relationship between the *Citizen* and the Labour-Progressive party, that can be summed up in four words: indifference tinged with hostility. Like other political groups the Labour-Progressive leaders evinced interest in the *Citizen* but this interest was curiosity, not support. Very shortly after the *Citizen* was incorporated, one of the Labour-Progressive leaders approached Dave Simkin and Dave and I were invited to meet a gathering of leading cadres in the back room of a shop on north Main Street, Winnipeg. As I remember the meeting there were present Joe Zuken, Jake Penner, Leslie Morris and William Kardash, the Labour-Progressive member of the Manitoba Legislature and a veteran of the Spanish Civil War who had lost a leg in battle.

Zuken and Morris took a very high tone with us. Did we not know that the Labour-Progressive party was launching its own daily newspaper and that we had no business encroaching on their territory? This did not particularly endear them to me. Dave was practical. He asked them how many copies of a newspaper published in Toronto they expected to sell in Winnipeg. They ignored this aspect of the matter as if dialectical materialism might enable them to overcome the fact that Toronto is eight hundred miles from Winnipeg and was then 24 to 30 hours away.

After we left Dave said to me, 'Those guys are crazy. Even the *Financial Post* can't do more than sell in Toronto and Montreal simultaneously. What are they going to do? Have a private aeroplane and sell their paper at two bucks a copy?'

Kardash, who ran a co-operative creamery which delivered milk and dairy products in Winnipeg, was personally friendly to the *Citizen*, but nothing more. At the first annual meeting Chester King, a machinist in the CNR shops and a Labour-Progressive party member, was elected to the board, but this was the only communist in the organization as far as my knowledge goes. King exercised no influence and was only moderately successful in selling shares at his place of work. The Labour-Progressive leaders on the other hand were, if anything, hostile to the *Citizen* and helped the enterprise and influenced it in no way.

Association with the University of Manitoba and disassociation from the *Citizen* wrought an improvement in my circumstances. The first was marginally more rewarding financially, less burdensome, and more interesting than working in United College. The second allowed me more time for study and reflection and the renewal of my interest in Anglo-Argentine history. I even wrote a fairly serious essay for the *Manitoba Arts Review* on the ideas of Mackenzie King and a gossipy series of sketches of the Prime Minister for the *Canadian Forum*. I went to night classes in order to improve my far from perfect Spanish. In short, I began to resume the academic career broken off seven years before.

But the world kept breaking in and I did not resist. In February 1948, Professor W.J. Waines asked me whether I would consider accepting a union nomination as a member of a conciliation board being set up to enquire into and report on a dispute between the Winnipeg Electric Company, which operated the urban transport system of Winnipeg and the employers organization, the One Big Union. I accepted the nomination and ironically the *Free Press* and not the *Citizen*, then a week old as a daily newspaper, reported the fact under the headline: 'Tram Workers Name Professor Ferns.'

Accepting nomination by a trade union to serve on a conciliation board set up under terms set by the Province of Manitoba would seem hardly worthy of notice were it not for the penumbra of memories which the dispute evoked in the community. This was 1948. The Winnipeg general strike of 1919, the largest and most complete general strike in North American history, was still an active recollection in the minds of older workers and employers alike. The *New York Times* had described the events in Winnipeg in 1919 as 'a beautiful demonstration of essential Bolshevism' (D.J. Bercuson *Confrontation at Winnipeg*, p. 131). And now in the late winter of 1947-48, the One Big Union under the leadership of R.B. Russell, who had been jailed in 1919, was threatening to bring

255

the public transport system and perhaps part of the electrical power industry in Winnipeg to a standstill. Events in Czechoslovakia had greatly stimulated red-baiting everywhere and thus the ghosts of the past found new substance from the events of the present.

But Winnipeg in 1948 was not Winnipeg in 1919. The fact of a conciliation procedure based on law was only one measure of how different labour relations were after the Second World War from what they had been after the First, when the federal government sent a supply of machine guns to Winnipeg. In 1919 Russell had preached a syndicalist millennium; in 1948 he wanted an additional 21 cents an hour for the tram and bus workers.

The conciliation procedures in Manitoba were a provincial version of the federal conciliation legislation, which was Mackenzie King's first claim to fame when he was one of Laurier's ministers before 1911. Its provisions were entirely voluntary. Unions could legally strike in Manitoba and employers could legally lock out their employees. Both could, however, resort to conciliation, i.e., each could nominate a member of a three-person conciliation board and the persons nominated by the parties in dispute were obliged to agree on a neutral chairman. The board heard the parties directly without the intrusion of lawyers or without the constraints of rules of evidence. Boards could report in any way they wished: unanimously, a split report, or three separate reports. Reports were not binding on the parties.

All this sounds rather feeble, but the psychological and moral consequences of public enquiry were beneficial and often very compelling. A unanimous report was a considerable barrier to strikes and lock-outs,and those who took action against a unanimous report usually enjoyed little success. On one occasion in 1949, the bakery workers refused to follow my advice to accept a unanimous report and they suffered a catastrophic defeat.

The One Big Union which nominated me to the board was a remainder of the endeavour of the left radicals of 1919 to bring together all the unions in Winnipeg in a single organization. Whether the leaders like R.B. Russell and R.J. Johns (who had been jailed and became a teacher of metal working in my old school, St John's Technical High School) were seeking political power in 1919 is an open question in their minds as well as in everyone else's. In 1948 the One Big Union was an industrial union in the urban transport industry in Winnipeg with only two peculiarities: it was independent of both the great international union organizations, the AFL and the CIO, and of the purely Canadian and Catholic trade union confederations. Its other peculiarity was its leader, who described himself as 'an armchair Marxist' with no political affiliation of any kind.

By 1945 R.B. Russell was more a figurehead than anything else. I had several discussions with him and it seemed evident to me that he followed the advice of the two other men who constituted the union leadership. He was, however, pretty firmly in favour of a settlement of the dispute without a strike, if a settlement could be found.

The effective, operational leaders were Ed Armstrong, a former tram driver who was the secretary, and Reg Slocombe, the business agent. Ed Armstrong was a tall, lean, elderly man who reminded me always of my maternal grandfather, a stone mason from Devonshire. He knew the membership individually and intimately and he seemed to me to spend most of his time chatting with tram drivers and conductors and mainte-nance workers who called at the poky, smoke-laden headquarters in down-town Winnipeg.

The tactical brain of the organization was Reg Slocombe, a young man not very much older than I. He was, of course, said to be a communist, but I never saw any evidence of this. He was an intelligent, immensely hard-working and literate man, who really did know how to present a case based upon comparative figures of wages in the industry in the several cities of Canada and on the history of wages in Winnipeg in his industry and in others. He, furthermore, understood the company's finances, better sometimes than the management of the Winnipeg Electric itself. He was scruffy in appearance and quiet in his manner, but always in the end he commanded respect from the management team, from the board and indeed, from everyone except W.H. Carter, the president of the company, who was, I think, incapable of respecting anyone.

W.H. Carter was a businessman of the age before public relations became a science, technology, and a form of religion. He was born in Bismarck, North Dakota. He proudly described himself as a 'descendant of a long line of Methodist horse-traders.' For most of his business life he had been a large building contractor in western Canada. His firm had constructed grain elevators, bridges, hospitals, railway shops and various civil engineering projects from Winnipeg to Vancouver. Now in 1948, he was the president of the Winnipeg Electric Company. If anyone could provoke a strike in Winnipeg it was Carter.

The man nominated by the employers was R.B. Hunter, the retired general manager in western Canada of Swifts Canadian, a subsidiary of one of the largest meat-packing companies in the world, the headquarters of which was in Chicago. In accordance with Ferns' Law of Occupational Resemblance, Hunter, like Adam Borg of the Packinghouse Workers Union, called to mind one of the raw materials of the slaughterhouse business, to wit, a bull. He was not a fat man. He was a heavy one, not tall but solid with a centre of gravity below the navel. When seated he appeared immovable, large feet flat on the floor and large hands palm down on the table or desk in front of him. He walked, of course, but he gave the impression of moving slowly like a tank or an armoured personnel carrier. He had a dark saturnine face, heavy hooded eyelids and lips which would have been sensuous had they had more colour. I never saw him in anything but a dark suit and out of doors he wore a black Homburg hat. At first one had the impression that he growled rather than talked, but with acquaintance this impression wore off and he turned out to be a quite lively conversationalist in a matter-of-fact way. He prided himself on being a hard man and he was hard but never boastful or overbearing. When we had become friends and he reflected in a relaxed way on his experiences of life, he once said to me: 'I never like doing business with weak men who let you have your own way. Nine times out of ten you run into trouble with weak, soft people. Either they can't deliver on their promises or they try to slide out of their obligations.'

Needless to say, I felt some trepidation when I first encountered this formidable man. I had no experience of labour negotiations and all I knew about the struggle between labour and capital came from books. 'Well, Professor,' growled R.B. Hunter, 'we have to find a chairman, Whom do you suggest?' Of course I had no answer. I did not know anyone sufficiently prestigious or powerful to stand between me and my opposite number and so I said, 'Whom do you suggest?'

'Well, Professor,' Hunter said, 'This is going to be a tough bit of business. I think we ought to ask A.K. Dysart. You know him, don't you?' I knew A.K. Dysart as I knew Winston Churchill or General Eisenhower. He was a remote and prestigious figure: the senior judge in the Court of the King's Bench in Manitoba, chancellor of the University of Manitoba, and the judge who years before had tried and hanged 'the strangler,' the terror of western Canada for some months in the 1930s.

So we agreed to ask Mr Justice A.K. Dysart to be our chairman.

He was then (1948) in his seventies. He had come to Winnipeg from the Maritime provinces before the turn of the century. Appointed to the judiciary comparatively young, he was the longest-serving judge in the province, but fully in possession of his faculties and a man of considerable intellect and powers of concentration. He was an austere, laconic, and patient man who listened carefully to all that was said, treated everyone with equal courtesy, and never betrayed the slightest bias in discussion. He did once say, however, apropos to the wage rates we were considering, 'You know when I was young, they got a dollar a day. And look what they are asking for today.'

This was early in our deliberations and the remark made my heart sink. I soon discovered that this was but the reflection of a conservative old man from a slow-moving, poor community and that the observation in no way influenced A.K. Dysart in his study of the facts before him. Even the 'they' did not truly indicate the assumption that the tram drivers and conductors of Winnipeg were a race apart with whom he had no connection.

Reaching a conclusion which could be embodied in a unanimous report proved to be a long drawn out affair. We met as often as three times a week through part of March, all through April, and during the first week of May 1948. The reasons for this were partly due to Judge Dysart's wish to hear all the facts and arguments which could conceivably be produced by both the company and the union, but mainly to the determination of the management of the Winnipeg Electric to make no concessions without being guaranteed an increase in tram fares. Hunter was rather inclined to favour a 'deal' along these lines, but the chairman was adamant on the point that the conciliation board was charged with the responsibility under the legislation of reporting on wages and nothing else. Judge Dysart belonged to the generation which regarded it as not only contrary to law but contrary to public morality for management and unions to resolve their differences easily by joining forces at the expense of the consumer of their services or products, by the manipulation of prices by regulatory bodies, and by fiscal devices ensuring constantly rising price levels. In spite of a great difference in our ages and our views Judge Dysart and I were at one in believing that the dispute between the parties was a real dispute which had, if possible, to be resolved in terms of the parties' interests and in no other way.

Although there were many complications connected with various levels of skill and experience, the main problem was the difference between the company's policy of conceding an increase of 11 cents an hour tied to fare increase and the Union's demand for an increase of 21 cents an hour with no strings attached and payable from 1 March. Although I never said anything on the subject in the private discussions of the Board, Ed. Armstrong, Reg Slocombe, and I were aware that for some reason W.H. Carter, if not the management of the Winnipeg Electric, would like a strike, probably because he wanted to unload the tram and bus system on the city of Winnipeg. We argued that it would be a triumph of some sort if we could avoid a strike and get a modest wage increase.

The company's argument was that they could not afford a pay increase without a fare increase. They produced a flood of figures going back over twenty years showing how poor they were. Poverty was, of course, the case from 1930 to 1940, but from 1940 to 1948 the Winnipeg Electric trams and buses had 'never had it so good.' True, wages and prices had been restrained by the wartime controls, but business had enormously increased as a result of wartime industrial activity and growth, the restriction on gasoline supplies, and the absolute stop on the manufacture of motor vehicles for civilian use. Furthermore, the Winnipeg Electric had spent pratically nothing on new equipment. No tram was less than twenty years old. The tracks were in very bad shape. The buses and trolley buses were not so badly run down, but the whole system needed replacement. A high percentage of the Winnipeg Electric's capital was in the bank, not in the equipment of the system, and Carter wanted to unload this junk heap on the city. A strike would be a great help in achieving this object.

Some interesting light was thrown on Carter's objectives, not at a meeting of the Board, but while we were taking some tea during a recess. When meetings had gone on for more than two hours, it was Judge Dysart's policy to adjourn and take tea. Everyone present sat around chatting and there was generally an atmosphere of friendliness and informality. Carter did not often attend meetings, but one day he was present. He was a man without manners and he had no sense of occasion or the fitness of things. He was always at work in his own interest, and taking tea seemed to be in his view an opportunity to do a little fighting on his own behalf. One day he singled me out for attack. He turned to me and in his best redneck manner said, 'And what do the socialist professors think about this nationalization which is going on in England?'

I replied that I did not think much of it. What was happening in Britain might be described by some as socialism, but as far as I could see the owners of the railways and coal mines in Britain were exchanging rundown plant, out-of-date productive enterprises, and derelict real estate for British government securities sellable on the stock exchange or good as security for new investment in activities which were profitable and free of headaches.

This reply seems to have touched Carter on the quick, because he then became really nasty, and started making dark allusions to the influence of reds in the universities and in the union. I lost my temper and said, 'Mr. Carter, you have been coming here for some weeks now telling us how poor you are. If you are so poor why don't you unload the Winnipeg Electric on the city of Winnipeg and take your bloody money and invest it in something profitable like uranium mining?'

At this juncture Judge Dysart intervened mildly saying: 'Didn't I see in the papers a few months ago that you were dickering with the city about the street cars?'

Carter then shut up, and later one of his junior managers who had studied economics with me in the University of Manitoba, said quietly, 'Don't let Carter get under your skin. He's like that.'

After six weeks or so of hearing and discussions Judge Dysart said to Hunter and me that we could not go on longer debating and getting nowhere; that we must come to a decision and that to this end we ought to hear the parties separately and in private with a view to ascertaining what they might settle for as distinct from their publicly announced positions. This was agreed.

I was pretty sure the Old Big Union would accept a modest increase, even the company's offer of 11 cents an hour provided it was not tied to a fare increase and was sweetened with something extra. Judge Dysart had already ruled out any reference to a fare increase and I could not see R.B. Hunter refusing to consider a sweetener, such as back-dating an increase of 11 cents an hour. What Carter might do was anybody's guess.

We heard the union officers first. I fed them questions which enabled them to satisfy Judge Dysart that they would take seriously a unanimous report provided there was some improvement in the company's offer. Then we sent for Carter. Hunter fed him some questions which enabled him to state that he would consent to an increase of at least 11 cents an hour provided the company lost no money by doing so. Judge Dysart then turned to me and said, 'And have you any questions for Mr Carter, Professor Ferns?'

'Only one question,' I replied. 'And it is this. Can Mr Carter tell us what he will do if we unanimously report that an increase of, say, 15 cents an hour be paid?'

Carter glared at me and said loudly, 'I can tell the professor this. If you recommend anything more than 11 cents an hour I'll close the car-barn doors and nothing will run in this town.'

'Thank you, Mr Carter. I have no further questions.'

This revelation that the president of the Winnipeg Electric would shut down a public service had, I think, a considerable effect upon Judge Dysart. When Carter withdrew Judge Dysart asked me what I thought we ought to recommend. I knew that the chairman would only go along with a proposal that would prevent a strike, and that if I could suggest something which had his support to this end he would persuade R.B. Hunter to make the report unanimous. I, therefore, said that I thought that Russell, Armstong, and Slocombe would not like a recommendation of 11 cents an hour and that I could not guarantee an acceptance of such a low figure, but the men themselves might very well accept 11 cents an hour if the increase were back dated to 1 March and that an additional $5\frac{1}{2}$ cents an hour were granted backdated to 1 January 1948. If one were going to secure acceptance by the employees, it was absolutely essential that they could look forward to thirty or forty dollars extra in their first pay packet after the signing of the agreement. R.B. Hunter nodded assent on this point. The whole package was going to cost the Winnipeg Electric $500,000. Both the chairman and Hunter knew in their heart of hearts that $500,000 was not going to break the Winnipeg Electric, fare increase or no fare increase.

And so we reported unanimously. The politics of acceptance were interesting to observe. The company said they would be $83,000 in the red in the next year unless they had a fare increase, and that they would not and could not accept the report unless fares went up. The union leaders said that 11 cents an hour was insufficient, and that they wanted at least 15 cents an hour. However, the proposal would be put to the membership, and a vote of the whole membership taken by ballot.

A meeting of the members of the union was called, and I was asked to address the gathering in one of the theatres. I said I admired the OBU as a strong sensible union that was not going to make trouble for the sake of making trouble. The union executive then asked the members to vote by ballot on the proposals of the board, but they did not declare for or against the proposals. Reg Slocombe, however, said that before voting every member of the union ought to think of his or her individual personal interest before voting, and he spelt out what acceptance would mean in terms of dollars and cents, what a strike would cost the individual members, and what the estimated advantages might be if a strike produced, say, an increase of 15 cents an hour after a stoppage of one to four weeks.

The union meeting was held on 30 May 1947. On 10 June the ballots were counted. They showed a substantial majority for acceptance of the report. The company still held out, and the union announced that they would strike for 21 cents an hour. It was pointed out that the report recommending 11 cents an hour being resisted by the company had been agreed to not just by A.K. Dysart and H.S. Ferns but also by R.B. Hunter. On 15 June, the company agreed to acceptance, and Ed Armstrong told the press. 'I consider this a splendid victory: one of the best we have ever won.'

During the next year I served on several conciliation boards. None of these compared in interest or importance with the Winnipeg Electric dispute, but the last one in which I was involved before I left Winnipeg presented some problems worth remembering. This was a dispute in the baking industry which, leading to a strike, had some effect on the structure of the manufacture and marketing of bread in Winnipeg.

I was asked to accept nomination by W.T. White, the business agent of the Bakery Workers Union, an affiliate of the Canadian Congress of Labour. White had been a founder director of the *Citizen*, one of those invited to create a public image for its board and not on account of his capacity to contribute to policy-making. He was a non-descript little man, who, I suspect, was out of his depth as a trade union leader. He certainly lacked judgement and shrewdness in the affairs of his union.

After some preliminary study of the industry I told White that in my opinion he could expect to get very little on behalf of his members whether the union struck or it did not. He, on the other hand, seemed to believe a strike was a sort of magic which could produce blood from a stone.

I said, no. You can marginally increase wages if we get a unanimous report, but a strike will be a disaster. In several discussions with the business agent I spelled out to him the obstacles to victory, which, as I learned more about the industry, seemed even greater than I had at first supposed. In the first place, the membership of the union was overwhelmingly employed in the three large mechanized bakeries in Winnipeg. All were local baking operations of large Canadian corporations. A strike in Winnipeg alone was not going to affect these companies very fundamentally, and they could stand a long strike.

Second, the large commercial bakeries were not in control of the total bread market. Winnipeg had many small family-operated bakeries producing the kind of real bread which Jews, Ukrainians, Poles, and Germans found an indispensable part of an agreeable diet. Furthermore, there were within a forty-mile radius of Winnipeg probably thirty or forty small town bakeries serving local markets. It would be no trouble at all for all these enterprises to double or triple their production to meet the needs of Winnipeg.

Third, the bread distribution system was changing, and home delivery dominated by the big commercial bakeries was having increasingly to compete with the supermarkets where prices were lower. The supermarkets were already buying bread from the small bakers, and it would not be difficult for the supermarkets to keep their customers supplied.

Finally, bread is something the housewives of Winnipeg still knew how to bake, and the ingredients were readily available. Furthermore, the end product of the housewives as well as the small Jewish, Polish, and German bakeries was in general superior to and cheaper than the products of the commercial bakeries. It was said that Canada produced the best wheat in the world and the worst bread. This was largely due to the methods and technological sophistication of the commercial bakeries. A strike in their plants could be a gastronomic blessing to the people of Winnipeg.

I figured that the employers could only be induced to improve wages if they were confronted with a unanimous report, and that unanimity could only be achieved if there was a chairman whom the employers could not challenge. The employers' nominee was Syd Halter, a lawyer known popularly for his part in the organization of ice hockey in the city. He was a cold hard man. I did not wait for him to suggest a chairman. I asked him, 'What do you think of R.B. Hunter as our chairman?'

I could see that Halter was a bit taken aback by this suggestion. He suspected a trick and he was right. No employer anywhere could reject the report of a board chaired by R.B. Hunter. Furthermore, Halter knew he would look a fool if he refused to accept Hunter. Whom could you get more sympathetic to employers in the food industry than the retired general manager of Swifts Canadian?

As it turned out, Hunter was a good chairman and surprisingly sympathetic to the union. He insisted on visiting the bakeries and we had some fascinating hours examining the marvellous devices which produced such appalling products as wrapped, sliced, tasteless, white bread. Because he was a clever man with a vast experience of the food industry, he was a perceptive enquirer. Once he said to me, 'You know, Ferns, I am surprised at what some of these bakers get away with.'

No matter what the chairman and I thought about wages in the baking industry in Winnipeg, we were confronted by a hard man and some hard facts. Neither a strike nor a generous recommendation by a board of conciliation could alter the circumstances in the baking business. The work force in the industry was largely unskilled. Only economic expansion of a kind which would offer more opportunities for the unskilled could possibly lift the wage levels of the below average work force of an industry which was easy to enter and easy to leave, where labour turnover and absenteeism were high. The employers could, if they wished, break the union because, if they so desired, they could recruit a work force from non-union workers willing to take jobs at any wages on offer. In Winnipeg in 1949 the market for unskilled labour was still surplus to demand. The rising level of expectation and the increasing desire for goods were impelling more and more unskilled into the labour market. Economic expansion during the war had broken down many inhibitions and fears, especially among women entering the labour market, and this had the effect of increasing the pool of people willing and able to work in an industry like baking where skill and experience were not important.

Syd Halter, and behind him the big bakers, knew these facts better than anyone else. They did not have to concede very much, and Hunter and I had to find an increase which they would accept rather than have a strike. This increase was of the order of 5 per cent, a figure far below what the union 'demanded.'

I knew very well I was in for trouble when I went to the mass meeting of the union members. White had steamed them up to expect a sizeable increase, and here was their nominee on the board of conciliation recommending next to nothing. When I rose to speak an effort was made to howl me down. I was a traitor, a Judas, and the like. I was, however, given a hearing. I invited the members to make some calculations about what they would earn in the coming year at the rates proposed and what their income would be in the coming year if they went on strike for three to six weeks and then won their demands.

I remember very vividly an intervention at this point, when I was asking the members to do some arithmetic so they could make up their minds. It came from a tall, thin, young man with heavy, black hair heavily greased and very shiny and smooth on his head, glistening in fact very like a glazed current bun. He almost sobbed his appeal to me. 'But tell us what to do! Tell us what to do!

'I am telling you what to do! To make a calculation of your interest.'

But these people were not rational tram drivers and conductors. They were a mob encouraged to believe in the magic of a strike. Like almost everyone else in Winnipeg they wanted more money. This made them blood brothers with W.H. Carter and tram drivers and university teachers and newspaper proprietors. But they did not know how to go about getting more money in the circumstances in which they found themselves. Such knowledge is very unequally distributed in society, and the bakery workers had a very small share.

They struck. Within forty-eight hours Winnipeg had an over-supply of bread. It would be an exaggeration to say that Winnipeg was bathed in the delicious odour of baking bread, but it suffused more homes than enough to defeat the union. For the bread delivery men, who were much the best paid in the industry, the strike was a total disaster. The big bakers ceased delivering bread to homes, and the supermarkets took over distribution. Never again did the citizens of Winnipeg see the familiar sight of the delivery wagons and trucks of Canada Bread, Westons, and Spiers Parnell.

Simultaneous to my endeavours to save the bakery workers from their union, I was engaged without success in an attempt to save myself as a teacher in the University of Manitoba. There had been some changes at the top in the University. The president of the university, Dr A.L. Trueman, had been fired by the Board of Governors for reasons that were never explained. The new president was a hatchet-faced Englishman who taught mathematics at McGill. He was an unknown quantity. It was in these circumstances of flux that I began to explore the possibility of my temporary appointment sponsored by two departments, economics and history, being converted into a permanent post in economic history.

I sought the advice and help of my old teacher, W.J. Waines. He was a disinterested friend whom I trusted and an experienced university politician, with a considerable knowledge of the wider community of Manitoba. It must be borne in mind that in 1949 there was no expectation, not even a hope, that the university would grow as it did in the 1960s. The expansion consequent upon the demobilization of the armed forces had peaked and it was anticipated that the university of the 1950s would not differ greatly from that which had managed to survive in the 1930s.

And there were good reasons for this view. The government of Manitoba was still the same kind of government which had controlled Manitoba for more than a quarter of a century. Its policy was 'economy.' Pay the public debt. Preserve the public credit. Spend as little as possible even on demonstrable economic necessities like roads and rural electrification. As for schools and the university it was regarded as a great triumph of enlightened policy that teachers were being paid regularly a living wage, something which had not been the case during the 1930s.

To suggest, as I was doing, that a new permanent post be created for me was to propose something nearly impossible of implementation. But there was more to the matter than this. There was me. Waines turned the matter over in his mind, consulted around, and came to the conclusion that I could not expect to make a career in Manitoba. I never pushed him to explain why this was so, but I did accept that it was so.

My own explanation at the time was hypothetical and incapable of positive proof. First there was the *Citizen*. At that time the *Citizen* was a 'going concern.' I was no longer associated with it, but I had started the enterprise. Furthermore I had defied the Winnipeg establishment in maintaining a connection with the *Citizen*. Even terminating my contract of employment with United College had not forced me to leave the city. It had not even forced me to stay on the campus and keep out of public affairs.

I was still young enough to feel hatred and contempt for the men like those on the Board of Regents of United College who seemed to assume that a university teacher could be dictated to as well as overworked, underpaid, and denied by a collusive agreement among university administrators the opportunity to accept a post with better pay and fewer burdens. The bullying and contemptuous attitude of the president of the Winnipeg Electric had not improved my regard for the Winnipeg business class, although the engagement in real work with men like A.K. Dysart and R.B. Hunter had a strong counter-effect. But when I added it all up, I found that I hated some of the business class of Winnipeg. I supposed that they hated me, and that this explained why I could not make a career in Manitoba. They had power and I did not.

I had defied 'them' in another way, which, keeping in mind the growing atmosphere of the cold war, must have had a real effect on my prospects. Academics then could safely venture out of their ivory tower to participate in the proceedings of approved bodies like the Canadian Institute of International Affairs. It was, however, imprudent to have anything to do with certain other bodies, for example, the Canadian-Soviet Friendship Council.

I never had any part in the formation, management or activities of the Canadian-Soviet Friendship Council, but in November 1947 I did accept an invitation to address a public meeting of the council. This invitation came from Lewis St George Stubbs. Judge Stubbs, as he was commonly called, was in his day a famous or notorious Winnipeg radical. An Englishman educated at Cambridge University he had, some years previously, been appointed a county court judge. This was a minor judicial office, but Stubbs had as strong a sense of the judicial independence of the Crown as any man who ever sat on the bench anywhere. Indeed, he carried the conception of judicial independence to the length of believing that he could himself make the law if that made by the legislature conflicted with natural justice or the common law as he understood it. The judgements of Lord Coke had had something to do with the English Civil War, and Stubbs appears to have believed that his historic duty was to play the role of Coke in Manitoba. At any rate his findings in the Macdonald will case were of such a character that Judge Stubbs' conduct was questioned by the government and Legislature of Manitoba with the result that he was removed from the Bench. Lewis St George Stubbs offered himself as a candidate in a provincial election and he was returned to the Legislature with a very large majority. When I knew him he was a very independent member of the Legislature – a one-man party.

I had first met Judge Stubbs when a student society in United College asked me to chair a meeting which he had been invited to address. In my introduction I said I was very much pleased to present to the students an old Cambridge man from Christ's College, whose most famous son was the poet John Milton. This did not please Stubbs. He said he was obliged 'to correct you, Mr Chairman, in your reference to Christ's College. Its greatest son was not John Milton. He was Charles Darwin, and I want everyone to remember this.'

When Stubbs called me up to invite me to speak to the Canadian-Soviet Friendship Council, I said that I was quite willing to do so provided I was free to say what I thought and would not be expected to engage in apologetics on behalf of the Soviet regime. This annoyed him. Undoubtedly I had been tactless and discourteous in making stipulations about free speech to a man of Stubbs' character and reputation. I apologized, and I agreed to speak.

What I had to say was nothing but a reiteration of my speech to the

United Nations gathering in 1945, i.e., that Canada was located between the two greatest military powers on earth and that Canada's interest was to work for understanding between these super-powers. This may have been a counsel of perfection but it was not a popular one at that time. One had to be anti-Soviet and 100 per cent American. I am sure, however, that, in the eyes of those who could determine whether I worked in Manitoba or not, what I said was not so important as to whom I said it. A colleague in the university, a man of mildly socialist views, who subsequently accepted an invitation to speak to the Canadian-Soviet Friendship Council, was seriously misreported in the *Winnipeg Free Press*. When he protested, he was told by the editor of the *Free Press* that if he spoke to organizations 'like that' he could expect to be misreported.

Although, or perhaps because, Waines could see no future for me in Manitoba, he suggested a way out, and one which met with my ready approval. He proposed to use his influence to get me a Canadian Social Science Research Council fellowship worth $1,800.00. He would, further, see that I was excused from the chore of marking examinations in April. With a research fellowship and six months freedom from teaching I could, perhaps, finish my work on British enterprise in Argentine, which I had begun at Cambridge in the autumn of 1938. Cambridge University agreed to revive my candidature for a Ph.D. after a lapse of nine years. There was the problem of finding a good library in which to work. I decided on the place nearest to Winnipeg, the University of Chicago. I was accepted in the Graduate School, as a visiting student of the University of Cambridge, with the right to attend courses if I so desired and to consult Professor J.F. Rippy, their authority on Latin American history.

CHAPTER TEN

An Interlude in the USA

On 2 April 1949 I set out for Chicago with two objectives in mind: at least to break the back of the work necessary to write a thesis on British enterprise in Argentina and to get a teaching job somewhere in Canada, the United States, or Britain. In 1949, this last objective was not as easy an attainment as it sounds. In those days the academic job market in the United States was like that in Canada – sticky. It was especially sticky for me on account of what I described as the system of academic feudalism. A graduate school was good if it satisfied three interdependent conditions: if it had good libraries and/or laboratories, good research scholars and directors of studies, and a good system of placing graduates in jobs. It was this last factor, the dependence or feudal aspect which affected me. The Graduate School in Chicago had no obligation to place me in a job and Cambridge University was far away and not of much weight or connection in the American or Canadian job markets. Earle J. Hamilton, the professor of economic history in Chicago, was very candid on this topic. After being a few weeks in his class, I asked him if he knew of any openings. He replied that he would be glad to help me, but only after he had placed his own students. Unless the job market altered significantly this was likely to be never.

Getting to Chicago involved a not unexpected pause. I required a visa from the US consul in Winnipeg. I filled in the required form, sent all the necessary documents including my Canadian passport and called at the consulate. The clerk produced the documentation and then said: 'You will have to see the consul.' The consul was Sherburne Dillingham III. I waited for an audience. I found it hard to get my mind off George III, and what Sherburne Dillingham III would think about him. As it turned out, the consul was a man of approximately my own age, the very image of an East Coast aristocrat, expensively dressed with a sort of tweedy insouciance. He was very fit and carefully barbered. He could very well have been a young teacher in charge, say, of Dunster House at Harvard. And he was embarrassed.

He politely asked me to sit down. I knew what was embarrassing him and he knew that I knew. This made it hard for him to come to the point. I would understand, of course, that he had a duty … Finally I said, 'Mr. Dillingham, in the present state of world politics, the United States government has the right and indeed the duty, to ascertain the character and connections of persons seeking to live in the United States. What do you want to know about me?'

The effect of this utterance was almost magical. He relaxed and smiled and I thought for a moment that he was going to embrace me. What a relief to encounter someone who did not make things difficult by talking about civil liberties or who questioned the ideal image of the land of the free and the home of the brave!

I knew, of course, that opinion being what it was in the United States, the consul could only give me a visa if he had something to put in the file supporting his judgement. I said I knew he must be worried by the fact that I had once addressed the Canadian-Soviet Friendship Council, but what I had said there was along the same lines as what I had put on record and in print in St Paul, Minnesota, in November 1946.

Could I send him a copy of this speech? I did and in a few days I had my visa and within 72 hours I was in Chicago.

What a city! I had come disposed to despise and within a week I was in love with the town. Within a fortnight I was even reading the *Chicago Tribune*. Whenever I could I went to Comiskey Park to watch the White Sox. Ravinia! One evening I heard there Heifitz, Rubinstein, and Piatagorsky in concert in the open air against the background noise of crickets and in the far distance the clash of steel freight cars in the railway marshalling yards. The pictures in the Chicago Institute of Fine Arts were as splendid and better displayed than anything I had ever seen in my life. The Chicago zoo was then incomparable in its display of wild animals uncaged so that they did not appear to be the prisoners of men. Many years later I saw a TV presentation by Studs Terkel in which he endeavoured to explain the appeal of the city and he made a point which did not occur to me but which seems to explain something about the city. Terkel argued that Chicago is a workers' city, a city of producers and merchants and not a city of financiers and bureaucrats.

And this is true. The exciting vitality of the place was related directly to producing the wealth of America. In those days Chicago was still the centre of the meat-packing industry and on hot humid days when the breeze was light but in the wrong direction, sitting in Jackson Park one could smell the sweet stink of death from the slaughterhouses. There were great steel mills, miles of engineering works. The railways were still a fundamental part of the economy of the United States, and they converged on Chicago and spread out from there across the continent.

Here in Chicago much more than in Boston and Cambridge, Massachusetts, I formed the strong impression that the United States is a very different society from what I had known in Canada and in Britain. How different? The Americans described themselves as a free people. There is something in this. I felt free in Chicago in the sense that internal restraints did not exist or were very weak. Anything goes. Anything is possible. This frightened me, but it also exhilarated.

The energy and vitality which surged in the city was just as present in the Graduate School of the University of Chicago as it was in Lasalle Street. Students could work all the year round. No one had to take a vacation unless one wished. No one was obliged to endure a long vacation. The atmosphere was highly competitive. Examinations occurred every three weeks. Grades were discussed and compared and everyone strove for the best grades possible. But the school was no degree factory. The students had a zealous intellectual interest in what they were doing. Frank Knight was the great guru in economics at that time and he was a widely learned man who illustrated his books and lectures with analytical examples drawn from the worlds of Greece, Rome, and ancient China. One gained from him the impression that economic problems were timeless and not just the result of that Man in the White House. Milton Friedman was just beginning to teach in Chicago, and he had a great and exciting impact. One of his admirers said to me, 'I can't understand how such an intelligent man can be such a reactionary.'

As an exercise in intellectual refreshment I enrolled in three courses: on price theory, on imperialism and on European economic history. The course on price theory was given at 8 o'clock three mornings a week by George Stigler. By European and even Canadian standards, 8 am for lectures suggests a Spartan devotion to duty. In fact, its wisdom emerged as spring passed into summer. How pleasant in those days before air conditioning had become general to stroll through cool morning air to the lecture room and sit in some comfort while Professor Stigler in a fresh white shirt chalked his equations on the black board and conducted his animated arguments.

I did not have enough mathematics to benefit from all he said, but none the less I found his analysis of price determination worthwhile. I particularly recall his discussion of the distribution of goods and services in society and how this was affected by political structure and values. In slave societies productive activity yields bare necessities for the work force and luxuries for the masters; in totalitarian societies bare necessities for the work force and munitions and instruments of power for the party in control. He did not, however, consider the effect on a free enterprise society of huge political expenditure on arms and the purchase of allies in political competition with dictatorship, or how dictatorships by their nature and dynamics force free societies to resemble themselves.

The course on imperialism was given by a long, lean, elderly Yankee with a grey moustache. When he closed the door behind him to begin his first lecture he said: 'Now, I don't want anything said in this class repeated outside this room.' Nothing was ever said in the class which could not have been repeated outside of the room. The remark was symptomatic, it seemed to me even then, of the growing confusion and uncertainty of intelligent Americans about the role of the United States in world politics. The conviction of moral superiority to the British, the French, the Japanese, and the Russians on the subject of the self-determination of nations and freedom from the taint of imperialism was in decline. It was no longer possible to dismiss as aberrations the political tendencies which had produced the Panama Canal and the Platt amendment to the Cuban constitution. Intelligent Americans really were becoming worried about the country's policies and they were well aware that thinking and the words which expressed their thoughts, might very well be misunderstood, misinterpreted, and misused. Hence the caution, but there could be no mistake about their intention earnestly to think about imperialism, not just other people's but their own.

I enrolled in a course on economic history given by Professor Earle J. Hamilton. My purpose was to encounter the man whom I regarded as the most prodigious scholar in the social sciences then teaching. Hamilton was not necessarily a great thinker. Indeed, he was probably not a thinker at all. What he had done was undertake to prove or disprove propositions about the quantity theory of money in relation to prices by examining detailed data about price trends in Spain during the first century and a half of the Spanish Empire in the Americas. During this period there had been an historically exceptional flow of gold and principally silver from Mexico and Peru to Spain. This increase in the supply of precious metals was the basis of an increase in the supply of money. Did this increase in the supply of money lead in this instance to an increase in the level of prices?

The volume and complexity of the data to be found in the Spanish records of a hundred and fifty years was quite incredible. To have examined these data, to have organized and interpreted them was an heroic feat of scholarship. I had never encountered before such an exhibition of painstaking attention to detail addressed to the solution of a general proposition in economic science and on such a scale involving such difficult archival material. It was, therefore, an experience in itself just to see and listen to Earle J. Hamilton. As it happened, *American Treasure and the Price Revolution in Spain 1501-1650* was one of the few works which my Cambridge supervisor, Sir John Clapham, and I had ever discussed in detail. Clapham agreed that Hamilton's book was an exceptional piece of work by any standard.

When I had been a few weeks in the class and had had several short discussions with Hamilton, I told him how much Sir John Clapham esteemed his work and that he had had a small but admiring body of followers in Cambridge back in the 1930s. I added by way of a joke that Sir John Clapham had one criticism: that he regretted that Hamilton had claimed in the preface that he and his wife had spent 30,750 hours in studying their material and that he felt that 'Hamilton had better be careful or he'll have us all punching the time clock.'

Hamilton was pleased to think that he had an ardent admirer in the Professor Emeritus of Economic History in the University of Cambridge, but he was puzzled by Sir John Clapham's worry about the time clock. Nothing, however, was said, until one day, as I was walking down 59th Street, a car stopped at the curb. It was Hamilton and he opened the door and asked me if I wanted a lift. I got in. No sooner was I seated and before he engaged the gears, Hamilton said: 'You know what you told me about what Clapham had to say. Well, we *did* work 30,000 hours!'

'Good God, Professor Hamilton,' I replied, 'Sir John Clapham never doubted for a moment that you worked 30,000 hours on the data in *American Treasure*. Probably more. Let me explain. You are an American and you are proud of working hard and why shouldn't you tell the world? I often wondered what it takes to write a book like yours and now I know. But Sir John Clapham is an Englishman. He is a gentleman and therefore he does not like to admit that he works hard, or that he works at all. I am quite sure that if he had undertaken a study of Spanish economic history and that it required 30,000 hours of work, he would have done the work, but he would never have told anyone about it. He would most likely have left the impression in Cambridge that he had been merely walking in Spain or visiting a few grandees or looking at some awfully interesting old convents. I am sure, too, that he would have referred to the travels of George Borrow and *The Bible in Spain,* but never to work. But I think you were right to tell the world how much work you and your wife put into *American Treasure,* because I do not think there is such a thing as effortless genius. It is a gentlemanly illusion.' This seemed to mollify and reassure Professor Hamilton. He let me out at International House, but he would not come in for a coffee. He had work to do.

My main purpose on entering the University of Chicago was to use the library. It was excellent. Professor J.F. Rippy, the expert in Latin America, was ill or absent and I saw him only once. He was a prolific but uncritical and undiscriminating scholar. I was able to follow the trail of his researches through the pages of *The South American Journal*, which he had marked up in black ink. It was evident that he was fascinated and impressed by numbers. It did not matter what they were or whence they came. A promoter's advertisement proposing to raise, say, £1,000,000 by a share issue was considered evidence of a British investment whether the issue was ever subscribed or not. Current values of shares or bonds on the Stock Exchange were thrown into the pot. Professor Rippy ranged very widely and I covered only a small segment of his vast terrain, but not surprisingly I found his estimates of British investment and mine differed considerably and both his and mine from the contemporary estimate made by the commercial secretary of the British minister in Buenos Aires. When I had finished my work, I wrote to Rippy from Cambridge, asking him whether or not he could throw any light on these differences. He thanked me and complimented me on my interesting information. That was all.

Two people I encountered in Chicago provided me with information flowing from their own experience of life which left marks on my mind and caused me eventually to think about society in new ways. These were a student in the Graduate School of the University of Chicago, Thelma Johnson, and a paternal uncle, Rolly Ferns.

Thelma Johnson was a young black woman whose parents lived in Winnipeg. She was an American negro and in 1949 to call a black person a negro was not patronizing or abusive. Thelma referred to herself as a negro, but she would, of course, have become angry and offended had anyone called her a nigger. She had attended the great negro university, Howard, and I first encountered her as a supervisor of studies when she was working for a Master's degree in the University of Manitoba. Although she had attended a party at my home in Winnipeg and I saw her in supervisions and in classes, I did not know her well. When I met her in a student cafeteria in Chicago on my second day in the city, I was delighted – the first person from Canada I had yet encountered.

Canadians of my kind tended to have a vague but horrified impression of race prejudice in the United States. The index of race relations in the American republic at that time was the statistics on the number of lynchings per annum. Lynchings, of course, happened in the South, and Canadians tended to have the impression that everything was all right on the race front in the North whose victory in the Civil War had ended slavery. Canadians thought of blacks as sleeping-car porters, jazz musicians, and boxers. We admired Paul Robeson and Marian Anderson, but I had never heard a Canadian, including myself, ask why there were no Canadian blacks in the employment of department stores or insurance companies, no black postmen or bus drivers. If the question had been asked we would probably have replied that there were not many blacks in Canada. That was the reason, not colour prejudice.

Here I was in the United States greeting a black girl like a long-lost friend and she was doing the same. We sat down for a cup of coffee. Thelma was working on a Ph.D. in economics. She nodded and smiled and exchanged a few words with white male American students. There was an easy atmosphere of camaraderie.

Thelma invited me to dinner in her flat on 61st Street. Then she added, 'I share it with a white girl.' I was not quite sure how to interpret this. I went to dinner. Thelma did not remark again on sharing a flat with a white girl, but she did say that it seemed to her some kind of progress that the landlord had made no objection so far to her presence in the flat even though it was several hundred yards on the white side of Cottage Grove Avenue, which divided the black South Side from the white South Side where the University of Chicago and Jackson Park were located. The liberal atmosphere of easy relations between blacks and whites on the campus of the University of Chicago seems, it was hoped, to have spilled over a block or two to the south.

After going to dinner at Thelma's flat a few times, I asked her whether she would let me take her out to dinner. She did not say yes. She wavered and she could see I was disappointed. Then she said: 'I know you think I think you are making a pass at me and that I am turning you down. But that is not so. If we go up town to some white place, we may run into nastiness. I don't say we will, but we might. Some damned redneck only has to make a remark and what are you going to do? Fight him and all there will cheer him on. Or be humiliated as I will be? And if we go to a black place, what are you going to do if some big black guy says, 'What are you doing with my woman?' I don't say that will happen but it might. No, it's not worth it.'

It was the very ordinariness of what I had proposed and the inability to do a simple thing like have dinner in a public place with a friend which enraged me. Henceforward, race relations in the United States became one of the staples of our conversation. When I came to see that she was deeply disturbed by the position of blacks in American society and that the way I felt at being denied the opportunity to dine in public with a friend was a momentary, passing feeling compared with the abiding anger which she had inside herself, I asked where she would choose to live in the United States, were she free to establish herself wherever she pleased. I was under the naive illusion that she might answer Iowa or Idaho or some state where there were comparatively few blacks, or in fact in some part of the United States the most like Canada in social composition. Her reply was illuminating. She said that she was ashamed to say so, but if she could choose she would live in the South.

'And not for the reason you may think. I don't go for all that jazz about southern culture. I would not like to live in a society where a spotty little white bank clerk calls me Thelma and not Miss Johnson, but a person like me with some education can live better in the South than in the North.' She went on to explain that in the North there was no legal segregation, but no one could judge the North by what one experienced on the campus of the University of Chicago. There were more educated blacks in the North and informal segregation and race prejudice obliged them to compete for opportunities among the black population.

'How many black doctors have white patients? How many black lawyers have white clients? How many black economists are there in white banks?' she asked me and she replied to her own question. 'In the North the blacks take in the blacks' washing. That's why I would rather live in the South. There's more washing there. There are more of us.'

I asked Thelma how she thought American negroes could break out of both the legal and the informal segregation which afflicted them. On this topic she was rather pessimistic. She argued that the American blacks are Americans and as such they are like all Americans: they want to 'make it good,' make money, make it to the top. Some American blacks see that American blacks cannot do this on their own, but the majority think they can. The best way to do this is not to cause trouble and be as much like the majority as possible.

She explained to me how this determination to be like the majority manifests itself, especially among the blacks who thought they were on the way up. Her observation of black male behaviour in black universities led her to the conclusion that, in selecting a mate, the black male's preference in a prospective wife was for the girl with the lightest skin and the longest hair, in short for girls who most resembled whites. Furthermore, how, she asked rhetorically, 'do boys and girls from Mississippi, for instance, who tend to have only real black ancestors, all of them real blacks,' how do they fare in their attempts to get into fraternities and societies in the black colleges? Not very well, Thelma observed. All they can do at college, she said, 'is beat the books and get good grades.'

I said that I found all this hard to believe. Thelma challenged me to look at the statistics for the sale of hair straighteners, bleaches, and cosmetics designed to make blacks look as much like whites as possible. I could not meet this challenge. I said the whole thing seemed to me crazy.

'You're right, it's crazy,' Thelma replied. On principle she refused ever to buy a hair straightening lotion or anything in the idiotic repertoire of transformation.

I argued that blacks had their own kind of beauty and if they needed artificial aids they ought to develop cosmetics which enhanced black beauty. She agreed. We did not invent the slogan 'Black is beautiful,' but we agreed about the principle behind the proposition.

Our discussions took place five years before the case of Brown v. the Board of Education was heard before the US Supreme Court. There seemed no way out of the injustices involved in segregation and race prejudices. A few years previously I would doubtless have sought an explanation of the prejudice and the injustice in the fact of capitalism and a remedy in socialist revolution. But having the problem put to me not in a book but at second-hand by knowing Thelma Johnson, such an explanation and such a solution seemed to me unreal. Thelma and I were afraid to go to dinner off the campus of the University of Chicago not because we would have been breaking the laws of the United States or of the State of Illinois. We were afraid of the American whites, not all of them, just some of them. And to tell the truth, we were afraid of the American blacks; not all of them, just some of them.

And yet out of this experience there were eventually born in me a respect for the American political system and some degree of optimism about the United States. The Supreme Court ruled against separate but equal public services for blacks and whites and found that segregation is in principle unjust and contrary to the constitution of the United States. After the decision in Brown v. the Board of Education, both blacks and the whites who wanted to end the monstrous hypocrisy of segregation in a free society had a stronger legal base from which to conduct political struggles for legislation outlawing segregation and opening up opportunities of employment. This struggle was an untidy business and has resulted in much foolishness like the compulsory bussing of school children, reverse discrimination, and much violence. But the big fact is that the political process in the United States under the constitution did create the possibility of blacks and whites being friends in public if they want to be and did beat down and isolate the people who capitalize on prejudice and race hatred. American whites now sometimes Afro their hair because black is beautiful. That this should have become a possibility makes me mildly optimistic about the United States.

My uncle Rolly Ferns was a most unlikely person to have afforded me an insight in politics. Upon first acquaintance he seemed to me a thoroughly unsatisfactory human being whom I was somewhat ashamed to acknowledge as a blood relation. He appeared to me an aging, dandified and silly man who lived on the margin of society because he had no capacity to do otherwise. He had been for some years, and remained until he died in his eighty-second year, a dependent of a crippled watchmaker named Oranger. Oranger ran a small watch repair shop in the Loop under the clattering shadow of the El. trains in downtown Chicago. Rolly lived in the back of the shop, kept Oranger's accounts, did his banking, and served as a messenger, shop assistant and night watchman of the enterprise.

Like my mother and father, Rolly had been born in London, Ontario. He left school early in life and had been apprenticed as a cigar maker. He had a certain facility with numbers and could add, subtract, multiply, and divide four figure numbers in his head. He turned from cigar making to office work and taught himself book-keeping and elementary accounting. So equipped, he migrated to the United States before the First World War when he moved from big city to big city. Sometime in the 1920s he became the auditor of passenger accounts for the Chicago and Northwestern Railroad and he seems then to have 'settled down.' He was generally in my family believed to be a bachelor, but he referred vaguely to having been married at some time in New York, but to whom and for how long was never clearly stated. He had become at some stage a Roman Catholic, but this, like his marriage, real or supposed, was vaguely alluded to as if it were a kind of embarrassment, not just to his family who were all Protestants, but to himself.

Rolly was a great reader of newspapers, but he never read books or magazines. He always left the impression that he was only interested in 'facts,' but it was plain from his discourse that out of facts he constructed many fantasies. He could, for example, talk in great detail about the affairs of the General Motor Corporation or American Tel and Tel as if he were a large shareholder very critical of what went on in the management at board level. Similarly he was fully informed about the affairs of the Chicago White Sox baseball team, but was very disappointed in the management. No mayor of Chicago had ever been any good and as for the state government of Illinois, it was beyond discussion. All this information and much else was conveyed in a flat monotone with a trace of a whine.

I felt that I had done my family duty by having dinner with Rolly, but he asked me, he almost pleaded with me, to come with him to see the new Chicago zoo, which he said was magnificent. Which, indeed, it was. Going there meant spending the best part of a Sunday with Rolly and it was then that I heard some things about his life and experiences which changed my view of the man. His account of the great depression in particular moved me and I found myself beginning to respect and even to like him.

By the time he was forty-five, he had found what seemed to be a safe and respectable niche in the Chicago and Northwestern Railroad. Then came the depression. Rolly seems to have been in some degree prudent, for he never played the stock market on margins. He always bought equities outright for cash. He invested, too, in the bonds of US public authorities. Most of his investments seemed to have been genuine savings out of his income and he owed little to profit-taking on a rising market. His only pleasure was watching the book value of his investments, which cannot have been large, grow.

Prudent he may have been, but the collapse of the stock market in the autumn of 1929 drastically reduced the value of his savings/investments. Then the Chicago and Northwestern Railroad went into receivership and he lost his job. He moved out of his apartment and into the YMCA. Bit by bit his assets went to pay for his rent and buy his food. Finally, one day in the late spring of 1933, he had no money.

'I did not have a dime, a single dime,' he told me. 'I could not pay for my breakfast and so I didn't have any.'

He went out and he found himself walking along Michigan Boulevard.

'My God, I was hungry,' he said. 'I was standing watching the traffic and a fellow with an unlit cigarette came up to me. 'Say,' he said, 'Have you got a match?' 'Sure,' I said, 'Here,' and I gave him a box of matches.

I wanted to say to him, 'Can you give me a dime for a cup of coffee?'
I wanted to say it but I couldn't. God, that was a low point!'

Rolly did not eat all day, but the next day he went to the Salvation Army. There one could get a bowl of soup free and no questions asked. He had a bowl of soup each day for a week. Then his elder brother, my Uncle Jack, who was a well-established business executive in a large corporation in California, sent him a cheque for a hundred dollars.

By chance in the YMCA he heard about a crippled watchmaker in the Loop whose wife had died. Oranger needed someone to help him. Rolly went to see Oranger. Oranger offered him a bed and $1.50 a day for food and cigars. For the rest of his life he remained with Oranger, doing for Oranger what Oranger could not do for himself. When he became feeble and useless Oranger cared for him until he had to go into a hospital a month before he died. As a last service to Rolly, Oranger summoned a priest who administered the last rites of the church.

In spite of his silliness and his illusions there seemed to me something noble in Rolly, something I could respect. He was prepared to starve rather than beg. And there was something to respect in a society which had within it a sufficiency of charity that he did not have to starve. From time to time I reflected on the experience of Rolly in the depression in the United States. Of course, it was a social disaster and Americans ought to do better than they had done in the management of their affairs. But Rolly and millions like him had not perished and somehow the Americans had got themselves out of their difficulties without vast idealistic planning which in other places resulted in the deliberate killing of millions of human beings.

When he talked about what he read in the newspapers Rolly was a tedious, pretentious bore, but when he reflected on his own personal experience there was some sense in him. On a Sunday in June 1949, he visited me at International House on 59th Street where I lived and we went walking in Jackson Park. At this time there was much written in the newspapers about reforming politicians who were cleaning up police corruption in one of the police districts in the city. This was the sort of news Rolly revelled in and I prompted him to talk. He said, yes, there was a clean-up in progress. One no longer saw cops going into an office building a few blocks from Oranger's place on a Friday afternoon for their pay-off.

'Oh,' I said. 'So there is a real clean-up?'

'I don't know,' said Rolly. 'They're probably going somewhere else. Reform doesn't mean the end of pay-offs.'

I was not especially surprised or shocked by this intelligence. I began to ask about crime in Chicago. Rolly displayed a certain amount of civic pride in Chicago's reputation for crime and he began to enlarge on the subject following the dramatic patterns of the newspapers. Then he checked himself and said, 'But you know, we don't have much crime down in the Loop. I've been fifteen years with Oranger and we've only had one stick-up, and a couple of instances of tough kids coming into the shop and snatching a watch or two.'

I asked Rolly to explain the comparatively crime-free nature of the Loop. He said that this could be explained by the system of paying off the cops. He informed me that Oranger gave one of the cops on the beat two dollars each week and he gave a special present of maybe 'five dollars for the kids' at Christmas and Easter. This amounted to about $115.00 a year. Rolly explained that this was good, cheap insurance. Of course, Oranger paid $500 or $600 a year for commercial insurance, but, Rolly argued, this was really re-insurance, a protection against the possibility of being cleaned out in a serious criminal attack. One had to be very careful not to make a claim on the strength of a commercial insurance policy because that would mean a big increase in the premiums. The real problem was to keep the crooks under control and out of one's shop and this involved a positive relationship with the police. Rolly invited me to consider what was involved in the one stick-up he had experienced.

It happened in the early evening shortly after the end of the war in 1945. Oranger had gone home and Rolly was keeping the shop open until a customer, who urgently wanted his watch, had collected it. Two young men entered, closed the door and one pulled out a gun demanding that Rolly give them 'all you got.' Rolly opened the till and placed on the counter ten or twelve dollars and some change and said, 'That's all there is.' The man with the gun demanded that he open the safe, which he said he knew was in the back room. Rolly said that he was only an employee, that the boss was not in, and he was the only one who could open the safe.

This angered the men. The gunman ordered Rolly out from behind the counter. One grabbed him around the neck and the other punched him in the stomach. Rolly was frightened and in pain. He decided to open the safe. He explained to me that he did so to escape a further beating, but also because he thought these thugs were mainly interested in cash and not in watches and jewellery left in for repair, which in total were worth far more than the cash in the safe. The money, amounting to only a few hundred dollars, mostly in five- and one-dollar bills, was done up in bundles held together by rubber bands and being bulky looked a larger sum than was really the case. The bundles of notes were open in the safe, but the valuable watches and jewellery were in a closed box.

Rolly believed that the thugs would go for the money and leave the rest. This turned out to be correct. They seized the bundles of notes, stuffed them in a shopping bag and departed. Rolly rang the police. In about fifteen minutes the policeman on the beat appeared.

'He was a big guy,' Rolly told me, 'with an Italian name but we always called him Al. Al was awfully upset by what had happened. He was full of apologies and he said he would report the details of what had happened. I pulled up my shirt and showed him where they had punched me. He said not to worry. I would have a lot of blue bruises, but I would be O.K. Old guys like me are tougher than you think, he told me.'

Nothing more happened. Oranger believed it would be prudent not to report his loss to the insurance company. After all he had lost only $200 or so and he did not want a big increase in his insurance premium.

'Then,' Rolly went on, 'one day about two months later I was talking with this big Italian cop, Al, in the entrance way of Oranger's place when suddenly I see the guy who had punched me. I nudged Al and told him, 'That's the guy who slugged me.'

Al looked around and then said, 'You absolutely sure that's the guy?' Rolly said there was no mistake. Al then followed the thug at a distance and both disappeared from view among the people and the traffic.

A few days later Rolly met Al and asked him whether he had been able to catch the thug. 'Oh, I caught up with him alright,' Al said. Rolly asked him whether there was going to be a trial. 'Nah,' Al said. 'There won't be a trial. It's no use charging a guy like that. He has no business being here in the Loop. Make him do time and he'll only learn bad habits. But you can tell Oranger he won't have any more trouble. You're not going to see that guy in the Loop for a very long time. It's not a healthy place for him.'

Obviously the police procedures in the Loop would not have had the approval of the Civil Liberties Union, but as Rolly said, 'There's not much crime in the Loop. We get personal service from the cops. We're friends with them and they are friends with us and it doesn't cost much.'

This episode related to me by my uncle remained in the back of my mind until I began seriously to study the writings of Hobbes some five years later. The episode seemed to illustrate the fundamental problem of politics and its solution. Many more years passed and in the mid 1970s I began to look more radically at politics. My memory of my uncle's encounter with crime in Chicago some thirty years previously and the 'Chicago solution' played a considerable part in formulating what I regard as the most fundamental and long-standing 'cause' in the emergence of the state and government – 'the robbery problem,' the inevitable emergence in any community of specialized producers and of specialists in the appropriation of goods and services who are not themselves producers. Producers need the police, but that is all they need. But how to control them?

CHAPTER ELEVEN

'One Can Never Get Justice from a Government'

The fascinating experience of living in Chicago and studying at the University of Chicago came suddenly to an end in the first week of August 1949. My work was disrupted and my prospect of life in Canada was destroyed by the Canadian government.

After a long and interesting morning in the university library on August 7th, I returned to International House and before going to lunch I looked in my pigeon hole for messages and letters. There were two notes from the telephone switchboard asking me first to call the number of a house agent in Victoria, British Columbia, and second, to call my wife in Winnipeg. Naturally, I called Maureen first.

Something had gone out of Maureen's voice and in a flash I thought that there had been some kind of terrible accident to one of our children. But no. She said, 'Today a letter came for you from Ottawa and I opened it in case it was important. It certainly is. Let me read it to you.'

In reply refer to file No.

ND-NE-3674 (AMS)
48-3098G
O.S.58177
4 August, 1949

H.S. Ferns, Esq.,
9 St. David Road,
St. Vital, Man.

Dear Sir:

I wish to refer to my letters of April 27, 1949 and May 2, 1949 wherein I advised you that you were selected for appointment as Associate Professor (Economics and History), Canadian Service College, Department of National Defence, Royal Roads, B.C.

The Department of National Defence has now indicated that your services are not acceptable. I regret to advise, therefore, that the Civil Service Commission has no alternative but to delete your name from eligible list 69.891.

Yours sincerely,

E.W. Sibley

for R. Morgan

Secretary

For a moment I felt pole-axed. Since late April, when I had been offered a teaching post in the naval college at Royal Roads, Maureen and I had rejoiced in our luck, in the prospect of having for the first time in our lives a reasonable income that would not oblige me to teach in vacations, a program of teaching duties which would enable me to do more research and both of us to have a little leisure and to do all this in a town where the climate is agreeable and the setting by the sea attractive. Maureen had sold our house and made a capital gain on the transaction of some $2,000. We were just about to sign a contract to purchase a house in Victoria.

I was utterly bewildered and we talked for a few minutes. Then Maureen said something which I think is one of the kindest, most intelligent, and most understanding suggestions that ever a wife made to a husband.

'I think we ought to get out of this country. You have never been happy in Canada. Let us go to England, which you like and where you have always done well.'

I asked her, 'What about you?' Post-war Britain was reported to be a land of hardship, poor and cold. She had only been briefly in Britain in 1939. She had no friends or family there and there was no evidence that she liked Britain as well as I did.

She said she would manage somehow. But what about the children? She said that our eldest son John, then eight years old, was apprehensive because he thought everyone in England had to go to boarding schools, that he had read somewhere about Eton and the caning of boys and the system of fagging. John was worried. I said I could guarantee to John that he would never have to go to Eton or a boarding school of any description.

And so the matter was settled in a few minutes by Maureen. I was anything but happy, but underneath I felt a great relief, because I could see what had to be done next. This was something I would never have seen on my own, certainly not so quickly.

As soon as we had terminated our discussion, I called Victoria and informed the house agent that our deal was off. Then I called Brockington in Ottawa. He had access to ministers and bureaucrats and I asked him to find out what had gone wrong. Brockington did his best, but the shutters had come down. No one would talk.

In order to understand this episode, it is necessary to go back to its beginning. In the early part of 1949, on one of the notice boards of the University of Manitoba, there was posted a printed advertisement of the Civil Service Commission of Canada inviting applications for the post of associate professor of economics and history in the Defence College at Royal Roads, BC. Ordinarily in Canada at that time university posts were never advertised, but the posts in colleges of the armed forces were exceptions being by law open to public competition. No feudal grapevines in the democratic government of Canada! I was reading the notice with not much interest when I was joined by a colleague, a historian named Richard Glover.

Dick was an odd character on the Canadian academic scene – probably no odder than I was myself but in a different way. He came from an English academic family. His father was T.R. Glover, the well-known classical scholar, sometime Public Orator of Cambridge University and sometime president of the Baptist Union. Dick had been educated at Oxford and Harvard universities. Politically he was very conservative and his academic interests were unusual in Canada. His field of study was the British army in the period of the Peninsular War and not just in its general role but in its organization, its drill, its provisioning and so on. One of Dick's characteristics was to throw himself back into history so that he entered into the fate and the politics of dead armies and governments with such enthusiasm that he might have been a participant himself. On one occasion he persuaded the BBC to do a program on the battle of Hastings addressed to the question of whether or not the English King Harold, who had fought a battle at Stamford Bridge on 25 September 1066, could have satisfactorily deployed an army at Hastings to fight the Normans on 14 October. To demonstrate this possibility he assembled a group of enthusiasts, weighed them down with the equivalent of the arms and accoutrements of an eleventh-century English soldier and marched them from York to Hastings over pathways similar to those which the English had probably used. All very interesting and it proved that Harold's soldiers could have done the job, but must have been rather tired. Not the sort of thing a Canadian historian would do or consider doing!

Dick read the notice. Teaching in a defence college seemed just the sort of thing which might interest him. I asked him if this was so. No, he said, he knew no economics and anyway the navy was not quite his cup of tea. But why did I not apply? I was looking for a job, wasn't I? I replied that he must be crazy to think of me applying for such a job. Why not? Dick said he was quite serious. I needed a job. Why not?

It is remarkable how one can begin to believe in one's public image whether it be of a god or a devil. I replied that 'a red like me' would never be allowed to teach the officers of His Majesty's Canadian Navy. But Dick was too much of an individual and an individualist ever to pay attention to popular impressions or gossip. He could only see me and not my image and he thought I ought to apply for the job. He had great trust in the objectivity, fairness, and so on of the Canadian government.

We left it at that, but Dick Glover had jolted me somewhat. I began to think about the associate professorship at Royal Roads and the more I thought about it the more I was tempted: good pay; not too much work; salubrious climate by the seaside seldom knowing frost and never below zero temperatures. It was actually 25° below zero Fahrenheit when I began to take Royal Roads seriously.

There was another aspect of applying for this post which I began to turn over in my mind. Whatever my political views and loyalties were in 1949 – and I seemed to be seeking to divest myself of all connections with causes – other people might very well have doubts about me. My name had been in Colonel Zabotin's notebook and obviously someone in Moscow thought of me as a potential Soviet agent. The best way to cut this albatross from my neck was to create a situation in which the government of Canada would have a free opportunity to do so privately in their own way and using their own evidence and resources. If they employed me to teach their naval officers, who then could say I was a red? If they did not wish to employ me, if they were not satisfied with my *bona fides,* I would be no worse off than I already was. If they thought me a risk all they had to do was not to put me on their eligible list, as the Civil Service Commission had done in 1937. This could do me no harm and there I was prepared to let the matter rest.

And so I decided to apply. Sometime in March I was invited for an interview in Winnipeg by a committee consisting of an owl-eyed civil servant and two naval officers plentifully covered with gold braid and embroidery on their sleeves and caps. We had a pleasant, informal talk. A few days after I arrived in Chicago, a letter came from the Civil Service Commission saying I had been placed second on the list and that the post had been given to someone else. I threw the letter in the waste paper basket and thought, 'That's that. I'll have to look elsewhere for a job, come September.'

I was in correspondence with the University of Alberta when on the last day of April 1949 another letter arrived from Ottawa, offering me the post of associate professor at Royal Roads. I accepted and shortly received a letter from Instructor Captain W.M. Ogle, RCN, telling me how pleased he was that I had accepted the post at Royal Roads, that he would fit into his program my plans to finish my Ph.D., that he would send me the program of studies. There followed a consignment of books used on the courses and we entered into a discussion of providing lectures on the economics of defence. I began to devote a couple of hours a day to designing a course on elementary economics related to the textbook in use in the college.

In Winnipeg, Maureen was preparing for our move to Victoria. She had sold our house and contracted to give vacant possession to the new owners on 15 September 1949. She found herself selling her household possessions, many of which had meant a hard struggle and much economy to acquire: fine reproduction Chippendale dining room furniture, a very technologically advanced electric cooker we had acquired from Jules and Gaby Léger, bedroom furniture, and so forth. Everything went except family gifts of linen, dishes and silver, my books, and a few of the children's toys.

Having now resolved to leave Canada, I had two personal objectives which I hoped might be achieved before departure: to obtain compensation for a gross breach of contract and to demonstrate to the clowns in Ottawa that I was not alone in the world and that I had some friends who respected me and would support me.

First, I went to see W.J. Waines in the University of Manitoba. When I told him what had happened, he was very angry. He did not hesitate a moment. He asked me to give him photostatic copies of my correspondence which he sent to the Minister of Justice in Ottawa, Stuart Garson, sometime premier of Manitoba. He told Garson that if they could do this to Ferns, they could do it to any academic and that the Minister of Justice would be wise to think of the implications.

Then I went to see Mr Justice A.K. Dysart. He listened to me and carefully read the correspondence. I can remember with great distinctness how, when he had finished reading, he took off his glasses, pressed his fingers to the bridge of his nose and said slowly: 'Ferns, I am deeply ashamed of the advice I am going to give you. Many years on the Bench have persuaded me that one can never get justice from a government. They have too many resources at their command. Therefore, I advise you not to waste either your time or your money on a legal action for breach of contract. But I will do this. I shall write to Ottawa expressing my indignation about what they have done to you.'

Next on my list was R.B. Hunter. All he said was, 'The bastards! I'll tell them what I think.' He sent me a copy of his letter to the Minister of Defence, Brooke Claxton. It is worth quoting in part as an example of Hunter's laconic prose style and his line of argument. After explaining how he had come to know me, he wrote: 'I found Professor Ferns particularly familiar with world labour conditions ... Have always found him very fair and with his wide educational training would consider him capable of handling any academic job to which he may be assigned. Summing up would say from my experience, Professor Ferns is a gentleman.'

I was even more grateful to R.B. Hunter for telling me that, if I wished, he would recommend me for appointment as a personnel officer in a large American paper-manufacturing corporation of which his son was the chief executive. But he added that he thought I would be a better academic than a businessman.

When word got round in Winnipeg about what had happened, there developed a current of sympathy and indignation. Dr W.C. Graham, the principal of United College, who had both made and terminated a contract with me, wrote me a very sympathetic letter and several others, particularly some of conservative disposition, expressed themselves in a similar way. I think that, had I asked for a job in the University of Manitoba, a place might have been found for me. But it was too late. Maureen was right: we had to get out.

We stopped in Ottawa, partly to see old friends and partly to get some satisfaction from the government. I had no difficulty in arranging an interview with C.H. Bland, the chairman of the Civil Service Commission. Brockington arranged for me to see a senior official of the Department of National Defence.

Bland was the same courteous and kind man I had first met in 1935. He explained, what I already knew, that the Civil Service Commission had prepared a list of persons eligible for appointment to the post for which I had applied. The Department of National Defence was obliged to appoint from the eligible list, but was not bound to appoint any particular person if, in their judgement, he or she was unacceptable. As far as the commission was concerned, I was a proper person to appoint, but the commission had no authority to enforce my appointment. Whether there had been a breach of contract or not and whether and what compensation should be paid was a matter for the Department of National Defence and the Treasury Board.

And so I went to see the ministry of National Defence. Years later, I read Robertson Davies' splendid novel *Fifth Business,* wherein one encounters a character named 'Boy ' Staunton. After reading for a time about Staunton, I said to myself, 'I've met this man before in real life. Who is he?' And then it dawned on me: this official in National Defence. Just the sort of man who would put a rock in a snowball, inadvertently destroy a person's sanity and go on from success to success: well-tailored, hands carefully manicured, sun-tanned, smooth, well-fed, well-exercised, complacent, self-confident and deceiving both himself and the world at large.

When I was ushered into the office he was not alone. Off to one side there sat a man with a notebook on his knees and a pencil in one hand. He was dressed in civilian clothes, that is to say, he wore a suit but he wore it uneasily as if he was more accustomed to a uniform. Even sitting he looked as if he were on duty: impersonal, distant, and stupified.

The official did not introduce me or explain the man's presence. Nothing so polite as that. As soon as I spoke, the man began to scribble in his notebook. 'What was my problem?' I replied that I supposed he knew. He said he did not. Brockington had asked him to see me, but he did not know what I wanted. I read him the letter from Instructor Captain Ogle, RCN. He said he knew nothing of Instructor Captain Ogle. In fact he knew nothing, nothing, nothing.

He then said that anything to do with employment by the government of Canada was a matter for the Civil Service Commission. The Department of National Defence was entirely in the hands of the commission as far as the employment of personnel was concerned. He advised me to consult the commission. I then read him the letter from the Civil Service Commission saying 'that the Department of National Defence has now indicated that your services are not acceptable.' He knew nothing about this. I said that perhaps I might speculate on why my services were unacceptable. Could it be that I had made a speech to the Canadian-Soviet Friendship Council? He cracked a little and said that there might be something in this. The interview ended.

To the very end he and his minister, Brooke Claxton, persisted in the lie that they knew nothing and had no responsibility. But when a settlement was finally reached in March 1950, the cheque for $2,000 which I received was drawn on the account of Department of National Defence.

The *modus operandi* of the bureaucracy in this instance is interesting to observe. The combination of lies, delays, and half-truths is well illustrated by their method of dealing with a protest made on my behalf by the widow of my friend William Paterson who, the reader may remember, had been invited by Claxton to become his executive assistant. She wrote to Claxton 10 September 1949. Four and a half months later she received the following reply from Claxton's executive assistant, W.R. Wright. His letter of 28 January 1950, read:

Before the Minister left for the West, he asked me to acknowledge your letter of 10 September in connection with Professor Ferns.

He asked me to tell you that he was sorry that he had not been able to reply sooner but that it was felt that it was desirable that some sort of decision should be reached before doing so.

While this is a matter purely for the Civil Service Commission who are responsible for the recruitment of personnel for positions such as the one in question, Mr. Claxton was very very glad to have this expression of your views.

He asked me to tell you the Civil Service Commission would be getting in touch with Professor Ferns in the very near future in order to reach a satisfactory settlement.

A satisfactory settlement! Had this been a breach of an ordinary contract between two citizens I would have been able to claim not only a year's salary – $4,200 – but damages into the bargain. As it was I was told that I would be paid $2,000 if I signed a release the last clause of which read: 'It is also understood and agreed that His Majesty does not admit any liability to the Releasor by the acceptance of this Release or the payment of the said sum of $2,000.00 and such liability.'

Lest anyone supposes that my treatment by the government was a unique instance of injustice dictated by superior authority, it must be recorded that the release I was obliged to sign was a standard duplicated form with blanks into which appropriate details were inserted according to the case. Breaches of contract similar in principle to the one affecting me would appear to have been frequent enough to warrant mimeographed forms, but insufficiently numerous to justify a long run set in type by the King's Printer. No wonder A.K. Dysart had said that it was impossible to get justice from a government!

By the time I was presented with this document, I was so tired of the whole business that I signed and let the matter rest. $2,000 was better than nothing and the means of making a down-payment on a house in England. I had achieved less that 50 per cent of what I aimed at by way of compensation, but like a football team in the relegation zone I was pleased enough with a draw.

In retrospect, this episode seems simple and straightforward enough and an example of reasonableness if not justice. One does not easily forget, however, the tension of the affair and the atmosphere of apprehension and fear which ran through it at that time. The day before we were due to move out of our home in Winnipeg, I observed an unmarked motor car parked opposite our house in which there was a man in civilian clothes.

He just sat there. After two hours of this I came to the conclusion that I was being watched. Was this, I thought, the prelude to a raid for the purpose of getting evidence to smear me and strengthen the case of the government? I decided I was going to take no chances and so I extracted the works of Lenin from among my books awaiting the packers, put them in the furnace and set them alight. In order to burn the works of Lenin it is necessary to stir them up with a poker and when one does this the blaze is quite impressive. There was roaring in the chimney and Maureen said in some alarm, 'For God sake, don't burn the house down before we leave.'

In Ottawa we put up with family friends. The head of the house was a Scotsman who worked as a laboratory technician in the National Research Council and his wife Betty was a pleasant woman with some interest in public affairs and some enthusiasm for flat-rate family allowances, the open legal sale of contraceptives, and such progressive improvements in public policy. Her husband welcomed us as friends, but the wife seemed mildly apprehensive at our presence. The evening before we left Bessie Touzel came to visit us to say hello and goodbye and mainly to see our children. This put Betty in a panic: Bessie's car parked in front of her house was a real danger. We were very sorry for our tactlessness in letting so dangerous a person as the director of social agencies come to visit us. When Christmas came we sent the children of our friends some small gifts from England as an acknowledgement of their parents' hospitality and kindness. The gifts were acknowledged by a brief, polite note from the elder child, but we never heard again from our friends.

There was no government-induced terror in Canada, but the press had created an atmosphere of fear and suspicion about reds. When I saw what this did to me and to friends I began to realize, not in theory but in practice, how useful real terror must be to tyrants. Suppose the bureaucrats and politicians in Ottawa wanted to seize power permanently and dispense with democratic institutions, how easy it would be to get control and silence opposition by creating an atmosphere of real terror through arbitrary arrests, the establishment of concentration camps, and so on. But how different was my experience from that of a Russian or a Czech or a Pole or a Chinese or a German in the Nazi Reich! I had merely encountered a few clumsy, lying civil servants and politicians who reached a compromise which did not cost them anything but which prevented me and those who sympathized with me from publicizing their behaviour.

I have sometimes speculated about what actually happened in my case. I had hoped that by applying for the post at Royal Roads I would be subjected to a careful intelligence check which would either clear me or not. When I was placed on the eligible list and then offered a post, I believed that I must have been found to be clean by what I imagined must the high security standards of the post-Gouzenko and the McCarthy era.

I was considered acceptable in April 1949, but by late July or early August I was found to be unacceptable. Why? Had intelligence got behind with their paper work so that a potential spy had been employed before they had finished their check? Or was the Department of National Defence so badly organized that they did not co-ordinate their several activities? This is a possible explanation, but I doubt whether it is the right one. A more plausible explanation for which I have some, but not conclusive, evidence connects this episode with my whole experience in Winnipeg. The first bit of evidence is a chance meeting I had on Portage Avenue, Winnipeg, in early July 1949, with the wife of a former colleague in United College. I was then at home in Winnipeg for a few days between terms at the University of Chicago and I was downtown on business connected with the sale of our house. This lady was not one from whom it was easy to escape by touching one's hat in passing. We stopped to say, 'How are you?' And she then said inquisitively, 'And what are you doing now?'

I was so full of enthusiasm about our new prospects in Victoria that I simply told her about my appointment at Royal Roads. The words had hardly passed my lips, when I felt a frisson of apprehension and the thought crossed my mind that I should not have given this information to this woman.

'Oh!' she said and I could see that the same thought was passing through her mind as had passed through my own before Dick Glover persuaded me of the possibility of applying for the post at Royal Roads. 'How could they give such a job to *you?*'

Later I learned that her husband had written a letter of complaint and warning to his member of Parliament about the appointment of a dubious red to teach naval officers. This may have been unjust gossip, but the possibility that he had done so was quite consistent with this man's reputation as a nasty creep. Tattle-taling was, too, in the spirit of the age of Senator McCarthy.

My guess is that I had never been positively vetted upon application for the post at Royal Roads. Intelligence work was at that time, and perhaps still is, very haphazard, inefficient, and ineffective. My difficulties stemmed from my over-confidence not just in their intelligence work but in the intelligent and efficient administration of the Department of National Defence.

When finally an MP warned Claxton about Ferns, there was a panic in the recesses of the Naval Branch, not, of course, on account of a possible penetration of the Navy by a Soviet agent but because of the adverse publicity the Department of National Defence might receive should there be a question in the House of Commons.

It is quite easy to understand the decision to dispense with Ferns at once. Their intelligence, ever defective, unfortunately let them down. Ferns was not entirely without resources to hit back. He had a few friends. If, for example, his case began to be discussed by members of the faculty of the University of Manitoba and then by students and then by supporters of the now defunct *Winnipeg Citizen,* and then by the One Big Union, and then by the CCF, and then and then and so forth, the political image of the Honourable Brooke Claxton would begin to tarnish somewhat. The questions asked in the House of Commons might begin to make it seem that Claxton was a red-baiter, not a vigilant guardian against the secret Soviet menace in our midst. The latent disdain and dislike of the United States, always so near the surface of politics in Canada, made it very difficult for red-baiting to flourish unabated in Canada. Red-baiting was a popular and profitable political sport in the United States and for this very reason, because it was American, red-baiting was never an unqualified sucess in Canada. Claxton was intelligent enough to know this. His assistants may have kept the shutters down and refused to admit that they knew what I was talking about, but behind the shutters there was evidently action enough. Before I left Ottawa for England, a message came to me from the chief examiner of the Civil Service Commission, who had once been a member of the faculty of United College in Winnipeg, to the effect that he was very sorry about what had happened and that something was going to be done for me.

Even my departure from Canada was loaded with political difficulties which required resolution by the government. If I went and was paid off, the matter would end in a blessed silence. If I went and Ferns was depicted as a political refugee, this would be ammunition for the opposition in the House of Commons. And so a sweet little example of the Canadian art of compromise was achieved. Ferns was paid a sufficiently small sum that no one was likely to charge the government with wasting public funds through a bone-headed error, but Ferns was paid enough to shut him up. None of his friends could say that he had been treated with total injustice. Too bad, of course. Everyone could be happy in his own way, or at least as happy as one can expect to be in this vale of tears. And this is not irony. Hundreds of thousands have been shot and millions have been put in labour camps in political circumstances which in principle are no different from those I experienced.

We left Canada from Halifax in the s.s. *Aquitania*, a magnificent ship making its last but one voyage before going to the breakers' yard. The second night at sea I was alone in my berth in our cabin. Maureen and the children were sound asleep, but I was awake thinking over the past. I began to weep with grief and I must have wept for half an hour or more. Then I felt a great sense of relief. I was through with Canada, and I went to sleep.

But one is never through with one's nationality. It stays with one like the religion learned in childhood. Like it or not, one is stuck with them, and they are a part of a person forever.

Many years later when I was the Dean of my Faculty in the University of Birmingham, I was obliged to accept on behalf of the university a gift of books from the government of the province of Quebec presented by the Hon. Hugues Lapointe, the son of Mackenzie King's great political ally. This presentation took place not long after the unpleasantness towards the Queen when she visited Quebec and Montreal. I referred to this and said that, while we might regret rudeness to the Queen, we Canadians would not attach much importance to this, because we understood each other even when we did not always like each other.

Subsequently, an official of the university wrote to me informing me that he was deleting my reference to the Queen from the text of my speech in the university *Gazette* because it was improper to dismiss as unimportant rudeness to the Visitor of the University. I wrote to the vice chancellor saying that if the university did not publish all of what I had said, it could publish none of it; that the irrelevance of rudeness to the Queen was something I as a Canadian had remarked on to a fellow Canadian; that it was the heart of the matter; and all else I had said was polite flannel.

After the presentation there was a luncheon for Hugues Lapointe. With a show of supposedly understanding tactfulness, the university had provided, it being a Friday, a menu with fish *and* a beefsteak and oyster pie as a main course. How thoughtful to take account of the Catholic taboos of our guest while indulging our own devotion to meat!

Hugues Lapointe and I sat side by side and ate beefsteak and oyster pie. We passed up the fish and we talked about Ottawa and how things were going in Canada. Suddenly, it came to me: how alike we were and how different from these British! We obviously disagreed in our understanding of aspects of Canadian public policy, but we spoke the same language – not French and/or English but the unspoken language of Canada. How right was Rousseau when he wrote of people living long together generating a general will stronger than laws and constitutions!

CHAPTER TWELVE

Bernie, King, and I: writing *The Age of Mackenzie King*

Mackenzie King died on 22 July 1950. We were then living in Bottisham, a village some eight miles east of Cambridge on the road to Newmarket. The day after Mr King's death, I was walking in the garden of the Village College and there came to me another sudden inspiration similar in kind and as complicating in its consequences as the idea of starting a third daily newspaper in Winnipeg. Why not write a book about Mackenzie King?

When *The Age of Mackenzie King: The Rise of the Leader* was published in Canada in December 1955, there soon developed a great spate of hostility, hatred, and denigration directed at the authors. The book was biased, unbalanced, distorted, prejudiced, muck-raking, disrespectful, unCanadian, obsessed, unscholarly, and so on. Why, some asked, should anyone write such a book?

'Why would two historians – both graduates of the University of Manitoba – labour so arduously for the sole purpose of blackening the reputation of Mackenzie King?' asked Grant Dexter, the high priest in the temple of Liberal party journalism *(Winnipeg Free Press*, 14 January

1956). 'The book affords no clue,' Mr Dexter concluded. But, of course, people in Winnipeg would know.

The mystery of the motives of the authors was taken up. In the *Canadian Historical Review,* Professor A.L. Burt, an ex-Rhodes scholar, an expatriate in the United States, suspected a hidden motive behind their denigration. Some found answers. One commentator writing in the *Vancouver Province* (30 December 1955) advanced the proposition that the 'unchallengeable moral code (of Ferns and Ostry) is nothing more or less than the economic-political dogma of the Socialist intellectuals of the British Labor Party.' Another, this time from the University of Manitoba, informed the readers of *Political Studies* that 'Mr. Ferns worked in King's office and King was notorious for being an incredibly inconsiderate employer.' This plus a rejection 'of the fundamental assumptions of liberal capitalist society' explained everything.

What were my motives on that warm summer day in July 1950? I can only remember one innocent and very Canadian motive which stirred my heart and mind: the desire to make money. I did not want to bring down the Liberal party, get a senatorship from the Conservatives, bring about an improved and ideal society, prove the great truths of Marxism, elevate the level of Canadian political discourse, or demonstrate my scholarship. No. I just wanted to make money and to do so by honest work.

Until this moment I had published anonymously and under my own name about ten thousand words on Mackenzie King's policies, ideas and personality. This had yielded me a total of $30.00. What I had written seemed to me fair and appreciative, but in no way sycophantic and apologetic in the manner of Professor Norman McLeod Rogers' book which had helped him into the House of Commons and into Mackenzie King's cabinet, nor was it the sort of drivelling guff produced by Bruce Hutchinson in his popular book so justly entitled *The Incredible Canadian.*

My idea was to produce a portrait of a credible Canadian and to make some money. But how? I knew relatively little about Mackenzie King and I was sure I could not improve my knowledge by reading what others had written about the man. Furthermore, I was located in a part of the world which was not rich in source material and I had no means of getting information. And finally, I was about to depart for the University of Birmingham to take up a post entitled assistant director of research and lecturer in modern history and government in the Faculty of Commerce and Social Science – a very unspecific job if ever there was one.

Then I had another flash of inspiration. Why not ask Bernard Ostry to join me in the enterprise?

Who was Bernard Ostry? Many Canadians will now know who Bernard Ostry is. My question is this: who was he in 1950?

He was a Manitoban born in Saskatchewan, then aged 23 and a graduate student in the London School of Economics. I knew him as a student in one of my classes in the University of Manitoba. If, in September 1949, I had been asked who is Bernard Ostry? I would have replied, 'He is the only student of mine who ever drove a Cadillac and the only one who ever addressed me by my Christian name before he had passed his examinations.' Otherwise, I had no recollection of him.

When we arrived in Britain and had established ourselves in Bottisham, there came one day in November a letter from Bernard saying how glad he was that I was now in Britain; maybe we could get together, etc. I was quite pleased to hear from a fellow Canadian and I suggested that he pay a visit sometime. Not many days later, he appeared in Cambridge, came to Bottisham, and stayed for a day or two. Maureen and I found him charming and pleasant. He offered to put me up in his flat if ever I wanted to work in London at the Public Record Office or in the British Museum. I needed to do just that and so I visited him in London.

There I formed a very favourable impression of the man. He had shed his Cadillac and his pretensions. There was evidence of money freely flowing through his pockets, but wisely into books and into an interest in several of the arts. He seemed to be working hard at his studies. What impressed me most was the fact that his director of studies in the field of diplomatic history, Sir Charles Webster, had agreed to enter him as a candidate for a Ph.D. after one year of work for his M.A. All in all I was attracted by the way in which escape from Winnipeg into a civilized capital city in Europe had transformed a young man with more money than was good for him into a serious scholar and an intelligent young man about town who might become a credit to himself and his country. What is more, Bernard seemed to be really likeable. Maureen and two of our three sons thought so too: only John was otherwise – never hostile, but always quietly reserved and unenthusiastic.

Bernard responded with alacrity to my suggestion. He was up to Bottisham within forty-eight hours and we were going over the proposition: I would write and he would research and we would split the take 50-50. Put that way one might think Bernie too was motivated to make money.

I never supposed this to be so and it was not. As I saw it, Bernie's rewards would be additional experience of research, an opportunity to acquaint himself with Canadian history and politics and a help in promoting the academic career upon which he seemed desirous to embark.

We agreed that there was no need for haste. I had the immediate problem of establishing myself in Birmingham and he of finishing his Ph.D. We set the summer of 1951 as a date for beginning serious work.

We did, however, discuss some of the problems which required investigation. I had already made some study of Mackenzie King's major book – *Industry and Humanity* – and I had written an article on the subject, but this was nothing more than an analysis of the argument between the two covers of the book. King was supposed to have a great knowledge of the 'labour problem' and to have built his career on this. Well, what was there in this often repeated suggestion? What were the facts? I recommended that Bernie begin to look into this.

Bernie began to do some reading in the British Museum. There he came upon the many volumes of the *Report of the United States Commission on Industrial Relations* published in Washington in 1915. These volumes contained among other items letters and documents taken from the files of the Rockefeller organization by a United States marshal commissioned to do so under the authority of Congress. Some of these letters and documents were written by Mackenzie King or were addressed to him.

Chapter VII of *The Age of Mackenzie King* records what was found in the *Report of the United States Commission on Industrial Relations*. The evidence Bernie presented shook me profoundly. Up to that moment I had regarded Mackenzie King as a fairly disinterested student of labour relations and the author of some useful legislation on conciliation, some of which, in a provincial form, I had myself operated with what seemed to me beneficial results for the community. Here was evidence of Mackenzie King supporting and recommending company unions and doing so while in the employ of one of the parties to troubles which had involved the killing of men, women, and children by rifle and machine-gun fire and by the use of kerosene as a means of incinerating families in their tent-homes. From that time forward I had a new view of Mackenzie King and the Canadian Liberals and one which I found was more consistent with my own experience and less in line with the apologetics generated by social scientists, journalists, and 'reliable scholars.'

When Bernie went to Canada in search of information he soon found that we would have to rely on what might be called 'peripheral sources.' Access to Mackenzie King's own papers was forbidden. This was a handicap, of course, but not an insurmountable one. So long as Mackenzie King was a secondary figure in Canadian public life, his activities could be traced in the records left behind by people like Sir Wilfrid Laurier, which were open for public inspection. An effort was made to close off even these sources. On one occasion in Ottawa, Bernie was working on the papers of Charles Murphy in the Public Archives. One of the officials inquired what was the purpose of his study. He replied that he was working on a life of Mackenzie King. Then he went to lunch. When he returned he was told that the Murphy papers were not available. A mistake had been made in allowing him to see them.

I had advised Bernie to seek the advice of L.W. Brockington if he ran into any trouble. This he did. Brockington rang up J.W. Pickersgill, then Clerk of the Privy Council and asked him to see Bernie. Pickersgill declared that he knew nothing about the problem; the Archives were not his responsibility and so on – in fact, the familiar civil service routine in the presence of difficulties from the public. Bernie, however, was an aggressive and determined young man. He told Pickersgill that he knew that the responsibility for the Public Archives of Canada rested with the Prime Minister and the Privy Council and that he intended to pursue the matter of being barred from the reading of papers open to the public. Pickersgill ordered Bernie out of his office, but when Bernie returned to the Archives he found that the Murphy papers were once more open to the public.

No one could have complained had the papers of Mackenzie King been placed under lock and key in the Public Archives or some library under a rule equally applied barring access for thirty or fifty years. This is a good rule and a necessary one if public men are to have any confidence in the preservation of their privacy. But this was not the rule applied in the case of the Mackenzie King papers. They were then being made available exclusively to the 'official' biographer, a man selected by the literary executors of Mackenzie King. The theory of these men seemed to be that truth is something discovered by 'well-qualified impartial people,' that the truth they tell is proven by documenting what they write and that there is an official kind of truth superior to all other kinds.

Unfortunately, truth concerning historical questions emerges in a quite different way and is never the same from age to age. Truth in any absolute sense is probably never achieved in historical study. Truth depends upon the open availability of sources and upon the study of the sources by many men and women. Students come to differing conclusions from the same body of material. More extensive study yields new conclusions. The selection of evidence and its meaning is influenced by the preconceptions of the students. Of course, if image-building in the service of a political movement is the object of students, then a monopoly must be established for one set of scholars so that no one can claim authority for an alternative image by using the sources. Monopoly was the policy of the literary executors of Mackenzie King because they wanted to see constructed an acceptable image *now* when the image would be of political advantage. If nothing more, they wanted 'the 'intellectual space' occupied at once so that alternative interpretations were impeded, delayed, or made impossible.

The great service to historical truth rendered by *The Age of Mackenzie King* was not the superior quality of its truth – we said specifically that it was *not* a definitive study and nothing more than a contribution to public discussion – but the quick occupation of the 'intellectual space' which the literary executors of Mackenzie King were seeking to pre-empt. After its publication no one, including the official biographers, could fashion an image on their own terms. In fact, the first volume of the official biography confirmed all the main points made in *The Age of Mackenzie King*. (See my review of *William Lyon Mackenzie King: A Political Biography, 1879-1923* by R. MacGregor Dawson in *Canadian Historical Review*, 1959. Better still, read the book.)

As a researcher, Bernie was an energetic bloodhound willing to follow every lead and to hunt down his quarry. When be brought it back in the form of notes, microfilm, and photostatic material we studied and analysed it and on the basis of this I wrote draft chapters. These we went over together, cutting and amplifying until we had things right in terms of consistency and their relation to the sources.

Analysis revealed a consistent pattern in Mackenzie King's behaviour. From the very first his attention was focused on making a career in politics and he was moved by a desire to emulate, justify, and surpass his grandfather, William Lyon Mackenzie. Very early, Mackenzie King devised a technique for success: first, to discover social problems which could be converted into political issues; second, to inform himself thoroughly on these problems; and finally then, to trade his knowledge for a public office. In this way, he recruited a following and made a reputation. He did not 'go into politics' by the front door of party constituency work. He went in by the back door, into the nascent bureaucracy. He established a foothold in the authority structure in Ottawa, not in the democratic voting apparatus in the constituencies.

As we discovered more and more of the ploys Mackenzie King used to advance his career, we became excited much as an explorer might have done traversing for the first time a virgin wilderness. We were both innocents and we often went into great gales of laughter at what we discovered. We had tremendous fun.

Upon reflection, I can see that our excitement, contempt, and amusement, seemingly so much one response to what we were studying, flowed in fact from our quite different characters. I was afflicted by a real innocence. I was governed by the simple-minded notion that success has a one-to-one relation with work, as if all of life is like writing university examinations or cultivating a garden. Native ability, of course, counts for something, but the main factor is work. In Mackenzie King's activities I discovered the explanation of why I had been a failure in Ottawa and indeed in Canada, but this explanation provoked in me contempt. It was not an encouragement to go forth and do likewise.

In Bernie's case Mackenzie King's example evoked contempt, as it did in me, but his was the contempt of innocent, idealistic youth. He was then only 25 or 26 years old. It is now evident that he was not just laughing, he was learning. This is how it is done in Canada, in Ottawa, perhaps everywhere. For Bernie working on *The Age of Mackenzie King* was, as it were, a part of his apprenticeship.

Working with Bernie was a happy, rewarding experience. We worked together, off and on, for two and a half years and there was never a cross word between us. In the end, however, we quarrelled and at one stage Bernie had an expensive firm of London solicitors threatening me with legal proceedings for the recovery of some rolls of microfilm which Bernie claimed belonged to him and the Public Archivist of Canada claimed were his.

I think we quarrelled because I misunderstood Bernie's ambitions and objectives. I supposed he was seeking an academic career and imagined I was helping him along. When I became established in Birmingham, I persuaded the university to appoint him to a research associateship in the Faculty of Commerce and Social Science at a salary of £400 a year: not much, but the same salary as others at the bottom of the academic profession and an appointment which implied that he was an independent research contributor and not a research assistant. This seemed to me and to the university fairly to represent the character of what he was doing.

It emerged, however, that Bernie's attitude to the academic profession was ambivalent. He admired academic achievement and he had a certain liking for the activity of study and research, but at the same time he despised people wholly committed to academic life. Although he was capable of hard work when it suited some purpose of his, he seemed to feel that work as such is a plebeian or peasant activity which, if too unremittingly undertaken, is demeaning. He was naturally enthusiastic about the working class and his heart went out to them in their sufferings and their noble struggle, but he himself was by preference and instinct a boss.

None of this came to the surface until the book was finished and the proof copies were available. Then trouble started. I am sure he would have been completely happy if I had disclaimed my part in the enterprise and declared him to be the sole begetter of *The Age of Mackenzie King*. All he asked as a preliminary, however, was to have his name put first: *The Age of Mackenzie King* by Ostry and Ferns. Inasmuch as I had initiated the project and written every word of the text, I demurred.

By the time the book appeared, Bernie and I were not on speaking terms. Alan Hill of Heinemann, the publishers, was an amused observer of our combat. He told me to console myself with the remembrance that Gilbert and Sullivan had quarrelled prodigiously and he related an instance of two authors of a successful textbook he had published making a scene on a platform of York station cursing each other with tears in their eyes.

Our quarrel had some very adverse repercussions. Bernie was determined not only to advertise the book but to put himself in the limelight. In my view the best tactic in selling the book was to say nothing and let the natural curiosity of the public in Canada cause people to buy it and read it. I regretted that the publishers in Canada, British Book Services, advertised it as a controversial book. Controversy is so much part of Canadian life and Canadians so sense its potential dangers for society and their individual interests that they do not like the thought of controversy. Bernie, however, was determined to advertise *The Age of Mackenzie King* in person and in his own way.

To this end he made contact with the Canadian Broadcasting Corporation's officers in London with a view to the production of a TV program about *The Age of Mackenzie King*. When he was asked about participation in the program of his fellow author, he told them that Ferns was deaf and could not take part in a program. Somehow or other Bernie seemed unaware that I lectured in the University of Birmingham, conducted seminars, sat on the faculty board, held tutorials and appeared on radio and TV programs in Birmingham, and that deafness did not seem to limit me for the simple reason that I used an effective hearing aid.

The CBC agreed to do a program with Bernie as the star of the show. Some of the program was shot in London and Bernie then went to Ottawa to arrange the rest of the program featuring Canadian politicians and academics. Unfortunately Brooke Claxton, who had left the Liberal cabinet and set up as a businessman in an office across the road from Parliament Hill, read the book. He became almost hysterical. In a letter dated 29 December 1955 he shared his *Angst* with Jack Pickersgill. 'The book is so nauseating,' he wrote, 'that I have to struggle hard to keep on with the exercise. At the club yesterday three (one of them myself) out of a table of six were reading the book. The other two agreed that it was self-condemning, but would this be the view generally held by the less enlightened people who have not the good fortune to live in Ottawa?'

'Almost worse than its malicious distortions of everything having to do with Mr. King is the tiresome emissions of Communist venom on every page ... The thought occurred to me that it would not be a bad thing if quite a few people across Canada sent letters to this effect to the newspapers.' (PAC, MG 32 B5, Claxton papers vol. 82-3).

Judging from the Claxton papers it would appear that Pickersgill did a little research in an endeavour to prove that the letters of Mackenzie King to William Jennings Bryan, the US Secretary of State, and Dr C.W. Eliot of Harvard were misquoted, but unfortunately Jack could find no comfort or ammunition in this exercise. The plan to discredit the book by rational argument was therefore abandoned. Instead, the CBC was advised to have nothing to do with *The Age of Mackenzie King*. It was such a thoroughly bad book of such a low standard that CBC would be doing itself a disservice to consider it. Although a program on *The Age of Mackenzie King* had been advertised in some advance publicity of the CBC, the program was cancelled.

I could imagine the passion into which this put Bernie. He took his case to the opposition in the House of Commons. Mr H.A. Bryson, the CCF member for Humboldt-Melfort in Saskatchewan, asked a question. The minister responsible offered to enquire. Then the CCF member for Winnipeg North, Mr Alistair Stewart, asked a witty question, 'Can the

Minister inform the House what medium the CBC will use to review the book on Mackenzie King?' Loud laughter.

Unfortunately, it was a very sober Conservative, Mr Donald Fleming, who spoke at length. There is no evidence that he had read the book. He treated the cancellation in terms of government dictation to the CBC and political censorship. This was, of course, right, but he said nothing to suggest why the government had used its influence. He did nothing but ask on what basis was the decision made by the CBC to cancel the program. Pickersgill gave the perfect one-line answer, which gave nothing away. 'They probably read the book,' he said.

Henceforward, the standard defence of the government was: the book is no good. By December 1955 the cash sales in Canada of *The Age of Mackenzie King* were 2,357 copies. Between January and June 1956 only 263 copies were sold. When my brother-in-law tried to buy a copy in Morgan's book department in Montreal he was told that they had no copies, but, of course, if he really wanted to buy a copy one might be obtained in three or four weeks. My mother was unable to buy a copy in Winnipeg. A friend in Halifax reported to me that no copies were available in bookshops there. In December 1955, the Toronto *Saturday Night* asked me to write 1,000-1,500 words on the experience of writing *The Age of Mackenzie King* and they sent me an advance of $75.00. The article never appeared and on enquiry I was told they found that they had no space. The same thing happened with *Maclean's*, except that I received no money from them.

The publicity given to *The Age of Mackenzie King* was enormous, all of it bad. The only perceptive and friendly reviews came from Grattan O'Leary, later a Conservative senator, and Arthur Ford, the editor of the *London Free Press*. Grant Dexter of the *Winnipeg Free Press* devoted almost half a page to denouncing the book and its authors. A syndicated columnist, Arnold Edinborough, went beserk in his denunciation and because it was mentioned on the dust jacket that I had written on Anglo-Argentine relations, he asked, 'Whatever has this to do with a biography of Mackenzie King?' In the communist vocabulary of political abuse there is a widely used phrase, 'the running dogs of the bourgeoisie.' The pack employed by the Liberal party of Canada was surely running loose and making a loud cacophony.

Elsewhere in the world where *The Age of Mackenzie King* was publicly noticed, particularly in Britain and Australia, comment was friendly and favourable. The book was accepted for what it is: a repository of facts, a rational, analysis and a tale told with a bit of acidulous wit. The few exceptions to the generally favourable comment outside Canada were the work of Canadians. Close inspection of these critics revealed in every case that they drew part of their incomes from the Canadian Broadcasting Corporation. Convincing, indeed, is the economic interpretation of history.

The sound and fury over *The Age of Mackenzie King* lasted from early January 1956 until the end of March 1956. By June 1957 the Liberals were out of office. The fuss about the book was a storm in a teacup, but it did signify something. It was the first political breeze which eventually turned into the gale-force winds of the pipeline debate. This ended the Liberal domination in Canadian politics.

Bernie's defeat in his endeavours to advertise *The Age of Mackenzie King* put him in a rage. The *Financial Times* of Montreal (17 February 1956) reported him as saying: 'My next volume will be much stronger. I have in it a lot about people who are now living. There will also be a tale of corruption, the like of which never occurred in Canada since the Pacific scandal.' After this it seemed to me imprudent to attempt to compose my differences with Bernie and detrimental to my interest and reputation to continue an association. Accordingly, on 20 April 1956 I informed *The Times* and the Press Association that, 'There will be no further volumes of *The Age of Mackenzie King*. I am satisfied that there is insufficient evidence available to the public to write a truthful and adequate account of Mackenzie King's life going beyond the year 1919. There are no papers open to public inspection comparable with those of Sir Wilfrid Laurier upon which *The Age of Mackenzie King: The Rise of the Leader* is largely based.'

In the ensuing months I made a few suggestions to the publishers about how to repair the damage done, but by the end of 1956 I had become so bored by *The Age of Mackenzie King* that I put it on the shelf and never looked at it again for another twenty years.

What annoyed and disappointed me most in the whole episode was the behaviour of academic historians in Canada. The book was given by the *Canadian Historical Review* to Professor A.L. Burt of the University of Minnesota for review. He put the stamp of academic authority and approval on every malign and false thing first uttered by the Liberal party journalist, Grant Dexter. When Professor Donald Creighton of the University of Toronto was asked to participate in a discussion of *The Age of Mackenzie King,* he excused himself on the ground that he did not wish to appear to be an authority on *two* Canadian prime ministers. A colleague in the University of Manitoba wrote to tell me how good he thought the book was and he urged me to 'answer Grant Dexter.' I replied, 'Why don't you answer him?' But he never did. The hosts of Israel kept well back just in case Goliath had a harder head than expected.

By 1958, however, when Goliath was stretched out on the benches of the opposition in the House of Commons, the *Canadian Historical Review* asked me to review volume I of the official biography of Mackenzie King, but just to play it safe, the editor invited another man to write a parallel review. This turned out to be more hostile than mine and for the very good reason that I always regarded and specifically said that Mackenzie King was a master politician who was successful because he had acquired by study a thorough understanding of the mechanics of society and never allowed himself to be confused by the superficial nonsense with which lesser men concern themselves. Furthermore, I was never so foolish as to judge him by his sentimental rhetoric or the strange quirks of his private personality. Mackenzie King was not a good man or a normal man or a straightforward man or a likeable man. He was simply a great man at his trade, in the way that Michaelangelo was a great artist or Marlborough a great soldier. Unfortunately, in the trade of politics, followers want their leaders to be like themselves, and they become very upset when someone tells them that this is seldom or never the case.

Most books die a natural death. They live for a few years and disappear into junk shops or libraries where they are seldom or never read. *The Age of Mackenzie King* is not an immortal work, but it has contrived to live on. At a meeting of the British Association of Canadian Studies two decades after its publication, something very pleasant happened to me. A young French-speaking Canadian historian introduced himself to me and said he had long wanted to meet the man who wrote *The Age of Mackenzie King*. 'Why?' I asked. Because, he answered, reading *The Age of Mackenzie King* when at college persuaded him that he wanted to become an historian.

Late in the 1970s a publisher in Toronto, James Lorimer, wrote to ask whether I would consent to the republication of the book. I agreed and Bernie agreed. *The Age of Mackenzie King* began once more to sell and people to buy. When this request came, I took the book down and re-read it. It is a good book and a rather humorous one, but I can see why it never appealed to Jack Pickersgill or Brooke Claxton. But then I never supposed it would. If it had, it would have been no good.

Bernie has not yet written the second volume of *The Age of Mackenzie King*. After a few false starts, he settled down to the task of surviving and prospering in Ottawa. The lessons learned in studying the career of Mackenzie King seem to have stood him in good stead. By the time Bernie was fifty he had reached the top of the bureaucracy: he was a deputy minister. He has not, however, matched the record of Mackenzie King. At fifty, Mackenzie King had already been prime minister for three years. But there is still time.

Whenever he was planning a metamorphosis from, say, a civil servant into a politician or from an ex-cabinet minister into a party leader, it was Mackenzie King's practice to write a book. Bernie seems to be following this pattern. He has written a book, *The Cultural Connection,* published in 1978. It compares favourably with Mackenzie King's great work, *Industry and Humanity*. It is, for example, shorter. It can fairly be said that it is in parts better written. It contains one funny joke. All this is to the good. In essentials, however, *The Cultural Connection* is like *Industry and Humanity*. It contains a message and the message is introduced with a quotation from *Proverbs:* 'Where There is No Vision the People Perish.'

The Ostry message can be simply stated. Canada, or at least the federal government of Canada, can be saved by culture. Culture has the role in present-day Canada that railways had in the nineteenth century. It can unite Canadians in achieving a new consciousness. Pour money into culture and Canada will live forever, or, if not forever, at least for the foreseeable future. Of course, torrents of money have already been spent on culture but we must keep up the good work. Provincial governments can and do spend money on culture, but it is the federal government which can get the mix just right for survival and the assurance of brotherhood and sisterhood in the here and the hereafter.

The tone of *The Cultural Connection,* like that of *Industry and Humanity,* is ecumenical. Each chapter is introduced by five or six quotations, 45 in all. These are a harvest from the wisdom of the ages, but with a strong Canadian flavour. They range from Matthew Arnold to Agnes MacPhail. Even Mackenzie King is represented in this Parliament of Owls.

There is in *The Cultural Connection* a truly original observation. 'Perhaps,' Bernie writes, 'only the armed forces have understood from the start the importance of developing a sense of identity and the connection of culture with morale and community relations.' When one considers the creative use of the Canadian armed forces in politics by Prime Minister

Trudeau, one is prompted to ask: 'Is Bernie planning a *coup d'état?'* Why, of course not! But talk like this is a staple rationalization in the armed forces of Argentina and Chile. Perhaps Bernie has achieved some sort of breakthrough to a new form of political consciousness for Canada.

Seriously, however, *The Cultural Connection* is a personal platform just as *Industry and Humanity* was. Critics have dismissed it just as critics dismissed *Industry and Humanity.* There is, however, no reason why Bernard Ostry should not dominate the Age of Taste as Mackenzie King dominated the Age of Unrest and War. As a youth, Bernie learned to spend his father's money on culture. Why should he not go on to spend Canada's money to the same end? There is now a vast vested interest in culture in Canada. Canada has problems. Persuade the vested interests that they have the solutions of the problems and the persuader is politically home and dry. If I were a Canadian voter, I would take Bernard Ostry very seriously indeed. And don't tell me he's not in Parliament. If one is aiming for the top in Canadian politics, one should never start in Parliament. Only Diefenbaker and Clark did, and look what has happened to them! And one must remember that the British Tories were in worse shape as a political party when they were rescued by Disraeli than the Canadian Tories are in the 1980s.

CHAPTER THIRTEEN

Marxism Transcended:
experience as a British academic

In 1978 I wrote and published a little book, *The Disease of Government.* It is based on the proposition 'that there are principles of law and politics which can and should be stated in language as simple and plain as that of the Constitution of the United States or the *Communist Manifesto.'* The book fell deadborn from the press. A nasty anonymous review in *the Economist,* an approving eulogy from Malcolm Muggeridge in the *Toronto Star*, and then oblivion.

The Disease of Government is, however, a station – perhaps the terminus – in an intellectual journey from innocent faith through liberalism, then Marxism, to a new understanding of politics. In a TV program broadcast in Britain eight days before the American presidential election of 1980, I was asked how I saw the contest in the United States. I replied that it was an event at the end of a long road which had begun in the 1930s when the Americans embarked on an endeavour to overcome the failures of a free enterprise market economy through the use of increasing state power, that the solutions embarked upon had now exhausted their possibilities, and that government intervention had ceased to be a solution and had become the problem; that the trouble with the United States was the government itself.

How had I reached this view not just of American but human affairs? How had I escaped the inertia of leftism into an atmosphere of freedom and hope that 1984 is merely a date and not a destiny, that my grandchildren will be neither dead nor red, that eternal life is still a metaphor with a meaning?

Britain turned out to be a happy place for me. Not because it was rich, not because it was full of opportunities, not because it was efficient, not because it was democratic, not because it was egalitarian, and not because it was semi-socialist. Why? Because it was, as it still is, a free society.

The freedom that one encounters in British society is not easy to describe or to analyse. There is, of course, an underlying social cohesion in Britain which can obliterate individual freedom, but this seems only to manifest itself in times of great danger such as war or the threat of profound economic disorganization and failure. Ordinarily, one encounters a strong sense of privacy among all classes and kinds of people which enables one, within wide limits, to be oneself, to live in one's own way without a numbing wariness of other people and other organizations to which one cannot or does not wish to belong, or to which one is loath to submit. There is some evidence that this condition is changing for the worse and that one cannot be too complacent about the character of British society, but on the whole the inarticulate responses of the British to overriding fanaticisms seems as strong, or nearly as strong, as they ever were.

When I left Britain at the end of 1939, I belonged to two organizations, first Trinity College and the University of Cambridge, and secondly to the Communist party. When I returned in 1949, I was still a member of the first organization but not the second. On the other hand, I was returning to a welcoming number of friends, many of whom were or had been members of the Communist party. One came especially from his laboratory in Stockholm to welcome me and my family in London. One provided the five of us with a home in his home for three weeks and we could have stayed as long as we wished. Another helped us to find a rented house sufficiently close to Cambridge for me to work there and in London. This was quite a different atmosphere from that I had left in Canada where some of my family even seemed to regard me as an embarrassing black sheep.

In picking up the threads of the past, I encountered only two disappointments. Soon after arriving back in Cambridge, I made a point of visiting a man who had been a very close friend in 1937-39. He was a don in St John's College. He specialized in laughing and smiling in all circumstances and now he laughed and smiled when he greeted me. But he said he was very busy. He was so sorry to be tied up. Remembering how he had once ordered up a splendid *creme brûlée* from the college kitchens when entertaining Maureen and me in the summer of 1939, I expected him to invite me to lunch. But this was 1949. He excused himself, and I could see he did not want to know me. Ten days later, I was turning into King's Parade with my son Pat when I encountered Eddie. He nodded and quickly passed by on the other side.

The other disappointment was a man in Pembroke, whose company I had much enjoyed in the past. I called on him. Just returned from playing tennis he asked me to stay to tea, but he so persistently discussed tennis with his partner that obviously he too did not want to know me.

Apart from these two brief and distasteful encounters, I met with nothing but friendship. Very little was ever said by anyone about why I had returned to Britain and for my part I limited my discussion to saying I wanted to complete my research at Cambridge and find a job. It was assumed that I was a refugee from the Cold War. I more or less assumed the same, but refugees of all kinds were so numerous in Britain and had been for so many years, that I could command no special attention nor did I wish to do so.

Objectively, as the communists say, I had become apolitical. This condition was a consequence of several factors: a prudence born of experience which caused me to attach more importance to making a career than to political activity of any kind; some serious, but not thoroughly worked out, doubts about the policies and practice of the communist parties and particularly of the Soviet Union; and finally, some unresolved doubts about Marxism as an explanatory theory of social and economic developments. On the other hand, I was neither politically nor theoreti-

312

cally totally unsympathetic to the left. The independence of India and Pakistan I counted as a great step forward, although I regretted that the political unity of the Indian subcontinent had been broken. I welcomed the news that the Soviet Union had exploded a nuclear bomb. This event seemed to me to create a balance of power in world affairs which would diminish the possibility of another world war. And I welcomed the victory of the Communists in China because I thought that at last China would have a government capable of arresting a revival of western imperialist activity in Asia and that this development complemented the anti-imperialist victories in India and the Dutch East Indies.

Although I was no longer a Communist or an uncritical Marxist, there was still some common ground politically between me and my old friends. They never sought from me a revival of the political commitment of my days as an undergraduate in Cambridge and I was never forced into a position of having to make up my mind about where I stood politically.

Another factor to be considered was the Communist party's view of me. When I joined the staff of the University of Birmingham in 1950, there was a party branch in the university numbering from fifteen to eighteen members.

I did not learn this fact from friends, but in a most dismaying way from the newspapers on the day I came to Birmingham to meet the Dean of the Faculty of Commerce and Social Science, Professor Philip Sargant Florence. On 29 March 1950, Lord Vansittart, speaking in the House of Lords, made a wide-ranging attack on Communist influence in the civil service, in the churches, and in the universities. Part of his attention was focused on the University of Birmingham and particularly on a member of the extra-mural department whom he described as a 'murderous priest.' His Lordship went on to ask how such a man could have been appointed to the staff of the University of Birmingham. Who was guilty?

The Vice-Chancellor of the University, Sir Raymond Priestly, promptly replied to Lord Vansittart; and so did 'the murderous priest.' Sir Raymond said, 'There are Communists in the University. It would be difficult to find any shade of political opinion not represented. I am not aware that the Communist party has been outlawed by the Government. We do not normally inquire into political convictions and, in my opinion, we shall be wrong to do so.'

This bold answer, so different from anything one might expect from a Canadian university president in similar circumstances, greatly relieved me. Lord Vansittart's endeavour to start a purge of British institutions fell flat and a witch hunt *à la américaine* did not develop in Britain. This seemed to me evidence of British freedom and a determination on the part of people at the top to preserve it. At the same time it made me aware that there was in Birmingham an organized Communist party in an institution where I hoped I might spend the rest of my life.

When I had established myself in Birmingham in September 1950, I did not seek out the Communists nor did they approach me. Some twenty years later I was told by a friend, who had been a member of the party branch at the time, that the comrades in Birmingham had been notified of my presence in Birmingham and that they had been instructed to treat me with reserve.

The Communists in Birmingham were not 'old friends.' I knew the name of Professor Roy Pascal, who was an ex-Cambridge man and a well-known and much respected Communist intellectual, but I did not know him personally. One man I had met very briefly at a gathering of 'party historians' in 1939, but he was not a friend. I did not remember him and I had no reason to suppose he remembered me. Another I had once encountered at a punt party in Cambridge and I had known his wife. As for the other Communists in Birmingham, I had no more knowledge of them than I did of the Conservatives in the university. It was this body of men and women completely uninfluenced by personal friendship who were instructed by the party organization to treat me with reserve.

In this matter I am bound to say that the Communist party exhibited more care and better judgement than the officials of the Canadian government. The party was right. I was an 'unreliable element.' For ten years I had never followed the party line in things which mattered. I had avoided organized contact with the party. Soviet intelligence had been given my name as a possible recruit, but I had approached the Soviet diplomats in Ottawa before they approached me. From their point of view I could conceivably have been a British or Canadian intelligence agent seeking to infiltrate their organization. On the question of India I had opposed the line of their Allies. Certainly I was not to be trusted. Certainly I had little potential as a soldier of the revolution.

In 1951 I once spent an evening in the company of a friend and James Klugman. Klugman was then a high party official and remained a faithful follower of the party until his death. He had a quick intelligence. His account of his activities as a British officer and party man in Yugoslavia during the war was extremely interesting and told with an ironic wit. He was obviously a brave and perceptive man with a profound knowledge of what he was doing. Then he wrote a book on politics relating to Yugoslavia. How could James Klugman ever have written such a book? Did he experience no mental and moral agony in producing such distorted garbage – i.e. distorted and garbage in terms of what he had to say privately about the events in which he had participated? I could only thank God and the party that I had been judged unfit – unfit to go through such mental contortions in the pursuit of power.

Of the Cambridge Communists whom I knew, James Klugman was one of the few who stuck to the party. I can think of only two others who seem to have kept the faith and continued to submit to the discipline of their church. The rest have left. Most have, however, retained their Marxism and a left political inclination. Some others seem to have turned completely away from politics and thinking about politics. I am probably not unique among the Cambridge ex-Communists, but I do seem to be one of the few who has retained an interest in politics and in thinking about politics, moved by a need to explore better alternatives to Marxist theory and better practice than that of the collectivists, whether communists, socialists, or fascists.

It may be argued that I have simply repented and returned to the liberalism I first learned in my youth. If this were so, it would be of no interest to anyone. But I do not think this is the case. Knowledge and experience of Marxism and the communists have not been wasteful mistakes, but encounters with political realities of positive value in coming to some understanding of the most lethal of all human activities; that from which most is expected and least gained.

That I have ever been able to come to a general understanding of politics owes much to the fact that from 1950 and for at least another ten years I ceased to think much about real politics. On 25 June 1950, the day when the war in Korea broke out, I was in Birmingham attending a meeting of the Faculty of Commerce and Social Science concerned with the teaching and tutorial arrangements for the session 1950-51. At tea after the meeting I fell into conversation with a young lecturer in economics who had been an officer in the British army during the Second World War. He said bleakly but confidently that he expected shortly to be back in uniform and a full participant in the Third. I remember how numb I felt. Somehow I did not believe that a new world war was about to begin, but I seemed to have lost the power to think about or comment on what was happening. My mind seemed to close. I turned away from the din, the hubbub, and the confusion, ceased to respond to events by

315

trying to understand them and gave myself over to the task, essential for me and my family, of establishing a secure career, if this were possible.

In this I was helped enormously by Trinity College, Cambridge. When I first arrived back I called on Kitson Clark. After examining me for a moment in silence he shook hands and said 'Hello.' Another moment of silence and then he reminded me that it was in 1938 that he had entered me as a candidate for a Ph.D. It was now 1949. Eleven years was a most unusual length of time working for a Ph.D.

Having put me in my place, Kitson Clark was civil enough. He invited me to dine at the high table. There he introduced me to M.J.K. Vyvyan who asked me to undertake the supervision of half a dozen undergraduates. There, too, I met my old comrade, Jack Gallagher, now a fellow. I invited him to tea at Bottisham.

Jack was warm and friendly. He told a few jokes which indicated that he had long since left the Communist party and had begun seriously to question the great truths of Marxism. I told a few jokes which indicated much the same direction of travel and there we left the questions of ideology and commitment. We were simply friends and Jack offered me the use of his rooms in Neville's Court for the purpose of my work as a supervisor.

One of the merits of Cambridge University as a place for graduate study is the wide freedom and responsibility accorded the students. One can work in one's own way without interference by others. One is judged on what one does and not on what someone else has recommended or even demanded.

I had a supervisor, of course: the Professor of Economic History, Michael Postan. Being a refugee from the Soviet sphere of influence, he was understandably an anti-Communist. Intellectually, he had a number of serious reservations about Marxism. He felt that I was in need of salvation, but my hearing and his English being what they were his efforts in this direction yielded little. Nor did his endeavours to persuade me that the writing of history needed a strong infusion of contemporary economic theorizing and his enthusiasm for the work of W.W. Rostow never influenced me. I conceived my task to be the discovery and analysis of a few basic facts about Anglo-Argentine economic relations and I was resolutely determined not to attempt to prove a theory of any description. If the facts proved something, well and good, but such was not my objective. As I said in the preface of the book, I eventually published on

316

the subject: 'It has been my method ... to avoid theorizing, model building and using the conclusions and reflections of others in order that, by submission to the authority of my sources, I might discover something about the conditions under which in this instance economic development did or did not take place. The only general conclusion I have come to is neither novel nor surprising. It would appear from this study that economic growth is not something that occurs by itself, but is dependent at every stage upon political decisions and organization and more remotely upon the faith and values of the community.'

More important at this juncture in my life than debating about the right kind of economic theory to be used in writing history was finding a job. In this matter Professor Postan was a real help. I would have liked to stay in Cambridge, but the place was swarming with eager, talented young people who wanted and needed opportunities. I was ten years too late, and I had nothing to show for those ten years which could possibly constitute a claim for preferment. I tried for two posts: Kenneth Berrill got one of them, John Street the other.

It was otherwise when I looked outside Cambridge. Late in February 1950 I answered an advertisement for the post of assistant director of research in the Faculty of Commerce and Social Science in the University of Birmingham. Within days Professor Postan was on the phone to say that Professor W.H.B. Court of Birmingham was in Cambridge and wanted to see me. It was not possible for me to see him, but Court left behind an invitation to visit Birmingham.

Settling in Birmingham is an instance of the extraordinary good luck in essentials which has governed my life. Some months after establishing myself and my family there, I came upon *A History of Birmingham* by William Hutton written in the closing years of the American Revolution and published in several editions between 1780 and 1810. Upon opening the second edition of 1783, I found these encouraging words in his dedication. They attracted me then in 1950 and they express the experience of thirty years in this great city; 'To the inhabitants of Birmingham. For to them I not only owe much, but all; and I think, among the congregated mass, there is not one person to whom I wish ill. I have the pleasure of calling many inhabitants friends and some of them share my warm affection equally with myself. Birmingham, like a compassionate nurse, not only draws our persons but our esteem, from the place of our nativity, and fixes them upon herself. I might add, I was hungry and she

317

fed me; thirsty, and she gave me drink; a stranger and she took me in. I approached her with reluctance, because I did not know her; I shall leave her with reluctance, because I do.'

The 'reluctance' to which Hutton referred is still with us. 1980 was only a few weeks old when I heard a supercilious twit on the BBC refer to Birmingham as 'that dreadful place.' Remarks like that – and they have not infrequently been heard for 250 years – tell more about their authors than they do about Birmingham. Almost invariably they issue from the mouths of people who are comfortable enough to despise work, to take the production of goods and services for granted and to esteem the beak, claws, and feathers of a bird more than its brains, muscles, and capacity to fly and feed itself.

On the first day of the autumn term in 1950 I descended from the tram on the Bristol Road near that old Victorian public house, *'The Gun Barrels'* set among trees and a fine old bowling green and I entered through the iron gates of the university. As I walked across the expanse of grass towards the hill crowned with the great bulk of the Aston-Webb Buildings, I experienced one of those moments – too few in life – of complete and happy peace. There may have been a war in Korea and a Cold War freezing the patterns of politics around the world, but I felt something I had not known for fifteen years, the sensation of security and freedom. I wanted nothing more than to stay where I then was and do what I had been appointed to do. Ambition seemed at an end and that I had arrived at a quiet destination. This was not altogether an illusion.

I climbed up to the 'temporary' huts where my office was. An office to myself! Something I had never known in Canada. I sat down at the desk and looked out across the playing fields below to the city stretched out as far as my eyes could see. I counted sixteen factory chimneys. I could hear the clatter and crash of the drop-forging plant across the Bournebrook beyond the boundaries of the campus. Intermittent rifle fire could be heard from a gunsmith's establishment opposite the foundry. Beyond lay a motorcycle works and a paper-box factory. All of it was real, the substance of life, not much appreciated or understood in some quarters.

I was fortunate to come to Birmingham while there still remained physical and moral evidence of its great age. Until the Second World War, Birmingham was unique among British cities: a town that had seldom or never in its history known depression; a town which had always attracted immigrants from other parts of the United Kingdom and abroad

318

because it was a place of social peace, political unity, economic opportunity, and freedom. Birmingham was so unlike other British cities in its political disposition and in its capacity for constructive social and economic reform that foreign students and observers like Ostragorski were prompted to ask why this should be so. Joseph Chamberlain, Birmingham's greatest, as his son Neville was its most unfortunate, politician, is remembered as an imperialist, but what is more easily forgotten is the fact that he is one of few Englishmen who ever made a public enterprise really work. When he brought the gas industry in Birmingham into public ownership there were within a year a reduction in the price of gas, an increase in wages in the industry, and a substantial contribution to the city treasury from profits. The same success came in electricity, transport, water, and banking.

The Birmingham I viewed in September 1950 has gone. For good, understandable reasons there are only five tall chimneys to be seen from the window of the office I first occupied. The motorcycle industry is gone. Where there used to be little or no industrial strife there are pockets of real antagonism blown up by the media so that British Leyland and Birmingham have become identified as a problem area. In fact, the problems are in just those industries which are uncharacteristic of Birmingham – large concentrations remotely or nationally owned and controlled and not the enormously various small industries on which Birmingham's reputation was built.

In the old Birmingham there was hardly a square foot of land outside the parks which was not used for the purpose of living and producing. National planning has ended that. Today, Birmingham has large areas of land in the dead hand of government and its agencies or inhibited in its use by private owners because national planners have ordained that industrial development must take place elsewhere in new towns or development areas or areas of unemployment. The deterioration of free enterprise caused by government has made Birmingham into a depressed area with higher than average levels of unemployment. But it is hard to kill a great city. The essential Birmingham of skilled workers and enterprising businessmen and women is still here and still working.

The post of assistant director of research turned out to be one with few responsibilities and ill-defined objectives. In the main, it consisted of putting into readable English the research findings of refugee researchers and semi-literate social scientists. Added to this not onerous task was an obligation to teach a course for one term on the institutions of government in the independent Commonwealth countries, which was a compulsory part of the program for students of accounting. And then there was some tutorial work. All in all, I had so little to do for others that I had much time for my own interests. It was a delightful set of circumstances marred only by the thought that, remembering the load of work I had had to carry in Canada, I was doing insufficient to justify my continued employment.

Quite by chance, I was put upon the road which led to a professorship of political science. The Faculty of Commerce and Social Science had a development plan and part of this involved the establishment of a Department of Political Science. The man in charge of this aspect of the plan was John Hawgood, the Professor of Modern History and Government. He was the head of the large department of history in the Faculty of Arts and the nominal parent of the embryo of a department of political science in the Faculty of Commerce and Social Science. The embryo consisted of Henry Maddick who taught courses in British government, local government, and public administration, and me, who taught part of a course on government of the Commonwealth, when I was not translating bad English into good and cultivating my garden.

John Hawgood was in many respects a remarkable man, but he was not much in Birmingham. He lived in a stone house in sight of Bredon Hill in Gloucestershire and he spent much of his time in the United States studying the history of the wild west beyond the Mississippi River. Whenever I saw him, which was not often, he seemed to be making a hurried departure for Gloucestershire or the United States and on most occasions he wanted me to do something for him in the way of a lecture or marking some examinations or seeing some students. I always obliged him as best I could and only once did I rebel. When he wanted me to take charge of appointing a new member of staff, I refused because I thought it improper to have responsibility for appointing someone on the same level of the hierarchy as myself and to do a responsible job for which I was not being paid. Hawgood amiably agreed to stay another day in Birmingham to make the appointment.

The people in the Faculty of Commerce and Social Science grew to dislike Professor Hawgood's frequent absence and they moved in the direction of establishing the Department of Political Science as a department in the faculty with a responsible head who would be continuously present in the university and wholly in the faculty. Academic judgements are often odd. They turned to me. I was not a political scientist and I did not pretend to be one. My lecturing on political theory was something I did because it interested me and because Professor Hawgood wanted me to do so as a contribution to one of his courses on aspects of world history. In *The Age of Mackenzie King* I had written on a political theme, not as a political scientist but as a Canadian and an historian.

My colleagues in the Faculty of Commerce and Social Science seemed to choose me because I appeared to them an unambitious intellectual who had a good degree from Cambridge, had published several articles in learned journals (but not in the field of political science) and never participated in the frequent fights for the control of resources and places in the university. In 1956 I was appointed a Senior Lecturer in charge of the Department of Political Science. When the money for the appointment of a professor became available in 1960, I applied for the post and was elected. After the election, one of the external assessors, Professor Michael Oakeshott of the London School of Economics said to me: 'I am delighted you were appointed, but my advice to you is never to appoint another man like yourself.' This was very good advice and I always followed it until the reforms in the university in response to student unrest deprived the heads of departments of the final authority in recommending people for appointment.

My unintended transformation into a political scientist with the responsibility of establishing the discipline in the university imposed upon me the task of acquainting myself sufficiently with the subject in order to develop a curriculum for undergraduates. The subject was developing at a very rapid pace from the mid 1950s onward, particularly in North America and on the continent of Europe. I believed that students in Birmingham ought to have the opportunity to acquaint themselves with the discipline as it was developing in the world at large and not as I conceived of it. I never tried to found my own church in Birmingham and to turn preacher of a doctrine. Instead, I launched courses imitative of what others were doing elsewhere and turned them over to young people more expertly specialized than myself as resources for new appointments flowed into the university from the seemingly bottomless well of public beneficence uncapped by Prime Minister Macmillan and handed over to Sir Harold Wilson for heavier pumping.

When I became Professor of Political Science in January 1961 there were three members of the department, including myself. By the time the tap was turned off in the mid 1970s, there were nine members of the department. But this is no measure of the expansion of the study of politics and administration in Birmingham. My first priority on appointment as a professor was to relieve Henry Maddick of the teaching burdens he had borne for ten years and to get him some recognition for what he had done. Once allowed to concentrate his attention on the subject of local government and appointed a senior lecturer, Henry displayed astonishing powers as an academic entrepreneur. He launched large programs for the education and training for administrators in the overseas territories of the dissolving empire and commonwealth and of local government officers in Britain. He himself found the finance for his enterprises and the teachers to bring them to fruition.

Being an anti-imperialist in world politics, I was resolved not to become an academic imperialist, by the exercise of my authority as head of the Department of Political Science. Using my powers and influence as Dean of the Faculty, to which office I was elected in September 1961, I severed the connection between Political Science and the study of local government. Henry Maddick then had full autonomy with the result that he developed an Institute of Local Government Studies as a department in the university which became vastly larger than the Department of Political Science and as large as the whole Faculty of Commerce and Social Science during my time as dean from 1961 to 1965.

The point in setting down an account of my activities as a political scientist in the University of Birmingham is to estimate the extent to which an acquaintance with modern political science affected my thinking about politics and assisted me to resolve the confusions so evidently present in mind whenever I asked myself where I stood on public issues.

Not very much, I fear. Perhaps I never went into political sociology, quantitative analysis, or the study of international politics in sufficient depth to learn anything significant. Perhaps I was too old a dog to learn new tricks. Very little that I encountered in the flood of books and articles, which constituted the political science of the 1950s, 1960s, and 1970s, was of any assistance to me personally, no matter how much light this abundance of intellectual activity may have brought to others. Indeed, much of the thinking of the time seemed to reinforce just those intellectual tendencies which I considered at the heart of the world's problems.

There was, however, one consequence of my duties as a teacher of political science which proved of great effect – the discovery and rediscovery of some insights from the past rather than from the present. When, at Professor Hawgood's behest, I began to lecture on political theory in 1952, I followed the very common practice of dusting off what I had learned as an undergraduate. When I did this I found that there were many gaps in my knowledge of the major figures in the history of political thought and many misinterpretations. In particular, I found that I had no working knowledge of Hobbes and that there were aspects of Rousseau's thought which illuminated contemporary experience in a most remarkable way.

Reading Hobbes' *Leviathan* was exciting. Here one encountered the clarity, simplicity and penetration of theory that illuminates so that one can see as one might suppose God sees – being aware of experience but outside it and understanding it. The hole in Marxist theory which had been opened to my view by 'the letter from Schlesinger' ceased to be. Here was a theory of greater generality and greater penetration, which covered more cases than Marx and Engels had dreamed of in their philosophy and which explained what they had ignored or could not face. The pitiless rationality and realism of Hobbes made me feel that my mind was full of political cant.

Re-reading Rousseau's *Social Contrast* affected me in another way. I was untroubled by the kind of arguments advanced by Rousseau so different from those of Hobbes. And for this reason. Rousseau's analysis of the general will, on which he based all legitimate public authority, seemed to me a concept which helped enormously in thinking about imperialism. Until re-reading Rousseau, my opposition to imperialism as a political phenomenon had been based partly on an appreciation of Canadian experience, partly on observation of the Indian movement for independence and sympathetic friendship with young people involved in it, and partly on the arguments of Hobson, Luxemburg, and Lenin. There was in my political response to imperialism a large element of moral preference and a smaller element of belief that my moral preferences coincided with the working of the inescapable laws of history. Study of Anglo-Argentine relations, the evidence of imperialist tendencies manifest by the Soviet and American governments and the disjunction between economic and political phenomena in inter-state relationships had, however, led me seriously to doubt the theoretical underpinning of my anti-imperialism.

Reading Rousseau and thinking about his concept of the general will and the social developments which bring it to birth and cause it to grow provided me with a theory which explained more than Marxist theories did. Marxist theories assert that imperialism is a political phenomenon which is peculiar to capitalist socio-economic relations; that the suppression of the capitalist order will end imperialism and produce a set of circumstances in which peoples are free and independent. This is so evidently not the case that the Marxist theories are deficient. They cannot, for example, explain why the Soviet Union is what it is and why Russian hegemony over non-Russian peoples, which had characterized the Tsarist regime, has not withered away, or why the Soviet Union has numerous client states under partial occupation by military force.

Rousseau's concept of the general will, however, offers a clue not only to what had caused the great empires of the western European nations to wither away but to what will happen to the Soviet empire and also why US policy towards client states has failed in Vietnam, in Cuba, and in Latin America. It explains why efficiency in administration, technological superiority, and economic and financial sophistication are not enough in the realm of politics. Indeed, Rousseau's brief analysis of the constituents of the general will suggest at once that Lenin's line on imperialism and even Stalin's on the national question are insufficient.

By themselves the ideas of Hobbes and Rousseau were not enough to clarify critically the experience of seeming enlightenment and positive dedication to political activity which I had found in Marxism. In 1956 I drew my thoughts together in a short paper entitled 'A Note on Faith in Politics.' In the 1950s we had in the university a society open to anyone interested in the social sciences, named after Sir William Ashley, the founder of our faculty, where it was still possible for economists, sociologists, students of administration and politics, social statisticians, historians and social psychologists to talk to one another in comprehensible English. It was to the Ashley Society that I read my thoughts on faith in politics.

They evoked no positive response. One young social psychologist asked how I could be so banal as to use a term like faith. It was not an operational concept and could not be quantified. This was the 1950s. When last I heard of this young woman twenty years on it was reported that she was 'into Zen.' The editor of *Political Studies* declined to consider my note and I came to the conclusion that, useful as the exercise was to me personally, it must be of no interest to anyone else.

In this note I draw a distinction based on experience between knowledge about which one can be reasonably certain and faith which is easily confused with knowledge. Knowledge has its origins in observation and reasoning about observations. One cannot make moral judgments about knowledge.

Knowledge, however, is used by man to build a mousetrap, for example, or to visit the moon. Why we use knowledge and for what purposes are the province of morals, politics, and religion. We can, of course, acquire knowledge based on observation about actions in the sphere of morals, politics, and religion, but we make a serious mistake if we regard such knowledge as in principle the same as our knowledge about molecular structures or the solar system or what happens if we dip our fingers in boiling water.

There was nothing very original in my argument. Fifty years previously, G.E. Moore had established that moral (and by implication, political) systems are founded on faith, not on knowledge susceptible to proof. Variants of the conclusion can be discovered in the thinking of at least two thousand years. Historically, the notion has been both the spoken and unspoken assumption of man for much longer than the contrary conception of moral science or scientific morality and politics. Even so severe a liberal dogmatist as von Hayek has in his old age conceded the point and acknowledges that one has to believe in something before one can think about anything.

This distinction between faith and knowledge led me to consider, not the discovery of a new comfortable faith for myself but the question of why faiths lead so evidently to social and personal disasters – why the reverse of the Marxist coin is the Gulag Archipelago or the reverse of the Roman Catholic coin was the Spanish Inquisition. Faith seems to be as necessary to life as oxygen and water, but is it necessary and inevitable that we poison ourselves with faith? Is it possible to transcend the ambigous nature and the consequences of faith, to hit upon a 'life-giving' faith?

A large question, and one which I did not attempt directly to answer. My route to a kind of answer was through experience, which for convenience of presentation can be divided in two: experience as a member of the government of the University of Birmingham during my term of office as dean of the Faculty of Commerce and Social Science from 1961 to 1965; and experience and study in the Argentine republic in 1966. Reflection upon these two experiences together led to the conclusion that the most general problem of politics is our faith in the state and government as a solution to the problem of self-destruction; that government is not the cure, that it has become the disease.

Before describing these two experiences it is worthwhile setting down

325

an instance of Marxist activism which finally extinguished in my mind the notion that a reasonable person can and should have no enemies on the left.

My election as professor of Political Science put me for the first time in my life in a position of responsibility where I was in some degree on my own and not a member of a committee or board where I was only one of many making decisions. In those days before the academic reforms of the late 1960s and the early 1970s heads of departments in universities like Birmingham had a wide and real personal responsibility for recommending persons for appointment as lecturers and research fellows. Such appointments were formally the business of appointments committees, but in real fact the heads of departments decided who or who would not be appointed to the staffs of departments from among those who applied in response to public advertisements. Not infrequently people were appointed who did not apply through advertisement, provided, of course, that the head of a department could justify his or her selection to a Faculty Board or to a Senate. Members of appointments committees were listened to, but the decision of heads of departments determined the outcome of the deliberations of appointments committees. A head of department had to be pretty feeble if he allowed others to over-ride him or left others to determine who were members of his or her department.

When I was elected to the chair of Political Science there was, of course, a vacancy in the lecturing staff in my department which had to be filled. This was my first encounter with a responsibility to the university which was almost entirely mine, and this was a very sobering circumstance. The job specification was determined and the post was advertised. Applications began to come in.

Then something began to happen which slowly assumed a recognizable shape. I had an unsolicited letter about one of the candidates. Then I had a phone call on behalf of this same candidate from someone who claimed to know me. Finally, a Marxist ideologue in the London School of Economics visited me on the strength of an acquaintanceship we had made some years previously through Bernard Ostry. He, too, spoke on behalf of this candidate. He did not say this man was a good Marxist. Quite the contrary, he emphasized the man's qualities of urbanity, wide travel in Europe, knowledge of European languages and so on. There was a pattern here, a pattern of behaviour which on the basis of experience in Ottawa I called lobbying.

When I looked at the applications and the references, this man seemed a pretty acceptable appointment. There were however, two or three other candidates who looked to be comparable. One candidate seemed to me rather good on the evidence in the papers: a first-class as an undergraduate, evidence of independent research and good references.

Let us call the man supported by the lobby X and the candidate without support Y. X and Y had two things in common. Both had been undergraduates at the London School of Economics and both had named as a referee a man Z on the staff of LSE. I read Z's letters of recommendation thoroughly. I read between the lines. Z was trying to say something, but it was not at all clear what he was trying to say beyond that he thought we ought to consider X and Y seriously. I decided then to go to LSE and talk personally to Z. After much discussion and being finally convinced that I would not report him to someone else Z said to me, 'If you are looking for an acceptable man of the left of moderate ability, appoint X; if you want brains, appoint Y.

When the interviews were held X turned out to be a smooth, polite, and urbane chap who had indeed travelled in Europe and knew his way around the world. Y, on the other hand, was shy and nervous, laconic, and cautious. But obviously, at least to me, he had brains, knowledge and capacity for research and writing.

The Dean, Professor T.W. Hutchison, was in the chair. After we had seen the candidates, he went around the committee, asking for opinions. X was the preferred candidate. The Dean then turned to me. This was the moment of decision. This was the moment when I had to ask myself what I wanted in the Department of Political Science.

I decided then I must base my judgement on the quality of the candidates themselves and not what others said about them or even what they said about themselves. I said that I wanted Y and I explained why I wanted him. The Dean simply said that we were recommending Y and that was that.

Subsequent events over some years suggest to me that I was then put in the Marxist activists' black book. Like MI5 and MI6 they too have files, long memories and a *modus operandi* in the political wars. Judging from their successes in securing left appointments in the right places they would appear to be at least as efficient as their enemies.

And now to the experience of university government in a time of big public spending. This was thrust upon me in a most unexpected way, as a result of bitter quarrels among economists concerning an appointment.

327

As a result, the Dean resigned in June 1961. The Vice Chancellor was so mortified by the dissension that he considered the appointment of a senior professor from another faculty to administer the Faculty of Commerce and Social Science in much the same way as a colonial secretary of Edwardian times might have appointed a governor with full powers to quell tribal warfare on the frontier of empire. An officer of the Registry advised him, however, against suspending the constitution and suggested as an alternative the election of a new professor with no record as an academic warrior. Consultations took place between the Vice Chancellor and a professor of the faculty in whom he had some lingering confidence. As a result I was asked to accept nomination as dean of the faculty. The Vice Chancellor promised to give me his full support. The Registrar wished me well. With some trepidation and many misgivings, I accepted the nomination and was, of course, elected.

There are two aspects of my experience as a dean which affected my thinking about general political questions: (1) the constitutional reform of the faculty as a means of relieving tension and creating a measure of stable co-operation in the teaching community, and (2) participation in the general decision-making of the university in a time of euphoric expansion.

Until I became the dean of the faculty, I had managed to stay out of university politics. Now politics and administration became the substance of my life away from home. Although I abandoned none of my teaching and continued to lecture for more hours a week than the average, I gave up entirely what is known as research, i.e., doing something or nothing which can occasionally result in papers or books. I immersed myself in politics and administration so that very soon the time and seemingly the power, to think and reflect on anything but immediate issues disappeared.

At the stormy meeting of the Faculty Board which provoked my predecessor to resign the office of dean, I had seconded the resolution to pass on to the next item of business, the standard procedure for cutting off acrimonious discussion and the means, sometimes sucessful, of sweeping unpleasant material under the carpet. In other words I was a supporter of the *status quo* and someone very reluctant to engage in academic wrangling.

I soon discovered that total conservatism was impossible and that problems would not go away if one turned one's back on them. They were real problems connected with the expansion of the university, changing fashions in the social sciences, and competition among teachers for funds,

328

opportunities, and promotion in the academic hierarchy. The focal point of the trouble at that time was to be found among the economists, the most numerous group in the faculty, but not confined to them alone. Among the economists there was an intellectual division which can best be described as a conflict between numeracy and literacy, between enthusiasts for quantitative economics and the others, who were described by their opponents as old-fashioned descriptive economists. The language of one group was mathematics and of the other English. Keynes, a transitional figure, had written in English and put his mathematics in appendices or special chapters remarking that 'Those who (rightly) dislike algebra will lose nothing by omitting ..' etc.' (*General Theory*, p. 280). The quantitative boys and girls of the 1950s, however, put algebra, calculus, geometry, and statistics in the main discourse and dispensed with English except as a means of moving from one operation to the next. Everyone in the quantitative camp was 'into' matrix algebra, which was supposed to have a special kind of magic.

Of course, all the combatants were full of zeal for truth. It is this enthusiasm which renders academic quarrelling particularly intractable. It serves to obscure, in the minds of the combatants and sometimes outsiders, the concern for money, prestige, and promotion which makes them kin with humankind. The leaders in these struggles attract followers in the shape of students and graduate students, and there is a strong tendency for the leaders, in their zeal to advance their cause, to endow some, if not all, their adherents with talents they do not possess. Time alone reveals that many of those described as swans turn out to be one-legged ducks which even promotion to the highest level cannot completely beautify. Great infusions of public money into the system tends to exacerbate, not to calm, contention among academics.

The natural propensity of university administrators is to rely upon authoritarian administrative devices for the control of dissension. Put full powers into the hands of vice chancellors, deans, professors, and senates packed with people endowed with prescriptive rights in the hierarchy. Theoretically there is something to be said for this. In practice, however, especially when the base of the pyramid is growing faster than the apex, authoritarian solutions have little to recommend them. Vice chancellors, deans, and professors are mere men. Even when they suffer an infusion of mere women the over-all character of authoritarian academic bodies remains the same. Election to a professorship does not automatically endow a scholar, however worthy and lively intellectually, with a talent

329

for human relations, politics, and administration. During my time in Birmingham, the university elected to a professorship a man whom trusted scientific friends assured me was a near-genius. Making him a professor turned this man into a power maniac who wrecked his department and quit the university because he was not allowed to bankrupt it.

I was instinctively sceptical about an authoritarian solution of the problems of the Faculty of Commerce and Social Service. By 1961 I more admired Madison, Hamilton, and Jay as political architects than Marx, Engels, and Lenin and more than George III and Lord North. I believed that the quarrels and the competition for places and control over policy had to be brought out into the open and the contending interests balanced one against the other.

My first move as dean was to call a general assembly of the faculty without regard to status: professors, senior lecturers, lecturers, assistant lecturers, research fellows, research associates. It was suggested that I invite stenographers, research assistants, and students. I said no to this. Teachers and researchers have responsibility and the others do not.

To the faculty assembly I made three points: that our quarrelling was making us ridiculous in the eyes of the university as a whole; that if we were considered ridiculous this would enable other faculties to justify a reduced income for us and an increased income for themselves; that changes in the faculty constitution would be considered which gave more voice in decision-making to a larger constituency than then obtained.

This message was received well enough, but it was hard to tell whether anyone believed me when I argued that our behaviour would adversely affect out interest. Even then academics were so secure that they did not readily grasp that there might be some relationship between what they do and what they get. Maybe they were right in supposing that nothing could injure their prospects and that the only true wisdom was to complain and ask for more. In any case that was what they tended to do.

My real task was to find a formula for quiet government which would be acceptable to the university administration, the University Council, to the Faculty Board of Commerce and Social Science, and to the teachers and research fellows and associates who were not on the Faculty Board.

There were two essential reforms which had to be made; one, to broaden representation on the Faculty Board and, two, to give the enlarged board full powers to decide all matters within its jurisdiction under the ordinances and charter of the university. As matters stood in September 1961, the Faculty Board was comprised of the professorial and non-professorial heads of departments, senior members of the faculty such as professors and senior lecturers who were elected by the Faculty Board for as long as they remained in the university, certain professors co-opted from other faculties, and three lecturers elected by lecturers for a period of three years. Thus the Faculty Board was heavily weighted in favour of the top level of the academic hierarchy. In practice, it meant that once promoted to a senior lectureship, one became part of the faculty government until resignation or retirement.

There was a further popular objection to the Faculty Board – its powers. The full board had no authority in the matter of salaries and promotions. Whenever these matters came up for discussion, as they did early every spring, the meeting of the full board was brought to a close and the Dean asked the heads of departments to remain. This truncated board decided on salaries and promotions and sent their recommendations forward to the higher bodies of the university government under a label of confidentiality. Only after the event did anyone learn of what had been decided in the matter of promotion and no one except the recipient was ever given information about increments.

It would be hard to point to any specific instances in which the 'unrepresentative' character of the board or the secret and hierarchical nature of the promotions procedure had resulted in manifestly bad policy or plain injustice. Academics may have trained intellects, but in the conduct of their relations with one another and the wider community they are as much afflicted by feelings as anyone else and as little disposed to be convinced by evidence. They can feel 'unfree' as much as my friend Kumaramangalam used to feel when he thought about the viceroy of India. The problem, as I saw it, was to create a set of political circumstances and institutional arrangements in the life of the faculty in which, when somebody started complaining about stupid academic policies or injustice in treatment by the university, the vice chancellor or the dean or anyone could reply, 'Do something about it! Get agreement from your colleagues. Your situation is not helpless or hopeless. If you don't like what is happening, make out a case to the Faculty Board. Get yourself elected to the Faculty Board. Otherwise, shut up!'

The question of the reform of the faculty government had been on the agenda of the board for at least a year before the explosion which caused Professor Hutchison to resign from the deanship. Papers had been written,

ten, proposals made and views expressed, but it looked as if all this would come to nothing. Because I had put reform back on the agenda at the informal faculty assembly, some action was now required. A committee was established to make concrete proposals to the board and through the board to the university authorities for the reform of Ordinance 7 which prescribed the faculty constitution.

Given the nature of the Faculty Board, it might be supposed that the board would never reform itself. The alignment of forces was depicted as the professor and senior teachers versus the lecturers who were numerically a majority. In fact, the professors were not a solid body with an over-riding interest in their prescriptive rights any more than the lecturers were a united body of active reformers. In both camps were those who cared not a fig for the fight. Among the professoriate in particular there were divisions of interest and personal antagonisms which I was astonished to discover among men with whom had I lived on generally friendly terms for ten years. Among the lecturers, on the other hand, there were none whom I ever discovered who were willing to stand up for the old order. If there were such they hid their conservatism behind a mask of indifference.

The committee struck off to consider reform consisted of Professor W.H.B. Court, Professor Alexander Baykov, the Sub-Dean, a senior lecturer named David Eversley, another senior lecturer, A.H. Halsey and a lecturer, R.W. Davies. I was the sixth member and the chairman.

The case for reform already had a majority in the committee, but I believed that reform could never be carried in the board or in Senate and Council of the university unless the recommendations for reform were unanimously supported. They would not carry even if the support was five to one. The key man was Court, because he was the only member who commanded wide respect in the university as a whole on account of his scholarship, his reputation for wisdom (based largely on a laconic disposition to say little and say it seldom), and a very cautious and conservative temper. And Court was very opposed to the reforms proposed.

Harry Court was my best friend in the faculty. He had invited me to come to Birmingham. He had advanced my interest and I liked and respected him more than any of my colleagues. It was a truly agonizing experience for me to find myself separated from him by a political difference and my strongest inclination was to go along with his judgement. But I had a public responsibility and I was expected to exercise my judgement in the interest of everyone. I steeled myself and determined, friendship or no friendship, to do what I conceived to be necessary. There was one night when I could not sleep a wink on account of my unhappiness about Court, but I got up still determined to be my own man in this matter.

I tried some friendly persuasion with Court, to no avail. As I distanced myself from him and he from me I began to judge the circumstances coldly. Court, I argued with myself, may yield to a majority in the committee if it is five to one. He does not like trouble and that's what he will get if there is a five to one majority.

To get a five to one majority required that Baykov come over to the side of reform. Could this be done? Alexander Baykov was an extreme authoritarian. He ran his department like a Gulag and his minions loved him for it. He never doubted the absolute rightness of his own judgement and he was tiresomely egotistical. None the less he was an intelligent, energetic, and able man.

Because he held me in contempt and thought I should never have been elected a professor of political science, I knew it was useless for me to attempt to influence Baykov. The key to Baykov was R.W. Davies. Davies worked in Baykov's department and was more or less Baykov's camp commandant. A hard working scholar, Davies' study of Russian history in collaboration with E.H. Carr added lustre to Baykov's department and was evidence beyond anything Baykov had done himself that Baykov's conception of Russian studies was a productive one. This was one aspect of the Baykov-Davies relationship.

But there was another. Baykov had been a schoolboy Bolshevik in Russia and even though he had fled from the reality of Bolshevism he was still a sympathizer with Marxism and was no enemy à outrance of the Soviet state. Davies was a member of the Communist party in the 1940s and 1950s, but I am pretty sure that by 1961 he was no longer a member. He, too, was still a Marxist and a not uncritical sympathizer of the Soviet regime. This common experience of commitment to revolution and change at one time in their lives seemed to me something on which I could build if I went about my business in the right way.

I said nothing to Baykov directly. Indeed, I kept silent in the committee. Privately, I stimulated Bob Davies to get on to Baykov, pointing out that if we who wanted a reform in the faculty were going to win, Baykov had to be converted from an opponent to an advocate. Baykov may have been an authoritarian and an egoist, but he was no fool. He recognized the possibility of dissidence in his own department if he opposed Davies too intransigently. Bit by bit Bob Davies wore Baykov down and in the end their commitment to change which both had experienced in their youth united them in support of some real changes in their place of work. It was a great day in the committee when Baykov drew himself up in his pompous way and pronounced judgement in broken English instructing us in what was the best course to follow. Court listened and in his customary few words said he did not want to oppose what seemed to be the unanimous views of his colleagues.

The reforms recommended by the committee were essentially two in number and they were in no way radical. The first was concerned with representation on the Faculty Board. The nine heads of departments, all professors, retained their prescriptive right to membership on account of their offices and the responsibilities attached to them. The election of senior lecturers and other senior members such as readers and professors who were not heads of departments was scrapped completely. The members of the faculty who were not heads of department were designated as a single constituency returning nine members to the board. Thus, the blessed word equality was invoked: a board of nine heads of department and nine others. The reform was advertised as the 'Nine plus Nine Constitution.' In fact, however, the board was still weighted in favour of the top of the hierarchy, for the vice chancellor, the vice principal and representatives of other faculties, nearly always professors, were also members of the board. None the less the majority of the teachers in the faculty had a place on the board through representatives sufficiently numerous to affect decision-making and policy formation. Above all, 'the masses' felt represented, not powerless.

The more difficult reform concerned the responsibility for salaries and promotions. For the sake of all concerned, decisions about salaries and promotions cannot be the subject of open debate. On the other hand, absolute secrecy breeds paranoia and discontent. The solution we found was to establish a salaries and promotions committee, the members of which were almost identical with the truncated Faculty Board which had, until the reform, decided on recommendations about salaries and promotions. The only change in membership was the addition of the Sub-Dean, who had long been an elected officer and was usually not a professor. This committee was obliged to make its recommendations to the full Faculty Board which could approve it without debate. If, however, five members of the board signed a motion to refer the recommendations back to the committee and stated their reasons in confidence to the dean, the salaries and promotions committee would be obliged to reconsider their recommendations. Thus was acrimonious debate involving personalities avoided, yet objections could be registered. Over eighteen years there have been two references back.

A unanimous recommendation of reform had no trouble before the Faculty Board. It passed, *nemine contradicente*. Getting the reform approved by the Senate Executive Committee, the Senate, and the Council of the University was another matter. The Vice Chancellor had promised me full support. Sir Robert Aitken always let me down whenever it suited him, but in this matter he was completely reliable. He did not wish to discuss the faculty proposals himself, but he handed me over to the Vice Principal, Professor (later Sir Kenneth) Mather.

The Vice Principal was a subtle and experienced academic politician. He did not suffer from a failing, only too common among natural scientists, of believing that, because a good scientist and perhaps a member of the Royal Society, all matters outside the laboratory are simple and can be either dismissed or dealt with in five minutes. Mather had the habit, when put a question, of asking another question designed to elicit an opinion or an argument without disclosing anything of his own mind. In spite of this, he was a listener and a thinker with some knowledge of political and social realities and without *idées fixes*. He was all cautious reservations which could be modified in response to reason and facts. We spent several hours arguing in a hut he occupied in the gardens where plant-breeding research was in progress. In the end, he was persuaded that we were not planning to burn down the university and destroy its sacred standards.

Once the Vice Principal signalled his approval to the Vice Chancellor, there were no problems. Considering that it took the university two and a half years to reform itself after the student disturbance of 1968, it is quite remarkable that the 'democratic' reform of the Faculty of Commerce and Social Science passed through all the formal stages in fifteen minutes, five of which were spent answering the objections in the senate of Professor Rudolf Peirels, one of the inventors of the atomic bomb. Peirels thought the reforms insufficiently democratic and I was able to point out that his view sprang from what was in his own mind and not from what was in the papers in front of him.

The reform of the constitution of the Faculty of Commerce and Social Science was my first experience of politics from the outside. I was a participant with objectives and responsibilities, but I was unidentified with any of the issues which had produced the divisions and antagonisms in the community. Whether the quantitative economists prevailed over the descriptive economists was a matter of indifference to me. Whether the professors and senior lecturers kept their supposed privileges or the lecturers had justice done to them moved me in no way. When I ceased to allow my friendship for Court to govern my view of the matter in hand, I finally escaped into objectivity and found a position which enabled me to think about peace and order and not about the victory of one point of view or one group over another. I was a doctor prescribing for someone else's fever.

The problem I was concerned with was, of course, a storm in a tea cup. None of the issues were matters of life and death and the divided community of which I was the governor numbered about forty souls. And yet it was this parliament of fleas which exhibited examples of some political problems as well defined as any I had observed in the parliament of Canada. From my place of observation as Chief Flea, I began to understand, say, Mackenzie King, if not better then at least differently than I had done when I had studied him through a Marxist microscope.

Hitherto in my life my excursions into politics had been in search of the improvement or even salvation of the world or society or city where I lived. With the missionary blinkers off, I began to see that in politics one can, and indeed should, seek to settle for less than salvation; that although individuals and groups inevitably take their own interests and obsessions seriously, it is possible to find the means of letting differences harmlessly flourish in a forum open to all. No very profound discovery, one may say, but one which was significant for me.

Although proofs of injustice to individuals and dangers to the purposes and practices of the university were wanting, it was evident that at least some of the members of the faculty were seriously anxious about something and that those who most loudly and persistently voiced anxiety found some degree of response from their colleagues. These responses tended to differ according to experience and position in the academic hierarchy.

Why should anyone be anxious? Opportunities to obtain posts in the university, to undertake intellectual endeavours of one's own devising, and to win recognition for one's achievements had never been better. Government and public opinion were becoming increasingly persuaded that 'higher education is a good thing' and increased wealth in the community at large made it possible to translate faith in higher learning into cash for university expansion.

This together with the rapidly changing volume and character of knowledge and the changing fashions in knowledge were the sources of the anxiety. Until the late 1950s the rate of change in British universities, particularly in the arts and the social sciences, had been slow enough for adjustments to be made within the traditional political and administrative structures. By the late 1950s there began to develop a set of circumstances which undermined the faith in old ways of doing things: of dividing resources, of making appointments, of promoting people, of deciding what to teach and how to teach. Hence the anxiety, hence the trouble.

Being Dean of the Faculty of Commerce and Social Science did not confer upon its holder any significant degree of power and authority. The faculty was the smallest but one in the university and it was not as highly regarded in the university and in the community at large as the Faculty of Science and Engineering and the Faculty of Medicine, nor was it regarded as highly as the Faculty of Arts supposed itself to be regarded. But being Dean did give one a share in the government of the university and an opportunity to observe this government in action. It was this experience that profoundly changed my views of public policy.

Experience in Canada had persuaded me of the importance of the independence of universities from not so much the government as from outside interference in their affairs. In the United Kingdom the independence seemed admirably protected so that within the limits of their charters from the state the academic communities governed themselves in a way which ensured as far as seemed humanly possible the personal independence of university teachers. Courts of governors who possessed the final authority in universities were so large and met so seldom that in practical fact the universities governed themselves not democratically but in a way which ensured that individuals were secure in their posts and able to do their work in their own way and in co-operation with their colleagues. Mainly, the individual was free because he or she was secure. Incomes may not have been large compared with other employments demanding equivalent mental capacity, but freedom to determine for oneself how one worked and what one worked at was beyond price.

All of this had to be financed. The British, I felt, had worked out the ultimately good solution of providing the wherewithal for universities without bringing universities under the control of those supplying the necessary cash. Oxford and Cambridge universities and the colleges which comprised the universities had substantial financial resources of their own derived from the ownership of property in a variety of forms and even Birmingham University had endowment funds of its own. But independently wealthy as Oxford and Cambridge were, all universities including Oxford and Cambridge depended very heavily on funds extracted from the public in the form of taxes and transferred to the universities by the Treasury through an intermediary independent of the government, the University Grants Committee. From the point of view of the academic community there could not be a better system, or so I supposed.

When I attended my first meeting of the Finance and General Purposes Committee of the Council of the University in the autumn of 1961, cash was already flowing from the Treasury, through the University Grants Committee, to the university more abundantly than at any time in the past. The treasurer, a Birmingham businessman and a lay member of the Council, warned us of the need for economy and declared that our financial resources required prudent husbanding. He said he would like to discuss this informally with the officers of the university and to this end he invited us to a dinner in the staff club.

I went to the dinner expecting to hear some harsh talk about finances and the perils of bankruptcy along the line familiar enough to anyone who had studied and worked in the University of Manitoba. Nothing of the kind. We sat down to an elegant and lavish dinner of five courses with aperitifs, two wines, brandy, and cigars. The talk was informal enough, but it amounted as far as finances were concerned to a few words on the need for caution if he was going to balance the books and provide for future expansion. Every academically legitimate and worth-while project could expect to be financed, if not now, assuredly in the future. And so on. Bread and cheese was not the atmosphere of this opportunity for the informal contemplation of our poverty.

The exhortations of the treasurer were not, however, phony. He was endeavouring to keep the growing euphoria of the academics within bounds. In this he and those who followed him in Birmingham had some success. The University of Birmingham never resorted to the policies of more than one institution of building up large annual deficits and using these as evidence that they were go-ahead, creative, innovative pioneers in the great enterprise of discovery, learning, teaching, and the general improvement of British culture and society.

If my experience of heavy public expenditure on higher education helped to turn me completely around politically, I am bound to say that I never witnessed in Birmingham anything corrupt, or any examples of thoroughly bad and wasteful administration, or the inauguration of any patently stupid academic enterprises. Any calculus based on concepts of good and bad does not equip one to judge what transpired in the world of higher education abundantly financed by the state during the 1960s and 1970s. Unless one believes that the discovery of new knowledge, the refinement of old knowledge, the transmission of knowledge and the cultivation of intelligence are themselves evils, as certain religious and political groups do, one is bound to approve of the intentions of those who believed that Britain should do more than hitherto in the sphere of higher education and research not connected with utilitarian purposes. This is precisely the difficulty. A good case for public assistance is often more loaded with eventual public evils than a bad one.

When student disorders developed in the United States, France, and Latin America in the late 1960s and spread to Britain, one of the cries of the disturbers of the peace was 'relevance.' The activities of universities were supposed to be insufficiently relevant to the immediate concerns of society. There is, of course, some substance to the argument about relevance and one which the advocates of complete independence for universities, like myself, tended to ignore. The student activists of the 1960s and 1970s were by no means the first people to discover the question of relevance. Members of the Foreign Office and the business community in the 1950s observed, for example, that in the social sciences, in the arts, and in legal studies in British universities there was an enfeebling inertia which prevented British students from learning very much about the life, politics, and economics of vast areas of the world such as Russia, China, and south-east Asia. Furthermore, that study of European communities was focused on literature and art, as if these important aspects of life are the only ones worthy of serious attention. In short, British universities tended to be less than universal in their interests.

Security and independence were at the root of this narrow-mindedness. Knowledge was what they knew. Academics responded to themselves. They examined one another and they chose one another. In this last matter of choosing one another the tendency was to choose people very like themselves in their interests and abilities. If Siam was not already studied in a British university, it was unlikely Siam would ever be studied in a British university. A colleague in London, for example, had for many years been interested in Latin America. No one tried to prevent him researching in the field, but when he attempted to offer a course in Latin American history to undergraduates, those who controlled the curriculum blocked his endeavour, because, they argued, there was insufficient evidence of a substantial and respectable bibliography on which to base undergraduate studies. This man was obliged to labour for some years to overcome the view that acceptability of a subject in a university depends on the existence of books and not on the existence of people or the importance of their relations with Britain or the need of British young people to know something about non-European civilizations.

Had there not been an intrusion from outside, it is unlikely that the devotion of British universities to comfortable ruts of their own making would ever have been seriously modified. This intrusion took the form of a committee of enquiry chaired by Sir William Hayter of the Foreign Office. Hayter and his committee found some deplorable areas of ignorance in the social sciences, numerous gaps in opportunities to study foreign languages such as Chinese, Russian, and Japanese, and over-weighted attention to the study of literature as the only significant aspect of life in foreign communities. They recommended that funds be earmarked by the University Grants Committee to stimulate new areas of study.

Earmarked funds! Those blessed words were the solution. In universities as elsewhere, ills can be cured by doses of money. Almost at once vice chancellors were vying with each other in their determination to launch the study of West Africa, East Africa, South-east Asia, China and Russia.

Unfortunately, the Hayter committee had overlooked Latin America as an object of academic attention. Indeed, they turned a blind eye to many areas of ignorance, e.g. the United States and the Commonwealth. Latin America was, however, given special attention. As a kind of afterthought, another committee under the chairmanship of J.H. Parry was set up to survey this gaping hole in British intellectual activity.

The handiwork of the Parry committee will serve as well as anything else to illustrate what caused me to revise radically my ideas on the role of government in society and gave substance to the uneasy feelings I had in the presence of the free spending on higher education in the 1960s.

Self-interest should have caused me to welcome any special stimulation given to the study of Latin America. Together with J.H. Parry and Professor R.A. Humphreys of London University, I was one of the small number of Cambridge men who had early in their academic lives touched

340

on Latin America. And I did welcome the enquiry and the evidence it provided of a determination on the part of the established authorities to take seriously what I had myself taken seriously.

The recommendations were another matter. Latin American studies are important, of course, but they are not so important that they warranted the establishment of *five* centres of Latin American studies. There were good practical reasons for establishing a centre in London. There was little justification for establishing one at Oxford. If Oxford, there must be one at Cambridge. If there were centres at London, Oxford and Cambridge there must be one in the English provinces and if there were four in England there must be one at least in Scotland. Poor Wales! The only explanation of this omission is probably that Parry, a Welshman and head of a Welsh university college, must have thought it improper to favour his own constituency.

The recommendations of the Parry committee, like that of the Robbins committee on university expansion, might have been satisfactory as a program to be implemented over a span of fifty years. As it was, the money for instant implementation was made available. Latin American studies have been firmly established. The output of academic writing on Latin America has grown enormously and the quality of much of it is very high. But the question to be asked is this: were not the resources put into this activity beyond the needs of the community? Did not the program encourage too many young people of good abilities to devote themselves to academic study as a career, to believe that society could support them for no better reason than having unravelled the mind of Bolivar or determined the pattern of kinship in the Matto Grosso?

The questions that could be asked about Latin American studies could be asked about the whole enterprise of higher education as it developed in the 1960s and 1970s. At first I had some enthusiasm for what was happening as a result of the government's willingness to increase abundantly the financial resources of the universities, but as I was pushed to make more and more claims on behalf of my faculty, I became increasingly uneasy. It was undoubtedly a pleasure to be able to tell people that more posts, more promotions, more research funds, and more equipment were available. At first I attributed my uneasiness to the fact that I had grown up in a world of small means and that I was insufficiently adjusted to a time of abundance; that maybe I ought to believe in Santa Claus after all.

Or maybe in Keynes. Had I eschewed Marxist politics when I went to

341

Cambridge in 1936 my first enthusiasm for Keynes might have blossomed into discipleship. As it was I considered Keynes' arguments a sound 'non-political' analysis of a capitalist economy and the one which had provided the means of preventing the return of the depression of the 1930s. Economic management by the governments of the United States, Canada, the United Kingdom and others obviously was working in terms of employment, increased productivity and improving standards of life. Perhaps I was wrong to feel uneasy about abundance as it manifested itself in the universities in the 1960s.

It appeared in the early 1960s that the British Tories had contrived to get control of the British government by their acceptance of Keynesian economics and by discovering in the stop-go policy a means of political control which would keep them in power for the foreseeable future. One turned on the tap before an election in order to mobilize a sufficiency of voters to win the election. Then one turned off the tap after the election in order to prevent the bankruptcy of the economy. Whatever one might think of the political morality of Tory practice, the stop-go policy seemed to me to ensure a long-term stability of the economy and was not seriously disruptive of what the western nations had learned from the experience of the depression of the 1930s. The stop-go policy was not inconsistent with the requirement of cyclical budgeting upon which the Keynesian school insisted as a necessary stabilizing feature of the management of an economy by a government. Furthermore, nothing in the stop-go policy was inconsistent with the international system of currency stability tied ultimately to the United States dollar which in its turn was tied to gold, the total amount of which was not susceptible to the fiat of any government. When Thorneycroft and his underlings at the Treasury resigned in 1959, I was inclined to agree with Macmillan that this was only a local difficulty and a result probably of the doctrinal pedantry of Enoch Powell. Reflection on the state of economic management at any time until 1965-66 did not lead me to believe that politicians and bureaucrats could be so mad as to destroy a mode of economic management which so evidently yielded better results than anything known in the 1920s and 1930s. But I was wrong.

The object in setting down my views of the economic and fiscal policies of the British government in the early 1960s is to show that the uneasiness I felt about the free flow of money into the universities was not inspired by any deep and critical objection to the Keynesian system of economic management as it was then working. The source of my doubts was not where the money came from, but where it was going: into, for example the proliferation of high-cost cottage universities scattered across England's green and pleasant land on the assumption that intellectual activity would be pure and disinterested in proportion to the distance these little centres of learning were from the daily, real life of an industrial and commercial nation. Even when these universities were located in cities like Coventry or York they were actually built as far as possible from the cities themselves as was consistent with any connection at all. It was as if a vast expenditure of goods and services produced by the British people were being employed to enable a minority to get as far away as possible from the society itself in order to engage in self-admiration of their cleverness and qualities.

When I came to Birmingham in 1950 there was already present in the Faculty of Commerce and Social Service some small evidence of this solipsism. A flash of it lighted up the first examiners' meeting I attended in June 1951. We were considering the case of a rather mediocre young man about whose merits there was considerable debate. This went on for what seemed to me a very long time, used as I was to the rapid, impersonal consideration of examination papers in Canadian universities. Finally, one of the lecturers in economics blurted out 'For goodness sake give the fellow a third and make him a businessman!'

This spontaneous revelation of social values shook me. Whether I was in the grip of ideas of Alfred Marshall or Karl Marx, I had never been able in good conscience to feel contempt for people who worked either on the shop floor or in a manager's office. The remark contradicted everything I had been led to believe was the purpose of the faculty to which I belonged and indeed of the University of Birmingham, founded as it had been by a businessman, Joseph Chamberlain, for the express purpose of improving the knowledge and intellectual qualities of the British business community.

A little enquiry into the faculty's history revealed to me that this contempt for businessmen was not the prejudice of an individual nor was it something new. Joseph Chamberlain may have been a formidable politician and a high-ranking member of the British cabinet, but he was not able to overcome the prejudices of the English academic community nor was he able to establish a parity of esteem for people who made and sold things. The inclination to live down rather than to live up to Napoleon's contemptuous description of a nation of shopkeepers was too strong. In order to establish a degree of Bachelor of Commerce on the same plane of acceptability as a Bachelor of Arts, Chamberlain had been obliged to threaten the academics organizing the university: 'No Bachelor of Commerce degree; no royal charter!'

A degree in business studies or not, the University of Birmingham had difficulty in attracting students to read for a Bachelor of Commerce. The Faculty of Commerce is the third oldest school of business studies in the English-speaking world, but in half a century it produced fewer graduates than the Harvard Business School produced in 1935. Before 1914 a significant percentage were not Englishmen; they were Japanese. The first employment of the Faculty's most distinguished academic graduate, Professor G.C. Allan, was in helping to establish an institution similar to the faculty in Japan. When I was Dean of the faculty, I was obliged to entertain the head of the great Mitsui family, one of whose members founded a chair of economics in Birmingham as a gesture of gratitude and respect. In those days we still had brown and white class photos on the walls and I showed them to Mr and Mrs Mitsui. They peered at them with chattering attention recognizing members of the Japanese business community who had thought it a worthy enterprise to study where Englishmen disdained to learn. Whenever I see more Hondas or Toyotas in a parking lot than Rovers or Minis, I reflect upon the divine justice and its reality.

In the early 1950s the study of economics at Birmingham was still in a healthy state based on an interest in the real life of the British economy and not in abstractions and techniques. Professor Philip Sargant Florence believed very strongly that the business of an economist was to bring to light aspects of productive activity, investment practices and labour relations which could only be discovered with difficulty, or not at all, by men and women themselves immersed in the production and distribution of goods and services. One of Florence's students, Michael Beesley, for example, challenged the contemporary business and financial wisdom which said that no further investments of huge sums in building more underground railways in London and elsewhere could be justified, that the future belonged to the motor car, and so on. Beesley made some complicated calculations which showed that what became the Victoria Line was a cheap option in the transport of people in London.

This was real economics as I understood the subject. There grew up rapidly, however, a *Kämpferbund* of young economists who asserted that Sargant Florence's book *The Statistical Method in Economics* was no good because Sargant Florence knew no statistics. What they meant was that he was unimpressed by the new science of econometrics, based on the assumption that by manipulating quantitative data truth would emerge, prediction would be possible and all the old nonsense about money, the division of labour, and the propensity of the rate of profit to fall could be dispensed with. Technique became more important than substance. They admired each other for their analytical skill. An elegant solution became the highest praise which could be recorded. What the elegance demonstrated was of little or no consequence. Invent a non-problem and find an elegant solution was the way forward, above all to promotion, more resources, and more jobs. Someone outside the mutual admiration society, a dean for example, was no longer able to judge whether an economist was any good or not, because only a master of the jargon of the economists could say whether the individual was worthy of blessing or otherwise. When one considers that it took the war in Vietnam to expose the inadequacies of systems analysis and a world depression to bring into doubt the expertise of economists in general, I do not feel too guilty about my inability to translate into administrative practice my private belief that modern economics, like much else in academic social science and aesthetics, is a kind of dressmaking for a lifeless god.

The economics *Kämpferbund* of Birmingham University was no band of provincial clowns. The young man who led the attack on the appointment of a mere descriptive economist which precipitated the mess I had to clean up in 1961 was Alan Walters, who eventually won fame by reducing his income to £50,000 a year in order to become an economic adviser of the Prime Minister. Two of the band became professors at Oxford, Cambridge, and the London School of Economics and presidents of the International Econometrics Association. All the lesser members flourished around the academic world, some in spite of mental and character defects which one might have supposed could disqualify them for employment anywhere.

Such is the way of the world, and one can point to many parallels in religion, the arts, literary criticism, sociology, political science, and so on. As far as this experience of the human comedy is concerned it generated in me profound doubts about the abundant public financing of higher education. Sanity, it seemed to me, can only be preserved by maintaining some degree of responsibility to society at large, for one's activities. The best way to encourage foolishness in any class of society

345

is to give people a prescriptive right to money and power. In such circumstances the least dangerous thing they can do is to engage in idle consumption.

How to restore the necessary connection of the universities with society while at the same time preserving their independence? By 1965 it was quite evident that the University Grants Committee was no guardian of university independence. It was a dispenser of money and quite naturally it was obliged to say what institutions got how much, and more and more it was obliged to say for what purposes. It decided on the number of square feet for a lecturer's room; what items of furniture should be ordered; what percentage of the staff should hold senior appointments; what they should be paid and so on. In prospect were prescriptions about teaching and research, if not by the University Grants Committee, by some other bodies appointed by the Government. In 1966 the pretence of university independence was exposed and the impotence of the University Grants Committee demonstrated by a simple decree of the Minister of Education that higher fees should be charged to foreign students than to British students.

A feeble protest was mounted. One vice chancellor resigned to demonstrate his displeasure. At Birmingham, a meeting of staff and students was called in the Great Hall. The Vice Chancellor spoke and so did I. Although it was raining heavily, the students organized themselves into marching columns under dripping banners which wound their way to the centre of the city. In the Senate of the University, the Vice Chancellor explained the implications of defying the government. If we continued to charge uniform fees, there would be less money for this and that. This dreadful prospect frightened the Senate and so Birmingham University caved in. Oxford and Bradford stood on principle for one year. Who cared about university independence? Nobody of any consequence and why should they? One's heart tends always to be where one's purse is and academics are no different from others in this matter. We have to be practical, it was argued.

At this stage in the mid 1960s I still subscribed to the conventional wisdom that the realization of any large worthwhile project not run for profit required the action of the government as a means of obtaining the financial resources necessary for capital and running costs. The University Grants Committee had ceased to be a mediator between the universities and the government and was turning into controller. Would not independence and responsible decision making be recovered if the students replaced the University Grants Committee as a mediating and controlling factor? Not the National Union of Students, but the students as a whole? Not by voting, but by paying full-cost fees?

In the summer of 1967 the *Political Quarterly* published an article of mine proposing that the subsidizing of universities by the government cease. Instead, the government should subsidize the students to the extent that they could pay in fees the full economic cost of their education. Not student grants of roughly £400 a year, but grants of £1,200 a year, large enough at 1960 prices to pay the fees which wholly independent universities would be obliged to charge in order to cover their costs.

Needless to say, the article evoked absolutely no response. The existing system involved the proliferation of committees and sub-committees making decisions or not making decisions as the case might be about the enterprise of higher education. A substantial part of the attraction of committees in and among universities is the power the committees have to influence the lives and activities of other people and to play games with one another. Not being much accustomed to committees in Canadian universities, I had often been struck by the atmosphere created when a committee assembled in the University of Birmingham. This atmosphere resembled that which prevails when people are settling down to a session at bridge or poker: an atmosphere of anticipating real fun matching wits with others. Any proposal which involved dispensing with a high-level complex of committees and replacing it with a simplified, impersonal market system of allocating resources and justifying one's existence was bound not to be greeted with enthusiasm.

Simultaneously to the publication of this article there was a considerable change in my ideas about university independence. When the University College at Buckingham graduated its first class in January 1976, I wrote to *The Times* (21 January 1976) in order to correct some of the misleading propaganda of the educational establishment concerning Britain's first university truly independent of the government. The letter encapsulated my ideas and my part in the enterprise and will suffice for the record of my change of mind. It read:

Sir, Your leader about the University College at Buckingham (January 5) contains the statement that the idea of an independent university 'was conceived in the late 1960s mainly as a response to the Government's decision to open

347

university accounts to the scrutiny of the Comptroller and the Auditor General but also in reaction against student disorder ... Before this becomes legend, may I correct you on the facts?

The idea of an independent university was first expressed in a letter to *The Times* in June, 1967, by Dr. J.W. Paulley, of Ipswich. When I discussed the idea with him on the seventh of July 1967, we were concerned solely with the moral, intellectual and political importance of independence of the state in university and professional education and with the practical steps which might be taken to achieve such independence.

At the two private conferences sponsored by the Institute of Economic Affairs in 1967 and 1968, the scrutiny of accounts and student unrest were never mentioned, let alone discussed. At the first public conference held in January, 1969, student unrest was referred to as a symptom of malaise and the scrutiny of university accounts by the Government as an inevitable consequence of dependence on the state.

May I restate the first reason for establishing an independent university set forth on page 1 of the pamphlet *Towards an Independent University* written by me in 1967 and published for sale by the Institute of Economic Affairs in 1968?

'The first reason is moral and social. For nearly three quarters of a century more and more people of all classes and occupations have become more and more dependent in one way or another upon the state and have accordingly come under its control. It is now becoming increasingly obvious that this dependence and control are doing the community more harm than good and that the moral and social energy of the people is diminishing through undue and prolonged entanglements in the web of government. The time has come to demonstrate on a large scale and in a sophisticated sphere of human endeavour and necessity that people on their own can meet a community need with no assistance from the state and entirely without state controls other than those designed to preserve the common law rights of individuals. To this end it is here proposed that an independent university be established for the provision of general higher education, the advancement of knowledge and the inculcation of habits of mental and moral discipline.

'Such an act of initiative and free cooperation among individuals will energize the community as a whole and serve to kindle the enthusiasm and focus the hope of all who are unwilling to believe that the fate of Britain is to become a stagnant society observing rather than shaping the fate of mankind.'

In 1969 a planning board for an independent university had been established. In 1971 a site was found in Buckingham, and within a year enough money was collected to think about physical accommodation for staff and students. In 1976 the University College at Buckingham was opened by the Rt. Hon. Margaret Thatcher. At the first graduation ceremony in 1978, John Paulley and I were made Honorary Fellows.

I had envisaged an independent university as a truly free enterprise unconnected in any way with the state, government, or political interests. This was not to be. The English are the English and they seem incapable of action unless they have a prospect of official approval and a hope of the House of Lords. The 'independent' planners felt they must seek a charter from the Privy Council. The right to act under the common law was not enough for them. Great was the rejoicing in Buckingham when a royal charter was granted in February 1983 and in the Labour party there were growls and threats. *Plus ça change,* etc.

CHAPTER FOURTEEN

I Cry for Thee, Argentina

Rather more important in changing my political thinking than reflections upon experience as a university teacher and administrator was my first visit to the Argentine Republic in 1966. I had contracted to write a general book on Argentina for the Nations of the Modern World series published by Ernest Benn and Company. The university gave me a year's study leave, a foundation granted me a modest sum of money for expenses and a privately financed research organization in Buenos Aires, the Instituto Torcuato di Tella, appointed me to a fellowship. On 1 January 1966 I set out by sea to visit Argentina.

The character of my relationship with Argentina has some inexplicable elements in it. When I embarked on the study of Anglo-Argentine relations I had absolutely no knowledge of the country and I chose my research project as a case history in the theory of imperialism. When I set out for Argentina in 1966 I could number on the fingers of one hand the Argentines whom I personally knew and on the fingers of the other the Argentines with whom I had talked for a few hours at most. I could not speak Spanish and my reading knowledge of the language was only sufficient to acquire the information I needed for my work. I could not, for example, pick up a novel or an essay by Borges and read it easily for pleasure. And yet when in January 1966 a fat, sweating immigration officer in an open neck shirt examined my passport, read the category of my visa granted in London, and said with a mixture of respect and sceptical contempt, '*Ah! Personalidad, eh?*' I felt suddenly in a familiar presence. When that same evening I left my hotel and walked alone down the Calle Florida I felt even more strongly that I was at home – more so, perhaps, than I did in Canada where my mother and father, sisters and brothers, uncles and aunts and cousins lived, where the spoken and unspoken languages were part of myself. Once an Argentine asked me, 'How is it that you know so much about our country?' In fact, I know very little about Argentina, but in some way I feel about the country in a manner that matters and which must convey the impression of understanding and empathy. In 1980 I was invited to Buenos Aires, all expenses paid, to present a paper to a gathering of historians. I did not go. I rationalized this in a variety of ways: I was too lazy or too busy to write the necessary paper; my interest in Latin America was exhausted; I might be kidnapped by the underground as a political demonstration against the government. The fact is I knew I could not bear to go. What has happened since last I was there in 1966 and 1971 is too terrible. I have cried for thee, Argentina, and I do not want to cry again.

Feelings apart, my business was to learn something about the country, its economy, its political history in the twentieth century and its prospects. What I discovered forced me to reconstruct radically my view of what politics is about, to redesign my map of the political world and the navigational charts necessary for staying afloat and reaching dry land somewhere.

In the mental luggage which I carried with me to Argentina was a strong impression that Argentina was a rather successful community, that its history could justify a certain degree of optimism about humanity. The United Provinces of the Rio de la Plata, which a variety of British visitors such as Charles Darwin, Woodbine Parish, and the Robertson brothers had described in the early decades of the nineteenth century were savage enough – anything but united and never peaceful. Barbarous as Argentine politics might have been at that time, my study of the British seizure of Buenos Aires in 1806 and the subsequent defeat of the invaders provoked a real admiration on account of an elemental determination and heroic self-confidence in the presence of European military expertise (Sir

Home Popham, the British commander of the first assault, was a master of combined operations). The mixture of greed and misinformation which animated Popham and the response in Britain which caused the government to reverse its condemnation of an unauthorized act of piracy was an instance of imperialism at its worst. The Spanish viceroy had fled when the British ships appeared off Buenos Aires. The fact that leaderless people united in a common determination to maintain their independence could defeat not one assault but a second well-organized expeditionary force seemed to me to expose all the apologetics of imperialists no matter how successful they might be when dealing with others around the world. Whatever else the Argentines might be, they seemed to me a people one could respect.

In their subsequent history, the great powers of Europe attempted on several occasions to force themselves upon the Argentines, and always they were sent packing by a combination of determination and subtlety. When, as they often now do, Argentine politicians, soldiers, and intellectuals have whined about imperialism, they deny the history and experience of their own country and employ a rhetoric which is false, misleading, and a cloak for their own incapacity. The Argentine Republic was born a free nation and has always remained one, and that, I think, is why I developed a kind of Argentine patriotism long before I ever walked down the Calle Florida.

The way in which the Argentines lifted themselves out of savagery and applied to their affairs the truths of liberal political economy are facts of compelling relevance in any consideration of wider political thinking. When Colin Clark wrote his book on *The Conditions of Economic Progress* in the late 1930s he found that the Argentines had achieved one of the highest standards of living in the world. Today this is no longer so. They have declined much further and much faster than Britain so that today the Argentine dream of the 1880s of overtaking and surpassing the United States will only be realized if the United States imitates Argentina to a much greater degree than it has so far done.

This is not the place to repeat an analysis of the policies of Juan Domingo Peron. In 1967-68 I set down my conclusion in the following words:

Peron was only an extreme instance of a state of mind common among politicians everywhere which blinds them to the facts of economic life. An industrial society, whether capitalist, socialist, or communist, requires constant attention to renewal, to technological improvement, and to expansion, and this involves dividing current production between spendable funds for consumption goods and spendable funds for the renewal of plant and expansion of equipment. If this constant attention is directed too long and resources are directed too completely to satisfying the desire for immediate consumption, upon conspicuous waste, upon war or the preparation for war, the productive system begins to run down, to become less productive, and people have either to work harder or go short. This happened on a great scale in Argentina under Peron, and the nation has not yet recovered. The evidence is visible on every hand: poor roads, poor railways, poor telephones, inadequate electric power, indifferent municipal services, shabby schools, overcrowded and under-equipped universities, and a brain drain to other countries. This has happened in a thoroughly modern community. It is not the result of some legacy of terrible poverty and backwardness in the past. This is precisely why Argentine experience is so important for others. It can happen in western Europe. It can happen in the United States of America.

Since that was written Argentina has experienced another bout of Peronism, even more debilitating than the first. And the political consequences have been much worse than the aftermath of Peronism, Mark I.

An economic analysis of what has happened in Argentina is, of course, not an explanation. Argentina was a wealthy community, and wealth seems to drive people insane. That is why Peron and Peronism are worth studying. Peron carried to extremes tendencies which are present in other rich democratic societies, and it is, therefore, possible to see in the Argentine example aspects of future developments elsewhere.

The most illuminating study of Argentina not based on economic arguments is the musical, *Evita*, by Tim Rice and Andrew Lloyd Webber. As entertainment it is splendid. It is music with a hard core of political intelligence which may be a factor in the show's popular success; an aspect of the public's disenchantment with do-good demagoguery. But *Evita* seems to me to have one fault. Juan Domingo Peron and Evita are depicted too completely as confidence tricksters. This they were certainly, and the tragedy of Argentina is that the majority could respond to Peron not once but twice. But, for example, Peron's first victory in a free election in 1946, was not effected, as Rice and Webber suggest, by corruption, but by skilful political manipulation of a kind only too readily practised in other democratic societies. The corruption came after the victory; it did not cause it.

Peron was not totally obsessional like Hitler. He was not a ruthless fanatic like Lenin and his successor Stalin. He was too intelligent to paint himself into a corner like Fidel Castro. Unlike Mussolini, whom he much resembled, he never allowed himself to become too dependent on outside political forces. He combined cynicism and charm with an element of genuine concern for his country which enabled him to repeat on a grander scale the disasters of his first presidency. The same could be said of Evita. She expressed in a powerful, popular way the ambivalent and wide-spread attitude observable in varying degrees in democratic societies towards the magnificence of the rich and their arrogant snobbery. Worship and envy. This element of sincerity was the worst and most effective factor in the evil they did and it is one which works the same way in other societies. One cannot eliminate sincerity in politicians and that is why some way must be found of depoliticizing society and of fixing more firmly customs and rules which contain their powers.

When I came to Argentina I discovered that I was something I had never been in Canada or Britain. I was comparatively well-known and respected on account of *Britain and Argentina in the Nineteenth Century,* published in 1960. Many doors were opened to me and I met and talked to a great variety of influential people in a way hitherto outside my experience. I was, for example, invited by Adelbert Krieger Vasena to lecture on inflation in Argentine history *before* he became the Minister of Economy and Labour in Ongania's second cabinet and one of the few men anywhere who have had some success in reducing inflation. I met and talked with the President, Arturo Illia, first in the baroque splendour of the Casa Rosada and again after his deposition in the sitting room of a shabby suburban villa in Buenos Aires against the background noise of a crying child and a vacuum cleaner in another room of the house. I met generals and admirals, foreign ministers and businessmen and *estancieros*. I met Luis Borges and a wide range of intellectuals of a variety of allegiances, views and obsessions. Everyone had their own understanding of the public *malaise,* and some had cures. This was, in fact, the Argentine problem. There was little agreement about anything – a vast amount of intelligence but little intelligibility.

I visited the President of the Republic only a few weeks before he was evicted from the Casa Rosada by the soldiers. My impression of Arturo Illia gained from the newspapers was of a feeble, ineffectual old man who was doing nothing and doing it badly. Cartoonists depicted him with a bird nesting in his white thatch of hair.

I found in the great ornate audience room of the president a vigorous man with, indeed, white hair but fit, weathered, and paternal but hard in appearance. He was a medical doctor by profession and he had been employed by one of the railways in Cordoba to attend to the health of its workers. When I asked him what he valued most in the present state of Argentina, he replied that he esteemed most that there was no one in prison in Argentina for a political offence and that only one man was in exile. He avoided mentioning the name of Peron. I then asked the President what he would do if the Peronistas won the election in the province of Buenos Aires as they had recently done in one of the small provinces in the interior. I could see that the man who had introduced me to the President was very upset by the tactlessness of this question. But not the President. He searched for a piece of paper, took a biro out of his pocket (the biro pen was invented in Argentina), beckoned me to come closer and proceeded to demonstrate with an analysis of voting in several areas of the province that the Peronistas were *not* going to win the province of Buenos Aires. He was going to defeat them. Even my capacity for tactlessness was unequal to asking President Illia what he was going to do about the generals in the Campo de Mayo.

When I saw ex-President Illia again in October I asked him about the probable consequence of the seizure of power by General Ongania. He replied mildly and with no bitterness. 'Poor Ongania,' he said. 'The problems of the Argentine Republic are much more difficult than he realizes.' How true! Already Ongania had launched his attack on the students of the University of Buenos Aires just as Peron in his time had attacked them. The jails began to fill with political prisoners. Political prisoners were released and others arrested. Always there were people in jail for political reasons, more and more, worse and worse. Looking back one can only say that Arturo Illia was the last good president of Argentina and even the economic indicators show that by doing nothing he did as well as any of his successors. When I recall this hardy old Cordoba doctor, I think that, like any good doctor does, he wanted to keep the patient quiet and let nature do its restorative work. But the damned journalists and generals would not let him.

Once at a dinner I found myself seated next to an admiral of the Argentine navy. To make conversation I asked him about the state of the navy. He launched into a long and bitter disquisition about the lamentable way 'the politicians' were preventing the Argentine navy from acquiring modern naval technology. Inasmuch as Argentina had no threatening enemies and its armed forces had not been engaged against anyone except

Argentines for nearly a century, I could not see what he was disturbed about. But he was disturbed – about the careers of his officers. I, then changed the subject and asked him about the Argentine economy. There emerged from the discussion the view that businessmen were all thieves and that the fortune of, say, the di Tella family was the result of persistent and malicious frauds effected by charging more for their products than their costs. I did not consider a dinner table the place to challenge this view, but later I came to an important conclusion: you, *almirante,* are the thief. Your officers are all thieves who nourish a myth and live off the proceeds. More than anything else, this conversation was the origin of my new theory of government. Government is theft.

There was one more conversation with an eminent Argentine, Luis Borges, which seemed to reveal part of the Argentine problem. Borges is, of course, an Argentine aristocrat. When I met him he was an impressive man, easy and courteous in manner rendered touching by his blindness and his gentleness. He received me in the National Library of which he was then the chief officer. I wanted to talk about Argentina, but he was full of his enthusiasm for the Icelandic sagas of which he was making a study and for which purpose he had learned Icelandic and Old English. When finally I got him around to speak of his experiences in the days of Peron, he told of the tortures at the hands of the police which some of his students had experienced. He was distressed and upset about this, but he was detached and mild. He might have been speaking of events in another century, events which were a sad reflection upon the conduct of men but events none the less with which he had nothing to do. Physically he was in Argentina, but he was elsewhere. When I asked him about the current circumstances of the country, he excused himself by saying it would not become him to comment on his present employers.

This detachment I encountered in other Argentine aristocrats. I met Señor Pueyrredon, a descendant of one of the founders of the republic. An American parallel might be an Adams or a Madison, if there are such still around. He received me in the exquisite little marble palace in the Calle Florida, which is the headquarters of the Sociedad Rural, the first of the farmers' unions of Argentine. How unlike the headquarters of the United Grain Growers in Winnipeg or the offices of the Canadian Wheat Pool! Pueyrredon moaned to me about the state of the agricultural and pastoral industry. I asked him what a big interest like the Sociedad Rural was doing to represent its needs and problems to the government. Nothing. No one could communicate with the government. He expressed this opinion as if my question was absurd, something unthinkable. I could not tell whether he disdained to take such a step, but clearly he had never tried and did not intend to. And yet the government of President Illia was accessible to all. Maybe it was just this which a Pueyrredon could not stomach.

In the end it seemed to me that the intellectual liveliness of the Argentines was part of their problem. In Buenos Aires or Cordoba one could hear and read theories and plans about everything from students, soldiers, trade union leaders, journalists, and businessmen. Every theory and fad current in Europe and America was examined, criticized, and modified in Argentina. Little groups of friends agreed with one another about public issues or moral questions or the need for this or the need for that, but no over-all commitment to anything existed. A friend, a banker whose forbears had come to the Republic from Switzerland once said to me: 'Two or three times a week I go to dinner with friends and colleagues. We eat and drink together from ten in the evening until two in the morning. The talk is always witty, intelligent, and sophisticated. Vast plans are projected. Splendid reforms are proposed. It is all very interesting and impressive. I go to my office at 9 in the morning. How many of these friends can I reach for business purposes before 11.30 or noon? None. Everything is just talk, talk, talk. With some friends I run a bank. By understanding the possibilities of inflation we make a good living.' And he gestured towards the elegance of his large apartment off the Plaza de Francia. 'But,' he continued, 'I can tell you I am ashamed of my life and the fact that so little of what I do produces real goods and services for real people. No, amigo, I fear we have lost our way.' This being 1971, Carlos could not know how lost the Argentines were.

CHAPTER FIFTEEN

From Left to Right

One day in 1971 in a lecture a student activist sarcastically challenged me with the question, 'Well, what do you believe in?' He obviously was in the grip of some faith of the moment. I had to find a quick answer. And I said, 'I believe in Hell, not as a place but as a possibility. That is what one has to hate.' Inasmuch as hate was rather fashionable at the time, this answer put the young man on the defensive.

It was then that I began to grasp that the important questions in politics and/or religion are the simple questions, like that which Martin Luther finally put to himself and answered with a text from St Paul's epistle to the Romans: 'The just are saved by faith.' Such questions are too general to produce immediate or concrete answers. How can they? But they determine the character of all subsequent and substantive questions.

This demand that I confess a faith and the answer I gave brought me back to questions which had been churning around unanswered for many years. It began to dawn upon me that for at least two centuries 'progressive' people, among whom I numbered myself, had been bit by bit and in a variety of ways abandoning the most important discovery the human species has ever made and the one underlying customs and laws for thousands of years: the discovery of the dual potentiality of human beings, the potentiality for self-destruction and chaos on the one hand and on the other the power to live and to create. Customs and laws are always the alternative to evil and self-destruction. Circumstances change and the appropriateness of customs and laws change too, but, if the purpose of laws and customs is forgotten and it is assumed that customs and laws are not directed to containing the potentiality for evil and chaos, they turn into their opposite and become the agencies of darkness and death.

Mankind's dramatic success in recent centuries, and one accelerating rapidly in recent decades, in the discovery and use of knowledge of the physical universe has tended to obscure and diminish the discovery of our nature by our more remote ancestors. Optimism about our character has supervened so that today a strong conviction has arisen *either* that the problem of our dual potential for what can be denominated by a variety of words – good or evil, heaven or hell, civilization or barbarism, darkness or light, freedom or slavery – does not exist *or* that, if it does, it can be overcome by some contrived human agency designed by ourselves and owing nothing to factors or forces beyond our knowledge. In short, God has been dethroned, and in His place the human species rules. O.K.

But is this O.K.? I certainly thought so when first I encountered Marxism/Leninism in September 1936. Marx in no way contradicted the Judeo-Christian archetypes implanted in my mind, but on the central question of man's power to realize a new and better world on his own Marx

357

liberated me and gave me what seemed at the time to be a new power. Away with the superstitions of the past! The future will be glorious and free! No more depression, no more war, no more restraints upon our capacity to live fully!

With God gone, History took His place. A knowledge of history revealed that the autonomous forces of economic development would produce heaven on earth and solve all mankind's problems. Churches, governments, literature, art and philosophy were all parts or aspects of a superstructure which would either be swept away or be marvellously transformed by the steady, inexorable working of the historical forces bearing us along towards the triumph of the proletariat.

Fortunately for me, John Saltmarsh spent his energy teaching me that history is something else than this. Saltmarsh's teaching worked directly on me so that in the detailed and particular historical work which I undertook, evidence took precedence over theory and rhetoric. It did not, however, seriously undermine at once the generalizations of Marxism or cause me to doubt Marx's laws of historical development. I remained a Marxist in theory and in political activity, even though as an apprentice historian I followed Saltmarsh's precepts and example.

Otherwise, all the intellectual influence I encountered from 1936 onward served to reinforce my fierce Marxist/democratic engagement against fascism and imperialism and my attachment to Soviet power as a means of destroying Nazi authoritarianism. I accepted completely and uncritically Lenin's doctrine of the party and I could see no problems, theoretical or otherwise, created by the concept of a political instrumentality consciously the product of the will of individuals and of the relationship of a party so created to the great, impersonal movement of the working class depicted by Marx and Engels as a titanic elemental force. Marxism-Leninism was a whole, seamless fabric of great intellectual splendour in my mind.

Experience has caused the splendour to fade in my sight and the seamless fabric to ravel and tear Why? Reflection suggests two factors.

In the years between my encounter with Major Hooper in September 1936, and Arthur Schlesinger Jr's letter of January 1942, I was a dogmatic believer in Marxism. I had not, however, entirely ceased to have a mind of my own, nor had I completely forgotten the argument I had advanced in my controversy with Lea Lardner about astrology, i.e., that a theory can only be said to be true if it explains an observation. This perception, seized on towards the end of my childhood, was never lost, and I knew that a theory can claim no status but that of a slogan or a myth if the weight of experience and observation fail to support it.

To Marxist activists seeking or holding power, their doctrine is not merely a hypothesis whose truth or acceptability depends on its power to explain a body of observed data. This does not mean to say that many Marxists, including Marx himself, did not labour away at ascertaining and analysing facts and data of all kinds. Indeed many of them are rather good at this. The critical factor is whether the facts contradict or impair the theory, or whether they are made to fit the theory in order to protect Marxism as a belief and as an inspiration to political action. At least this is how I saw the matter.

In his letter Schlesinger was inviting me to look at historical evidence for one of the basic assumptions of Marx's economic interpretation of historical development. January 1942, when the world wondered whether the *Wehrmacht* had been stopped temporarily or permanently before Moscow, was not an appropriate time for responding to this invitation. None the less, I was disturbed by Schlesinger's argument, even though at the very moment when I encountered it, one could reasonably begin to hope that victory over the Nazis was a possibility, and to recognize that the Soviet Union was a major factor in this.

It would be untruthful for me to suggest that, as the victories of the Red army grew in number, my doubts about Marxism increased. Rather, the grain of doubt implanted in my mind by Schlesinger's argument lay dormant, but apt to flourish because of what I had learned in the science classes in St John's Technical High School, in the University of Manitoba, and in the lectures of John Saltmarsh. This was the first factor in my abandonment of Marxism.

The second was experience and meditation upon its meaning. Schlesinger had the advantage over me of knowing something about the American thinkers who had laid the foundations of the constitution of the United States. When I came to study them I was surprised to find that men like James Madison, Alexander Hamilton, and John Jay had entertained views of politics which had anticipated the Marxists by three-quarters of a century and were more general and embraced more possibilities than were conceived of in the philosophy of Marx and Engels.

For Madison, Hamilton, and Jay as for Hobbes from whom they drew some of their ideas, the central problem of politics derives from the nature of man, from his natural disposition, in the absence of laws and customs and often in their presence, to define and assert for himself his self-interest and to seek to satisfy his own wants and desires. 'The latent courses of faction are ... sown in the nature of man; and we see them everywhere brought into different degrees of activity, according to the different circumstances of civil society,' James Madison had argued. 'So strong is this propensity of mankind to fall into mutual animosities, that where no substantial occasion presents itself, the most frivolous and fanciful distinctions have been sufficient to kindle their unfriendly passions and excite their most violent conflicts.'

Madison, Hamilton, and Jay attached great importance to economic factors in politics, but they had a more general conception of what makes for economic antagonisms. Differences between workers and employers were not the only, and were not necessarily the most significant, differences between economic interests. 'But,' wrote Madison, 'the most common and durable source of factions has been the various and unequal distribution of property. Those who hold and those who are without property have ever formed distinct interests in society. Those who are creditors and those who are debtors, fall under a like discrimination. A landed interest, a manufacturing interest, a moneyed interest, a mercantile interest with many lesser interests grow up of necessity in civilised nations and divide them into different sentiments and views.' *(The Federalist,* no. 10).

This was clearer and more comprehensive than anything Marx and Engels had to say on the central question of economically generated antagonisms. Furthermore, Madison, Hamilton, and Jay were not dogmatic about economic factors in politics. They were important, and in North America at the end of the eighteenth century were perhaps of overriding importance, but in principle the central problem of politics arises from the differences in the thoughts, behaviour, and objectives of individuals and groups which have no common character, economic or otherwise. Marx's view of the origin of politics was, by contrast, limited and historically blinkered. But what has this to do with believing in Hell as a possibility?.

The enlightened liberals who devised the constitution of the United States were, in the essence of their thought, as much atheists as Marx and Engels, or Lenin and Stalin. The constitution of the United States does not require that the president of the republic swear an oath of allegiance to the constitution. He or she can affirm the commitment to uphold the constitution on his or her own responsibility, and this is a legal obligation as much as if he or she swore to do so on the Bible or invoked some other sacred symbol to witness to their good faith. The constitution of the United States separated the public authority from all religious organizations and forbade the government of the United States from making 'laws respecting the establishment of religion or prohibiting the free exercise thereof.'

The purpose in calling attention to the essential atheism of the American revolutionaries is to focus on the fact that Marxism and the classical liberalism of eighteenth-century America shared a common understanding that men and women make themselves and that politics is the essence of everything. Apart from the brilliant polemicist, Tom Paine, the American revolutionaries did not, however, assert their atheism as a principle. Religious belief for them was a private sentiment, which some of them entertained, but it had no place, nor should it have a place, as an organizing principle of public life. In the constitution the American revolutionaries devised a neutral mechanism which, they hoped, would balance interests and views of all kinds against one another so that the people of the United States would form a political community, establish justice, ensure domestic tranquillity, provide for the common defence, promote the general welfare, and secure the blessings of liberty to themselves and those who came after them. The constitution of the United States left it up to the people themselves whether they went to Hell or not.

So far, the Americans have not done so completely. For some years I used to lecture to students in Birmingham on American politics and, in the late sixties, to tutor an able American student who later became a partner in a large law firm in Chicago. He was unsparing in his criticism of my account of the American political system and we had many hours of argument over many months. My thesis was that the American political system produced some dreadful forms of human behaviour, but such was the American constitutional system that what was wrong could be and often was put right. I instanced slavery, racial discrimination, unequal opportunities, the use of state power to benefit private interests, and so on and so on. 'Think about McCarthyism,' I used to say. 'When I left North America in 1949, I believed that the US was turning into a fascist state dominated by ugly, selfish interests. Look what has happened. McCarthyism is gone with the wind. The American system works if people have the courage to work it.'

Bob would not accept this. He argued that the 'US has had it.' The future is dismal. 'You are crazily optimistic,' he used to say to me.

I replied using the same argument as Svetlana Stalin subsequently did

361

when Malcolm Muggeridge sought to equate the US with its hedonism, pornography, and slaughter by abortion with the USSR with its tyranny and repression. I said that in the United States men and women are free. Some are wicked and many become so. But they are also free to be as good and decent as they can be. Sometimes the wicked prevail and sometimes the good people do. It was mainly a matter of asserting oneself and fighting for one's values with words, arguments, demonstrations, and the example of a good life.

But where do compelling conceptions of good conduct and the means of defeating Hell come from in the United States with its constitutional system which is morally and religiously neutral and which acknowledges no authority except itself? The mechanism established by the constitution of the United States produces laws, but what kind of laws? In the beginning the constitution protected slavery and so for some years did the laws produced by the constitutional organs. Slavery was wrong, but it was legal and indeed widely supported. Subsequent study suggests that slavery was economically efficient and that the slaves themselves were on the whole materially better off than free labourers. Nonetheless it was a wrong, wicked, and hellish institution. How do I know? How did William Lloyd Garrison know? How did John Brown?

Whence comes the knowledge of good and evil? How do we avoid Hell? What can we do to be saved? These are fundamental questions. Marxism and Marxists in their proliferating variety offer no answers. 'But,' as Solzhenitsyn has said, 'if we are deprived of the concepts of good and evil, what will be left? Nothing but manipulation of one another. We will sink to the status of animals.' *(Alexander Solzhenitsyn Speaks to the West*, pp.45-6).

It may be fairly said that a liberal open society offers no answers either. But the United States, as an example of a free, open society, differs from the USSR as an example of a Marxist society, in an important respect. It is possible in the United States to have a knowledge of good and evil, to proclaim it and to seek to translate the knowledge into public policy.

Slavery was so ended in the United States. The politicians operating the constitutional machinery of government were determined at all times to contain differences about the evils of slavery within the bounds of constitutional procedures. When the break came, Lincoln declared the war to be about the maintenance of the union and not about slavery. He was willing to maintain the union on any terms as far as slavery was concerned. The energizing force in the crisis, however, was revealed not in a congressional resolution or a presidential proclamation but in a song 'The Battle Hymn of the Republic':

As He died to make men holy, let us die to make men free ...

Lincoln himself acknowledged as a result of the suffering in the Civil War that the dead must not be allowed to have died in vain and that 'this nation, under God, shall have a new birth of freedom ...'

It seems pretty clear to me, both from experience and from study, that the impulse to fundamental change in society is not generated in society itself. Society or societies on their own have a tendency towards static equilibrium, as China did for thousands of years and may do again. If the Soviet government can maintain its mechanisms of political control and can eliminate the religious inclinations of the Russians and other races of the Soviet empire, the USSR will likely become, too, a stagnant society.

Wherever the belief is entertained that man is not God but has some of the power of God, has some knowledge of God's will, and has a disposition to obey His will and to hearken to His wisdom, there can be no equilibrium, no stagnation, and no imprisonment in Hell. Which is what, I suppose, I believed all the time.

Index

366

Illia, A. 353-4

Imperialism 70, 78, 82; dogmas about imperialism in India, 95; British students not interested in imperialism, 101; importance of understanding, 101; theory of tested, 124-7; abuse of theory, 127; Soviet form of, 133; awareness of in Graduate School in Chicago, 272; Rousseau and, 323-4; Argentine resistance to, 351; Argentine whining about, 351

Independent Order of the Daughters of the Empire 51, 59

India 79, 91, 94; British policy of modernization in, 98; failure of Cripps' mission, 165; 171, 173

Indian nationalism (*also* Indian National Congress) 39, 69, 82; argument for legitimacy of Indian independence, 94, 95; leaders jailed, 165

Indians, Canadian 54, 77

Inkster, C. 12

Innis, H.A. 39, 64, 124

Insch, N. 238

Institute of Canadian-American Relations speech to, 247

Institute of Economic Affairs 348

International Typographical Union 229; issues of strike by, 229-31; 232; attitude to the *Citizen*, 237, 251

Jack (Wing Com. J.E.J. Sing, DFC) 71

Japan 77; assault on Pearl Harbour, 147; effect on white imperial power in Far East, 165; 172; 196; H. Norman's experiences in, 200-2; language of, 205; respect for Japanese intelligence services, 220

Jesus Christ 15, 16, 66

Jha, L.K. 94

Johns, R.J. 256

Johnson, T. 275; her explanation of black response to racial prejudice in USA, 277

Judeo-Christian religion archetypes of, 65-8; 357

Keenleyside, H.L. 168, 169

Kenyatta, J. 86

Keuneman, P. 101, 104

Keynes, J.M. 43, 329, 341-2

Kiernan, V.G. 75, 76, 89, 104; subsequent career, 104-5; 122, 124, 127, 197, 198, 203; information from diary of, 213

King Edward VIII 85

King George V 4, 24, 57

King George VI 151, 173

King, W.L. Mackenzie 4, 59; expands office, 139; practice of ministerial government, 139; lamentable impression of from diaries, 139-40; possible explanation of his personal life, 141-2; encounters bats in the East Block, 146; Prime Minister's account of day of Pearl Harbour, 147; policy *re* Indian independence, 166, 169, 172, 173; calls chauffeur a 'red,' 179; 184, 185, 195; concilation legislation, 256; dies, 297; books about, 298; study of *Industry and Humanity*, 300; as labour relations expert, 300; official biography of, 301

Kingston, Ontario 61

Kirkconnell, W. 52

Kitson Clark, G.S.R. 72ff; worries about Guy Burgess, 74; 77, 97, 122, 206, 316

Klugman, J. 74, 113, 169, 314-15

Koestler, A. 131, 171, 211

Korea 202; war in, 315

Koudrieatsev, S. 183; blows his nose, 184

372